Managing Global Organizations

'This is an important book dealing with the increasingly important phenomenon of international business ventures and the globalization of management, markets, and careers. Drs Bhagat, Triandis, and McDevitt have produced a challenging and highly readable book in which they analyse such key concepts as intercultural communication, job satisfaction in culturally diverse workplaces, the additional workplace stressors brought on by international business alliances, the importance of working with others in groups and on teams charged with task completion, and the transfer of technology among people with different but overlapping skill sets and knowledge. This book will find a valued place in the libraries of international managers, graduate students contemplating careers in international business, and trainers who take on the challenge of preparing people for assignments in countries other than their own.'

– Richard Brislin, University of Hawaii, USA

'Issues of cultural variation in the management of global organizations are of great importance in the twenty-first century. In developing this book, these three authors bring a wealth of academic knowledge and practical insights from their consulting and worldwide travels to present us with a coherent picture of how the world of work organizations has changed in response to cultural differences and synergies. The 14 chapters cover all of the important aspects of organization behavior and theory including recent topics like global management focused on the creation and transfer of organizational knowledge. This book is a must-read for all students interested in understanding the fundamentals of cultural differences and how they affect the management of global organizations.'

– Kwok Leung, City University of Hong Kong, China

Managing Global Organizations
A Cultural Perspective

Rabi S. Bhagat

University of Memphis, USA

Harry C. Triandis

University of Illinois, USA

Annette S. McDevitt

University of Memphis, USA

Edward Elgar
Cheltenham, UK • Northampton, MA, USA

© Rabi S. Bhagat, Harry C. Triandis and Annette S. McDevitt 2012

Published by
Edward Elgar Publishing Limited
The Lypiatts
15 Lansdown Road
Cheltenham
Glos GL50 2JA
UK

Edward Elgar Publishing, Inc.
William Pratt House
9 Dewey Court
Northampton
Massachusetts 01060
USA

A catalogue record for this book
is available from the British Library

Library of Congress Control Number: 2012940184

MIX
Paper from
responsible sources
FSC
www.fsc.org   FSC® C018575

ISBN 978 1 84720 595 7 (cased)

Typeset by Servis Filmsetting Ltd, Stockport, Cheshire
Printed and bound by MPG Books Group, UK

Contents

About the authors

Rabi S. Bhagat is Professor of Oganizational Behavior and International Management at the University of Memphis in Tennessee. He was awarded the Distinguished Research Award in Social Sciences by the University of Memphis in 2004. In addition, he has been a recipient of numerous research awards from the Society of Industrial and Organizational Psychology, including the James McKeen Cattell Award and W. Scott Myers Award (co-recipient). He was a co-recipient of the Best Symposium Award from the Academy of Management and Best Paper Award from the Eastern Academy of Management. Rabi is author or co-editor of six books in the area of international management and organizational behavior, including the *Cambridge Handbook of Cultures, Organizations, and Work* (2009) and *Work Stress and Coping in the Era of Globalization* (2012), and has published widely in major journals of the field. He is a fellow of SIOP, APA, APS, International Association of Applied Psychology (IAAP), and the International Academy for Intercultural Research (IAIR). For the past 30 years, he has maintained a strong interest in understanding the role of cultural variations in different organizational processes in dissimilar nations of the world. Currently, he and Annette McDevitt are working on a book on global mindset in multinational corporations (forthcoming from Stanford Business School Press, 2013).

Harry C. Triandis is Professor Emeritus of Psychology (1997–) at the University of Illinois. He received his Ph.D. from Cornell University in Ithaca, New York in 1958, and an honorary doctorate from the University of Athens, Greece, in 1987. He was Chairman and Secretary General of the Society of Experimental Social Psychology; and President of the International Association of Cross-Cultural Psychology (1974–76), the Society for the Psychological Study of Social

Issues, the InterAmerican Society of Psychology, and the International Association of Applied Psychology (1990–94), as well as of Divisions 8 and 9 of the American Psychological Association (APA). He was also Ford Foundation Faculty Fellow, 1964–65; Fellow of the Center for International Studies, Cornell University, 1968–69; and Guggenheim Fellow at the Center for Advanced Studies, University of Illinois, 1972–73 and 1979–80. In addition, he received an award for significant contributions to the development of psychology from the Interamerican Society of Psychology, 1981. He was an Honorary Fellow of the International Association of Cross-Cultural Psychology, 1982; a Distinguished Fulbright Professor to India, 1983; Fellow, American Association for Advancement of Science, 1984; and University of Illinois Scholar, 1987. In 1992 Harry received the Centennial Citation from the APA "for significant contributions to the establishment of cross-cultural psychology as a distinct discipline." He was an APA Distinguished Scientist Lecturer in 1994 and in the same year received the Klineberg Award of the Society for the Psychological Study of Social Issues. He was also a recipient of the American Psychological Association's Distinguished Contributions to International Psychology Award, 1995; the American Psychological Society's James M. Cattell Award, 1996; and the APA's Division 52 (International) named him Distinguished International Psychologist of the Year in 2002. He also received the Lifetime Contributions Award from the Academy of Intercultural Research, May 2004 (in Taiwan), and the Society of Personality and Social Psychology in January 2012. He received the Eminent Scholar in International Management Award from the Academy of Management in 2009. He was a Master Lecturer at the meetings of the American Psychological Association in 2009. His 2009 book, *Fooling Ourselves*, received the William James Award from Division 1 of the APA. The Society for Personality and Social Psychology gave him its Lifetime Contributions Award in 2012.

His research interests concern (a) the links between behavior and elements of subjective culture and (b) differences between individualistic and collectivist cultures. His work has focused on the implications of these links for social behavior, personality, work behavior, intergroup relations, prejudice, attitude change, and cultural training; and applications to intercultural training for successful interaction in other cultures. He is currently writing a book on self-deception, which discusses the relationship between culture and religion.

His 200+ publications include *Attitudes and Attitude Change, Analysis of Subjective Culture, Interpersonal Behavior, Variations in Black and White Perceptions of the Social Environment, Culture and Social Behaviour,* and *Individualism and Collectivism*. He was the general editor of the six-volume *Handbook of Cross-cultural Psychology*, and editor of the 4th (international) volume of the *Handbook of Industrial and Organizational Psychology*.

 **Annette S. McDevitt** is on the faculty in the Department of Management of the University of Memphis. She has been keenly interested in understanding cultural variations in organizational communication for a long time. She has published in the *Cambridge Handbook of Culture, Organizations, and Work* and the *Asia Pacific Journal of Management*. She has presented papers at the international conference of the Society of Cross-Cultural Psychologists. Her travels in Japan and all over Western Europe and Egypt have been instrumental in developing her insights into the role of indigenous culture on management of organizations across nations.

Dedications

RABI S. BHAGAT

I dedicate this book to my wife, Ebha, my daughters, Monika and Priyanka and my son-in-law, Timothy F. Kennedy. My wife and daughters were particularly patient during the various holidays and festivals when I needed to spend my time away from the family discussing and working on this book with my colleagues and doctoral students in Memphis and abroad. It is also dedicated to the loving memory of my parents, who encouraged me to think and dream big and explore the world through my travels and advanced studies. In addition, my mentor during my high school and college years, Mr Bibekananda Roy (who recently retired as the editor of the *Planning Commission Magazine* of the government of India) played a pivotal role in encouraging me to view the world with a multicultural lens. Finally, I thank my sisters, Bharati and Neelaxmi Jaiswal of India. Sincere appreciation is also expressed for Dr Bharatendu N. Srivastava, the former dean of the Indian Institute of Management in Calcutta, and Dr S. Raghunath of the Indian Institute of Management in Bangalore for their encouragement and insights at various stages of the writing of the book.

HARRY C. TRIANDIS

The idea of writing this book developed when Rabi approached me with observations that there were no good books in the area of comparative management that incorporated cultural variations in an appropriate fashion. Rabi was my student during the 1970s and always maintained a strong interest in understanding cultural variations in organizational behavior and theory. I supervised his doctoral dissertation in the mid-1970s and, since then, he has been an active researcher in the area of cross-cultural organizational behavior and processes. While the idea of doing this book with Rabi was interesting, it took several years before the project got off the board. During the 1990s and in the first two decades of the 21st century, Rabi traveled widely and lectured in various universities in Asia, Western and Eastern Europe, and Australia. He realized the need for a book on managing global organizations from a cultural perspective. At that time, Annette McDevitt, who was working with Rabi on several cross-cultural research projects, also became interested in the project, and from 2006, she worked on this book.

At age 85 this is bound to be my last book. It all started when I took a seminar with Robert Joyner, at the University of Toronto. The title of the course was "Human Relations in Industry." We read widely not only on that topic, but also in anthropology, psychology, and sociology. This seminar resulted in my decision to change from industrial engineering, which was my undergraduate degree at McGill University, to psychology. Since I had no undergraduate psychology, in order to get into graduate school I went back to McGill for one year to pick up the basics – history of psychology, experimental psychology, social psychology, statistics, and the like. Wally Lambert, at McGill, was just out of graduate school and did not want to direct my dissertation, so he sent me to his brother, Bill Lambert, an eminent cross-cultural psychologist at Cornell University. There I took many courses that shaped my future, but especially a course of "Methods in the Social Sciences" that included training in the methods of anthropology, political science, psychology, and sociology. Thus, I became a multi-method social psychologist. During graduate school I collaborated with Charles Osgood, of the University of Illinois, in a study on the generality of affective meaning across cultures. Upon graduation, with a Ph.D., Osgood arranged for me to come to Illinois, and though other universities asked me to go to other places, Illinois always matched their offers and so I stayed there for 40 years. All these scholars made significant contributions to my thinking. I thank them all, and many others, like John Adamapoulos, Marilyn Brewer, John Berry, Richard Brislin, Juris Draguns, Marv Dunnette, Michele Gelfand, Yoshi and Emiko Kashima, Walter Lonner, Shalom Schwartz, and Peter Smith. I am grateful to all of them.

ANNETTE S. McDEVITT

I dedicate this book to my loving husband, Ian McDevitt for his sustained encouragement and support through my doctoral education and the many hours spent working on this book. It is also dedicated to John M. Hodges, M.D., F.A.C.S. for his continuous inspiration and for sharing many stories of cross-cultural encounters.

Foreword

Conventional thinking tells us that globalization is eating away at the sharp differences that characterized life in different parts of the world in former times. Nowhere are these effects said to be more evident than in the field of international business. To be sure, it is true that we can now communicate with one another a great deal faster, more readily meet up with one another, dress more similarly and eat more similar foods. However, these convergences need to be placed into a broader context. Commerce has always involved a good deal of mingling between cultural groups, yet the differences between these groups have converged little over centuries. So, caution is needed in assuming that one global business model is currently in the process of construction. We now have transnational organizations within which only a tiny percentage of employees are located in the nation where that organization is headquartered. But do transnational organizations headquartered in the USA, Japan, Germany, India, the UK, France, Sweden, China or elsewhere operate in similar ways? What we need is careful scrutiny of the evidence relating to the many processes that contribute to successful organizational performance in different parts of the world, and in the joint ventures and enterprises that bring together organizational units from different cultural settings.

For better or for worse, we are all now engaged in communications and transactions with persons from differing cultural perspectives and each of us must struggle with the limitations of our own worldview. This struggle affects the authors of books as much as the rest of us, and it is commendable that this book draws together three authors with distinctive and complementary perspectives. They were born on three separate continents, and they face one another as representatives of three different generations of researchers into the relations between culture and organizational behavior. Having themselves worked together in different ways over several decades, this places them well to be sensitive to the distinctive and sometimes subtle cultural differences that can make the difference between organizational successes and failures. They have provided you, the reader, with a welcome and refreshingly accessible account of key aspects of 21st century organizational behavior.

Peter B. Smith
Professor Emeritus, University of Sussex, UK

Preface

> Growth takes place whenever a challenge evokes a successful response that, in turn, evokes a further and different challenge. We have not found any intrinsic reason why this process should not repeat itself indefinitely, even though a majority of civilizations have failed as a matter of historical fact.
>
> Arnold J. Toynbee, *A Study of History*

Globalization has been reshaping the world in many ways, and it will continue to do so in the future. Consider the emerging economies of the BRIC countries (Brazil, Russia, India, and China). These countries were hardly players in the global marketplace in the 1970s. However, these four countries are being touted as the four emerging giants of the global economy. In fact, China is the second largest economy in the world, having surpassed the economic miracle that Japan was known to be in the 1980s. Globalization has also been altering our conceptions of how organizations are managed, ought to be managed, and whether they should be managed for improving profitability and stakeholder value or should also incorporate a concern for human welfare in the process of international expansion.

Financial markets have become highly interdependent and sometimes with dramatic consequences for the world economy, as we have recently witnessed since the autumn of 2008. Volatility in the global marketplace is a given, and multinationals from both globalized and emerging economies are competing at a rate not seen before. Money, other tangible assets, and intangible assets like technological know-how, as well as organizational knowledge are becoming increasingly global and accessible to many private and public organizations worldwide. Given this development, it is only natural that multinational and global organizations are searching for new ways of improving their operations (i.e., finding effective ways of managing the global organizations). While there are many facets to managing the global organization (e.g., financial, market-related, technology-related), cultural differences have been emerging as being rather important.

The goal of this book is to provide theory-specific and research-based knowledge in the area of cultural differences that are germane to managing global organizations. We start with the concept of societal culture, which has been a focus of research in numerous social science disciplines including anthropology, sociology, political science, and psychology. Even legal scholars have struggled with the notions of equity and fairness as a function of cultural differences that exist across nations. The specific contents of this book are designed to address the following:

In Chapter 1, we discuss the concept of culture, cultural variations, and the various theoretical frameworks that are designed to understand cultural phenomena across nations. Then, in Chapter 2 we address the scope and significance of globalization as it exists today and as it is expected to grow and change the economic map of the world. Chapter 3 presents a detailed analysis of how cultural variations can influence effectiveness of communication in the interpersonal, intergroup, and interorganizational contexts. It is indeed true that media can sometimes be more important in transmitting the significance of a message compared with the explicit content of the messages.

In Chapter 4, we discuss the role of negotiation and decision-making involving cross-border transactions. The roles of cultural beliefs, biases, and values are explored at some length. Implications for the conduct of successful negotiation are discussed.

Chapters 4, 5, 6, 7, and 8 discuss the issues of sustaining high levels of work motivation, job satisfaction, and organizational commitment across borders and cultures (e.g., in various subsidiaries of the multinational and global corporation, in the context of joint ventures and strategic alliances), and effectiveness of work groups and teams. Globally dispersed work teams are becoming commonplace in many multinational companies. Strategies for effectively managing such teams need to be formed on an ongoing basis. Theoretical foundations for managing the multicultural and cross-border teams are discussed in Chapter 8. The relentless pace of technological changes and the spread of globalization have increased work stresses in various industries and countries in the world. New ways of coping with stressful experiences at work and non-work need to be devised. Multinational and global companies are emphasizing the growth of employee assistance programs in managing stressful experiences that can and often have debilitating consequences in the global workplace.

Then, in Chapter 9 the topic of leadership, a topic of perennial interest in the field of US management, is discussed from a cultural perspective. Individualists view the phenomenon of leadership with a different lens compared with collectivists. Interestingly, about 70 percent of the world's population are collectivists or are typically inclined to endorse collectivistically tailored practices and leadership behaviors. We discuss in that chapter also the evolution and sustenance of leadership at different levels of multinational global organizations. In the process, we remind ourselves that leadership, especially how it is perceived and exercised, varies considerably across cultures. Implications for developing leaders at different levels of the multinational organization are presented.

The nature of organizational structures and designs is addressed from a cultural perspective in Chapter 10. The fact that German and Japanese multinational organizations are designed differently from their Anglo counterparts (US, UK, Australia, and Canadian multinationals) is not only interesting from a scientific point of view but has significant implications for the development of various management methods as well as for developing global careers. We provide a framework for understanding the nature of the interplay between cultural variations and organizational structures.

In Chapter 11, we discuss a topic that emerged in the 1990s as the major springboard for ideas on the path to creating superior products and services in multinational and global organizations. While it was well known from the dawn of the 20th century that the transfer of technological know-how was of critical importance in sustaining excellence, creation of scientific and system-specific knowledge that can be diffused, transmitted, transferred, and absorbed in various subsidiaries and strategic alliance-based contexts is a new phenomenon. In addition, it is a rather important development. Understanding how cultural variations interact with technological developments is crucial in addition to understanding the economic and infrastructure-related costs. The implications for effective management of technology transfer and organizational knowledge management are presented in this chapter.

Chapter 12 deals with the cultural variations of international human resource management. Cultural values are bound to cause preferences in the way individuals like to be treated, rewarded, and develop in the context of their work organizations, and especially in the context of multinational and global organizations. The careers of executives in the era of globalization are in a state of flux. While senior managers realize the importance of cultivating and retaining executive talent, a new development is on the horizon. The workforces of multinational and global organizations are becoming more diverse in terms of the cultural backgrounds of the workers. The preferences of these workers are rooted in their cultures but also change as a function of changing realities in the global economy.

Finally, Chapters 13 and 14 present the emerging scenario of managing multinational and global organizations from a cultural perspective and also discuss the future that awaits it. It is going to be an exciting future— one that is full with possibilities but also fraught with challenges on many fronts. The challenge of cultural variations to the management of multicultural global organizations is examined in these chapters. We hope that they shed some light on the future of managing multinational and global organizations.

In order to manage global organizations, the managers of the 21st century will not find help by simply searching for a book called *Global management 101* or *Global management for dummies*. The topic is too complex to make such books possible. There are many challenges to managing and developing global organizations which are not only profitable but are also exciting places to work and develop a career and sustain a high quality of work life in a multicultural environment. It is hoped that we have addressed many dimensions of the cultural aspects of managing global organizations. A book like this is not designed to be free from our own values and biases, but we tried to present our biases as we moved along.

The idea of writing a book focusing on the management of organizations across cultures was discussed between the first two authors in the late 1980s when the first author was a professor at the University of Texas at Dallas. The idea led to several meetings between Rabi Bhagat and Harry Triandis. Some of the preliminary frameworks were presented by Rabi Bhagat at graduate and undergraduate seminars on international and global management at the University of Memphis. The 1990s and 2000s were spent writing several research articles in the area of cultural variations. The idea of reviving the book and making it available for students and researchers all over the world took place when Annette McDevitt joined the endeavor in 2006. She completed her doctorate at the University of Memphis in the area of cultural variations on negotiation and worked closely with Rabi Bhagat in writing several research chapters and articles in the area of organizational knowledge management, robustness of Asian management styles, and culture conflicts.

In writing this book, we were able to draw on our research and teaching experiences in various countries and regions of the world, including Australia, Argentina, Brazil, China, Denmark, Finland, France, Germany, India, Japan, Malaysia, The Netherlands, Poland, Russia, Singapore, and South Korea. Annette McDevitt lived in Japan in her earlier years and developed insights into the functioning of Japanese culture—both urban and rural. Harry Triandis has been to about 70 countries, on all inhabited continents, doing research and lecturing. The ideas presented in this book have evolved over the years.

Any book of this kind is a joint endeavor between the authors and the publisher. We are indeed thankful to our editor, Alan Sturmer, and his assistant, Alexandra Mandzak for their patience and encouragement. We also thank Kulraj Singh and Robert Vickery, two of Rabi Bhagat's doctoral assistants, for help in manuscript preparation.

A project like this has been demanding on our families. We thank them very much for their patience and support for the past four years. We sincerely hope that this book will encourage readers to explore the role of cultural variations in the management of organizations, and particularly global organizations. The journey of a thousand miles begins with a single step, and we sincerely hope that our book has taken a bold single step in that direction.

Rabi S. Bhagat and Annette S. McDevitt
Memphis, Tennessee

Harry C. Triandis
Urbana-Champaign, Illinois

Acknowledgments

Several individuals assisted at various stages in the preparation of the outline of the book, and also in the preparation of the manuscript. We thank Kulraj Singh in particular for his assistance in preparing the various figures and diagrams for the book. Also, appreciation is expressed to Dr Bharatendu Srivastava of the Indian Institute of Management, Calcutta and Dr S. Raghunath of the Indian Institute of Management, Bangalore for their sustained interest in my research and teaching in the area of International and Cross-Cultural Management. The Doctoral and MBA students at the University of Memphis provided interesting examples of cross-cultural episodes in International Business which were helpful in our thinking.

Several colleagues in countries where Rabi Bhagat went as Visiting Distinguished Professor were also helpful with their insights. They are Kwok Leung of the City University of Hong Kong, China; Mansoo Shin of Korea University Business School in South Korea; Ilan Arvishir of the ESPM Business Institute of Sao Paulo, Brazil; Ronald Burke of York University, Canada; and Anna Bokszczanin and Anna Bronowicka of the Institute of Applied Psychology at the University of Opole, Poland.

1. Introduction to managing the global organization

The internationalization of businesses has become a reality all over the world. It is not just the richer countries of the world, such as the US, the UK, Germany, France, Japan, and Italy, that are expanding their international operations to culturally dissimilar countries, but there has also been significant growth of international business activities on the part of corporations from the emerging economies. The 2003 BRIC report (on Brazil, Russia, India, and China) by the global financial firm of Goldman Sachs states that in 2040 the largest economies of the world will be the US, followed by the People's Republic of China (including Hong Kong), and India. The economies of Brazil and Russia are currently behind the economies of China and India.

Such a phenomenon was inconceivable in the early 1960s when Gunnar Myrdal coined the term "the Asian drama" in his classic inquiry into the riches and poverties of nations (1968). Myrdal, a Nobel laureate in economics, inquired into the economic and non-economic factors that are responsible for spurring as well as sustaining economic growth in different regions of the world.

While not explicitly concerned with the concept of cultural differences in fostering or impeding the economic growth of nations, he observed that China, India, and other central Asian countries are probably destined to remain poor nations for an indefinite period, including the early parts of the 21st century. The leaders of the world respected greatly the analyses provided by Myrdal at that time. However, as we look at the comparative economic statistics of these huge Asian economies, as well as of the countries that did not encourage capitalistic forms of growth, it is remarkable that it is precisely the countries that Myrdal was pessimistic about that are doing so well in the 2010 world economy. They are destined to become the largest importers and exporters and are also providing foreign direct investments to the first nations of the world, including the premier economy of the world. In the US 1.5 trillion dollars of the foreign deficit was financed by China.

There are a number of historical, economic, political, institutional, and cultural factors that are responsible for the very slow growth of the Asian,

Latin American, and African economies of the world after World War II. While we will briefly discuss the importance of the first four factors, it is our objective in this book, and especially in this chapter, to discuss the role of cultural differences, which is one of the important determinants of economic growth and organizational performance in various economies of the world, regardless of their location. The next section is dedicated to the concept of culture and cultural differences. We adopt an evolutionary perspective in that we like to trace the importance of this phenomenon over the historical development of countries. In other words, the role of cultural differences (and how they influence various economic activities on which the prosperity of the people and the growth of the country depend) is remarkably different in different geographical regions of the world. The nature of relationships between the phenomenon of culture and the economic prosperity of a country will be traced from an evolutionary perspective. It is only then that we can begin to appreciate the complete role of cultural differences and their significance in managing across cultures.

HISTORICAL BACKGROUND OF THE CULTURE CONCEPT

A team of renowned cross-cultural psychologists (Berry, Poortinga, Segall, & Dasen, 2006) provide a framework that is very helpful for understanding the evolution of the phenomenon of culture within an eco-cultural framework. We present an adapted version of this framework (Figure 1.1) which shows that culture evolves within the geographical context of a nation as a function of ecological (the nature of the physical environment and climate, the way people make a living in that culture) variables as well as cultural diffusion. Socio-political and economic (history of various political and administrative systems in the country, the nature of wars and other serious conflicts) factors are also very important. The kind of adaptation that humans make to their environment is a product of the interaction between the ecological factors and the influences of historical, economic, social, and political factors.

For example, the physical characteristics of people from sub-Saharan Africa and the Middle East are remarkably different from people of the Nordic countries of Europe and also from Slavic countries in central Asia. Skin pigmentation of the people of Africa is a function of the temperature and sunlight that have affected Africans for centuries. In contrast, the light skin colors and blonde hair of Scandinavian people are a function of long dark winters which provide very little exposure to the sun's rays. The Slavic people from central Asia and people from the Middle East tend not

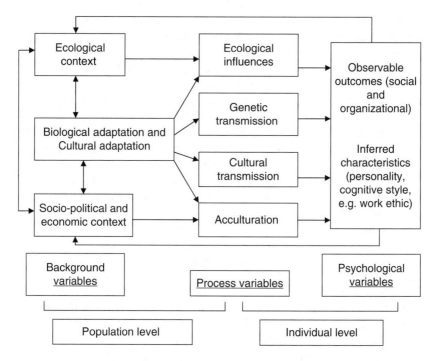

Figure 1.1   An eco-cultural model of cultural transmission

to be as tall as people from Northern Europe as a general rule, but they are somewhat heavier.

In a similar fashion, the cultural values of the societies of Africa, the Middle East, Northern Europe, and modern-day America are quite different from each other. This is largely due to the processes of adaptation of humans in these societies which have been quite different from each other in the past and continue to be different even today. For example, the history of freedom struggles in the North American context which took place around the late 1700s was quite different from the kinds of historical struggles that Slavic people encountered in Czarist Russia of the 1700s. The social behavior of Russians in general is more sensitive to the approval of higher authorities than is the behavior of European Americans. American behavior is in part the consequence of freedom struggles with the British Empire in the late 18th century. Americans tend to do what they like to do as individuals, without much need for social approval from groups or organized hierarchies.

On the other hand, people on the African continent are group-oriented and are more averse about accepting risks than are Americans. The history of colonialism in Africa shows us that those who took risks and fought for independence from their European rulers were punished most severely and this resulted in a collective tendency of Africans to avoid taking risks. The differences that African people exhibit compared with their European and American counterparts result in the development of work organizations and management systems which do not encourage risk-taking behaviors. This is especially important in the area of investments, important strategic endeavors, and the development of technology and innovations associated with the creation of new types of technologies.

The Berry et al. (2006) framework shows that these two types of adaptation result in the development of four types of processes and systems that are relevant for understanding the behaviors of humans in various social and organizational contexts. In addition, the various inferences that we make about how human beings are motivated in different parts of the world, and the extent to which they depict different levels of work ethic, are a direct function of these four processes. Work behaviors are a function of the ecological-, genetic-, cultural-, and acculturation-related influences depicted in Figure 1.1.

This framework is also found in the work of researchers in the field of culture and personality (e.g., Kardiner & Linton, 1945; Whiting, 1974) as well as culture and management (e.g., Haire, Ghiselli, & Porter, 1966; Kerr, Harbison, Dunlop, & Myers, 1964). Berry et al. (2006) are careful to emphasize that this framework is a conceptual scheme and is not a theoretical model in the sense that it provides a general guide to the kinds of variables that we should be studying. The framework is based on the seminal work of Malinowski (1924) and Rivers (1901), who attempted to develop a scientific theory of culture in 1924. The views of these scholars are known as *functionalism*. They tend to explain the manner or the mechanism by which various elements within a system are related to each other and then how the system itself is related to the physical surroundings. For example, the reason people from sub-Saharan Africa are averse to taking risks can be explained by referring to their collective experience during their struggles against the colonial European countries.

In a related vein, the tendency for North Americans to be not so risk averse in their various social and organizational endeavors can be explained by the struggles of the early settlers (from 1607 to 1776) to adapt to a new continent when taking individual risks was rewarded. Therefore, the differential nature of independence as a central construct in the study of cultures can be traced to the differential experiences of humans in dissimilar social, historical, and political contexts. However, while we focus on the rewards provided by different environments we should not forget the role of ecological and physical demands on human behavior. One has to be highly concerned with work-related activities, not only in order to survive but also to prosper, in the harsh climates of northern states of the US. In contrast, the warmer climates of Central America make it difficult for people to work for sustained periods of time, which results in a collective de-emphasis of the value of work.

CULTURE: DEFINITION AND RELATED ISSUES

In the social sciences, it is imperative that we provide a robust definition of a concept. In the physical sciences, this is not typically the case. The concepts of mass, temperature, time, and light, which are essential concepts of physics, do not need elaborate definitions. However, the concept of culture is complex, dynamic, and fluid (Chiu & Hong, 2006). No single definition of culture can fully capture the complexity of the concept. In fact, it is a construct that is useful not only for scholars in cross-cultural management but has provided also significant explanatory perspectives in anthropology, psychology, sociology, and these days even in the discipline of economics and finance.

The anthropologist Kluckhohn (1954) stated that culture is to society as memory is to humans. Triandis (1989) elaborates this suggestion: culture is what works in a particular ecology, so that it is important for humans to transmit it to the next generation. Human beings cannot function without relying on memory. Those with Alzheimer's disease (such as President Ronald Reagan a few years before his death in 2004) need continuous care from an attendant in order to perform the daily activities which most of us take for granted. A culture without memory would be equally dysfunctional. No society can function without shared norms and knowledge of its physical, historical, social, political, and economic environments.

If a group of people in a society has a drastically different understanding of its history compared with another group in the same society, then that society cannot function in a harmonious way. For example, if a significant portion of the US population strongly believed in 1776 that British colonial rule was desirable while another group believed the opposite, then the US would not be able to function as a harmonious society. In fact, in the late 18th century those with the first point of view generally moved to Canada. For another example, differences in views of slavery resulted in the devastating US Civil War that killed about 600,000 people. In short, it is imperative for the members of a society to have similar perspectives on the significance and functioning of important institutions and practices of the society.

Here is another example, this time from the field of management.

Leadership, in the sense of focusing on getting things done, is highly valued in the US, the UK, France, Canada, and so on. On the other hand, in countries such as Japan, South Korea, India, and China, managers are regarded as most effective when they are nurturing, help their subordinates, and care about their well-being, even if their productivity is not as high and the contributions to the performance of the work group or the organization are in question. For example, in some cultures good managers find a spouse for employees needing one, which would be very unlikely in Western cultures.

There are numerous definitions of "culture." We provide a range of definitions to give the reader a sense of the meaning of this concept.

The anthropologist Redfield (1962) defined culture as "shared understandings made manifest in act and artifact." In short, culture is shared behavior and shared human-made aspects of the society. Thus, it includes "practices" (the way things are done here) and "values" (the way things should be done).

These older definitions of culture focus on what is outside the person (e.g., do people drive on the right or left?). The more recent definitions also stress what is inside the person (e.g., is the self independent or interdependent of in-groups?). Almost every aspect of psychological functioning is influenced, to some extent, by culture. Thus, it is best to view culture and psychology as complementing each other to make appropriate social behavior possible (Nisbett, Peng, Choi, & Norenzayan, 2001; Shweder, 1991).

Triandis (1972 and in later years) emphasizes the *subjective elements* (the shared way concepts are defined, attitudes, beliefs, norms, values) of a society as being the important ingredients of its culture. Systems of beliefs (how things are linked in one's physical and social environment), norms (what is the right way to behave in a given social situation), attitudes (how to feel and react to an object, event, or person in accordance with one's beliefs and norms), behavioral intentions (expressed desire to perform certain acts in a social and organizational context), and values (preferred states of being in one's physical and social context) are included in the definition of culture according to Triandis (1972). The subjective culture of a nation or society is different from its *objective culture* (tools, roads, bridges), which is concerned with the structure of the physical surroundings. It is obvious that the objective culture of the state of Alaska in North America is quite different from the state of Guadalajara in Mexico. These two regions of the world are located in very dissimilar physical environments and are subject to different kinds of variations from the rays of the sun (resulting in very cold, temperate, or hot climates). Triandis observes that while objective cultures (just like in the eco-cultural framework we discussed above) are important for the evolution of subjective cultures, it is this latter type of culture which is most important in the prediction of social behavior. Subjective culture influences the conduct of human affairs and especially the conduct and functioning of work organizations and management processes.

This does not mean that material culture is unimportant. When an American comes across a man wearing an Arabic headdress or a turban, he or she may think that this person has a culture very different from his or her culture. Countries in different parts of the world have distinctive architectural preferences and even the curves associated with the roads are different. Most buildings in Cairo and Moscow are quite different from buildings in New York City or Vienna. However, such differences in the objective- or physical environment-related features of the countries are not especially important in the development of cultural norms and preferences of the people in these countries. While there might be a little importance attached to historically significant buildings and monuments (such as the Pyramids in Egypt, the Acropolis in Greece, the Taj Mahal in India, the Sears Tower in Chicago, and the Parliament Building in London), the point is that the subjective culture of a country evolves primarily based on the continuous interaction between the various facets of the eco-cultural model as suggested by Berry et al. (2006).

The next definition of culture that has had an impact on the conceptual foundations and empirical research in the management field is that advanced by Geert Hofstede (1980, 1983, 1991, 1995, 2001). He defines the culture of a society as the collective mental programming of a group of people in a given nation or geographic locale who speak the same language and have had considerable history in common.

Adopting this definition would immediately suggest that even though the Arabian Peninsula has numerous countries, the cultural milieu in which they find themselves is the same. The Arab culture is to be found in the Middle East and in North Africa, even though there are considerable differences in the political philosophies and economic values of these countries. However, consider the case of Turkey—a country located between the continents of Europe and Asia does not necessarily share the Arabic culture, and neither do Iran, Indonesia, or Malaysia for that matter. The countries of the Middle East and parts of northern Africa (i.e., Saudi Arabia, Iraq, Oman, UAE, Syria, Jordan, Lebanon, Egypt, Libya) share a strong religious orientation founded on Islamic principles. However, the degree of religiosity differs from country to country, with Saudi Arabia being strongly Islamic, having strong foundations in the Wahabian principles of Islam, and the UAE and Jordan being more relaxed in terms of strict adherence to Islamic values and practices. In

Saudi Arabia in particular, a substantial percentage of women are not allowed to work outside their homes, which results in extremely low levels of participation of women in the workforce. Given the current foundations of the economy on petrochemical industries, the economic growth rate of Saudi Arabia is not affected by the lack of participation of women in the workforce. However, as the country slowly adapts to globalization and oil industries begin to lose their prominence in the global economy, this country is likely to experience a strong economic shock and perhaps a sharp decline in its standards of living.

Contrast this with the Islamic countries of Turkey, Indonesia, and Malaysia, where women work outside the home in large numbers and these countries do not share the philosophies of Islam that evolved in the dry, desert climates of the Arabian Peninsula. Recent reports show that growth rates of nations which have low rates of participation of women in the labor force are typically around 2 percent (Zakaria, 2011). Examples like this abound. The point is that the cultural underpinnings of a nation have profound implications for many aspects of economic, social, political, and organizational life. This is not to say that modern cultures of the West are necessarily superior to those of the East and of sub-Saharan Africa, central Asia, and Latin America. In a later section we will discuss the possible impact of ethnocentric thinking on the quality of scientific findings in the field of cross-cultural and international management research.

Students tend to confuse the concept of culture with the performing arts or refinements that are found within a nation. While the basic foundations of the societal culture can affect the evolution and quality of performing arts, let us be clear about the distinction between the concept of subjective culture and the notions of culture and cultural refinements as discussed in the realm of performing arts. The evolution of the Western classical music tradition has been largely possible due to the organized nature of activities that were possible in Europe, especially in Austria, Germany, and Italy. The greatest composers of the Western classical tradition were born and learned their trade in Central and South Central parts of Europe. Compare the structure of Western classical music with the musical traditions found in China, Japan, India, and the Arabian Peninsula. The number of musicians involved is quite different, and in Asia a great significance is given to musical instruments like the sitar, which are played by individual musicians and not necessarily in an orchestra, which is more common in Western classical music. A final analysis of the musical traditions of the world will reveal that they deal with the complexities of human emotions as well as destinies of humans expressed in the form of love, hate, anger, revenge, and peace. The forms of musical expression in the East are quite different from those in the West, but the essential purpose of music, drama, and other forms of the performing arts is to present the mosaic of human emotions in the cultural context of the countries.

Studies involving the construct of culture reject the idea of *high culture* or *culture as artistic refinement* of a group of individuals who speak the same language, live in the same geographical region of the world, and share a common history.

Culture should be distinguished from genetic influences on the one hand and personality on the other. A large part of human nature is a function of genetic heritage and upbringing: observable parts of human nature are relatively easily investigated but not the inferred characteristics. Personality characteristics reflecting aggressiveness versus submissiveness, activity versus passivity, introvertedness versus extrovertedness, and so on are not easily assessed in individuals, no matter what their national or cultural origins are. However, observable characteristics of human interactions and behaviors are studied by social psychologists, political scientists (the role of political and legal institutions and organizations), sociologists (studies of families, the role of authority relationships, significance of social movements, etc.), and economists (the growth and flow of money across national borders, growth rates of nations, entrepreneurial orientation, etc.).

The study of culture and cultural values is cultivated differently in different nations of the world. There has been a great deal of interest in understanding the underpinnings of *national character* (Kelman, 1968) of people in different countries. In fact, all over the world people have stereotypes about the attributes of peoples from other cultures. However, while these stereotypes have a "grain of truth," they are largely invalid. There is some truth in the notion that the Japanese tend to be more polite than Westerners; the British tend to be reserved and display very little emotion even during times of stressful interactions; and the Brazilians are fun-loving. However, when you meet a Japanese or British national, you may not necessarily find these qualities present in the specific person with whom you interact. Behavior is very strongly influenced by the situation. National character reflects the modal tendency of a group of people who have an identical language and have spent a significant amount of time with each other during a historical epoch. Triandis (1994) observed that the cultural values of the people living near the central square in Barcelona, Spain, which has been historically known to reflect some of the central characteristics of the Spanish, have remained more or less unchanged for several centuries. The central square has been a physical setting of considerable symbolic importance in Spanish history and has not been subjected to architectural innovations as has been the case in other parts of Barcelona. Families and businesses tend to interact in the same fashion as their ancestors did several centuries ago and the cultural characteristics are preserved. In contrast, modern urban centers in the US, Western Europe, and other advanced G-8 economies have undergone structural changes since World War II. The structure of inner cities in the US keeps changing (see Florida, 2008), resulting in continuous shifts in the evolution of the cultural patterns in these cities. Scholars conceptualize national characters to be enduring; however, we note that they are more enduring in traditional societies where scientific and technological changes have not affected the physical environment.

An earlier tradition that has influenced current research approaches in cross-cultural management is based on the social anthropologist perspective, which was largely derived from intensive, qualitatively designed fieldwork from different parts of the world. The American anthropologist Ruth Benedict (1946) was an important contributor to this perspective. She asserted that the national characters of various nations tend to be based on different historical, political, and cultural factors and also tend to be relatively resistant to change. Following this perspective, she noted that the national character of Japan was based on *shame*, whereas in the US, it was based on *guilt* (Benedict, 1946). She acknowledged that some individuals in either society might not fit the overall pattern, but believed the goals of the cultural anthropologist should be directed at understanding the overall cultural profile of a given nation or society. Her famous work, entitled *The Chrysanthemum and the Sword* (1946), was considered a classic and continues to be important even today in helping investigators discern some of the persistent patterns of Japanese character. Anthropologists like Ruth Benedict and Malinowski (1924) were strongly encouraged by psychoanalytic theories. The development of the massive Human Relations Area Files (HRAF), at Yale University in 1949, which includes paragraphs of the world's ethnographies, organized by topic, made it possible to test hypotheses linking different styles of child-rearing with some of the predominant practices of societies.

This culture and personality school of anthropology was useful in developing insights into nations that were small and quite homogeneous. Compared with this perspective, the psychometric perspective espoused by cross-cultural psychologists (e.g., Triandis, 1972; Berry, Poortinga, Segall, & Dasen, 2006) emphasizes the notion that some psychological processes are of universal significance and utility because of their functional significance. These processes are termed *etic* processes and reflect the psychic unity of mankind. For example, in all cultures the idea of reciprocity (if you do something nice to me I will do something nice to you, but also if you hurt me I will hurt you) can be found. In contrast, there are nation-specific processes. These processes are called *emic* and connote the notion that while a large portion of the human experience in dissimilar geographical locales can be understood and interpreted using similar kinds of analytical lenses, there are other processes that are of unique significance in the socio-historical context of that society. The natives of the Tierra del Fuego in the southern tip of South America have a word (*mimihlapinatapei*) that means "looking at each other hoping that either one will offer to do something that both desire but are unwilling to be the first to do" (Triandis, 1994, p. 67). Clearly that concept is an emic; it does not occur in other cultures. The Maori people of New Zealand have some special practices that they initiate while confirming the passage to puberty for both boys and girls. These practices are not present in the Anglo-Saxon Protestant population of the Euro-centric New Zealanders.

In the next section we describe the broad goals of cross-cultural management. We will also be concerned with the relevance of the goals for helping us understand the process of globalization as it unfolds in different forms in different cultures.

GOALS OF CROSS-CULTURAL MANAGEMENT

The goals and objectives of cross-cultural management are discussed below.

1. It is important for students of human behavior as well as managers of multinational and global corporations to understand the nature of the specific mechanisms underlying the influence of cultural variations on people who work in organizations—whether they are for-profit or non-profit. It is also imperative that we get a better appreciation of the influences of cultural variations on organizational structures (Lincoln, Hanada, & McBride, 1986). For example, why is it that Japanese multinational and global companies such as Toyota, Honda, Hitachi, Canon, and Fitzhugh tend to be much larger in terms of the number of individuals employed compared with US-based organizations in the same industries and pursuing similar strategies for increasing market share in the global economy? Increased understanding of the role of culture and cultural variations will be of significant value for designing large organizations in different societies, and also for enhancing their effectiveness.

2. As we have noted already, culture affects both observable and not so clearly observable states of humans in all parts of the world. If we gain increased understanding of the role of cultural variations in

phenomena such as motivation to work, the significance of working and work ethic (MOW International Research Team, 1987), leadership effectiveness, and the ability of people to absorb increased volumes of information and knowledge, we will be in a better position to improve work effectiveness in different societies of the world. In other words, if we gain better insights in terms of how cultural factors selectively influence the process of energizing individuals to perform on the job and sustain their motivation over time, we will be a step closer to designing a global workforce that will be better equipped to deal with the turbulent character of global work environments in today's uncertain economy.

3. An understanding of the role of national character in the functioning of organizations in dissimilar cultural contexts of the world. For example, is the effectiveness of Japanese organizations a clear reflection of the fact that the Japanese national character is highly concerned with respect for social hierarchy and authority and has a strong in-group orientation, fostering loyalty and commitment to members of one's in-group? In a related vein, why is it that work organizations in sub-Saharan Africa, the Middle East, and Central America are not particularly effective in their ability and willingness to absorb technological innovations to sustain organizational growth and development (Steers, Nardon, & Sanchez-Runde, 2010)? The fact that there are variations within countries due to differences in cultures of industries and corporate cultures is well known. Some industries, for instance, are more hierarchical than others. What is not yet developed is a body of practical insights in terms of utilizing these patterns of scientific knowledge in developing innovative techniques that are especially suitable in enhancing organizational growth, individual and group effectiveness, and satisfaction, as well as principle-oriented leadership. The gap from scientific insights that have developed in the field of cross-cultural psychology and cross-cultural management has not often been successfully filled. Advanced knowledge in the various topics covered in this book should be helpful in making organizations of the world and the people who work in them more effective as well as happy with their work lives.

4. Cultural variations can also tell us about the processes of organizational innovation and change. Anglo-Saxon Protestant cultures in nations such as the US, the UK, the Netherlands, the Scandinavian countries, and Australia have been successful in initiating various phases of industrial and information-based renaissance. Despite the fact that 20 percent of the world's population is Islamic and inhabits most of the Middle East and northern parts of Africa, this cultural

region has not witnessed much technological innovation in recent years. This contrasts with the Islam of the 12th century, when Arabic was the language of science, when new techniques in medicine, algebra, and the work of the ancient Greek philosophers were transmitted by Arabs to medieval Europe. The closing of the Arab mind occurred when the Ottomans, in the 15th century, came from central Asia, and became the dominant culture in Islam. They were more interested in conquest than in science. Allawi (2009) is a Moslem who laments these developments. On the other hand, organizations in Scandinavian countries (characterized by low levels of population densities) and Israel (despite having to contend with hostile neighbors) have been springboards for important scientific and technological innovations in healthcare and other industries.

5.   Globalization of businesses is creating a movement of both educated and not so educated workers from developing and poorer countries of the world to countries of the European Union, US, Canada, Australia, New Zealand, and the Middle East. The pattern of movement of these workers is discussed in the field of social demography. In fact, recent demographic trends show that Japan is experiencing a significant decline in the number of workers in the most productive years of their lives. The policy of immigration in Japan is restrictive and very different from that of Western countries, especially Canada, Australia, and New Zealand, where the influx of immigrants is key to sustaining economic activities on an ongoing basis. New Zealand, for example, has a population of about 3 million, and this population is primarily Euro-centric and has favored a relaxed lifestyle which is not necessarily conducive to major technological breakthroughs. New Zealand is pursuing an active immigration policy which encourages professionals from Asia (e.g., India, Indonesia, Singapore) to migrate permanently to this land, which has been known as a country "down under." The cross-cultural issues in the assimilation and functioning of these immigrant workers, whether they are educated or not, are vitally important for the government of New Zealand.

In a similar vein, Canada has a policy of immigration whereby immigrants are encouraged to retain their ethnic cultures and actively pursue entrepreneurial and professional activities which are typically enshrined in those cultures. In this aspect, the US, which has absorbed the largest number of immigrants during the past 150 years, is somewhat different. The policy in the US is one of assimilation, that is, encouraging immigrants to absorb the norms and values of the mainstream culture (i.e., Euro-centric) and not necessarily be highly vigilant in retaining the unique values of their ethnic cultures. In fact, the US is known as a country of immigrants and Silicon Valley in California has a workforce that is 25 percent foreign-born. A large number of high-tech professionals in Silicon Valley and parts of the northwestern US are from culturally dissimilar countries (i.e., dissimilar from the US), such as China, India, South Korea, Indonesia, Spain, and Mexico. Global corporations in these industries have realized the important need to encourage the valuing of cultural diversity in their organizational cultures. There have been many scientific research and training programs in the area of sustaining cultural diversity in order to enhance international competitiveness. Global consumer companies, for example Procter & Gamble and Vicks International, organize international weeks in which members of various cultural groups display the significant objective and subjective artifacts of their culture. The idea is that members of ethnic groups tend to exhibit more organizational citizenship (e.g., help other workers even if that is not required by their job description) when they take pride in their ethnic heritage.

Knowledge of the dominant values of the various ethnic groups which actively seek immigration in advanced global economies (e.g., the US, Canada, and the European Union) and the oil-rich gulf countries (e.g., Saudi Arabia, Oman, and UAE) will be important in maintaining harmonious workforces at various levels of organizations. In this work it is helpful for people to learn to see the social behavior of members of other ethnic groups the way the ethnic groups perceive it (Triandis, 1994, Chapter 10).

SOME OBSERVATIONS ON THE PRECEDENCE OF METHOD

The method of cross-cultural psychology as well as related areas of inquiry (i.e., cross-cultural management, the role of cultural variables in management of subsidiaries of global corporations, etc.) is quite explicit in that it involves empirical study of members of different cultural and ethnic groups who have had different historical, social, and psychological experiences in different parts of the world. Such differences lead to predictable as well as statistically significant differences in both observed and implicit dependent variables of interest (Brislin, Lonner, & Thorndike, 1967).

Recent work has conceived of culture both as an independent variable and as a dependent variable (Shweder, 1991). Experimental work is now done by priming a bi-cultural population, with stimuli that come from one or another culture, and by checking their behavior after the priming. The findings indicate, for instance, that if one uses a collectivist prime the collectivist responses of the samples increase and if one uses an individualist prime the individualist responses increase. This way it is possible to make sure that culture is the cause of a behavior (Hong, 2009).

In cross-cultural research, *culture* has the status of an independent variable whose influence is to be determined. Were culture a truly independent variable (i.e., one which would permit random assignment of subjects to it), the problems of drawing causal inferences that culture causes group behavior would be no more difficult than for any other independent treatment variable in experimentally controlled research, either in the laboratory or in field settings.

It is obvious that cultural experiences that different groups of populations have in different geographical locales of the world cannot be controlled, and hence culture has the status of a quasi-experimental variable (Campbell & Stanley, 1966). Reviews of cross-cultural organizational research (Bhagat & McQuaid, 1982; Bhagat, Kedia, Crawford, & Kaplan, 1990; Child, 1981) began to reveal that there was a strong move from merely documenting descriptive and ethnographic differences across cultures to understanding the ideology of cultural differences as causal agents in various organizational phenomena. Yet, the attempts to delineate the roles of cultural differences in organizational behavior were too narrow, focusing on bivariate comparisons of important organizational phenomena (e.g., comparing job satisfaction levels of US workers with those of Mexican workers; Slocum, Topichak, & Kuhn, 1972). Current studies are more sophisticated, and there seems to be a considerable amount of emphasis on the cultural variation of individualism–collectivism (I–C) to explain numerous organizational phenomena across the cultural divide (Bond, 1997). Despite some conceptual and empirical confusion surrounding the I–C construct (Oyserman, Coon, & Kemmelmeir, 2002; Brewer & Chen, 2006), this variation of cultural difference seems to arouse the interest of international organizational behavior scholars all over the world.

To be sure, this dimension is fundamental to understanding the nature of cultural variations that are found in different geographical locales of the six continents (Asia, Europe, North America, South America, Africa, and Oceania). However, there are other dimensions of cultural variations that are perhaps better suited for studying organizational phenomena such as complex decision-making processes, creativity, problem-solving tasks, and irrational approaches for solving organizational problems. In a sense, the field is ready to explore the theoretical foundations along with empirical research of other dimensions which might be less powerful—that is, predictive—in explaining certain kinds of dependent organizational phenomena. Such a focus will begin to shed light on unexplored territories relating to behavior in and around organizations.

Cultural differences are also a function of the strength of social norms and mores (Gelfand, Erez, & Aycan, 2007), nature of roles (McAuley, Bond, & Kashima, 2002; Smith, Bond, & Kagitcibasi, 2006), and traditional beliefs regarding the nature of the physical and social environment in which one lives (Leung, Bond, de Carrasquel, Munoz, Hernandez, et al., 2002) and domain-specific implicit or explicit theories (Chiu, Hong, Morris, & Menon, 2000). Sources of cultural differences might also lie outside the domain of consciousness, which means that unobtrusive approaches for assessing these influences may also be needed.

Level of analysis tends to confuse cross-cultural researchers. The individual-level bias in assessing cultural differences is strongly grounded at both the level of theory and measurement. Organizational research involving cultural differences continues to apply culture-level theories (such as Hofstede's framework) in predicting individual-level phenomena (such as the job satisfaction of managers in a high-tech organization). In future research investigations regarding cultural differences, it is crucial that issues concerned with the level of analysis be examined and applied with more precision. Detection of cultural differences at the individual, dyadic, team, work-group, and at the organizational level of analysis should be made by employing constructs that are appropriate for multi-level (i.e., meso) research. Both conjunctive and disjunctive formulations of influences from different levels of analysis need to be integrated in order to explain group-level and organizational-level phenomena.

CONCLUDING REMARKS

In the current era of globalization, opportunities for expanding business transactions across borders and nations have increased greatly. Gone are the years after World War II when the US was the dominant economy in the world, having over 380 multinational and global corporations within its territory. During the past decade, there has been significant growth in some of the economies which were regarded as not being particularly effective in absorbing the scientific and technological advances that typically accompany economic globalization. Some of these countries are also moving ahead of some of the Western economies (Zakaria, 2011). For example, China and India, and lately Brazil and Russia, are experiencing economic growth rates in the range of 8–9 percent (since 1978 in the case of China and 1991 for India). The BRIC economies are countries that do not reflect the cultural values of the dominant economies of the West (i.e., the US, UK, Canada, France, Germany, etc.). However, the citizens of these countries are just as interested in enjoying a global and affluent lifestyle as the citizens of the Western countries. In order for the organizational researcher to understand the role of cultural differences in the evolution of globalization as well as global patterns or thoughts in the countries of Asia, Latin America, Southern Europe, and Africa, it is important to develop appropriate theoretical models using multilevel-based analyses. We hope this chapter has provided some of the primary impetus in understanding the significance of cultural differences that exist in differing nations of the world and their implications for creating a better, more affluent and just world tomorrow.

REFERENCES

Allawi, A.A. (2009). *The crisis of Islamic civilization.* New Haven, CT: Yale University Press.
Benedict, R. (1946). *The chrysanthemum and the sword.* Boston, MA: Houghton Mifflin.
Berry, J.W., Poortinga, Y.H., Segall, M.H., & Dasen, P.R. (2006). *Cross-cultural psychology.* Cambridge: Cambridge University Press.
Bhagat, R.S. & McQuaid, S.J. (1982). The role of subjective culture in organizations: A review and direction for future research. *Journal of Applied Psychology,* 67(5), 653–85.
Bhagat, R.S., Kedia, B.L., Crawford, S.E., & Kaplan, M.R. (1990). Cross-cultural issues in organizational psychology: Emergent trends and discussion for research in the 1990s. In C.L. Cooper & I.T. Robertson (Eds). *International review of industrial and organizational psychology* (pp. 59–99). New York: John Wiley.
Bond, M.H. (1997). Adding value to the cross-cultural study of organizational behavior. In M.H. Bond, C.P. Earley, & M. Erez (Eds). *New perspectives on international industrial/organizational psychology* (pp. 256–75). San Francisco: The New Lexington Press/Jossey-Bass.
Brewer, M.B. & Chen, Y.R. (2006). Where (who) are collectives in collectivism? Toward conceptual clarification of individualism and collectivism. *Psychological Review,* 114(1), 133–51.
Brislin, R.W., Lonner, W.J., & Thorndike, R.M. (1967). *Cross-cultural research methods.* New York: John Wiley.
Campbell, D.T. & Stanley, J. (1966). *Experimental and quasi-experimental design for research.* Chicago: Rand-McNally.
Child, J. (1981). Culture, contingency and capitalism in the cross-national study of organizations. *Research in Organizational Behavior,* 2, 303–56.
Chiu, C. & Hong, Y. (2006). *The social psychology of culture.* Principles of Social Psychology Series. New York: Psychology Press.
Chiu, C., Hong, Y., Morris, M.W., & Menon, T. (2000). Motivated cultural cognition: The impact of implicit cultural theories on dispositional attribution varies

as a function of need for closure. *Journal of Personality and Social Psychology,* 78, 247–59.

Florida, R. (2008). *Flight of the creative class.* New York: Harper Business.

Gelfand, M.J., Erez, M., & Aycan, Z. (2007). Cross-cultural organizational behavior. *Annual Review of Psychology,* 58, 479–514.

Goldman Sachs (2003). *Dreaming with the BRICS: The path to 2050.* http://www2.goldmsachs.com/ideas/brics-dream-html.

Haire, M., Ghiselli, E.E., & Porter, L.W. (1966). *Managerial thinking: An international study.* New York: John Wiley & Sons.

Hofstede, G. (1980). *Culture's consequences: International differences in work related values.* Beverly Hills, CA: Sage.

Hofstede, G. (1983). The cultural relativity of organizational practices and theories. *Journal of International Business Studies,* 14, 75–89.

Hofstede, G. (1991). *Cultures and organizations: Software of the mind.* London: McGraw-Hill.

Hofstede, G. (1995). Multilevel research of human systems: Flowers, bouquets, and gardens. *Human Systems Management,*14, 207–17.

Hofstede, G. (2001). *Culture's consequences* (2nd edn). Thousand Oaks, CA: Sage.

Hong, Y.-Y. (2009). A dynamic constructivist approach to culture: Moving from describing culture to explaining culture. In R.S. Wyer, C. Chiu, & Y. Hong (Eds). *Understanding culture: Theory, research and application* (pp. 3–24). New York: Psychology Press.

Kardiner, A. & Linton, R. (1945). *The individual and his society.* New York: Columbia University Press.

Kelman, H.C. (1968). International relations: Psychological aspects. In D.L. Sills (Ed.). *International encyclopedia of the social sciences* (Vol. 8, pp. 75–83). New York: Macmillan and Free Press.

Kerr, C., Harbison, C.A., Dunlop, J.T., & Myers, A. (1964). *Labor and management in industrial society.* New York: Oxford University Press.

Kluckhohn, C. (1954). Southwestern studies of culture and personality. *American Anthropologist,* 56(4), 685–97.

Leung, K., Bond, M.H., Reimel De Carrasquel, S., Hernandez, M. et al. (2002). Social axioms: The search for universal dimensions of general beliefs about how the world functions. *Journal of Cross-Cultural Psychology,* 33(3), 286–302.

Lincoln, J.R., Hanada, M., & McBride, K. (1986). Organizational structures in Japan and U.S. manufacturing. *Administrative Science Quarterly,* 31, 338–64.

Malinowski, B. (1924). Special foreword. In W.H.R. Rivers, *Social organization.* London: Kegan Paul, Trench, Trubner.

McAuley, P.C., Bond, M.D., & Kashima, E. (2002). Toward defining situations objectively: A culture-level analysis of role dyads in Hong Kong and Australia. *Journal of Cross-Cultural Psychology,* 33, 363–79.

McClelland, D. (1961). *The achieving society.* Princeton, NJ: Van Nostrand.

MOW International Research Team (1987). The meaning of work: An international perspective. London: Academic Press.

Myrdal, G. (1968). *The Asian drama.* New York: Pantheon.

Nisbett, R.W., Peng, K., Choi, I., & Norenzayan, A. (2001). Culture and systems of thought: Holistic versus analytic cognition. *Psychological Review,* 108(2), 291–310.

Oyserman, D., Coon, H.M., & Kemmelmeier, M. (2002). Rethinking individualism and collectivism: Evaluation of theoretical assumptions and meta-analysis. *Psychological Bulletin*, 128, 3–72.

Redfield, M.P. (1962). *Human nature and the study of society. The papers of Robert Redfield*. Chicago: University of Chicago Press.

Rivers, W.H.R. (1901). 'Vision'. In *Physiology and psychology. Part I: Reports of the Cambridge anthropological expedition to Torres Straits* (vol. II, pp. 44–58). Cambridge: Cambridge University Press.

Shweder, R.A. (1991). *Thinking through cultures: Expeditions in cultural psychology*. Cambridge, MA: Harvard University Press.

Slocum, J.W., Topichak, P.M., & Kuhn, D. (1972). Do cultural differences affect job satisfaction? *Journal of Applied Psychology*, 56, 177–8.

Smith, P.B., Bond, M.H., & Kagitcibasi, C. (2006). *Understanding social psychology across cultures: Living and working in a changing world*. London: Sage.

Steers, R., Nardon, L., & Sanchez-Runde, C. (2010). *Managing across cultures: Challenges and strategies*. Cambridge: Cambridge University Press.

Tanaka-Matsumi, J. & Draguns, J.G. (1987). Culture and psychopathology. In J.W. Berry, M.H. Segall, & C. Kagitcibasi (Eds). *Handbook of cross-cultural psychology* (pp. 449–92). Boston: Allyn & Bacon.

The Economist (2010). Country report on South Africa and new political strategies in Japan. 5 June.

Triandis, H.C. (1972). *The analysis of subjective culture*. New York: Wiley.

Triandis, H.C. (1989). The self and social behavior in differing cultural context. *Psychological Review*, 96, 506–20.

Triandis, H.C. (1994). *Culture and social behavior*. New York: McGraw-Hill.

Whiting, J.W.M. (1974). *A model for psychocultural research. Annual report*. Washington, DC: American Anthropological Association.

Zakaria, S. (2011). *The post-American world 2.0*. New York: W.W. Norton.

2. Culture and cultural frameworks

In the last chapter, we emphasized the idea that culture evolves when a group of people living in close physical proximity and sharing a common language develop a way of interpreting and enacting on their social environment in a shared fashion. Therefore, cultural patterns evolve when the following ecological and demographic factors are present:

1) A group of people who need to work cooperatively in order to survive and maintain a sense of connectedness and belonging in a distinct geographical locale.
2) As a direct consequence of the need to cooperate and collaborate a system of language, symbols, codes, and ways of communication is developed. A sense of collective identity begins to evolve as a common language makes interpretation of subjective and objective experiences within the same frame of reference.
3) Interactions among the members of this collective are of an enduring nature. A group of people who pursue common objectives and speak the same language begins to develop ties of emotional interconnectedness and bonds. Consider the following scenario: A group of travelers who are stranded due to an ice storm in an airport begin to develop ways of coping with the situation by sharing information regarding the closest hotels to stay in overnight, and so on. It has also been observed that many of these stranded individuals are likely to form relatively long-term bonds which would not have existed had they not been confronted with the common objective of sharing helpful information and cooperating with others during an unforeseeable event. The classic experiments of Sherif et al. (1961) with Boy Scouts in Oklahoma revealed that bonds can be developed and conflicts can be resolved when groups confront hazardous conditions such as road hazards, earthquakes, and other natural disasters. Ecological and historical factors which require that individuals in a large group or two or three groups must cooperate in order to guarantee survival and prosper lead to the development of commonly shared patterns of beliefs, attitudes, norms, values, and behavioral intentions (Triandis, 1972, 1994). Different societies develop their

own shared patterns of understanding based on unique ecological and historical experiences.

4) Cultures of traditional societies, such as China, India, Japan, Egypt, Greece, and Italy, have existed for thousands of years—resulting in strong heritages that are not easily changed. While globalization-related pressures, socioeconomic developments, and activist national governments can induce cultural changes, deep structures of cultural differences do not change easily (Hofstede, 1980, 2001). Major events like the experience of the Holocaust during World War II can precipitate significant shifts in fundamental cultural values—anti-Semitism began to disappear in Central Europe where it was a hallmark of the culture before the war. Newer societies which have been evolving for a couple of centuries such as the US, Australia, and New Zealand are more prone to accept changes induced by globalization, technological advances, demographic shifts, and major world events. In contrast to traditional societies, the cultures of these societies are "loose", that is, the social norms are not as strictly enforced as they are in "tight" societies (e.g., Japan and the Koreas, and Saudi Arabia) (Triandis, 1989, 1994, 1995; Imai & Gelfand, 2009). Tightness evolves when norms governing social conduct are clear. This requires a relatively homogenous composition of the society. The existence of dissimilar norms for behavior in a particular social or organizational situation leads people to take individual initiatives in deciding which norms are to be observed. Existence of different kinds of norms is likely in a society characterized by heterogeneity (e.g., the US, Canada, and Australia). Triandis (1994) observes that loose cultures may evolve in societies that are geographically located between two large traditional societies. For example, modern Thailand lies at the intersection between two large traditional societies (i.e., India and China). In tight cultures, deviations from social norms are not tolerated, and sanctions are rather high. An extreme example is provided by the Taliban, which had a myriad of rules (e.g., you may not fly kites) and punished severely those who did not behave according to those norms. In loose cultures one does not get upset if some members behave in a manner which is different from the established mores.

Tight cultures are products of long-term and successful interactions among a group of people in a collective. The Chinese, Japanese, and Indians (especially from rural parts of China and India) tend to have relatively tight cultures. Japan is perhaps the most tight highly modern society of the 21st century—whereas India and China are relatively less tight, that is, many individuals may deviate from the normal expected patterns of behavior. The point is that long-term associations between members of a culture are vital for the development of a mature and stable culture, even though such stabilities are not particularly conducive for embracing the changes in structural values that accompany globalization.

MORE RECENT DEFINITIONS OF CULTURE

Culture is to society what memory is to individuals (Kluckhohn, 1954). It consists of what "has worked" in the experience of a group of people so it was worth transmitting to peers and descendants. Another definition of culture was provided by the anthropologist Redfield (1941): culture is shared understandings made manifest in act and artifact. There is some consensus among anthropologists that Redfield's definition is a good one (Borowski et al., 2001). The earlier definitions were primarily concerned with external events (i.e., those which were observable in the physical and ecological contexts) and also were interested in rules and customs of societies. More recent approaches stress the importance of the cognitive aspects of the individual (i.e., what people feel about themselves and their groups). According to these approaches, every aspect of human psychological function is influenced by cultural factors, and thus they complement each other (Shweder, 1990; Cole, 1996).

We can distinguish between material and subjective culture. The tools, dwellings, foods, clothing, pots, machines, roads, bridges, and many other entities that are typically found in a culture are examples of *material* culture. *Subjective* culture includes shared ideas, theories, and political, religious, scientific, economic, and social standards for judging events in the environment (Triandis, 1972). The language (e.g., the way experience is categorized and organized), beliefs, associations (e.g., what ideas are linked to other ideas), attitudes, norms, role definitions, religion, and values of the culture are elements of a cultural group's subjective culture. Ideas about how to make an item of material culture constitute subjective culture as well (e.g., mathematical equations needed to construct a bridge), so the two kinds of culture are interrelated.

Subjective culture also includes shared memories, ideas about correct and incorrect behavior, the way members of the culture view themselves (auto-stereotypes) and other cultural groups (hetero-stereotypes), and the way members of the culture value entities in their environment. Categorizations, associations among the categories, values, attitudes, norms, role definitions, and socialized expectations (e.g., what behaviors are likely to lead to what kind of rewards) are important elements of the subjective culture of a group of people.

Members of different cultures have characteristic lifestyles that correspond to subjective events, and shared habits for paying attention to specific aspects of their environment (e.g., cues about hierarchy or hostility), and weigh these aspects differently (e.g., in hierarchical cultures people weigh cues about hierarchy much more than cues about kindness). Such shared perceptual habits and weightings are parts of subjective culture, too. Beliefs about whether or not one can trust other people, about supernatural beings, about work and about being healthy, about what happens after death are further aspects of subjective culture.

Cultures emerge because ecologies (climate, geographic features, ways of making a living) are different from place to place. For instance, if the environment has fish, people will go fishing, will buy and sell fish, will cook fish, will eat fish, will develop a rich lexicon about fish, and so on. They will also have ideas about how to fish, where to fish, when to fish, with whom to fish, will value fish, they may link their religious ideas with fish, will have theories about how fish developed, will have ideas about how valuable fish are at different times and places, will have norms about how to eat, when to eat, what other foods should be eaten with fish, with whom to eat fish, and so on. Fish will be an important element of the economy of the culture, will be on the educational curriculum, will get involved in politics (e.g., one party advocates restrictions of fishing, another opposes restrictions), the gods will help or spoil fishing, social life will require exchanges of fish, and so on.

LANGUAGE LEARNING AND CULTURE LEARNING

Individuals in all societies grow up learning the native language of the land and cultural mores and beliefs. In Table 2.1, we depict the parallel processes of language learning and culture learning as aptly described by the cultural anthropologist George Guthrie (1975).

In a monograph entitled *Culture: A critical review of concepts and definitions*, Kroeber & Kluckhohn (1952) cite no less than 164 approaches to the concept of culture, classified into such categories as descriptive, genetic, structural, normative, historical, and, finally, psychological. Examples of such definitions have been proposed by pioneers in cultural anthropology (e.g., Ruth Benedict and Margaret Mead):

Benedict: . . . that complex whole which includes all the habits acquired by man as a member of society. All of the customs and practices that humans acquire in their interactions with others.

Table 2.1   Similarities and contrasts in learning a new language and a new culture

Learning language	Learning culture
Learned in early childhood, generally by age five.	Learned in early childhood, generally by age five.
New languages can be learned somewhat easily by children.	New culture can be learned somewhat more easily by children than by adults.
One's native language largely determines one's style of thinking.	One's native culture largely determines one's values.
One's native language largely influences the mistakes made in learning a second language.	One's native culture introduces errors of judgment in interpreting the new culture.
One must learn a new set of pitch levels and intonation patterns in learning a second language.	One's native culture has some unique gestures and body language that are always correctly interpreted by members of that culture.
An accent remains, which reveals the nature of the native language.	Values of the native culture often introduce "noise" when learning the values of the second culture.
In dealing with significant difficulties and stressful experiences, one is usually more comfortable thinking in the native language.	In dealing with significant difficulties and stressful experiences, one is usually more comfortable with coping styles learned in childhood.
One's most affectionate feelings are best expressed in one's native language.	One's behavior is best understood in terms of one's long-standing, deeply rooted values. It is easier for us to learn to appreciate a different cuisine than to learn a new way of expressing affection or love.
One tends to think in one's native language when reflecting on personal values or problems.	One's native culture determines how one views and values an event, either favorably or unfavorably. Profound emotions are generally determined by one's native culture.

Source: Adapted from Guthrie (1975), pp. 95–116.

Boas: Culture embraces all the manifestations of social habits in a community, the reactions of the individual as affected by the habits of the group in which he lives, and the products of human activities as determined by these habits. Culture is seen as the expressions of patterns of communication of individuals and the interactions of these patterns with others.

Kroeber: . . . the mass of learned and transmitted motor reactions, habits, techniques, ideas, and values—and the behavior they induce—is what constitutes culture.

Sapir: . . . culture . . . is . . . the socially inherited assemblage of practices and beliefs that determines the texture of our lives.
Mead: Culture means the whole complex of traditional behavior which has been developed by the human race and is successively learned by each generation.
Kluckhohn and Kelly: By culture we mean all those historically created designs for living, explicit and implicit, rational, irrational, and non-rational, which exist at any given time as potential guides for the behavior of men.
Morris: A culture is a scheme for living by which a number of interacting persons favor certain motivations more than others and favor certain ways rather than others for satisfying these motivations. The word to be underlined is "favor." For preference is an essential of living things . . . To live at all is to act preferentially— to prefer some goals rather than others and some ways of reaching preferred goals rather than other ways. A culture is such a pattern of preferences held by a group of persons and transmitted in time.

Two definitions which remain in use in current research efforts are offered by Clifford Geertz (1973) and Kluckhohn & Strodtbeck (1961). Geertz defined culture as consisting of those religious, philosophical, aesthetic, scientific, and ideological programs of the mind that provide a systematic template or blueprint for the organization of psychological and social processes, much like the way human genes provide a template for the organization and behavior of human beings.

The perspective of Kluckhohn and Strodtbeck is empirically testable. They define value orientations as being complex and rank-ordered. Such orientations result from the interplay of three distinct elements in the evaluation process dealing with cognitive, affective, and volitional facets. These elements provide order and direction in order to control the flow of human thoughts and actions as they relate to solving common problems encountered by humans in distinct geographical locales.

KLUCKHOHN AND STRODTBECK'S FRAMEWORK

Kluckhohn and Strodtbeck developed a framework to describe the emphasis a culture places on various dimensions. These are called *dimensions of value orientation*, and are described in Table 2.2.

The dimension of *relation to nature* is concerned with the extent that a culture copes with its relation to nature most of the time by subjugating to it, being in harmony with it, or attempting to master it. Polynesians from islands in the South Pacific have a *subjugation* orientation. They believe that what happens to them is their luck or destiny, and they are not able to change it by their behavior. A culture that emphasizes *harmony*, like the Japanese, emphasizes the value of coexisting with nature, rather than changing it. For example, Japanese planned areas of parks within

Table 2.2   Cultural emphases on important dimensions

Dimensions	Emphasis in culture		
Relation to nature	Subjugation	Harmony	Mastery
Basic human nature	Evil	Mixed	Good
Time orientation	Past	Present	Future
Space orientation	Private	Mixed	Public
Activity orientation	Being	Thinking	Doing
Relationships among people	Hierarchical	Group-based	Individualistic

Source: Adapted from Kluckhohn and Strodtbeck (1961).

cities before it became popular in city planning in the US. Cultures with a *mastery* orientation, like the US and most of the Western world, as well as the leaders of current China, believe that some of nature's forces can be controlled. Continuous emphasis on technology, such as air-conditioning systems and flood control, reflect this tendency to seek mastery over nature to the greatest extent possible.

The dimension of *basic human nature* reflects how cultures socialize individuals to develop beliefs about the inherent character of human beings: as *evil*, *good*, or *mixed*. Cultural values greatly determine whether people believe that the fundamental nature of humans is changeable or not. In Japan, for example, executives have historically trusted each other enough so that verbal agreements are used for major business deals. In a culture that believes that people are basically evil, there is a lack of trust in business deals and explicit contracts are needed. The *Wall Street Journal* reported that American workers are among the most carefully watched workers in the world, due to electronic monitoring devices. The primary reason for careful monitoring was to check on the rate of production and theft as well as for industrial espionage. We might speculate that such tendencies have increased in the US after the incident in New York on September 11, 2001 when suicide bombers demolished the World Trade Center's twin towers. The notion that human beings can be easily trusted has been completely discarded in favor of tight monitoring at airports and in many office buildings. A society with a mixed orientation views people as basically good and trustworthy, but recognizes that they are capable of committing criminal acts in some situations that violate society norms. Norway reflects this orientation in that there is a general atmosphere of goodwill and trust among its citizens, but very strict laws governing the use of alcohol.

The dimension of *time orientation* reflects a society's emphasis on the past, present, or future. A *past* orientation emphasizes customary, tradition-bound, and time-honored approaches. Indians from the subcontinent of Asia, Middle Easterners, and those from Mediterranean countries, such as Greece, Italy, and Turkey, have a tendency to emphasize past precedents in resolving important issues. Whether such past approaches are relevant or not is not the point. One has to examine how a similar issue was resolved in the past and to what extent deviating from the past pattern might be considered inappropriate in that culture. A *present*-oriented culture generally focuses on short-term approaches. Americans are particularly present-oriented in terms of time orientation, and managers are socialized to look at quarterly financial reports and daily returns of stock market performance. A *future*-oriented society emphasizes long-term approaches. Many Japanese and Korean global companies have plans for improving their performance in the long term, which may range from 5 to 10 years. East Asians often engage in activities that are designed to benefit future generations rather than providing immediate gratification for themselves.

The dimension of *space orientation* indicates how people define the concept of space in relation to other people: is it public, private, or mixed? In a society that emphasizes a *public* orientation, space belongs to not just one person but to all. It is not uncommon in Japanese companies to arrange office space in the form of an open layout. In societies that value *privacy*, such as Germany, the UK, and the US, employees consider it important to have their own space. Senior managers and other high-status employees are often provided private office spaces. In societies reflecting a *mixed* orientation, the tendency is to combine both public and private emphases on space. In India, for example, while lower-level employees may share a common area of work, senior managers have private offices that are not easily accessible.

The *activity orientation* of a culture focuses on doing, being, or thinking. In a culture emphasizing *doing*, such as the US, people are always moving from one activity to another, and their days are heavily scheduled or organized to accomplish a series of things from morning to evening. When people are busy they feel virtuous. Continuous focus on getting tasks done is the primary orientation of these cultures, and it contrasts with those cultures where a *being* orientation is emphasized. Rural areas of India, Mexico, and other countries of Latin America are examples of such cultures. A *thinking* orientation is also known as a controlling and containing orientation. Individuals are socialized to take time off from work, enjoy each other's company, exchange greetings, and achieve a balance in their work and non-work life. The French, the Spanish, and those from the other Mediterranean countries sometimes adopt this mode of functioning.

The dimension of *relationships among people* reflects the extent to which a culture emphasizes individualistic, group-oriented, or hierarchy-focused ways of relating to one another. Cultures emphasizing the *individualistic* orientation tend to focus on people, relating to each in terms of their personal characteristics and achievements. In the US, Canada, and most parts of the Western world, employees receive rewards for their own achievements, work on their own personal agenda, and relate to each other one on one. In a *group*-oriented society, people relate to each other by focusing on the needs of the group to which they belong. Emphasis is on harmony, equality, unity, and loyalty to the group objectives. The Japanese make decisions by referring to group consensus and working from lower levels and moving upward. In *hierarchical* societies, while valuing group relationships, one must be aware of the status of the individual that one is talking to or relating with. Venezuela, Colombia, Mexico, the Philippines, and India reflect this orientation.

HOFSTEDE'S FRAMEWORK

Geert Hofstede, a Dutch researcher, used five dimensions of culture to explain differences in behaviors among cultures. His work came from questionnaires completed by IBM employees from 70 countries, and is one of the largest studies in international management ever conducted. Although Hofstede's work has been criticized because his data were obtained from a single company, he believed that using employees from the same company would clearly show national cultural differences because the IBM employees were matched in other respects, such as their type of work and educational levels for similar occupations. Hofstede's five dimensions are: (1) individualism and collectivism, (2) power distance, (3) uncertainty avoidance, (4) masculinity and femininity, and (5) time orientation.

Individualism and Collectivism

Hofstede identified this as an important dimension of cultural variation. A number of other scholars have argued that this dimension of cultural variation is the major distinguishing characteristic in the way that people in various societies of the world analyze social behavior and process information. *Individualism* and *collectivism* are social patterns that define cultural syndromes. Cultural syndromes are shared patterns of beliefs, attitudes, norms, values, and so on organized as one theme. Some countries are more individualistic than others. Individualism may be defined as a social pattern that consists of loosely linked individuals who view themselves as independent of groups and who are motivated by their own preferences, needs, rights, and contracts. Collectivism, on the other hand, may be defined as a social pattern that consists of closely linked individuals who see themselves as belonging to one or more groups (e.g., family, co-workers, in-groups, organizations, tribe) and who are motivated by norms, duties, and obligations identified by these groups. People give priority to the goals of these groups over their own personal goals. People of a given culture emphasize and sample different segments of information from a given body of knowledge and believe that their ways of thinking about themselves and their groups are obviously correct and do not question their validity.

Included in Hofstede's work is the idea that countries with higher per capita gross national product exhibit more individualism. In other words, countries that are more individualistic are also wealthier, more urbanized, and more industrialized (reported in Hofstede, 1991). Hofstede also found that countries with moderate and cold climates tend to show more individualistic tendencies, and speculated that this finding was a result of the personal initiative required for survival in these climates.

Power Distance

Another dimension proposed by Hofstede deals with power distance—the extent to which members of societies located in the lower rungs expect privileges, wealth, and power to be distributed unequally and naturally. Power distance scores inform us about the nature of dependence relationships in a society.

In countries characterized by small power distance scores, subordinates do not necessarily depend on their supervisors as much as is the case in countries characterized by large power distance scores.

In high power distance societies, it is common to have a centralized authority designating the procedures for employees to follow, and inequalities in rewards are easily accepted. On the other hand, centralized authority and severe inequalities in rewards are difficult to maintain in low power distance societies.

Lower-level employees in low power distance societies follow procedures outlined by their superiors, but not when they disagree or when they feel that the directions are wrong. In high power distance countries, strict obedience to superiors is expected even when their judgments are considered to be wrong. Power distance is reflected in the way that companies are organized. In high power distance societies, centralized organizations are the norm, while decentralized decision-making is more common in low power distance societies.

Table 2.3   Individual differences between individualistic and collectivist societies

Collectivist	Individualist
People are born into extended families or other in-groups which continue to protect them in exchange for loyalty.	Everyone grows up to look after himself or herself and his or her immediate (nuclear) family only.
Identity is based in the social network to which one belongs.	Identity is based in the individual.
Children learn to think in terms of "we".	Children learn to think in terms of "I".
Harmony should always be maintained and direct confrontations avoided.	Speaking one's mind is a characteristic of an honest person.
The purpose of education is learning how to *do*.	The purpose of education is learning how to *learn*.
The employer–employee relationship is perceived in moral terms, like a family link.	The employer–employee relationship is a contract based on mutual advantage.
Hiring and promotion decisions take into account the employee's in-group.	Hiring and promotion decisions are based on skills and rules only.
Management is management of groups.	Management is management of individuals.
Relationship prevails over task.	Task prevails over relationship.

Source: From Hofstede (2001). Reprinted with permission of the author.

Individualism and Collectivism versus Power Distance

Hofstede compared societies that scored high on individualism or collectivism with their scores on power distance. Cultures that are relatively individualistic generally have lower power distance, while those that are relatively collectivistic generally have higher power distance. There are exceptions. Costa Rica is a strongly collectivistic country with small power distance. France is individualist but its power distance is rather high. Other countries rank toward the middle on both dimensions, such as Spain and India.

Uncertainty Avoidance

The degree to which individuals avoid uncertainty in their environments and the resulting anxiety vary from society to society. Hofstede found

Table 2.4   Key differences between low and high power distance societies

Low power distance	High power distance
Inequalities among people should be minimized.	Inequalities among people are both expected and desired.
Teachers are experts who transfer impersonal truths.	Teachers are gurus who transfer personal wisdom.
Hierarchy in organization means an inequality of roles, established for convenience.	Hierarchy in organization means there are inequalities between superiors and subordinates.
Decentralization is popular.	Centralization is popular.
The salary range between the top and bottom of the organization is narrow.	The salary range between the top and bottom of the organization is wide.
Subordinates expect to be consulted.	Subordinates expect to be told what to do.
The ideal boss is a resourceful democrat.	The ideal boss is a benevolent autocrat, or good father.
Privileges and status symbols are frowned upon.	Privileges and status symbols for managers are both expected and popular.

Source: Hofstede (1991), p. 37. Reprinted with permission of the author.

this dimension as a derivative of power distance and coined the term *uncertainty avoidance* to define the "extent to which the members of a culture feel threatened by uncertain or unknown situations" (Hofstede, 1991, p.113) or by ambiguity in a situation. Cultures that are high in uncertainty avoidance tend to be more expressive, that is, they use body language to release their anxiety and to ensure their message is conveyed.

Masculinity and Femininity

The use of masculinity and femininity as dimensions has been controversial, but Hofstede indicates that he developed these from male and female stereotypical gender roles.

Masculinity pertains to societies in which social gender roles are clearly distinct (i.e., men are supposed to be assertive, tough, and focused on material success whereas women are supposed to be modest, tender, and concerned with the quality of life). *Femininity* pertains to societies in which social gender roles overlap, that is, both men and women are supposed to be modest, tender, and concerned with the quality of life.

In masculine societies, success and money are dominant values; in

Table 2.5   Key differences between weak and strong uncertainty avoidance societies

Weak uncertainty avoidance	Strong uncertainty avoidance
Uncertainty is a normal feature of life and each day is accepted as it comes.	The uncertainty inherent in life is felt as a continuous threat that must be fought.
Low stress; subjective feeling of well-being.	High stress; subjective feeling of anxiety.
Aggression and emotions should not be shown.	Aggression and emotions may be ventilated at appropriate times and places.
Ambiguous situations and unfamiliar risks cause no discomfort.	Familiar risks are accepted; ambiguous situations and unfamiliar risks raise fears.
What is different is curious.	What is different is dangerous.
Rules should be limited to those that are strictly necessary.	There is an emotional need for rules, even if they will never work.
Comfortable feeling when lazy; hard work only when needed.	Emotions need to be busy; inner urge to work hard.
Tolerance of deviant and innovative ideas and behavior.	Suppression of deviant ideas and behavior; resistance to innovation.
Motivation by achievement and esteem or belongingness.	Motivation by security and esteem or belongingness.

Source: From Hofstede (1991), p. 125. Reprinted with permission of the author.

feminine societies, the quality of life is the dominant value. For example, in masculine societies such as Japan, the workplace is generally high in job stress and supervisor oversight. However, in more feminine societies, such as Scandinavia, cooperation and security are emphasized. Female managers are more common in organizations in feminine societies than in masculine societies. The comparison between high and low power distance and masculinity and femininity is not as distinct as the comparison between individualism and collectivism versus power distance.

Time Orientation

Societies place different emphasis on time. In some cultures, efficient use of time is emphasized. In the US, a common phrase is "time is money," denoting the fact that time has value. Time can be saved, computed, exchanged with other resources and the like. Western Europeans and Canadians are also very time-conscious. However, in other countries

Table 2.6   Key differences between feminine and masculine societies

Feminine	Masculine
Dominant values in society are caring for others and quality of life.	Dominant values in society are material success and progress.
People and warm relationships are important.	Money and things are important.
Everyone is supposed to be modest.	Men are supposed to be assertive, ambitious, and tough.
Both men and women are allowed to be tender and concerned with relationships.	Women are supposed to be tender and take care of relationships.
Sympathy for the weak.	Sympathy for the strong.
Work in order to live.	Live in order to work.
Managers use intuition and strive for consensus.	Managers should be decisive and assertive.
Stress on equality, solidarity, and quality of work life.	Stress on equity, competition, and performance.
Conflicts are resolved through compromise and negotiation.	Conflicts are resolved by fighting them out.

Source: From Hofstede (1991), p. 96. Reprinted with permission of the author.

time is not considered to be limited and valuable, but is an inexhaustible resource. This attitude makes individuals in these cultures very casual about such things as keeping appointments and deadlines. The differences in time orientation can cause anxiety and frustration on the part of individuals from both types of cultures.

In the US, the time spent waiting for a person beyond the appointed time is a measure of the importance of the person kept waiting. The longer the waiting time, the less important the person kept waiting is deemed to be. This is why Americans consider having to wait to be an affront. In other countries, such as in the Middle East, there is no such interpretation of waiting time. A visitor may wait for a long time, but once the visitor is seen, the interview will last as long as necessary to complete the business between the individuals. However, the next visitor may be kept waiting a long time as a result of this practice. This happens at all levels of society. The following incident during Secretary of State Warren Christopher's visit to Saudi Arabia illustrates this point.

Secretary of State Christopher was on a visit to Saudi Arabia to discuss critical Middle East issues with King Fahd. The King kept his guest waiting for more than six hours beyond the expected meeting time and

met him shortly before 10 p.m. Mr Christopher used the free time to tour
the old section of Jedda, rest, and have dinner. The King apologized for
the delay but offered no explanation. The whole incident was written
off by the US State Department saying that it was nothing personal and
that such things happen all the time in that part of the world. If the individuals involved had both been from countries where "time is money," the
incident would have caused a furor.

When two individuals engaged in a business transaction have different time orientations, problems are likely to develop. For example, in
most Middle Eastern cultures, deadlines are considered an affront in the
same way that Americans would be offended if someone backed them
into a corner in a threatening manner. Americans set deadlines to get
things done. Middle Easterners use a different method, which Americans
consider rude: needling. During a discussion with the first author at a
conference on cross-cultural psychology in Istanbul in 1986, an Arab
businessman explained how he gets his car repaired in the UAE:

> First, I go to the garage and tell the mechanic what is wrong with my car. I
> wouldn't want to give him the idea that I didn't know. After that, I leave the
> car and walk around the block. When I come back to the garage, I ask him if he
> has started to work yet. On my way home for lunch, I stop in and ask him how
> things are going. When I go back to the office, I stop by again. In the evening,
> I return and peer over his shoulder for a while. If I didn't keep this up, he'd be
> off working on someone else's car.

Due to differences in the way various societies perceive and manage
time, Fed-Ex, a Memphis-based global corporation, entered the European
market with a final pick-up time set for 5 p.m. However, in Spain, the
pick-up time was 8 p.m. since the Spanish work as late as 8 p.m.

TROMPENAARS' FRAMEWORK

Another European researcher, Fons Trompenaars, examined data of
15,000 managers from 28 countries, representing 47 national cultures. He
describes cultural differences using seven dimensions. Five dimensions are
concerned with how people relate to each other. They are: (1) universalism versus particularism, (2) individualism versus collectivism, (3) neutral
versus affective relationships, (4) specific versus diffuse relationships, and
(5) achievement versus ascription. The sixth dimension deals with time;
whether the culture emphasizes the past, present, or future and whether
time is sequential (one deals with one client at a time) or synchronic (one
may deal with several clients at the same time). The final and seventh

dimension is the relation to nature, which focuses on internal or external orientation.

Universalism versus Particularism

In cultures emphasizing a *universalistic* orientation, people believe in the definition of goodness or truth as being applicable to all situations. Judgments are likely to be made without regard to situational considerations. On the other hand, people in *particularistic* societies take the notion of situational forces more seriously, and judgments take into account contingencies that affect most circumstances. In universalistic cultures, such as the US, the UK, and Germany, there is a tendency to rely on legal contracts defining a business relationship. These legal contracts are considered to reflect what the parties should do and are referred to in times of dispute and conflict. In particularistic cultures, such as China and parts of Latin America, legal contracts do not carry much significance. The contract may reflect an initial agreement, but how the parties relate to each other depends on many factors in the situation.

Individualism versus Collectivism

This dimension is almost identical to the Hofstede dimension. In *individualistic* societies, an individual pursues his or her own personal goals, and the focus tends to be on continuous improvement of one's self-worth. Laws and regulations make the rights of individuals of paramount importance. Most Western cultures share this value orientation. *Collectivistic* societies emphasize group well-being and an individual learns to subordinate his or her personal goals to group goals. Cultures in most parts of East and South Asia, as well as Latin America, the Middle East, and Africa, are collectivist in their orientation. About 70 percent of the world's cultures are collectivist.

Neutral versus Affective Relationships

In this dimension, Trompenaars focuses on the appropriateness of expressing emotions in different cultures. In *neutral* cultures, the tendency is to control one's emotion so that it does not interfere with judgments. In contrast, *affective* cultures encourage expression of emotions as one relates to others. In a business situation, members of affective cultures, such as Brazil, Mexico, and Italy, may express emotions such as anger, joy, or frustration more freely compared with members of neutral cultures, such as the UK, Singapore, and Japan.

Specific versus Diffuse Relationships

This dimension of culture focuses on how a culture emphasizes notions of privacy and access to privacy. In *specific* cultures, individuals have large public spaces and relatively small private spaces. The distinction between public and private spaces is clear, and the private space retains its private character with limited access to people except those in one's inner circle. The US is a good example of a specific culture, but the UK is even more specific. One often must go through several levels of receptionist, secretary, and personal assistant to reach the manager, even for a specified appointment. On the other hand, members of *diffuse* cultures, such as those found in parts of Latin America and Southern Europe, have no clear distinction between public and private spaces. In diffuse cultures, a businessman's office and home are not divided as clearly as they are in specific cultures, and work relationships often extend into personal relationships. Business associates are often invited into each other's homes.

Achievement versus Ascription

This dimension of culture describes the methods that are employed to achieve status, power, and prosperity in different societies. Achievement-oriented cultures such as the US, UK, and Germany emphasize the role of competence (special occupational skills and knowledge, talent, etc.) in attaining such desired outcomes. However, in cultures which emphasize ascription, as is the case in many countries in the Arabian Peninsula, Middle East, South Asia, and sub-Saharan Africa, one may achieve the desired outcomes from membership in special groups (i.e., elites—those born into influence). The role of membership in clans or groups is relatively unimportant as a prerequisite for achieving these valued outcomes in achievement-oriented societies.

Relationship to Time

The first aspect of Trompenaars' time dimension is similar to Hofstede's; there are different emphases on the past, present, and future. The second, sequential versus synchronic, is quite different. In *sequential* cultures, time is viewed as being linear and divided into segments that can then be divided and scheduled. In sequential cultures such as the US and the UK, schedules rule the business and private lives of individuals and are generally more important than interpersonal relationships. On the other hand, in *synchronic* cultures, time is viewed as circular and indivisible, and relationships are more important than schedules. In synchronic cultures, such as Portugal and Egypt, activities are not scheduled with definite starting or ending times, and individuals move from event to event, rather than from deadline to deadline.

Relationship to Nature

This dimension is similar to Kluckhohn and Strodtbeck's dimension. In *internal-oriented* cultures, individuals control situations. In America, for example, if someone is late for an appointment, it is his or her fault. In *external-oriented* cultures, individuals do not control situations. In Argentina, for example, if someone is late for an appointment, it is not considered to be his or her fault, but the fault of the situation that prevented a prompt arrival.

RONEN AND SHENKAR'S FRAMEWORK

In this framework, shown in Figure 2.1, countries of the world are clustered based on attitudinal dimensions that Ronen and Shenkar (1985) found by

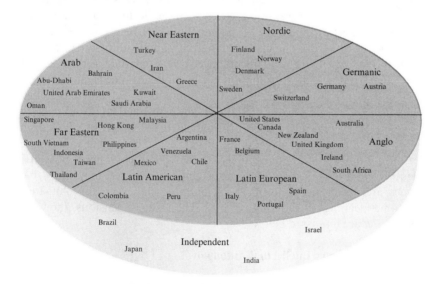

Source: Ronen and Shenkar (1985). Copyright © 1985 by Academy of Management. Reproduced with permission of Academy of Management via Copyright Clearance Center.

Figure 2.1   Ronen and Shenkar's framework

conducting a smallest-space analysis of their data. This framework provides another interesting way of clustering countries and naming them in a fashion somewhat consistent with the regions of the world from where they come. Nine clusters were found based on employee attitudes toward importance of work roles, need fulfillment, job satisfaction, managerial and organizational variables, work role, and interpersonal orientation. In addition to the country clusters resulting from smallest-space analysis, per capita gross national product was used to determine the relative placements of the countries in the circle. It seems as though most highly developed countries are on the right side of the circle. While this may indicate some consistency between a country's level of economic development and generally endorsed patterns of values and work attitudes, no firm conclusions can be drawn about the relationship.

SCHWARTZ'S FRAMEWORK

Another important framework is based on the work of Shalom Schwartz, an Israeli cross-cultural researcher, and his collaborators from different parts of the world. They were interested in identifying the content and organization of human values based on their similarities and differences. Schwartz (2004) proposed that fundamental issues facing mankind need to be identified before one can meaningfully sample all of the important value differences. Three fundamental needs were regarded as the basis for this value study: social coordination needs, biological needs, and survival and welfare needs. Working from this foundation, Schwartz identified 56 values and constructed a method in which respondents from over 50 countries in all regions of the world indicated the extent to which each value was "a guiding principle in his or her life." The human values were grouped into three dimensions, based on the fundamental needs Schwartz identified. Schwartz's dimensions are significant because they show that values are important concepts in all cultures and have approximately the same meanings in different cultures. The value dimensions, shown in Figure 2.2, are discussed below.

Conservatism versus Intellectual Autonomy

In countries where *conservatism* is emphasized, maintenance of the status quo and restraint of personal actions that disrupt solidarity, cohesiveness, and traditional order are especially valued. Examples of such values include obedience, respect of tradition, family security, social order, and reciprocation of favors. *Intellectual autonomy*, in contrast, emphasizes

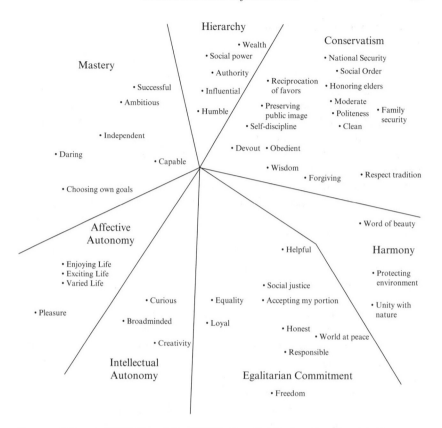

Figure 2.2   Schwartz's value dimensions

independence of ideas and the rights of an individual to pursue his or her own intellectual goals. Examples include values of curiosity, broadmindedness, and creativity. *Affective autonomy*, which is also opposite to conservatism, focuses on individuals' rights to have pleasurable experiences, such as enjoying life, having an exciting life, having a varied life, and pursuit of pleasure. Countries that emphasize conservatism include China, India, and those in the Middle East. Emphasis on intellectual autonomy is found in countries which are also high on Hofstede's dimension of individualism, such as the US, UK, Australia, and Germany. Affective autonomy is especially emphasized in the US and other individualist countries, such as Australia and the UK.

Hierarchy versus Egalitarianism

In countries that emphasize the value of *hierarchy*, individuals are social-ized to respect the obligations and rules attached to social roles. Sanctions are imposed if they deviate from these expectations. This value type accepts the unequal distribution of power, wealth, authority, and influence. On the other hand, countries emphasizing the value of *egalitarianism* reinforce the need for individuals to cooperate voluntarily and feel a sense of genuine concern for everyone's welfare. This value type de-emphasizes society's interests in favor of equality, responsibility, and freedom. Hierarchy is particularly found in countries that are also high in Hofstede's dimension of power distance, such as Latin American countries, Middle Eastern countries, and some East and South Asian countries. Egalitarianism is found in countries that are low in power distance and high in femininity, such as the Scandinavian countries of Denmark, Sweden, and Norway.

Mastery versus Harmony

In countries that emphasize *mastery*, people are socialized to control and change the natural and social world, to exert some degree of control, and to exploit it. This value type emphasizes the importance of getting ahead through assertiveness. Ambition, success, independence, and individual capability are highly valued in these countries. *Harmony*, on the other hand, emphasizes leaving the ecological and social worlds as they are. This value type emphasizes protection of the environment and unity with nature. The value of mastery is found in the US and other Western European countries, whereas the value of harmony is found in East Asian countries, particularly those influenced by Confucius. However, the ecological movement is becoming very strong in the US and Western European countries, and time will show whether the values of mastery retain their hold on these countries.

HALL'S FRAMEWORK

Edward T. Hall (1966), an American anthropologist, used the concept of *context* to explain cultural differences between countries. Context refers to cues and other information that are present in a given situation. In *high-context* cultures, such as Japan, Spain, and the Middle Eastern countries, information is embedded in the social situation and is implicitly under-stood by those involved in the situation. Use of body language and tone of voice in conveying sentiments and messages is common. An Indian friend told Triandis that he was "a meat-eating vegetarian." That concept makes no sense in the US so Triandis asked him to explain it in more detail. He said, "I am a vegetarian, but when others eat meat I eat meat." In short, context is all-important. In *low-context* cultures, such as Switzerland, Germany, and the US, information tends to be more explicitly stated. Use of words to convey meaning is emphasized, and little information is left that is not explicitly stated. For example, the Swiss and Germans are much more direct in their style of communication, whereas the Japanese and Chinese expect that implicit messages that are in the context will be easily understood.

This dimension is extremely important, as can be seen from this incident. In 1991 US Secretary of State James Baker met a delegation of Iraqis in Geneva. He told them very clearly, "if you do not move out of Quwait we will attack you." The Iraqis understood that the Americans would not attack. They reported back to Baghdad that "the Americans are just talking." How could they make such a mistake that cost them billions of dollars and many lives? They observed *how* the Americans delivered their message not *what* was the message.

TRIANDIS' FRAMEWORK

Harry C. Triandis (1996), a cross-cultural researcher, developed a framework around the concept of subjective culture. He advanced the notion that to analyze culture systematically, one needs to understand the significance of four *cultural syndromes*: (1) cultural complexity, (2) tightness versus looseness, (3) individualism versus collectivism, and (4) vertical versus horizontal cultures.

Cultural complexity is largely determined by the ecology and history of a society. Societies where people are hunters and gatherers of food tend to be simple. Agricultural societies become a little more complex, and then industrial societies tend to be more complex. Societies where large volumes of information are continuously being exchanged tend to be most complex. According to this scheme, the culture of the Eskimos is relatively simple, whereas the culture of cities like metropolitan New York is one of the most complex. Most international business occurs in more complex societies and has an established infrastructure. One of the best measures of complexity is the size of settlements. Very simple cultures include relationships among 50 or so individuals. Very complex cultures include a myriad of relationships.

The second aspect of the syndrome, *tightness versus looseness*, is concerned with the degree of enforcement of social norms in the society. In the US, the culture is relatively loose; in most of the country deviation from social norms is tolerated more easily than in tight cultures, such as those found in most East Asian (e.g., Japan and China), Mediterranean (Greece and Egypt), and Arabian countries. But there are subcultures (e.g., the Amish) that are tight even in the US. Impulsive behaviors and those that lead to self-gratification are more frequent in US and Western television programs, compared with countries that are tighter in the enforcement of norms. Tight cultures do not tolerate deviation from norms and expected role behaviors, and severe sanctions are imposed on those who violate expectations. Triandis noted that self-control and control of impulsive behavior are learned more easily in cultures that are tight. The significance of this aspect of the cultural syndrome will be discussed in the chapter on leadership (Chapter 9) as well as the chapter on negotiation and decision-making (Chapter 5). One clue about tightness is found in the percentage of the population that is left handed. In loose cultures the percentage is about 15; in tight cultures it is less than 1 percent. In all cultures the right hand is the "correct" hand, but in loose cultures parents do not force children that prefer their left hand to use their right hand. In tight cultures children are punished if they use the left hand and that forces them to become right handed.

The third syndrome is *individuals and collectivism* that has been discussed above.

The fourth syndrome is vertical vs. horizontal cultures. In vertical cultures hierarchy is very important. In horizontal cultures people favor equality. Of course, there are no cultures with *complete* equality. Hunters and gatherers tend to be largely horizontal in terms of their relationships (i.e., there is not much of a hierarchy in these collectives). They do not have refrigerators to store food, banks to put away their money and the like, and therefore have fewer resources and privileges to differentiate themselves from others in their collectives. However, it is safe to note that the best hunters might possess a slightly higher status compared with those who are not as skilled at hunting.

Among contemporary cultures there is more verticality in South and East Asia, especially India, and more horizontality in Scandinavia and in Australia. Within culture there are also differences. In the US, corporations and academia are vertical; most voluntary organizations are horizontal.

Interactions among the Dimensions

There is a tendency for simple, tight, collectivist and vertical cultures to be more common than complex, loose, individualist and horizontal cultures. Correlations of about 0.4 have been found between tightness and

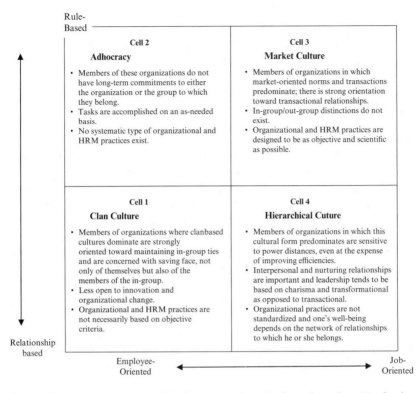

Figure 2.3 A cultural matrix of organizational culture based on Hooker's (2003) framework

collectivism (Carpenter, 2000). Triandis and his colleagues (1995) suggest that there are two kinds of collectivism and two kinds of individualism.

The first kind of collectivism, *horizontal collectivism*, emphasizes interdependence of action and equality with others. The Israeli kibbutz is a good example. The second type of collectivism, *vertical collectivism*, emphasizes interdependence of action and conformity to high-status persons (Bond & Smith, 1996). Vertical collectivism cultures are traditional China, India, most of Latin America, and many African countries. The first kind of individualism, *horizontal individualism*, emphasizes independence of action and equality with others. Australia, Sweden, and Denmark are good examples of countries that are high on horizontal individualism. The second type of individualism, *vertical individualism*, emphasizes independence of action and the need to stand out from others. This is a characteristic of most wealthy Western countries, and is particularly prevalent in the US, UK, and France.

Triandis' framework is important because the preference for management style differs, in part, due to these cultural syndromes. The significance of the framework will also be seen in the chapter on managing technology and knowledge (Chapter 11).

HOOKER'S FRAMEWORK

John Hooker (2003) offers a framework which is also helpful for understanding cultural differences. The major dimension of this framework is concerned with the relative emphasis that members of societies put on rules versus relationships. *Rule-oriented societies* are those which rely on proven guiding principles, schedules, rules and procedures, and contracts, both in dealing with the formalities of the organization and in the informal relationships among the members of the organization. *Relationship-oriented societies*, on the other hand, emphasize harmony and working together peacefully, even at the expense of productivity. By superimposing the rule- versus relationship-oriented dimension with the dimension of employee-orientedness versus job-orientedness (Hofstede, 2001), we arrive at a scheme for classifying organizational cultures.

We describe four types of culture: cultures that are called clan, adhocracy, hierarchical, and market cultures. *Clan*-based organizations are found in traditional societies which have not yet embraced globalization. In fact, these societies are called *partially globalized* or *semi-globalized* nations (Leung et al., 2005; Ghemawat, 2008). *Adhocracies* are found in societies which are transitional in nature; Middle Eastern countries which are experiencing transitions from the strict Islamic code of transactions to norms and transactions preferred by globalizing countries tend to have adhocracies in their organizational contexts. While adhocracies are effective in accomplishing goals conceived in the short term, they are not particularly suitable for launching long-term developmental projects needed for building nations.

Hierarchical organizations are found in collectivistic societies in Asia, Southern Europe, South America, and Africa. Strong emphasis is placed on status; job incumbents and new employees are always reminded of their appropriate roles in the organizational chart or hierarchy. Excessive centralization of decision-making leads to "red-tape-ism" and lower emphasis on innovation, if any at all. Globalization, when embraced by the national leaders, may have the effect of flattening these hierarchical organizations and making their cultures become closer to the market cultures. Finally, organizations which reflect *market* cultures are found in societies where rules and regulations and proper observance of codes

Table 2.7   Central themes invoking the culture concept

Theme	Important questions	Implications for international and cross-cultural management research
Cultural convergence and divergence	Are cultures becoming more similar under the force of globalization?	Whether standard business practices will emerge.
Cultural change	What are the dynamics of cultural change?	How business practices will change over time.
Novel constructs of culture	What is new about culture?	New concepts for understanding cultural differences in business practices.
Moderating effects of culture	When is culture important?	When to adopt standard business practices.
Experimental approaches	How to test the effects of culture experimentally?	Causal inferences about the effects of culture on standard business practices.

of behaviors and ethics are of paramount importance. Individuals are evaluated according to their skills and abilities and not because of their membership of in-groups. Organizations in North America, Western Europe, and Australia and New Zealand reflect this pattern. Perhaps the strongest determinant of these cultures is their almost complete acceptance of the norms and practices of economic globalization (Ghemawat, 2008). We might note that the cultures of these organizations are most suitable for absorbing innovative practices in management of technology and routine absorption of various new types of organizational knowledge.

Some of the major themes that are of interest to cross-cultural researchers are shown in Table 2.7.

Since the publication of the landmark study *Industrialism and Industrial Man* by Kerr, Dunlop, Harbison, & Meyer (1964), researchers have been interested in identifying both similarities and differences among patterns of beliefs, attitudes, norms, behavioral intentions and the like in different societies. The issue of convergence versus divergence of cultures in different parts of the world is important for two reasons. Theoretically, we will gain better insights into the role of ecological, historical, political, and economic variables in the evolution of cultures. If cultures of the world do indeed tend to converge over time (i.e., if cultures of the Middle East, not only the consumer culture but also the basic value orientations of the dominant groups, become similar to the Anglo-Saxon cultures of Western Europe and the US), then issues of clashes of civilizations and culture conflicts will be increasingly less frequent in the future.

On the other hand, if cultures of the world are diverging (whether relatively rapidly or slowly), then the theoretical implications of such a trend are quite different from the phenomenon of convergence.

When cultures of the various locales of the world do converge (Heuer, Cummings, & Hutabarat, 1999) then international management and business-related practices will become increasingly similar. Standard, culture-free, and innovative business practices will emerge in all geographical locales of the world where globalization is widely accepted. Inefficiencies and complexities as well as distrustful attitudes toward dissimilar and foreign cultures will disappear.

SUMMARY AND CONCLUSIONS

We have presented the concepts of culture and cultural differences among societies as a way of seeing beyond the obvious in social and organizational contexts. Employing the concepts of cultural differences enables us to arrive at a better understanding of why and how people in a given society act differently from others in another society, even toward identical social and organizational phenomena. Consider the fact that a major wing of the Jedda's King Abdul Azziz International Airport is devoted to a mosque for pilgrims to Mecca. Such a phenomenon is not likely to occur in India, China, Brazil, or Russia—the four emerging economies— or in Western secular societies like the US, Canada, Australia, Germany, the UK, and so on. Obviously, the culture of Saudi society is quite different and despite high per capita GDP, Islamic religious practices and rituals are likely to exercise major influences on belief systems and patterns of behavior—regardless of whether they occur in the general social context or in work contexts. Such cultural differences affect the way employees are selected, promoted, compensated, and the like, the kinds of management styles that will be effective, the way innovations are likely to occur and to become accepted, and many other aspects of organizational behavior.

Consider the importance of equal opportunity in the workplace in US society. The fight for equal opportunity across gender, race, ethnicity, and national origin has been a long and difficult one, not only in the US, but also in other globalizing countries such as India, Indonesia, and Brazil. Some societies find it necessary to emphasize sex-role differentiation (i.e., much of the Middle East, Africa, and Latin America), but such differentiation is of no consequence to Nordic countries (i.e., Sweden, Denmark, Finland, and Norway). Ecological conditions, belief systems, and historical experiences are clearly responsible for the evolution of such culturally distinct practices. To what extent these practices are going to diverge and, in the long term, disappear depends on the ability of the cultures to absorb new information which may or may not be congruent with traditional beliefs.

One of the major problems of classifying cultures into a set of fixed dimensions is that cultures are rather stable yet undergo major changes over time. For example, in the US South until about 1970, blacks could not use the toilets, restaurants, or hotels that whites used. Now they can use them. Organizational behavior was much more different in the South compared with the North of the US 50 years ago than it is now. Japan is a masculine society and low on individualism, but today's Japanese youth are different from this established cultural norm. Even in a rather tight culture like Japan, cultural changes are becoming noticeable in both patterns of consumption and in other aspects of social and inter-personal behavior. In a recent report on Saudi Arabia, *The Economist* (January 2012) noted that some Saudi women are now allowed to drive cars in response to demands from Saudi businesswomen who find the ban outdated. Another example is found in the organizational context of outsourcing operations in India. The organizations that perform a lot of outsourcing operations for Western companies employ a large percentage of women, many of whom are working mothers. Shift work is difficult to adjust to for working mothers, regardless of whether the work context is an advanced globalized country or an emerging economy like India. Managers of organizations who oversee outsourcing operations need to foster growth of a different kind of workplace, where family-friendly personnel policies (i.e., work–family balance programs) are emphasized (Kossek & Lambert, 2005).

Another problem is that though a dimension of cultural variation may apply to most people in a culture, there are subcultures that do not conform to the dimension. Triandis (2009, p. 77), for example, argues that one must pay attention to a number of factors in determining whether a sample of individuals is collectivist:

1. Homogenous cultures (cultures with one ethnic group) are more collectivist than heterogenous cultures (e.g., cultures with many immigrants).
2. The lower social classes are more collectivist than the upper classes.
3. Those who live in isolated environments, such as an ethnic neigh-borhood in a large city, are more collectivist than those who live in

an environment in which they have to deal with people from other cultures.

4. Those who live in the same place are more collectivist than those who have changed neighborhoods, villages, cities, states, or countries.
5. Older sample populations tend to be more collectivist than younger samples.
6. Those who were socialized in large families tend to be more collectivist than those who were socialized in small families or were only children.
7. Those who have experienced a common fate (as in wars, earthquakes, labor unions) are more collectivist than those who have not had such experiences.
8. People who have had strict religious upbringing tend to be more collectivist than secular samples.
9. People who have had little education and have never traveled are more collectivist than people with much education or who have traveled widely.
10. People who have not been exposed to the mass media (movies, television, magazines) are more collectivist than those who have been exposed to the mass media.

We have discussed the role of homogeneity versus heterogeneity in the existing population as a major determinant of tightness versus looseness. Statements like "Germans are highly methodical and punctual" and "the Japanese go the extra mile to avoid overt conflicts" may be descriptive of broad cultural patterns, and they may contain a kernel of truth. But they may be inaccurate in describing the behavior of an individual or a small group of people. Cultural dimensions as described in Hofstede, Trompenaars, Triandis, and others are helpful in capturing the essence of etic elements of societies. Etic elements are those that are culture-general, that is, concepts such as motherhood, brotherhood, and sympathy for an unfortunate one. However, they do not capture the emic elements of cultures, which reflect idiosyncratic characteristics of those societies. Consider the cultural script concept of *simpatia* (Triandis, Marin, Lisansky, & Benancourt, 1984). Hispanics are more collectivistic than non-Hispanics, and the aspect of collectivism that fosters greater harmony in in-group relationships is known as simpatia. Hispanics who are high on simpatia display more politeness, friendliness, affection, and, more importantly, loyalty to the members of the in-group. Triandis (1994) notes that this emic tendency can lead to misunderstandings and conflicts between Hispanics and non-Hispanics, that is, Anglos and others. Criticizing poor performance is considered normal in Anglo cultures and is rather common in Anglo managers of maquiladores. However, Hispanics interpret this tendency to criticize as an act of hostility and prejudice displayed by Anglos toward them. There are other culture-specific characteristics which do not generalize in the same fashion as the concepts of power distance, individualism–collectivism, and so on. In order to have a rich understanding of specific cultures, it is necessary to adopt a robust etic-based perspective with a cultural anthropology-based perspective (i.e., emic). While arriving at a complex and more accurate picture of cultural functioning in a given societal context involves a longitudinal perspective and many years of sustained field-work, one can get a reasonably correct picture of the role of cultural variations from previous analyses. From the point of view of managing a global organization, this perspective is going to be quite useful.

Some societies are composed of distinct groups of people with their own ethic and subcultures. The US, France, the UK, Australia, Canada, South Africa, and India are examples of countries which have distinct subcultures. International migrations of labor including forced migration help create distinctive subcultures—the US being a prime example of this kind of society (Bhagat, McDevitt, & Segovis, 2011). Australia is a good example of a modern 21st century country which seeks to encourage immigration of skilled professionals from countries such as China, India, Greece, and Italy. In these countries, a mainstream culture representing paramount values of the society (i.e., individualism in the case of the US, Australia, New Zealand, and the UK, and collectivism in the case of India, Singapore, Indonesia, and Turkey) exists along with idiosyncratic modes of cultures in the subgroups. Currently, over 70 million people in Western globalized democracies are foreign-born, and their numbers keep increasing with the growth of multinational and global organizations. This development makes it even more difficult to generalize from broad cultural patterns of societies to individuals who are members of their distinctive ethnic groups. Expecting an Asian-American manager to be as efficient at laying off people in times of recession as an Anglo manager is perhaps correct when we think of the dominant value of the Western society which is based on equitable exchanges without encouraging emotional dependence of the worker on the employing organizations. However, Asian-Americans think rather differently in regard to the unique significance of employment; their view reflects a more benevolent and paternalistic orientation. Therefore, summarizing the experiences of Asian-American managers in dealing with the laying off of workers to reflect the general tendencies of mainstream, that is, Anglo managers, in the identical work situation is misleading. The socialization pressures exerted by one's ethnic group tend to have profound effects compared with those of one's mainstream culture.

Taken together, the various theoretical perspectives presented in this chapter highlight the importance of a multicultural perspective in managing the workers of multinational and global organizations. While the culture of the country where subsidiaries of global organizations are set up has profound local effects on the operations, the fact remains that managers of multinational and global organizations need to be cognizant of the necessary cultural frameworks in order to grasp the evolving reality of managing these organizations. Managing global organizations in the future will not only be a challenging task, but we hope it will be a rewarding one as well.

REFERENCES

Bhagat, R.S., McDevitt, A.S., & Segovis, J.C. (2011). Immigration as an adaptive challenge: Implications for life-long learning. In Manual L. London (Ed.). *Oxford handbook of life-long learning* (pp. 402–21). New York: Oxford University Press.

Bond, R. & Smith, P.B. (1996). Culture and conformity. A meta-analysis of studies using Asch's (1952b, 1956) line judgment task. *Psychological Bulletin*, 119, 111–37.

Borowski, R., Barth, F., Shweder, R.A., Rodseth, L., & Stolzenberg, N.M. (2001). A conversation about culture. *American Anthropologist*, 103, 432–46.

Carpenter, S. (2000). Effects of cultural tightness and collectivism on self-concept and causal attributions. *Cross-Cultural Research*, 34, 38–56.

Cole, M. (1996). *Cultural psychology: A once and future discipline*. Cambridge, MA: Harvard University Press.

Geertz, C. (1973). *The interpretation of cultures*. New York: Basic Books.

Ghemawat, P. (2008). *Rethinking global strategy*. Cambridge, MA: Harvard University Press.

Guthrie, G.M. (1975). A behavioral analysis of culture learning. In R.W. Brislin, S. Bochner, & W.J. Lonners (Eds). *Cross-cultural perspective of learning* (pp. 95–116). New York: Sage.

Hall, E.T. (1966). *The hidden dimension*. New York: Doubleday.

Hall, E.T. (1976). *Beyond culture*. New York: Anchor/Doubleday.

Heuer, M., Cummings, J.L. & Hutabarat, H. (1999). Cultural stability or change among managers in Indonesia? *Journal of International Business Studies*, 30(3), 599–610.

Hofstede, G. (1980). *Culture's consequences: International differences in work-related values*. Beverly Hills, CA: Sage Publications.

Hofstede, G. (1991). *Cultures and organizations: Software of the mind*. London: McGraw-Hill.

Hofstede, G. (2001). *Culture's consequences: International differences in work-related values*. Thousand Oaks, CA: Sage.

Hooker, J. (2003). *Working across cultures: managing the high-performance team*. Palo Alto, CA: Stanford University Press.

Imai, L. & Gelfand, M.J. (2009). Interdisciplinary perspectives on culture, conflict, and negotiation. In R.S. Bhagat & R.M. Steers (Eds). *Culture, organizations, and work* (pp. 334–72). Cambridge: Cambridge University Press.

Kerr, C., Dunlop, M., Harbison, M., & Meyer, J. (1964). *Industrialism and industrial man*. New York: Oxford University Press.

Kluckhohn, F. (1954). Culture and behavior. In G. Lindzey (Ed.). *Handbook of social psychology* (Vol. 2, pp. 921–76). Cambridge, MA: Addison-Wesley.

Kluckhohn, F. & Strodtbeck, F.L. (1961). *Variations in value orientations*. Evanston, IL: Row, Peterson.

Kossek, E.E. & Lambert, S.J. (2005). *Work and lift integration: Organizational, cultural, and individual perspectives*. Mahwah, NJ: Lea Publishers.

Kroeber, A.L. & Kluckhohn, C. (1952). *Culture: A critical review of concepts and definitions*. Papers of the Peabody Museum of American Archaeology and Ethnology. Cambridge, MA: Harvard University.

Leung, K., Bhagat, R.S., Buchan, N., Erez, M., & Gibson, C.R. (2005). Culture and international business: Recent advances and their implications for future research. *Journal of International Business Studies*, 36(4), 357–78.

Redfield, R. (1941). *The folk culture of the Yucatan*. Chicago: University of Chicago Press.

Ronen, S. and Shenkar, O. (1985). Clustering cultures on attitudinal dimensions: A review and synthesis. *Academy of Management Review*, 10(3), 435–54.

Schwartz, S.H. (1994). Beyond individualism/collectivism: New dimensions of values. In U. Kim et al. (Eds). *Individualism and collectivism: theory, application, and methods*. Thousand Oaks, CA: Sage Publications.

Schwartz, S.H. (2004). Mapping and interpreting cultural differences around the world. In H. Vinken, J. Soeters, & P. Ester (Eds). *Comparing cultures: Dimensions of culture in a comparative perspective* (pp. 43–73). Leiden, NJ: Brill.

Sherif, M., Harvey, O.J., White, B.J., Hood, W.R., & Sherif, C. (1961). *Intergroup conflict and cooperation: The robber's cave experiment*. Norman, OK: University of Oklahoma Institute of Group Relations.

Shweder, R.A. (1990). Cultural psychology. In J.W. Stigler, R. Shweder, & G. Herdt (Eds). *Cultural Psychology* (pp. 1–46). Cambridge: Cambridge University Press.

The Economist (2012). Women and Islam: God daughters. 5 January, p. 27.

Triandis, H.C. (1972). *The analysis of subjective culture*. New York: Wiley.

Triandis, H.C. (1989). The self and social behaviors in differing cultural contexts. *Psychological Review*, 96(3), 506–20.

Triandis, H.C. (1994). *Culture and social behavior*. New York: McGraw-Hill.

Triandis, H.C. (1995). *Individualism & collectivism*. Boulder, CO: Westview Press.

Triandis, H.C. (1996). The psychological measurement of cultural syndromes. *American Psychologist*, 51, 407–15.

Triandis, H.C. (2009). *Fooling ourselves*. New York: Praeger Publications.

Triandis, H.C., Lisansky, J., Marin, G., & Betancourt, H. (1984). Simpatica as a cultural script for Hispanics. *Journal of Personality and Social Psychology*, 47, 1363–75.

Trompenaars, F. (1993). *Riding the waves of culture: Understanding diversity in global business*. London: Economist Books.

3. Culture and globalization

The trading of goods and services among various traditional societies such as China, India, Greece, and Egypt has been in existence for over a thousand years. It is not just since the advent of the Internet that economies of the world have started to become highly intertwined with each other. Humans have realized the significance of trading goods of various kinds (e.g., gold, diamonds, silver, silk, food products, spices, and handicrafts) since the time of Alexander the Great or earlier. The development of the Silk Road, which connected the distinct economies of West Asia with China and some countries in the West, has had a long history and was a major factor in encouraging the development of international trade routes and the early stages of globalization. Since the end of World War II, trade barriers have been falling in most parts of the world, and trade among countries involving manufactured goods, agricultural products, and recently service has grown faster than the rate of domestic production in almost all countries. In other words, the rate of growth of international trade involving two or more countries is higher than the rate of growth of the domestic economies in these countries when considered one at a time. This phenomenon is unique and is a product of major improvements in global travel and faster access to sea routes for international trade. In the latter part of the 20th century, especially from the 1970s, the economies of the eastern region of Asia have continued to expand at an unprecedented rate—and at rates faster than those observed in the economies of Western Europe and North America.

Gunnar Myrdal, a Nobel Prize-winning economist who was interested in examining the patterns of economic growth in Asia in particular, wrote a path-breaking book entitled, *The Asian Drama* in 1968. In this book, Professor Myrdal observed that the economies of Asia were not likely to participate vigorously in the world economic system that was pioneered by the UK in the 1880s and then sustained by US entrepreneurial activities in the 20th century. He noted that Asians were not knowledgeable about the various facets of the global marketplace. In addition, they were high on 'familialism' (concern for the immediate and extended members of one's family). Myrdal's work created controversy in the various ministries of finance in large countries with substantial populations such as China, India, and Indonesia. He was invited to explain the significance of his findings to the intellectual elites of these large countries and numerous controversies surrounding his work characterized their economic development activities, including attempts to participate in the global economy in the 1960s. J. Kenneth Galbraith (1967) echoed a similar concern that India was characterized by numerous issues that were not economic in nature. For those of us growing up in South Asia in the 1960s, it was inconceivable that India would be a major economic powerhouse at the start of the 21st century. However, as can be observed in the patterns of international trade and commerce, and also in the analyses made by the World Bank and Goldman Sachs (a large investment bank in New York), India and China (two large and relatively less affluent countries at the end of World War II), Russia (a country with a centralized economy and very low reserves of foreign capital at the end of World War II), and Brazil (a large country which was largely ruled by the military junta in the 1960s) are the four most important emerging markets in the global economy. While the role of the government in creating such a state of affairs is certainly important to consider, one should not forget the role of cultural factors that can either foster or impede the progress of globalization. The role of cultural values in affecting globalization is not only present in these countries but is important in many other parts of the world that have developed or are developing (Parker, 2005). In the next section, we define globalization and examine its various facets.

DEFINITION OF GLOBALIZATION

Globalization is the worldwide trend for businesses expanding their operations beyond the domestic boundaries of the countries in which they were founded. Globalization means that the world is becoming highly interconnected in economic terms, and transactions involving capital, goods, services, and people are taking place on a routine basis involving a large number of countries that are members of the World Trade Organization (WTO). This is not to say that countries that don't belong to the WTO are not participating in the global commerce or that they are fundamentally reluctant in their propensity to benefit from economic commerce. In a truly global economy, any company from any country can become a competitor of any company from another country in its respective attempts to seek larger shares of the global market. This was inconceivable in the 1960s and in earlier periods following World War II because of the following factors:

1. Political factors (e.g., high levels of governmental interference, centralized command economies not willing to participate in global commerce).
2. High cost of inter-country transportation (e.g., involving air transportation and sea lanes).
3. Lack of appropriate technological innovations (e.g., limited abilities to communicate across national borders, no Internet, computer-mediated communication, or tele- and video-conferencing, or satellites across various countries).
4. Lack of an educated workforce in various parts of the world (e.g., limited abilities on the part of many countries to absorb scientific and technological innovations from the West and lack of adequate training in the local manpower in the areas of science, technology, economics, and business disciplines).
5. Lack of physical and technological infrastructure (e.g., lack of wide/ multi-lane highways, and inefficient transportation, lack of wide-scale telephone networks and computer networks).

There are other factors that were clearly responsible for the relatively low levels of participation of large countries from the continents of Asia (e.g., India, Indonesia, Malaysia), South America (Brazil, Argentina, Chile, Mexico), and Africa (Nigeria, Egypt, Kenya, Tanzania). These factors were largely concerned with lack of entrepreneurial spirit among the ruling classes in post-Colonial periods. Many of these countries were plagued by waves of institutional corruption which are still responsible for much of the lack of progress in these parts of the world. It is difficult to embrace globalization when a vast majority of the business elites have difficulty conducting their operations in the domestic context, let alone the global economy. This is due to widespread institutionalized corruption, official red tape, and the continued existence of a political class who are largely unconcerned with the economic fate of the average citizen (Zakaria, 2008).

However, the situation is quite different today. There are four facets of globalization: economic, political, social, and cultural. Of these four facets, the economic is the most important in improving the standard of living of citizens. Media such as *The Economist*, *Wall Street Journal* (both Asian and European editions), and *International Herald Tribune* cover developments in the area of economic globalization in various societies of the world. When viewed collectively, we get the impression that certain cultural values play important roles. Economic planners and finance ministers of the emergent economies correctly assume that some cultural factors (as discussed in Chapter 1) are of crucial importance in fostering or impeding the progress of economic globalization. A study by Franke, Hofstede, & Bond (1991) reported:

1. Collectivistic countries in East Asia were registering higher levels of economic growth than the individualistic countries of Western Europe and North America.
2. A culture-specific syndrome of values termed *Confucian dynamism* (see Chapter 1) was primarily responsible for rapid economic growth.

These authors found that Confucian dynamism—an emic construct operationalized by items developed by Chinese scholars which stresses dynamic rather than static values, as reflected in the teachings of Confucius—was the primary determinant of rapid economic growth. The second cultural value was *individualism*—generally considered a liability in those parts of the world where group cohesion has generally been emphasized as a prime requirement for collective economic action. In addition, in multiple regressions with economic growth rate as the dependent variable, these authors also found that relative equality of power (lower power distance) and a tendency toward competitiveness at the expense of friendship and harmony (lower emphasis on integration) were also important predictors. Therefore, the most important predictor of economic growth in the era of globalization was Confucian dynamism, followed by individualism, and then by lower power distance and lower tendencies toward integration with one's in-group.

This research by Franke, Hofstede, & Bond (1991) was the first empirical investigation to reflect findings opposite to what Myrdal, Galbraith, and other leading economic theorists had suggested in the 1960s. The findings were rather surprising given the earlier reports by Myrdal and Galbraith which clearly depicted a majority of the Asian economies being relatively unconcerned with economic growth. In fact, Edward Luce, an economic reporter and analyst for *The Economist* who covered South Asia, noted in *In spite of the gods* (2006) that various parts of India would manage to prosper and participate effectively in the global marketplace despite the strong tendencies of the large majority of Indians to remain preoccupied with various religious practices and rituals. The point is that the observations made by Myrdal were correct, and it reflected the state of affairs of the Indian economy and other Asian economies in the 1960s. However, due to significant positive interventions by national governments starting with Hong Kong, Taiwan, Malaysia, Indonesia, and South Korea from the 1960s and then in China and India from 1976 and 1991, these countries are now members of the G-20 nations which are important players in the global economy. Chairman Mao, who strongly discouraged participation of Chinese state-owned enterprises in the global economy, died in 1976, and immediately after this significant event in the history of Mainland China, Deng Xiaaping instituted a series of economic reforms by emphasizing the value of creating wealth for personal prosperity along with collective welfare. This would not have been possible during Mao's lifetime because of the Communist ideology that characterized his regime. In 1991, India's foreign reserves reached their lowest point since independence in 1947. India's finance minister, who was an Oxford-trained economist, was able to reach a series of negotiated agreements with the International Monetary Fund (IMF) and the World Bank and began to liberalize many sectors of the Indian economy. Indian businesses began to participate most rigorously in the high-tech sector and in particular were able to secure a large number of contracts from multinational companies at the turn of the century. India's economy is now the fifth largest in the world in terms of purchasing power parity (PPP), and China's economy is the third largest in terms of PPP.

In the next section, we discuss in detail the role of cultural variations in globalization and the activities of global corporations.

CULTURAL VARIATIONS

The types of cultural variations that are important to consider in explaining the growth of globalization in different countries are as follows:

Individualism

At the country level of analysis (where data from many countries are used in the analysis), *individualism* is defined as a social pattern in which individuals in a given geographical locale are loosely connected with one another. They pursue their individual goals and are not inclined to suppress their aspirations in favor of group-generated alternatives. Triandis (2006) noted that a simple way of thinking about individualism is to consider it as a social pattern consisting of the behavior of many Hollywood movie stars. Their social relationships are in continuous flux—they do what they consider to be fun and pursue their objectives for their own economic welfare and hedonistic outcomes. Since in countries characterized by higher levels of individualism people do not derive their identities from group membership, they are likely to pursue economic activities that are entrepreneurial and are geared toward enhancing the economic benefits for themselves and their immediate in-groups. A country composed of a large number of individualists is likely to think of situations as largely variable and their own personalities as relatively stable. Individualists have very positive self-concepts (Heine, Lehman, Markus, & Kitayama, 1999) and are quite optimistic (Lee & Seligmann, 1997). When we analyze the economic history of Western Europe, in particular of Great Britain, which started the Industrial Revolution in the 18th century, and later of the Americans who sustained the rate of economic growth and globalization in the 20th century, we find that the movements were largely led by individualists. Individuals such as Andrew Carnegie, Henry Ford, the Rockefellers, and the Vanderbilts were driven by their own ambition and largely unconstrained by the societal mores of their times. The economic visionaries of the 21st century are largely individualists. They emphasize self-reliance, competition, and the value of uniqueness in their entrepreneurial activities. They also tend to be hedonistic and maintain considerable emotional distance from their in-groups. They value intelligence, creativity, persistence, and forward thinking—which are all attributes of individualists. In vertical individualistic cultures (see Chapter 1) (e.g., US and UK corporate cultures) competitiveness tends to be high and the race for being the "best" among one's peers is strongly emphasized. In horizontal individualist cultures (e.g., Sweden, Denmark, and New Zealand corporate cultures), individuals are unlikely to differentiate among themselves based on achievement, privileges, and other resources. Self-reliance, independence from others, and uniqueness in the pursuit of economic and other activities are emphasized (Triandis & Gelfand, 1998).

Societies characterized by strong tendencies toward individualism, whether they are of the vertical or horizontal type, are more likely to foster as well as to embrace various opportunities created by advances in globalization. Economic globalization not only has its origin in this context, but is largely nurtured by values of individualism at the societal level, at the group level, and at the level of the person.

Collectivism

Collectivism is almost opposite a cultural value to individualism. It is found in those societies which are largely traditional (Egypt, China, Greece, India, and Japan), simple (Mongolia, Siberian region of Russia, a larger part of the Arabian Peninsula), and tight (Japan, much of the rural part of the Arabian Peninsula, much of rural China and India). The self-concept of people in collectivist cultures has a strong social content and is highly connected with the self-concept of others (Triandis, 1989)—for example, "I am a member of this family, and I know their preferences quite well." Collectivists largely describe themselves by using information sampled from interpersonal and social domains in their lives. However, they tend to increase the number of personal attributes used in describing themselves in situations strongly characterized by values of individualism (e.g., "I am an introvert—I like classical music by Mozart or Beethoven").

Vertical collectivistic cultures (i.e., those in Franke, Hofstede, & Bond, 1991) emphasize traditional values—those which have been handed down from generation to generation and are generally found to be effective in conducting social transactions. Members of such societies stress cohesion with members of in-groups. Harmony is important. Respect for authority and norms of the in-group is strongly emphasized. In such cultures, since people are socialized to be interdependent with members of their in-groups (family, community, nation, etc.) and give priority to the goals of the in-group, they are likely to engage in economic activities whose roots lie primarily in the family or in-group context. A closer examination of the economic activities in the vertical collectivistic societies of Hong Kong, Taiwan, Singapore, Indonesia, and Malaysia during the 1970s and 1980s would reveal that family businesses were the dominant pattern. Japan, on the other hand, has been more successful than these Southeast Asian countries in developing large-scale multinational and global companies which are major players in the world economy. The major difference between Southeast Asian countries on the one hand and Japan on the other, lies in the fact that institutional collectivism (House et al., 2004) is much stronger in the Japanese context than in the context of Southeast Asian countries.

Japanese workers of all stripes see the success of any Japanese company as a source of national pride regardless of whether the successful company happens to be a major competitor of the company for which they work. For example, the successful exoneration of the Japanese carmaker Toyota (the largest automaker in the world) will be regarded as a sign of national pride. The nearest competitors of Toyota in the global marketplace are Nissan, Honda, Mitsubishi, and Mazda. The executives and workers of these companies would be happy to see Toyota being honorably cleared of the current difficulties involving defects in its products. This kind of situation is almost inconceivable in the individualistic context of the US, UK, France, and even Spain. If a competitor from one's home country experiences difficulties in the global marketplace, it is a source of much pleasure and comfort to its competitors.

One of the aspects of collectivism that might hinder the progress of globalization is that collectivists do not necessarily relate very well to individuals they consider members of out-groups. In a global economy where norms of universalism are the most important norms governing international transactions, such tendencies can severely impede the process of winning contracts from clients from different parts of the world.

The desire to know the individuals who are involved in a global transaction is rather high on the part of collectivists—especially those from the countries of Southeast and East Asia. This is not always possible and, as a result, many small businesses from these countries do not get opportunities to transact on a worldwide scale. When organizations in these societies become large, then a shift occurs. The senior managers of large multinational and global organizations from the collectivistic context train themselves to be effective in conducting business transactions with members of societies whom they consider out-groups or with whom they have had historical conflicts. The case of Japanese businesses conducting large-scale business transactions with US-based importers and companies is a good example. Companies from Communist China undertake major business transactions with countries from the capitalistic bloc. The US has the largest trade deficit with the People's Republic of China—its one-time nemesis. After US–Chinese relations were normalized following the historic visit of President Nixon in 1971, Chinese companies began to develop trade relations with their US counterparts, and then, after the death of Chairman Mao in 1976, engaged in large-scale exports to the world's largest economy.

The point is that the cultural values of collectivism might hurt the potential for expansion of family-owned businesses—businesses which are run primarily by members of in-groups and where trust-based considerations with members of one's in-group are of paramount importance. However, this cultural orientation does not seem to deter the participation of large-scale enterprises in the global marketplace.

In summary, both collectivism and individualism play important roles in the process of making the progress of globalization either rapid or slow in a given country. It is not necessarily correct to note that the collectivistic orientation of the large majority of Asian countries would be a significant deterrent to the progress of globalization and economic growth in these countries. The important work of Franke, Hofstede, & Bond (1991) demonstrates the importance of collectivism in fostering high economic growth—a finding that was most counter-intuitive in the early 1990s. Individualism, as has been noted by previous research on this cultural variation, is a major factor that encourages risk-taking, entrepreneurship, and creative participation in the dynamics of the global economy. Witness the membership of the G-8 countries—a majority of them are individualistic in their cultural orientations (i.e., the US, Canada, Germany, the UK, France, Italy, and Spain). The remaining member of the G-8 countries, by no means a lesser economy, is Japan, which is a pure collectivistic country where institutional collectivism is the hallmark of the culture.

Power Distance

This dimension of cultural variation is an important determinant of the progress of globalization. Power distance is concerned with the extent to which members of a given society who find themselves at lower strata accept the fact that power and privilege are distributed unequally. Hofstede notes that power distance scores in his 1980, 1995, and 2001 studies inform us about the nature of dependence relationships in a country. In large power distance countries, the dependence of subordinates on these superiors is rather high, whereas in low power distance countries, there is limited dependence of subordinates on superiors. There is a strong preference for consultation, that is, interdependence between superiors and subordinates in organizational (and in social) hierarchies. It is not uncommon to find subordinates expressing considerable emotional dependence on their superiors to the point of shedding tears in the presence of one's colleagues when unfortunate news strikes the person. Subordinates reveal the nature of their personal relationships including the state of their material and non-material well-being with their supervisors—something that is inconceivable in low power distance cultures such as Sweden, Denmark, Norway, and Finland.

Lower-level employees in low power distance societies also follow rules and regulations outlined in organizational routines and codes and developed by their superiors. It is only when they disagree or feel that directions are wrong that they do not follow the procedures. In high power distance societies, on the other hand, employees at both lower and higher levels of hierarchies like to follow the procedures outlined in the company manuals and do not entertain any thoughts about changing or breaking the rules even if they are wrong or unreasonable.

Globalization—especially economic globalization—might necessitate that lower-level participants of organizations (Mechanic, 1965) have more decision-making latitude in matters pertaining to certain ongoing manufacturing processes and involving quality improvement-related activities. If superiors insist on being the major players in making all of the decisions when their company is competing in the global marketplace and the need to make decisions pertaining to product quality and innovation is high and also needs to be executed rapidly, it is essential that the power distribution not be so rigid and hierarchical. One of the major reasons for the lack of competitiveness of multinational organizations from Central and South America stems from this precise phenomenon, that is, the unwillingness on the part of superiors to share power with their subordinates.

During the 1960s, there were ample opportunities for multinational and global enterprises from Latin American countries, for example Brazil,

Argentina, Chile, and Venezuela, to absorb technological innovation and various types of organizational knowledge-related developments. However, the senior executives of these companies looked the other way and did not make adequate attempts to absorb these various techniques for improving products and services that they could offer in the global marketplace. The salient reason was that absorption of technological innovation often meant that the distribution of power would change after the adoption of techniques from North America and Western European countries. This explains why Latin American countries started lagging behind the massive economic changes taking place in Japan, South Korea, Taiwan, Hong Kong, Thailand, Malaysia, and Indonesia. It behooves us to note that the Latin American countries had every incentive to adopt appropriate technological innovations from the Northern neighbors, particularly the US. There were also various incentives being offered to the various South and Central American countries (Brazil, Argentina, Mexico, and Chile) by the Commerce Department of the US government in order to facilitate the adoption of technological advances from the US. Undoubtedly, the politics of economic development played a significant role; however, one has to recognize the important role of power distance-related cultural variations as a significant dampening factor in affecting the absorption of technological advances and various knowledge management-related methods.

Uncertainty Avoidance

The cultural variation of uncertainty avoidance refers to the degree to which individuals in a given nation like to avoid uncertainty in their daily transactions. They also prefer to reduce risks and uncertainties in their dealings with various aspects of their work and social environments in both routine and non-routine situations. Hofstede (1980, 1995, 2001) noted that this variation of cultural dimension is a derivative of power distance and chose to label it *uncertainty avoidance*. It is defined as the extent to which members of a given society feel threatened by uncertain or unknown situations. If individuals go to great lengths to avoid ambiguities in their routine and non-routine transactions with people and with various situational demands, then they are said to be high in uncertainty avoidance. Cultures that are high in uncertainty avoidance tend to be more expressive, that is, there is a great deal of reliance on body language and non-verbal expression to release their anxieties and to make sure that their message is conveyed without any ambiguities and, in fact, in a fairly precise fashion.

Globalization of all types induces uncertainties (Grieder, 1997). Farmers and those who earn their livelihoods by working the land are often induced to working in new environments (often high-tech and information-based industries) established in special economic zones (SEZs in countries such as China, South Korea, India, Brazil, and Russia). The degree of uncertainty that these new workers undergo in urban work environments as a result of being uprooted is enormous and highly stressful. If adequate assistance is not provided to these workers in the form of employee assistance programs or work-related counseling, they are likely to experience high levels of job stress, job depression, and poor occupational health (Bhagat, Steverson, & Segovis, 2007). In particular, workers in countries such as Greece, Poland, and others characterized by higher scores on the dimension of uncertainty avoidance are likely to experience negative job-related experiences during times of rapid globalization taking place in their countries. Therefore, it follows that countries which are materially predisposed toward healthy acceptance of uncertainty avoidance in their work and non-work contexts are likely to embrace various technological and organizational changes that are brought about by economic globalization in SEZs of the country.

Masculinity and Femininity

The relationships between this dimension of cultural variations and the progress of globalization are somewhat unclear. The use of the term *masculinity versus femininity* to reflect the degree of differentiation between the gender roles in a given society has been somewhat controversial. In Hofstede's use, masculinity refers to societies in which the gender roles are clearly distinct (i.e., men are supposed to be assertive, tough, and more focused on material success whereas women are supposed to be more modest, concerned with tenderness, nurturing, and quality of life as opposed to materialistic success). Femininity, according to Hofstede, pertains to societies in which expectations from the two gender roles largely overlap, that is, both men and women perform similar social and occupational roles, tend to be modest, and are equally concerned with the quality of life. Recently, there has also been a trend to link feminine countries with high concern for preservation of the environment.

In masculine societies, success and money are the dominant concerns, whereas in feminine societies, the quality of human life as well as the environment are valued more than material accomplishments in the domain of work organizations and society. In masculine societies such as Japan and many of the countries in the Arabian Peninsula, job stress and a considerable amount of supervisory oversight are common. In contrast, in more feminine societies such as those in Scandinavia, the Netherlands,

Israel, and Austria, cooperation with one's colleagues is emphasized, and there is also significant concern for occupational health and psychological well-being of workers and managers at all levels of the organization. Women are found in higher echelons of corporations and other non-profit organizations more often in feminine societies than in masculine societies. Interestingly, Japan, the second largest economy in the world, has not been able to effectively integrate female managers into the higher levels of organizations. It is generally believed by cross-cultural management researchers that this is largely due to the high masculine orientation (95 for Japan in contrast with 5 for Sweden, 8 for Norway, and 14 for the Netherlands) of Japanese multinational and global organizations and of wider Japanese society.

The implication of this cultural orientation is that masculine societies are likely to be quick to embrace large-scale projects such as bigger buildings, skyscrapers, large manufacturing facilities, and technologically complex projects involving aerospace, computers, electronics, and so on. Feminine countries, on the other hand, are likely to emphasize higher levels of innovation in projects that are relatively smaller in scope. Compare the scale of Hitachi Industries or Mitsubishi Corporation of Japan with Nokia of Finland or Volvo of Sweden. Uniformity of pressures for producing various manufactured goods increases with globalization, and it is likely that the differences between masculine and feminine countries are likely to slowly disappear over time in terms of their preferences for larger versus smaller but high quality-oriented projects.

Temporal Orientation

In Western cultures, efficient use of time is emphasized. By efficient, we mean getting a lot of real work done in a defined span of time. For instance, Americans prefer segmenting activities according to clock time, resulting in less attention being paid to the quality of events, particularly those which focus on enhancing interpersonal aspects of life (Bhagat & Moustafa, 2002). In the US, Switzerland, Germany, Austria, Japan, and the UK, time has the same connotation as money. Wasting time is equivalent to wasting money in an unproductive fashion. Western Europeans (as opposed to Southern Europeans and Turkey) are much more concerned with efficient use of time. In a recent international conference at Nizhny Novgorod University in Novgorod, Russia, the focus was on the cultural foundations of differential perception of time and time-related phenomena in organizations. Scholars from Russia, Germany, the Netherlands, and Asia noted that Russians (Eastern Europeans in terms of their national origins) are much less concerned with efficient use of time. Time spent on activities to sustain interpersonal affect and romantic relationships takes precedence over work-related activities in the Russian and other Slavic countries in Eastern Europe. The focus of the conference was to increase the sense of temporal orientation on the part of Russian managers, who are increasingly being called upon to manage their enterprises in a manner so as to be highly competitive in the global economy. What this means is that efficient use of time in executing organizational activities and various tasks in a monochronic fashion is becoming important—an activity that was largely frowned upon in Soviet Russia.

Long-Term versus Short-Term Orientation: Confucian Dynamic

This dimension of cultural variation—discovered by Hofstede in his re-analysis of the IBM data and reported in his 1991 book *Cultures and Organizations: Software of the Mind* and later in a larger volume in 2001— is concerned with the extent to which different societies are concerned with differential emphases on time and temporal activities in their social and organizational contexts.

In a follow-up to Hofstede's IBM studies, Bond & Smith (2006) based their long- versus short-term orientation on values which are reminiscent of the teachings of Confucius. Characteristics such as harmony, tolerance of others, contentedness with one's position in life, trustworthiness, and kindness are associated with the Confucian dynamic. Confucianism is not seen as a religion but as a set of pragmatic rules by which one lives. According to Confucianism, there are several key principles involved with this way of life:

1. The stability of a society is based on unequal relationships between people.
2. The family is a prototype of all social organizations.
3. Virtuous behavior toward others consists of treating others as one would like to be treated oneself.
4. Virtue with regard to one's task in life consists of trying to acquire all skills and education, working hard, not spending more than necessary, being patient, and persevering (Hofstede, 2001).

According to Hofstede (2001), Confucian values refer to long-term versus short-term orientation. China, Japan, Korea, and Thailand are countries which have a long-term orientation. Values such as persistence allow individuals to pursue goals which are entrepreneurial in nature and ordering relationships by status allows these individuals to experience harmony and stable relationships which facilitate long-term business relationships. Another value associated with the Confucian dynamic is thrift, or the ability to use financial resources wisely and save money. In times of economic pressure, the ability to control and preserve resources is essential in order to maintain profitability in global markets. However, these same attributes that lead to cohesion, social harmony, and respect for tradition can also impede innovative processes that can lead to improved products and services in accordance with the ever-changing demands of the global marketplace.

In contrast, in those countries which are characterized by short-term time orientation, such as the US, UK, Australia, New Zealand, Germany, France, and Finland (generally members of the individualistic family of countries), quick feedback from their efforts to penetrate or win the market share in the global economy is valued more. Sometimes, this is achieved at the expense of maintaining harmony in the workplace and with vendors and clients. The tendency to invest resources in projects that are likely to yield results in the short term is valued more. Respect for precedence in accomplishing organizational goals and missions is not valued as much as spontaneous actions that might result in success in the marketplace.

The consequences of short-term versus long-term time orientation on globalization are clear-cut. Where countries characterized by short-term orientation are likely to make quick strikes for learning from their globalized brethren, the chances that they might commit some irreversible errors are also rather high. On the other hand, organizations and countries characterized by long-term orientation will be slow in absorbing technological and process-related innovations, but the chances of organizational learning (Argote & Todorova, 2007) that yields accurate outcomes also increases. A review of the economic history and development of countries with collectivistic and long-term orientations reveals that they have been successful in avoiding knowledge disavowal and at the same time launch market-friendly products and services on an ongoing basis. Franke, Hofstede, & Bond (1991) noted that the economic growth of the future is likely to belong to those countries which are high in long-term orientation and Confucian dynamism.

A likely hallmark of countries characterized by short-term orientation is *analytic thinking*, whereas *systemic thinking* is the more dominant norm of societies characterized by long-term orientation. Analytic thinking may lead to radical breakthroughs and scientific discoveries; however, it does not guarantee success in the global marketplace. In other words, countries characterized by high levels of analytic thinking in the R & D laboratories of multinational and global corporations are not necessarily more successful in winning large shares of the ever-expanding pie of the global marketplace in many consumer sectors. Systemic thinking leads to a complete acceptance of the innovative tendencies initiated by the senior managers on a system-wide basis, and this is precisely the strength of large-scale Japanese, Chinese, South Korean, and even Indian global and multinational companies. While the global organizations in these countries might be less effective in radical scientific innovations, they are nonetheless quite efficient and make system-wide efforts in creating products that are user-friendly for today's market as well as for the future. We suggest that countries which favor long-term orientation are likely to be higher on uncertainty avoidance compared with those which prefer a quicker way of responding to the markets and various signals in the global economy. Japan, the second largest economy in the world, is characterized by high degrees of uncertainty avoidance (92 as opposed to 46 for the US and 65 for Germany, the first and the third largest economies in the world).

CULTURAL VARIATIONS AND GLOBALIZATION: WHERE DO WE GO FROM HERE?

Globalization is often easier to describe in anecdotal terms than to define in a fashion making it amenable for an analysis based on cultural variations among nations. In general, it reflects the growing interdependence of various countries and regions of the world. It is a process as opposed to an outcome that aims at integrating not just the various diverse economies of the world but their cultures, technologies, and systems of political governance as well. People everywhere are becoming increasingly interconnected, and in fact are affected by events taking place in the far corners of the world. There is no doubt that globalization has become the most important economic, political, and cultural phenomenon of the late 20th and now the 21st century. It is going to play an increasingly important, if not the dominant, role in the political governance of the countries and peoples of the world. Integration of the world economy is not only changing the nature of businesses but is also reordering the priorities of various economic and international institutions, such as the WTO, IMF, World Bank, and UNESCO, and business organizations of all kinds (not just large transnationals like Microsoft and General Motors but small family-owned businesses as well). The lives of individuals and goals and objectives of national governments and labor unions of all kinds are also affected by the kind of globalization that eventually grows roots in a given country.

Globalization as a process is neither new nor complete. It has been in existence for the past few centuries. However, its importance in recent times has increased many-fold—not only in terms of economic importance, but also in terms of its potential role in affecting the social, political, and cultural characteristics of the various countries and regions. Take for example the case of the Arabian Peninsula—the latest world report in 2011 by *The Economist* noted Qatar as the most efficient economy of this year, whereas Somalia in Northeast Africa was rated the most miserable nation in the world in terms of economic growth rate, violence in society, and overall quality of well-being of its citizens. For some world leaders, such as George Bush and Barak Obama of the US, Gordon Brown of the UK, Nicholas Sarkozy of France, Angela Merkel of Germany, Yukio Hatoyama of Japan, Hu Jintao of the People's Republic of China, Dmitri Anatolyevich Medvedev of Russia, and Manmahan Singh of India, globalization is synonymous with modernity and economic progress in their respective countries. While there was considerable ambivalence regarding the liberalization of domestic markets in countries such as China, India, Brazil, Mexico, South Africa, and Russia, the failure of the Soviet Union to sustain a viable economic alternative to the US and Japanese model of capitalism has enshrined the path of globalization in all geographical regions of the world. According to current estimates (The year in 2010, *The Economist*), the most globalized continent in the world is North America, and the least is Africa. The overall contribution of Africa to global domestic product is less than 5 percent, whereas Japan by itself contributes over 22 percent of global GDP and China is a close third (the US being first and Japan second). It has been predicted that the 21st century will be the "Chinese century" (Shenkar, 2005).

Collectively, there have been dramatic changes in the economic history of the world since the 1980s: *Chindia Rising* (Sheth, 2007), *The Chinese Century* (Shenkar, 2005), and *Africa Rising* (Mahajan, 2007) portray some of these major transformations. The people of the world as well as scholars of international business and cross-cultural management long for the day when the economic inequality that characterizes the current income distribution in the world will be diminished. Cultural factors clearly play major roles in either accelerating or impeding the progress of globalization in a given country context or in specific geographic locales.

The expansion of global corporations such as General Motors, Ford, IBM, Sony, and Coca Cola in culturally dissimilar (i.e., dissimilar from the West) countries is often held responsible for many of the adverse consequences of globalization. To be sure, no one is immune from the far-reaching consequences of globalization: it creates growing inequalities between countries, social classes, and individuals (Stiglitz, 2002). Moreover, the benefits of globalization are not distributed as either the proponents or critics of globalization espouse. During the last two decades, many noted critics of globalization have feared that it was counter-productive for cultural expression and development. It was also thought that forces of globalization would ultimately lead to the sacrifice or discarding of indigenous cultural values, norms, and practices, thus extinguishing the native and weak cultures of the world in various regions.

REFERENCES

Argote, L. & Todorova, G. (2007). Organizational learning. In G.P. Hodgkinson and J.K. Ford (Eds). *International review of industrial and organizational psychology* (Vol. 22, pp. 193–234). New York: John Wiley.

Bhagat, R.S. & Moustafa, K.S. (2002). How non-Americans view American use of time: A cross-cultural perspective. In Pawel Boski, Fons J.R. van de Viver, & A.M. Chodynicka (Eds). *New directions in cross-cultural psychology. Selected papers from the Fifteenth International Congress of the International Association for Cross-Cultural Psychology* (pp. 183–192). Warsaw: Polish Psychological Association.

Bhagat, R.S., Steverson, P.K. & Segovis, J.S. (2007). International and cultural variations in employee assistance programmes: Implications for managerial health and effectiveness. *Journal of Management Studies*, 44(2), 222–42.

Bond, M. & Smith, P.D. (2006). Cross-cultural and social and organizational psychology. *Annual Review of Psychology*, 47, 205–35.

Franke, R.H., Hofstede, G., & Bond, M.H. (1991). Cultural roots of economic performance: A research note. *Strategic Management Journal*, 12, Special Issue: Global Strategy (Summer), 165–73.

Galbraith, J.K. (1967). *The new industrial state*. New York: Houghton-Mifflin.

Grieder, W. (1997). *One world: Ready or not: The manic logic of globalization*. New York: Simon Schuster.

Heine, S.J., Lehman, D.R., Markus, H.R., & Kitayama, S. (1999). Is there a universal need for positive self-regard? *Psychological Review*, 106, 766–94.

Hofstede, G. (1980). *Cultural consequences: International differences in work-related values*. Thousand Oaks, CA: Sage Publications.

Hofstede, G. (1991). *Cultures and organizations: Software of the mind*. London: McGraw-Hill.

Hofstede, G. (1995). Multilevel research of human systems: Flowers, bouquets, and gardens. *Human Systems Management*, 14, 207–17.

Hofstede, G. (2001). *Culture's consequences* (2nd edn).Thousand Oaks, CA: Sage Publications.

House, J., Hanges, P.J., Javidan, M., Dorfman, P.W., & Gupta, V. (Eds) (2004). *Leadership, culture, and organizations: The GLOBE study of 62 societies*. Thousand Oaks, CA: Sage.

Lee, Y.-T. & Seligman, M.E.P. (1997). Are Americans more optimistic than Chinese? *Journal of Personality and Social Psychology*, 23(1), 32–40.

Luce, E. (2006). *In spite of the gods*. New York: Random House.

Mahajan, V. (2007). *Africa rising*. Philadelphia, PA: Wharton School Publishing.

Mechanic, D. (1965). Sources of power for lower participants in complex organizations. *Administrative Sciences Quarterly*, 7(3), 349–64.

Myrdal, G. (1968). *The Asian drama*. New York: Pantheon.

Parker, B. (2005). Globalization. In S.R. Clegg, C. Hardy, & R. Nord (Eds). *Sage handbook of organizational studies*. Thousand Oaks, CA: Sage Publications.

Shenkar, O. (2005). *The Chinese century*. Philadelphia, PA: Wharton School Publishing.

Sheth, J. (2007). *Chindia rising*. New Delhi: Tata McGraw-Hill.

Stiglitz, J.E. (2002). *Globalization and its discontents*. New York: W.W. Norton.

The Economist (2011). The year in 2010. Available at: http://www.economist.com / theworldin/2010?d=2010 (accessed 23 July 2011).

Triandis, H.C. (1989). Cross-cultural studies of individualism and collectivism. In John J. Berman (Ed.). *Cross-cultural perspectives* (pp. 41–133). Lincoln, NE: University of Nebraska Press.

Triandis, H.C. (2006). Cultural aspects of globalization. *Journal of International Management*, 12(2), 208–17.

Triandis, H.C. & Gelfand, M. (1998). Converging measurements of horizontal and vertical individualism and collectivism. *Journal of Personality and Social Psychology*, 74, 118–28.

Zakaria, F. (2008). *The post-American world*. New York: W.W. Norton.

4. Cultural variations in communication

Communication is ubiquitous in 21st century multinational and global organizations. The variety and the volume of communication that characterize the process of getting work done are much higher than in any preceding century. Along with the proliferation of different types of media (e.g., face-to-face, computer-mediated, network-based) through which people communicate, there is clearly a growing confusion about what to communicate, to whom, and at what time, and what is the eventual usefulness of such communication. The difficulty arises primarily because of national and cultural differences in the emphasis on the process of communication and the role that communication and the media play when conveying information, so that it is consistent with the cultural norms of the various societies.

WHAT IS COMMUNICATION?

Communication is the process of exchanging information between two or more individuals, in a group or in an organization. Managers of multinational and global organizations need to communicate on an ongoing basis to coordinate and disseminate information, and to control as well as implement organizational initiatives. There are times when communication is essential in order to share information about an important event, such as the closure of a plant or factory in the domestic or international market—as was the case with General Motors closing the Opel manufacturing facilities in Germany. Communication functions as the glue that develops valued interpersonal relationships, tasks, and social networks in organizations—regardless of the cultural contexts. Effective cross-communication is of pivotal importance in all types of transactions across national borders and cultures. While effective patterns of communication facilitate ongoing business transactions, breakdowns of vital communication in the various networks of multinational global organizations have an adverse impact on international competitiveness. The process of communicating across borders and cultures is generally well understood.

However, here we present a model that incorporates some of the recent complexities created due to the heavy emphasis on computer-mediated methods of communication across borders and cultures.

CULTURAL INFLUENCES ON THE PROCESS OF COMMUNICATION

Figure 4.1 depicts normative beliefs (beliefs about the right kinds of information to convey or not convey) regarding appropriate ways of communicating. It also describes the culture-specific preferences for the type of communication media, and the history of experiences (for instance, successful experiences when communicating with members of other cultures) that are important when beginning and when sending a communication. The receiver of a communication should have appropriate cognitive abilities to construe and interpret both the direct and indirect information content inherent in the messages. Familiarity and preferences for the medium used can facilitate the accurate receiving of the information. In addition, the histories of success or failure in communicating with members of the culture of the sender are also important. Factors that moderate the communication process are:

1. The extent to which the communication styles used by the sender and receiver are compatible with their cultures.
2. The extent to which the parties prefer communication that is explicit or implicit; for instance, how much articulation is needed to decipher the messages.

According to this model, characteristics inherent in the cultural environments of the sender as well as the receiver help determine the normative beliefs about how to conduct a successful communication. Cultural factors strongly influence the extent to which the communication should be open and frank or subtle and indirect. Also, the degree of confrontation or open conflict that can be reflected in the communication process depends on the cultural backgrounds of the sender and receiver of the information. As Figure 4.1 depicts, the history of success or failure during past communications is also a determinant of the effectiveness of the communication. If a manager from Culture 1 has generally been successful in communicating without distortion with members from Culture 2, then the perceived probability (and possibly the real possibility) of communicating effectively improves.

Communication behaviors that are typical in modern multinational and

Sender (Culture 1)

Normative beliefs about appropriate
ways of communicating

Preference for communication medium

History of communication-related
experience with members of Culture 2

Cultural differences in communication style
Preference for explicit vs. implicit messages

Receiver's response (Culture 2)

Ability to decode and interpret both explicit
and implicit messages

Preference for communication medium

History of communication-related
experiences with members of Culture 1

Situational influences on communication process
Normative beliefs about appropriate ways of communicating

——— Presumed causal inferences
- - - - Presumed moderating influences

Figure 4.1 Cultural influences on interpersonal communication

global organizations are usually verbal and non-verbal, as well as virtual. Virtual forms of communication include e-mails, teleconferencing, and other forms of computer-mediated communication. Virtual communications have increased dramatically in the 21st century. It is not possible to manage global organizations, of the type and scale that exist today, by simple verbal and non-verbal methods. Communication among geographically dispersed units of organizations requires the use of global information technology. This facilitates the effective sharing of information, data, and knowledge among the various decision-makers.

In today's global economy, there has been an unprecedented growth of multinational and global corporations. Many cultures are involved in transactions in the global marketplace. In order to survive in this competitive global environment, organizations must develop new strategies and re-train their workforces to be better equipped to operate in the global arena. The organizations that address the importance of understanding others, and of effectively *communicating* with other cultures, will be the organizations that succeed.

Cultural differences reflect cultural dimensions, such as individualism–collectivism, power distance, and uncertainty avoidance. Personal-level attributes such as self-construals, communication styles, and face work are also important factors that determine the effectiveness of cross-cultural communication. Self-construals are psychological processes that involve separation or integration of important concerns about one's "self" with others. In the European–American view of personhood, one's self evolves by emphasizing an independent mode of construal, whereas in the East Asian view of personhood, one's self evolves in an interdependent mode. Face work involves conscious and unconscious actions in order to preserve one's reputation in the immediate social context.

Social exchanges or decision-making may emphasize getting things done or good relationships. In individualist cultures achievement is of the greatest importance, but in collectivist cultures good relationships are of the greatest importance. Managers of multinational and global organizations must understand not only the fundamentals of communication but also the importance of building and sustaining personal relationships. Through the building of these relationships, trust and mutual respect can be established, and these two elements will lay the groundwork on which to build effective communication and achieve desirable outcomes. With the advent of globalization, organizations are expanding into international markets, forming strategic alliances, and/or are subject to mergers and acquisitions. Those organizational members who exhibit cross-cultural communication competency will be in a better position to succeed in this environment.

CULTURE AND COMMUNICATION: A CLOSER LOOK

Of the many factors that influence the effectiveness of communication (the accuracy of receiving messages without much noise or distortion), issues of cultural variation are perhaps the most important. Other factors that play important roles include the distance between various subsidiaries of the multinational corporation and the speed with which communication can be conveyed—either by using telephone or by computer-mediated means such as e-mail, faxes, and satellite-based communication systems. Cultural variations in enhancing or impeding communication across national boundaries influence the degree of shared beliefs, attitudes, meanings, and values that are central to particular cultures. In the 1980s, there was little understanding of the culture of virtual work teams and how distinctive orientations of virtual work teams selectively influence communication across national boundaries. Cultures provide appropriate platforms or forums for directing a variety of opinions and judgments made by the important members of a specific group—ethnic, national, or virtual. It is common knowledge that the groups that speak different languages or dialects or have not learned the languages of the other group experience communication difficulties. In fact, often the performance of a team composed of members speaking different languages or dialects is not as good as one where the members speak the same language or dialect. One of the most important components of training expatriates is to improve their language skills so that they can function effectively in another culture. People are unlikely or unable to make isomorphic attributions while communicating with others using different languages (i.e., languages that are not native to one's home country).

Effectiveness of communication is also largely dependent on some of the unique beliefs and values that emerge in historical, economic, political, or social contexts.

COMMUNICATION CHARACTERISTICS

Communication can take place using verbal, non-verbal, virtual, and computer-mediated media. Most communications which occur in face-to-face situations are usually language-dependent, but in some cultures non-verbal cues are more important than the verbal ones. For example, Bello, Brandau-Brown, Zhang, & Ragsdale (2010) examined the use of verbal and non-verbal methods of expressing appreciation among Chinese and Americans. They found that Americans relied about evenly on verbal and non-verbal methods but Chinese favored non-verbal significantly more than verbal methods.

Non-verbal cues must be properly interpreted and assimilated. Miscommunication is often the result of a significant gap between what is interpreted as being said—that is, the verbal content of the message—and the cues conveyed by a variety of gestures, body language, silence, and eye contact (or lack of it). Much non-verbal communication is involuntary and often does not involve a lot of calculation on the part of the sender. However, non-verbal communication reflects the content of the message often more correctly than what is being conveyed verbally. Verbal messages tend to be more calculated in situations involving intercultural communication. People tend to be diplomatic and not as straightforward as is the case in a monocultural context. Verbal communication includes words whose meanings may be changed by inflection, intonation, pitch, volume, and speed. Words can be denotative (representing an entity) or connotative (associating entities with each other) and can also be concrete or abstract. For example, English is highly idiomatic and many non-native speakers find it difficult to learn. Even with the use of a translator or interpreter, idioms may not be understood correctly. Certain words do not translate well, and sometimes they are associated with concepts that are quite different across cultures. For example, when an American auto company marketed the Nova in Latin America the promotion was a disaster, since *"no va"* means "it does not go." Use of connotative forms of language may result in a richer message, but unless the individuals who are involved in a particular discourse share similar connotative meanings, the richness of the message may be lost. This is why poetry is so extraordinarily difficult to translate. To be sure, both non-verbal and verbal forms of communication are needed. Accurate interpretations of both of these forms will result in the message being successfully understood and without much effort.

BARRIERS TO EFFECTIVE COMMUNICATION

The art of communicating fluently is difficult to master. It becomes more difficult when communicating with members of cultures that are very different, that is, belong to different language families. For instance, it is easy to translate a Latin-based language such as Spanish into another Latin-based language such as French. It is much more difficult to translate English into Chinese. Cultural distance (Triandis, 1994, p. 33) makes communication difficult. In addition to language, people who differ in social class, past experiences, and values will also have communication difficulties. People with different cultural backgrounds also may have less common information (about heroes, religion, geography, politics, economics, philosophy), which decreases the effectiveness of communication. Additional factors that act as barriers include:

- stereotypes of the other culture;
- ethnocentric tendencies;
- beliefs about what it is correct to communicate;
- attitudes toward the content of the message;
- cultural preferences regarding the medium used;
- educational level and professional competence of both the sender and receiver;
- habits of paralinguistic communication (looking or not looking in the eyes, posture, gestures, appropriate distance between the bodies of the communicators, touching or not touching, loudness of speech, use or no use of silence, and the like);
- different conceptions of politeness;
- the structure of messages (Triandis, 1994, p. 190).

Ethnocentrism reflects a sense of superiority that members of one culture feel in relation to members of another culture. Ethnocentric individuals believe that their way of thinking and communicating is the best. It is difficult to change one's ethnocentric biases in communication unless one has experienced communication failures which resulted in learning a lot about effective communication across cultures. Such learning will include identifying different patterns and styles of communication in dissimilar societies. Cognitive schemas and mindsets of adults are relatively stable and internally coherent (Fazzi, 2001). More often than not, individuals screen out information and ideas which are incongruent with their beliefs and values.

Stereotyping of another culture acts as a barrier to effective cross-cultural communication. *Stereotyping* is the process of attributing traits to members of another group. Stereotypes tend to define people by their demographic, ethnic, organizational, and national memberships. For example, some stereotypes about members of other cultures, held by some Americans, are that Italians are emotional and Germans are highly methodical. Stereotypical beliefs often guide patterns of communication across cultures. While stereotypes may contain a grain of truth, more often than not they inhibit effective communication. Stereotypes often are oversimplifications. For instance, in many places people have the stereotype that Americans are rich. That is obviously not true for the 20 percent of the American population that survives on minimum wages.

Often a particular attribute is over-emphasized at the expense of other attributes. That Germans are generally methodical may be true for most but not all Germans. If one communicates with a particular German assuming that it applies to that person, it may result in a miscommunication. Some German members of the work group may not be methodical at all, and therefore may be annoyed when receiving information that assumes the validity of the stereotype. This can lead to potential misunderstanding in communication and even conflict. However, Lee & Duenas (1995) found that when communication between Mexican and American business persons was free from ambiguities and distortion, emphasizing some aspects of stereotypes could result in better forms of negotiation. This happens because stereotypes contain a "kernel of truth" (Allport, 1954), and they can provide a provisional basis for one's interaction with others—thus promoting intercultural effectiveness in the initial stages of encounters. It follows that multinational and global managers who are not as effective in cross-cultural communication are likely to be unable to change their stereotypes. This can persist even in situations when members of the other dissimilar culture have acted counter-stereotypically (Riatu, 1983).

The content of communication is valued differently in dissimilar cultures. One may exaggerate some peripheral elements of the message more strongly in some nations than in others. For instance, compared with individuals from Western cultures (the UK, Germany, France, the US, and Switzerland), individuals from Middle Eastern cultures (e.g., Saudi Arabia, UAE, Egypt, Jordan) place more emphasis on social and interpersonal aspects of the message, especially content that concerns differences in status. Such emphasis may not be necessarily linked with the central message(s) that are being conveyed. As a general rule, individualists prefer to emphasize as well as like to receive *specific* aspects of the message that are immediately relevant for their thoughts or actions. Individualists are interested in knowing the exact content of the message that is necessary for decision-making or action—whether it is in the context of work or non-work. In fact, peripheral elements of communications are likely to be regarded as extraneous to the message and a waste of time. Continuous emphasis on peripheral information is likely to annoy and frustrate individualists. However, collectivists tend to focus on many peripheral aspects of the content before discussing the central themes that might be relevant for immediate decision-making. This happens because collectivists are more interested in developing cordial relationships prior to engaging in business transactions than in focusing on the task.

The issue of developing and maintaining trust is especially important when communicating with collectivists. It may not be wise to communicate something that might be damaging to the self-esteem of collectivists: an opportunity for saving face should be either present or created. In contrast to this pattern for communicating, managers from multinational and global corporations of individualistic countries are more inclined to get to the specifics ("nitty-gritty") of the communication and do not necessarily see the relevance of developing trust in matters that are purely related to business decisions. Collectivists, on the other hand, feel a degree of comfort when they know that they are communicating with someone that they can trust in matters other than those related to the business transaction. As multinational and global businesses extend their reaches in dissimilar nations and cultures of the world, we will begin to develop more insights into the role of trust in sustaining both short-term and long-term patterns of communication.

Attitudes toward the content of the message are also valued differently in different cultural contexts. Collectivists pay more attention to messages that come from individuals who are at higher levels of the organizational or social hierarchy than do individualists. In fact, individualists are not necessarily likely to favor messages coming from high-status individuals. The tone and the sense of respect that need to be conveyed during the communication are of greater significance in collectivist than in individualist countries. In India, for example, the manner (i.e., the style of addressing) used by a subordinate interacting with a supervisor is very different from the way that person would address a fellow co-worker or colleague. The word "you" in the English language has only one connotation in English-speaking countries, but it has three different status connotations in India. In Japan also one has to use different words to address a person of equal, higher, or very high status. In addressing the Emperor, one must use a term that is only used in addressing the Emperor. Furthermore, the terms used by women are not exactly the same as the terms used by men.

The use of sophisticated information technology, management information systems, and computer-mediated communication allows managers of multinational and global corporations to communicate with each other easily and frequently. However, cultures differ in their preferences for the choice of media. Members of some cultures have a strong preference for face-to-face communication and communication that uses a lot of context. In many cultures, non-verbal cues are given much more weight than verbal cues. In short, *how* one says something may be all-important and *what* one says may be of little importance. Non-verbal and contextual aspects of communication are valued by members of some cultures (e.g., the Japanese, and members of Middle Eastern, African, and Latin American cultures) much more than verbal aspects.

Communication difficulties usually tend to diminish when educated members of dissimilar cultures engage in sending messages to one another. There is a culture of the "jet-set" which is different from national cultures. Communication in that culture tends to be similar to communication in individualist cultures. Increases in the educational levels of individuals are correlated positively with cognitive complexity. The more educated and professionally qualified persons develop skills that make it possible for them to understand the nuances and subtleties of communication from dissimilar occupational, national, ethnic, and other geographically diverse populations. International conferences which are attended by members from dissimilar countries and cultures are usually free of misunderstandings. All attendees understand the language of the conference, which tends to be English, French, or German (one of the languages of the Western European countries), and the immediate focus of the attendees is on the scientific content of the papers being presented and the discoveries that are being discussed. In fact, scientific disciplines, such as mathematics, communicate in the languages of the discipline, so that a talk at a conference may be understood by just following the presentation of mathematical equations.

THE ROLE OF IDEOLOGY VERSUS PRAGMATISM

Some nations as well as cultures put a strong premium on the role of ideology in various types of communication—whether they are conducted within the work organization or in a social context. The ideology can be political (such as Marxism), religious (Judeo-Christian, Islamic, Hindu, Buddhist), or a worldview (i.e., strong emphasis on self-interest versus strong concern for the less fortunate). It may also involve a theory of economics, politics, philosophy, education, or aesthetics. The center of the communication tends to start with the assumption that the other party— that is, the recipient of the communication—is broadly aware of the central values held in the nation or the culture of the sender. Members of Socialist and Communist countries tend to emphasize the role of ideology (such as emphasis on central economic planning and state ownership of lands, factories, etc.) as a general guiding principle in communicating with members of capitalist and market-driven countries. Managers from countries where market-related transactions govern the economic enterprise tend to be more pragmatic, that is, less concerned with ideology. They expect the content of communication to be direct, expressed in specific terms, and free from ideological concerns and jargon. Individualists from market-driven economies are not inclined to waste their time worrying about ideological concerns. They feel that excessive communication concerning ideological issues is bound to slow the speed of decision-making and the efficiency of cross-border transactions. Ideology may also make decision-making less linked to "reality."

Communicators from ideological cultures are likely to begin the communication with the assumption that their ideology is correct, and the facts must fit the ideology. They often present a generalization, and then add facts that they consider consistent with it. Communications from pragmatic cultures are more likely to start with many facts, and end with a generalization that fits the facts. As a result, the structure of communications is quite different. The ideologists present the broad framework and place the facts within it. The structure is *deductive*. Facts that do not agree with the framework are ignored. The pragmatists present the facts first, and the generalization emerges *inductively*.

ABSTRACTIVE VERSUS ASSOCIATIVE NORMS

Associative norms tend to characterize many rural areas in highly homogenous and tight cultures. Parts of Japan, Korea, China, Mexico, countries in sub-Saharan Africa, and a majority of the countries in Eastern and Southern Europe communicate by using associative modes of processing information. The countries of South America are also fairly associative. In associative cultures, the elements in a communication may not be linked logically to each other. For example, in one case a communicator asked for a 3 percent change, and the recipient of the communication said "No." When the communicator suggested a change of 2.9 percent, the recipient said "Yes." How could this trivial change account for the difference in the response? It turned out that a few years earlier the predecessor of the recipient was fired after he agreed to a 3 percent change. Thus 3 percent was associated with a bad outcome, but 2.9 percent did not have this connotation. Historical factors, past precedence, and relationship-oriented issues play dominant roles. Associative modes of thinking are found more commonly in the collectivistic contexts of Asian and Latin American cultures (Glenn & Glenn, 1981). Circular thinking is also often used (Nisbett, 2003) in China. Thus, if something (say the stock market) is good, it is likely to become bad, and then again it is likely to become good.

Communication that is heavily skewed toward scientific and abstractive forms of information is likely to be highly valued in Western cultures. Abstractive as opposed to associative cultures (United States versus Mexico or Bolivia) emphasize logical, systematic, and linear modes of thinking (Nisbett, 2003). Members of abstractive cultures are much more inclined to absorb communications that are high in explicit content and tend to disregard tacit or indirect information. In contrast, members of associative cultures prefer information that is more contextual and implicit. In general, communication tends to break down when members of collectivistic cultures, who emphasize associative modes of thinking, communicate with members of individualist cultures, who emphasize abstractive modes of thinking.

THE ROLE OF SYMBOLS

Throughout the history of mankind, the role of symbols in communicating a distinct idea or thought has been important. Consider the sickle and hammer sign on a red flag. It indicates a Communist regime such as China, Russia, or North Korea. Symbols are usually highly culture-specific. They can create noise or confusion when used without adequate accompanying explanations. Just as symbols have to be appropriately developed and the nature of meaning associated with each symbol must be taken into account, the sender and the receiver must also be skilled in adopting appropriate media to convey the message containing the symbol. Consider the theme of the best-seller, *The Da Vinci Code* (2003) by Dan Brown; the symbol depicted in the book was supposed to reveal some special message regarding the life of Jesus Christ, the founder of Christianity. The message was so powerful that it created severe conflicts and clashes among various parties with dissimilar interests in different parts of the world.

Uniformities in the use of symbols are developing in much of the globalized and advanced countries of the world. Their use has also spread to the globalizing and emergent economies, but we have not reached the stage where the importance of symbols and symbolic processes can be either ignored or given lesser importance when communicating across nations and cultures. Managers should learn as much as possible about the use of various types of symbols in the cultures in which they are doing business. They should do so not only to be more effective in the immediate future but also to develop an understanding of the underlying cultural foundations of the countries that are important in the global marketplace.

Other barriers that cause difficulties in cross-cultural communication include the use of etiquette, humor, self-disclosure, elaborate versus succinct discourse, silence, and the role of truthfulness. Discussion of these barriers follows. First, we deal with the issues concerning etiquette, humor, and self-disclosure.

ETIQUETTE, HUMOR, AND SELF-DISCLOSURE

Cultures differ in what they consider to be the polite forms of communication and etiquette in communication. For instance, the way one requests an action, or specifies how to perform a task or hope to fulfill a given role or obligation, can be conveyed in many different ways. Depending on the skill of the communicator, the request may be approved or denied. For example, the way one interacts in Japanese, Korean, or Brazilian cultures emphasizes smooth interpersonal relationships. Saving face is particularly important in East Asian cultures. Americans assigned to the Philippines as Peace Corps volunteers were instructed to be frank and direct in requesting information or supplies from the vendors in the local community. This turned out to be a big mistake—the American directness was considered impolite and inconsiderate. That is, the Philippinos saw the Americans as ignorant and rude. Note the following examples.

The Chinese are known to be somewhat ambiguous while communicating with members of Western European countries and the US, mainly because of their greater emphasis on face-saving. The Chinese feel that members of these Western cultures often ask direct questions that they might not be able to answer easily or deal with as readily as Westerners would like (Lin, 1997).

The Japanese in discussions tend to take shorter turns and create opportunities for everyone to participate in group discussions. Americans take longer turns, and the amount of time that one spends depends a lot on one's status in the work group. A person with higher status normally spends more time talking to the members of the group compared with listening to others. Similarly, the initiator in the Japanese context takes no more time than others in making a point, whereas in the US context, the initiator of the discussion may take a long time to express his or her point of view.

The use of the word "no" is infrequent in many Asian countries, so that a "yes" can sometimes mean "maybe" or "no." Remember that in East Asia it is most important to maintain a relationship. Saying "no" feels as if one cuts off the relationship. For example, a request made to a Japanese manager might elicit a deep breath and the words "It is difficult." That generally means "No" but that word is not used.

Rules about extending and accepting invitations from one's colleagues and superiors in dissimilar cultures are also related to communication etiquette. An Asian subordinate may invite his or her American superior for dinner at home and may not receive an affirmative reply. Most Asians are likely to be somewhat hurt or offended if their superior does not accept the invitation. The Asian response to an American superior not coming to his or her home may simply be interpreted as indicating that the boss does not like Asian ways of entertaining. Therefore, as a result of this denial, the Asian may be offended. The American superior, on the other hand, probably had no intention of hurting the subordinate's feelings (Brein & David, 1971).

Who walks first through a door can be an important issue among individuals who are supposed to be of equal status. Traditional Japanese women sometimes insist on walking behind a male colleague. On one occasion, Triandis realized that he and a woman colleague were not moving forward, because he wanted to walk behind her and she wanted to walk behind him.

Triandis (1975) reported the story of an American visitor asking his Greek acquaintance what time he should arrive for dinner. The Greek villager replied, "Any time." In the United States, the expression "any time" is considered vague and is often synonymous with a non-invitation that people give in order to be polite. It is not necessarily a serious invitation. The Greek villager, however, meant that the American would be welcome any time at all, because in his situation and culture, it is considered impolite to give the guest a definite time of arrival. In some cultures, "thank you" is expressed in written form, but in other cultures, "thank you" can be conveyed by appropriate and polite verbal and non-verbal gestures. In some cultures one does not say "thank you" because a kind act is rewarded in heaven and the kind person has already received the "thank you" from heaven.

The intensity of speaking, that is, how loud the speaker is, varies around the world. Arabs and those from countries around the Mediterranean tend to speak loudly and Northern Europeans interpret such loudness as shouting or as a disagreement. Americans, the French, Italians, and Greeks tend to speak louder than the English, the Swedes, or other Scandinavians. The English find the art of speaking loudly sometimes overly assertive and pointless.

The Japanese apologize more than people in many other cultures. In Japan, a remark that might cause a co-worker to lose face in public requires immediate attention and a verbal apology. In the US, by contrast, an apology from a co-worker or a superior may come much later and may be in writing.

The role of *humor* in communication is interesting. Although smiling is associated with happiness in all cultures, a smiling face may not be appreciated as communicating direct and honest information regarding a product or service in all cultures. The Chinese may associate smiling with a lack of self-control and a deceitful way of getting things done, that is, a clever way of selling inferior wares. Research has shown that

Americans tend to associate smiling and humorous ways of communicating information with intelligence, but the Japanese do not make such attributions. Individuals from Thailand are known to laugh when dealing with embarrassing situations. Such expression can be misconstrued by members of cultures not familiar with the significance of smiles among the Thais. Americans tend to get offended when they are told that they lack a sense of humor when communicating or in executing tasks in the workplace. However, the knowledge that one does not possess a significant sense of humor is not considered offensive in many parts of East Asia. Humor is not seen as an unqualified good attribute in many collectivist cultures.

Self-disclosure is the process of revealing personal information about oneself to others. There is little doubt that some degree of self-disclosure is important in maintaining communication ties in Western and in individualistic cultures. Consider the movies directed by Woody Allen—a large majority of them portray Allen disclosing a great deal about his personal tastes and distastes in various events, to different people, and in a range of situations. Excessive self-disclosure regarding social and personal situations, especially if the information is unfavorable to the speaker, is often inappropriate in collectivistic cultures, unless it takes place among in-group members. Barnlund's (1975) study of the private and public self in Japan and the United States illustrates the importance of self-disclosure in the communication process. The Japanese prefer a communication style where relatively little about oneself is made available to others in everyday interaction. A majority of information that one knows about oneself is strictly kept private and the private self is relatively large compared with the public self. In contrast, the preferred style of communication in the United States is one in which an apparently large amount of information about oneself is given to others—the public self is relatively large with little information about oneself hidden from public exposure. The private self is considered relatively small, but tends to be highly guarded and information is not often revealed even to the most intimate members of one's in-group, that is, one's spouse, children, friends, and so on. This is depicted in Figure 4.2. The French consider Americans easy to make friends with at work but difficult to develop deep and meaningful relationships with in social contexts. The difficulty in getting to know an American manager in Greece, Egypt, China, and other cultures is also reported in various business periodicals. What information is considered private also depends on culture. For instance, one does not reveal one's income as readily in America as in Greece. The refusal of Americans to reveal their income can be construed by Greeks as unwillingness to be friends.

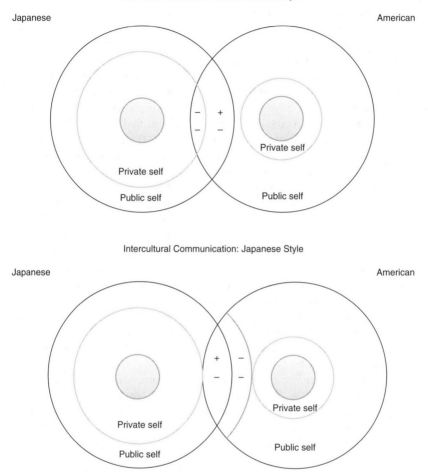

Source: Adapted from Barnlund (1975), p. 50.

Figure 4.2   Self-disclosure and intercultural communication

ROLE OF ELABORATE VERSUS SUCCINCT COMMUNICATION, SILENCE, AND TRUTHFULNESS

Another obstacle that is important to consider in cross-cultural communication is the extent to which members of a given nation or culture prefer *elaborate* versus *succinct* ways of communicating. Elaborate com-munication uses many words, and often tends to exaggerate the content of the communication by using various analogies and proverbs. Members of associative cultures have a preference for elaborate communication whereas members of abstractive cultures have a clear preference for more succinct forms of communication. Succinct communication uses few words to convey a message. Inflated statements and exaggerated ways of describing a given episode are avoided by members of Western and abstractive cultures. Arabs in particular are expected to make hyperbolic statements to those who are not members of their in-groups such as Western visitors. For instance, one does not say "This food is delicious." One must say, "This is the best food I ever had!" If they do not make inflated statements in communicating with Westerners, even in business-related transactions, they are likely to be considered poor communicators. An example concerns the manner in which former US president, George Bush and the Pentagon communicated plans for attacking Iraq because of its failure to disclose its stockpile of weapons of mass destruction. Since it was conveyed in a rather abstractive and non-inflated fashion, the Iraqi president did not take it seriously, resulting in Gulf War II and the even-tual fall of the Saddam Hussein regime in Iraq. The war cost the US the loss of more than 4000 young people and one trillion dollars so far, and if we include the cost of taking care of wounded veterans for the next 50 years it will cost 3 trillion dollars. This may be the best example of how cross-cultural mistakes can be extremely costly.

The point is that while members of Western cultures are inclined to prefer crisp forms of communication without much exaggeration or hyperbole, the situation tends to be just the opposite in most of the coun-tries of the Middle East. While historical factors have contributed to this state of affairs, the fact remains that Westerners and Middle Easterners communicate differently.

It might be surprising that the absence of spoken words, that is, silence, is regarded as an effective method of communicating in many parts of the world. While Westerners describe talking in most situations as pleasant and emphasize the importance of keeping the conversation going as a means for maintaining smooth relationships, such is not the case in many countries. In many countries the news of a death is best conveyed by silence. When a silent messenger arrives at the door of an Army wife, she knows that her husband is dead. Silence in funeral parlors is the correct norm and is regarded highly in all parts of the world.

The main difference is that, while American executives in particular and European managers to some extent, prefer to engage in talking and discussing various scenarios, the Chinese sometimes perceive silence and quietness as the proper method of responding to a situation. Studies with Western expatriates who have worked in Japan note that Japanese women prefer husbands who are likely to remain silent much of the time. They had the stereotype that men who are more silent than vocal in the workplace are likely to be more successful (Adler, 2008). Experienced expatriate managers from the Western countries working in cultures where the use of silence is a valued practice recognize its importance and often appreciate and respect its use.

The concept of *truthfulness* in communicating across cultures is tricky. In cultures that emphasize universalistic values (see Chapter 2), messages are often applicable to all persons regardless of rank or status. However, in non-universalistic cultures, rank and status considerations may make it appropriate not to reveal the whole truth. Furthermore, social sensitivity and the use of tact can override the importance of direct and blunt communication. "White lies"—vague or ambiguous and untrue statements that are said to preserve harmony in a closely knit group—are likely to be forgiven in particularistic cultures. The importance of saving one's face during a communication is extremely significant. This is true in computer-mediated communication as well as face-to-face communications. It is especially important in collectivistic countries such as China, Japan, South Korea, Thailand, Indonesia, and even in parts of the Indian sub-continent (Earley, 1997). Saving face means preserving the reputation of the other party. The other party should not feel embarrassed or experience loss of self-esteem among those who are aware of the communication.

Cultures may differ on their views of *proxemics*, which may be defined as the distance between people during interaction (Hall, 1976). Proxemics are those aspects of cultural, behavioral, sociological, and spatial characteristics that are relevant to the process of communication. The amount of physical distance that one should keep from the receiver of the message varies greatly across cultures—members of individualistic countries and especially people from Western Europe and the US tend to maintain considerable personal space while communicating face to face. If one encroaches on the personal space of the sender of the message, the sender will typically back away. This will continue until he or she resumes a comfortable physical distance again. The process is an automatic one and both parties may not be fully aware as to what is happening. However, such is not the case in the cultures of the Middle East, Latin America, Southern Europe, and in parts of India. Westerners are sometimes perplexed at observing the closeness (i.e., little or no physical distance between the speaker and the receiver of the message) that characterizes interpersonal communication in these cultures.

Sussman & Rosenfeld (1982) asked Japanese and Venezuelans to place their chairs where they wanted, when talking in Japanese or Spanish. The Japanese placed their chairs far apart, while the Venezuelans placed them close to each other. In both cultures men placed their chairs more apart than did women. When instructed to speak in English the Japanese pairs and the Venezuelan pairs placed their chairs in the same place where Americans usually place their chairs, that is, the cultural difference disappeared. Thus, culture, language, and gender determined the comfortable conversational distance.

Haptics is another concept that describes the use of touch during an interpersonal communication. High-contact cultures are characterized by considerable use of touch, contact greetings such as hugging and kissing, and small personal space during interpersonal and intra-group communication (Hall, 1976). Brazilians, for example, touch each other more frequently during communication than their US and Japanese colleagues. Because of the cultural differences in the use of haptics, an American or Japanese may feel uncomfortable and experience negative affect from frequent physical contact (Graham, 1986; Adler, 1997). As another example, German businessmen are likely to be offended and may experience negative affect when a Mexican businessman hugs them as a sign of trust (Adler, 1997). In general, the Japanese do not touch any part of the body except the hands (Triandis, 1994, p. 200). When President Bush visited the Japanese Prime Minister he touched his shoulder, which was quite inappropriate.

In the Mediterranean and in the Middle East and Russia, it is common for men to embrace when greeting each other, whereas in North America this is likely to be regarded as a violation of personal space. Even a simple gesture, such as the shaking of hands during a formal event, may be approached quite differently by members of different cultures. An American may display a strong, prolonged handshake, whereas an individual from an Eastern culture (Japanese or Chinese) may prefer a gentler clasp of hands. In addition, individuals in South and East Asian cultures do not like to shake hands for an extended period of time. In France one shakes hands with co-workers when arriving and leaving the workplace every day, while in America one shakes hands only when meeting a co-worker for the first time.

LOW- AND HIGH-CONTEXT CULTURES

According to Hall (1976), human interaction can be defined in terms of either a low-context or a high-context communication system. In low-context cultures, intention and meaning are expressed through explicit verbal messages; that is, the emphasis is placed on words. On the other hand, in high-context cultures, intention and message can best be relayed through the context. Social roles or position and non-verbal channels such as pauses, silence, or tone of voice (Ting-Toomey, 1985) are crucial in high-context cultures. In high-context cultures, people understand a message's meaning by examining its context—that is, *how* and *where* something is said outweighs *what* is actually said.

Low-context communication uses the direct verbal mode, which includes straight talk, and is sender-oriented. The speaker in a low-context situation is expected to be responsible for constructing a clear message that can easily be decoded. Since low-context communication is based on the literal, the concept of face may be viewed as a transient signal during a specific interaction (Triandis & Albert, 1987; Ting-Toomey, 1988; Erez & Earley, 1993; Earley, 1997).

High-context communication refers to communication patterns involving indirect communication behavior. Indirect communication includes non-verbal subtleties, self-effacing talk, and interpreter-sensitive values. The receiver of the message assumes the responsibility to infer the hidden or contextual meaning (Ting-Toomey, 1985). In high-context communication, the receiver is expected to "read between the lines," that is, to infer the intent of the verbal message. Coupled with this, the receiver is also expected to consider the non-verbal messages that are associated with the verbal message.

In essence, low-context communication stresses the importance of human verbal messages to relay personal thoughts, opinion, and feelings. In contrast, high-context communication emphasizes historical context, social norms, roles, and situational and relational contexts (Ting-Toomey, 1999).

Low-context communication characteristics emphasize individualist values. Other characteristics of low-context cultures include self-face concerns (concern with one's own face or reputation in the immediate social context), linear logic, direct style, person-oriented style, self-enhancement style, speaker-oriented style, and verbal-based understanding. Low-context countries include the United States, UK, Germany, Switzerland, Denmark, and Canada.

In contrast, high-context communication emphasizes group-oriented values, mutual face concern, spiral logic, indirect style, status-oriented style, self-effacement style, and listener-oriented style, as well as a context-based understanding. Examples of high-context countries include Saudi Arabia, China, Japan, and Mexico.

Using Americans and Japanese as the comparative model, Americans have a tendency to be more verbal in their communications. In contrast,

Managing global organizations

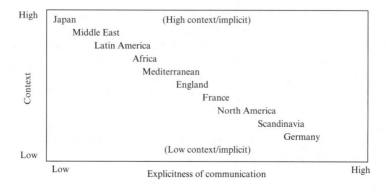

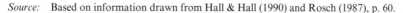

Source: Based on information drawn from Hall & Hall (1990) and Rosch (1987), p. 60.

*Figure 4.3   Contrasting patterns of communication in low- versus high-
context cultures*

the Japanese are apt to employ non-verbal mechanisms. Also, the Japanese and other Asian cultures use silence as part of their communication process. Often, Western cultures misconstrue silence as a negative or "not interested" message when dealing with an Asian counterpart—however, in reality the Asian counterpart may be using this silent time for reflection about the issue at hand.

Individuals from low-context cultures (such as the United States, Germany, Switzerland, and Scandinavia) have been found to communicate more directly than members of high-context cultures such as Asian cultures (Chua & Gudykunst, 1987). More recently, however, some researchers have found that the more important difference may be in the actual goals of the communication and not the amount of direct communication (Weldon & Jehn, 1995).

Methods of communication may vary across borders. Some cultures may use either verbal or non-verbal methods, or may use a hybrid of the two communication methods. Whatever the case, the more varied the method of communication, the more complex the communication context will be, and the more likely mis-communication.

Although high- and low-context communication are two essential components which are present in different degrees in dissimilar cultures, there are indeed multiple factors that may complicate cross-cultural communication. Factors that may complicate the process of communication across nations and cultures are: (1) the extent of persuasiveness inherent in the message, (2) the nature of trust that characterizes the relationship between the sender and the receiver, (3) the difference in power and status between the parties, (4) differences in propensities for taking risks that might accompany the process of careful listening and actions that may follow, (5) the significance and the use of time in communicating with culturally dissimilar individuals in the organizational context.

The role that individuals play in their job is an important element in understanding their communication—both within culture and across cultures. For example, supervisors and managers at higher levels of the organization may communicate with someone in a lower position with a tone of voice that is unlikely to be used when the same individual communicates with someone at the same or higher level.

SAVING FACE

The concept of saving face is important to understand because it plays a crucial role in communication across cultures. *Face work* involves a series of processes that one engages in order to preserve one's face (i.e., one's reputation and social identity) and the face of the party that one is communicating with (Ting-Toomey, 1999). Saving one's face is of crucial importance in collectivistic cultures—especially when communication involves members of one's in-group or one's supervisor and co-worker. It involves such acts as hiding one's emotions and facial expressions that are typically associated with experiences of difficult emotions (i.e., shame, guilt, and even strong feelings of joy and pride). Face is more than just an issue of self-presentation—face can also capture the sense of family and honor (Earley, 1997). Within the context of cross-cultural communication, face plays a vital role.

Face is a universal phenomenon, but the use of face work can differ across cultures (Ting-Toomey, 1988, 1999; Earley, 1997; Earley & Ang, 2003). The concepts of face and face work can be meaningfully interpreted within the communication ideals of a larger cultural system. Face refers to issues of respect. Face is tied to a claimed sense of self-esteem or regard that other persons have for one. Face can be seen as a vulnerable identity resource during social interactions because face can be threatened, enhanced, undermined, or bargained for (Ting-Toomey, 1999). Face has generally been defined as the claimed positive aspects of self. Earley's work on the concept of face was based on the 1900s work of Asian scholars. These scholars viewed face as a predominantly Chinese concept and two categories of face were described: *lian* and *mianzi* (Earley, 1997). *Lian* refers to the rules underlying the moral character and ethics of an individual. *Mianzi* mirrors the interaction with others in a society. Thus *lian* is an attribute of individuals and *mianzi* is an attribute of a relationship.

Saving face is particularly important while conducting negotiations across borders and cultures—especially in collectivistic contexts. Protecting the face of the other party with whom one is negotiating is valuable in building long-term relationships, even though the outcome of negotiation in the initial stages may not be favorable. Ting-Toomey's (1988) approach addresses issues of managing conflict from the perspective of "face-saving strategies" with which one must necessarily be involved. The styles of managing conflicts that often arise while conducting negotiations across cultures may indeed clash. Some specific aspects of saving face are related to managing conflicts (Ting-Toomey et al.,1991; Earley, 1997). Showing respect and consideration for others may vary from one culture to another, but an understanding of how other cultures engage in face-saving and competence in carrying out these strategies can facilitate cross-cultural communication.

Face considerations are especially important in high-context cultures (Cohen, 1997). The structure of the situation, which pits the wills and skills of the negotiating parties, is undesirable in societies that value social harmony and have an aversion to confrontation. Looking past the issues that are being negotiated, there is a psychological dimension in which pride of place is given in considerations of psychic, non-material gains and losses. According to Ting-Toomey & Oetzel (2001), intangible issues such as national representation, status, pride, honor, power, dignity, and face often reflect the hidden dimension of the overt negotiation process. Indeed, face is related to a sense of honor (Earley, 1997), and in high-context cultures it is important to have honor and to give honor to the other person.

ROLE OF AFFECT

Three types of cultural processes determine the nature of affect or emotions that individuals are likely to experience while communicating across cultures: (1) values ingrained in one's culture; (2) norms, rules, and roles associated with the act of communication; and (3) differences in styles of communicating (Ting-Toomey & Korzenny, 1993).

Every culture has its own set of values and norms that guide the members of that culture. People internalize these cultural values and norms and are continuously influenced by them while communicating both within their own culture and across cultures. Rules, norms, and values regulate the standards of what is considered the proper ways of communication.

POWER DISTANCE

Hofstede described power distance as the extent to which the less powerful members of institutions accept that power is distributed unequally (Hofstede, 1980). People in small power distance cultures tend to value equal power distribution, equal rights and relations, and equitable rewards and punishment based on performance (Ting-Toomey, 1999). On the other hand, people in large power distance cultures tend to accept unequal power situations, hierarchical rights, asymmetrical role relations, and rewards and punishment based on age, rank, status, title, and seniority (Ting-Toomey, 1999).

According to Hofstede (1980), power distance refers to the relative prevalence of social or professional hierarchies in a society. High power distant societies reflect inequalities among individuals on the basis of these hierarchies, whereas low power distance societies reflect more egalitarian values.

In cross-cultural communication, the communication itself can be facilitated or impeded, depending on the perceived power distance of the culture. This can also reflect the degree to which communication is open. Having an understanding of the dynamics of power distance in intercultural communication will benefit the global manager. In general, the greater the power distance, the less effective is the communication. In large power distance cultures most communication is from the top to the bottom, and thus useful information available at the grassroots is missing.

UNCERTAINTY AVOIDANCE

Hofstede's dimension of uncertainty avoidance may play a significant role in determining the speed of communication and in the decision-making process (Hofstede, 1998, 2001).

Uncertainty avoidance describes the degree to which members of a culture are threatened by the unknown or the uncertainty of a situation and reflects the extent people avoid uncertain situations. Those cultures that are considered to be low in uncertainty avoidance encourage risk-taking. In contrast, those cultures that are high in uncertainty avoidance prefer to avoid any risk; they seek clear procedures and direction from their organizations. People in low uncertainty avoidance situations prefer informal behavioral rules, whereas high uncertainty avoidance cultures seek formal structures and rules that reduce their anxiety in dealing with uncertainty. In low uncertainty avoidance cultures, innovation and creativity are more likely to occur because there is less aversion to risk.

Cross-cultural communication involves a certain amount of risk. The communicator is uncertain of the outcome of the communication. Considering the position of a culture on the uncertainty avoidance dimension will determine if people will be receptive to new ideas, suggestions, or compromise, or if they will choose to remain within the confines of their expected boundaries and agreements. For comparison's sake, based on Hofstede's ranking of cultures on the uncertainty avoidance continuum, Americans are relatively open to risk and they accept new ideas, whereas the Japanese prefer familiar situations. While the Japanese are not too keen on adopting innovations, they are extremely good at carrying out structured activities, such as producing a high-quality industrial product. The Japanese are likely to take an American invention and perfect it so that it is even better than its original version. Furthermore, a culture can be high in uncertainty avoidance in one domain, such as in socialization (or education), social, political, religious, economic, or aesthetic matters, and yet be low on another of these domains. Such complexities should be considered in anticipating how uncertainty avoidance may influence cross-cultural communication.

GENDER DIFFERENCES

It has been known for centuries that men and women communicate differently. Deborah Tannen (2001) notes that men communicate to make a point—to be understood. They do so regardless of the impact of the communication on the emotional state of the recipient. In her extensive research on gender differences in communication, Tanner found that women emphasize relationship-building and related aspects of the communication process. When communication is examined cross-culturally, women are likely to speak softly and be less impatient in making a point. They want to be properly understood, interpreted, and to convey the message without much distortion. Male executives, especially those from individualistic countries, are likely to emphasize the validity of their points more than their female counterparts. Male executives are more likely to fail when communicating across cultures than are their female counterparts. Glenn & Glenn (1981) note that females are likely to be more associative in their styles of communication compared with males, who prefer a more abstractive style of communication.

Even though gender differences in communication are disappearing rapidly in the era of globalization and computer-mediated communication, the fact remains that gender differences make communication difficult.

TEMPORAL ISSUES

The importance and availability of time can also make communication across cultures challenging. Members of Western cultures report scarcity of time as a persistent feature of their daily lives (Robinson, 1982; Levine, 1997; Florida, 2007). They prefer to communicate in a succinct fashion. They often communicate a lot of ideas or issues in a limited amount of time and then move on to the next task in their daily agenda (Bluedorn, Kaufman, & Lane, 1992; Bhagat & Moustafa, 2002). Members of cultures where time is limited experience stress when communicating with members of cultures where time is more available. People from leisurely cultures are not in a hurry to express their thoughts and ideas and do not understand why their Western supervisors tend to be so curt and quick in expressing their views regarding work-related activities. Punctuality, adhering to schedules, and defined agendas are important in modern cultures, and as a result people prefer to come to the point quickly and then to move on to the next task.

Research by Levine & Bartlett (1984) showed that people move faster in large than in small cities, and are very fast in Japan, moderately fast in Taiwan and the US, and rather slow in Indonesia.

THE ROLE OF COMMUNICATION IN DECISION-MAKING

Different cultures approach decision-making in different ways. The power of decision-making may fall in the hands of one individual, or a group may make the decisions. In a group, individuals may accept the decisions of higher-status or more senior group members. On the other hand, some cultures may embrace a decision that reflects the agreement of the majority of the group members. Other cultures, such as the Japanese or other Eastern cultures, value the consensus of group members. Decision-making is carried out through a communication process which includes the exchange of ideas and the weighing of options. In some cultures the group may continue discussions for a long time until there is unanimity.

In some cultures, a formal written agreement, such as a contract, is required; however, in other cultures "sealing the deal" is consummated with a handshake. Some organizations may require a point-by-point agreement, which might also address contingencies and potential unexpected events. In other cultures people may prefer a more encompassing general agreement, and address issues as they emerge or evolve. Some cultures expect the agreement to be legally binding, whereas other cultures place very little faith on legal contracts and have a tendency to emphasize a person's obligation to keep his or her word.

In a cross-cultural setting, some organizations may turn to other professionals to augment their communication capabilities. Some businesses may use cultural experts, translators, attorneys, advisors (both financial and technical) who have at least moderate and preferably high familiarity with their counterparts. Some organizations in other cultures commonly may use brokers or intermediaries as effective assistants of cross-cultural communication. The use of these bicultural brokers may significantly increase the chances of success (Hendon, Hendon, & Herbig, 1999).

ROLE OF LANGUAGE AND LINGUISTIC STYLES

In considering barriers to effective communication, the issue of language (i.e., same or different language, patterns of enunciation, and speech) and the role of the interpreter are crucial. Executives of multinational and global firms often need to communicate with members of countries and cultures who speak totally different languages. The results are often frustrating as well as time-consuming. Use of interpreters certainly helps communication, but it can also produce distortions. In negotiations between Greeks and Americans, in one study (Triandis, 1977), the Greek bilingual interpreters took the side of the Greek negotiators!

CONCLUSION

Communicating across borders and cultures is a complex process that requires skill and patience. Being fluent in another language, or at least having a working knowledge of the language, is a desirable first step. However, having an understanding or at least being sensitive to cultural differences facilitates cross-cultural communication. Knowing that other factors come into play—that is, cultural variations such as individualism–collectivism, power distance, and uncertainty avoidance as well as differences in communication styles—helps develop efficient and effective communication strategies. Whether the communication act is an encounter between two individuals from dissimilar cultures or between cross-cultural teams negotiating business transactions, cross-cultural communication competency is a core component for ensuring the success of multinational and global firms.

As multinational and global organizations begin to deal with massive amounts of information, knowledge, and data in their communication activities across cultures, the importance of sophisticated computer-mediated mechanisms is going to increase. However, we note that the importance of communication between two individuals from dissimilar cultures as well as from an individual to a group (composed of members of different functional groups in a corporation and dissimilar cultures) is not going to wane. Complications will arise as globalization introduces both convergence and divergence of cultural values in different countries. When members of a given culture become more globalized, affluent, and individualistic, they are likely to change their cultural orientations in the way they communicate. The communication patterns of the past may be devalued in favor of more assertive and explicit communication which is consonant with the values of individualists. In a similar vein, members of individualistic cultures might become more sensitive to the benefits of communicating in a subtle and less forceful and assertive fashion, as has been characteristic of collectivist cultures. These kinds of changes are going to be interesting and at the same time have important implications for communication across cultures. It is necessary for multinational and global management to be sensitive to the changes in the global environment and communicate in ways that are both culturally sensitive and at the same time enhance organizational effectiveness.

REFERENCES

Adler, N.J. (1997). *International dimensions of organizational behavior*. Cincinnati, OH: South-Western.

Adler, N.J. (2008). *International division of organizational behavior*. New York: Thompson Learning.

Allport, G.W. (1954). *The nature of prejudice*. Cambridge, MA: Addison-Wesley.

Barnlund, D. (1975). *Public and private self in Japan and the U.S.* Tokyo: Simul Press.

Bello, R.S., Brandau-Brown, F.E., Zhang, S., & Ragsdale, J.D. (2010). Verbal and nonverbal methods for expressing appreciation in friendships and romantic relationships: A cross-cultural comparison. *International Journal of Intercultural Relations*, 34, 294–302.

Bhagat, R.S. & Moustafa, K.S. (2002). How non-Americans view American use of time: A cross-cultural perspective. In P. Boski (Ed.), *Advances in cross-cultural psychology* (pp. 183–91). Warsaw: Wydawnictwo Intytutu Psychologii.

Bluedorn, A.C., Kaufman, C.D., & Lane, P.M. (1992). How many things do you like to do at once? An introduction to monochronic and polychronic time. *Academy of Management Executive*, 6, 17–26.

Brein, M. & David, K.H. (1971). Intercultural communications and the adjustment of the sojourner. *Psychological Bulletin*, 76, 215–34.

Brown, D. (2003). *The Da Vinci code*. New York: Random House.

Chua, E. & Gudykunst, W.B. (1987). Conflict resolution styles in low- and high-context cultures. *Communication Research*, 4, 32–7.

Cohen, R. (1997). *Negotiation across cultures.* Washington, DC: United States Institute of Peace.

Earley, P.C. (1997). *Face, harmony, and social structure: An analysis of organizational behavior across cultures.* New York: Oxford University Press.

Earley, P.C. & Ang, S. (2003). *Cultural intelligence: Individual interactions across cultures.* Stanford, CA: Stanford Business Books.

Erez, M. & Earley, C. (1993). *Culture, self-identity, and work.* New York: Oxford University Press.

Fazzi, C. (2001). Theories on conflict take special significance during crisis. *Dispute Resolution Journal*, Nov., 87.

Florida, R.L. (2007). *The flight of the creative class: The new global competition for talent.* New York: Harper-Collins.

Glenn, E. & Glenn, P. (1981). *Man and mankind: Conflicts and communication between cultures.* Norwood, NJ: Ablex.

Graham, J.L. (1986). Across the negotiating table from the Japanese. *International Marketing Review*, Autumn, 58–70.

Hall, E.T. (1976). *Beyond culture.* Garden City, NJ: Anchor.

Hall, E.T. & Hall, M.R. (1990). *Understanding cultural differences.* Yarmouth, ME: Intercultural Press.

Hendon, D.W., Hendon, R.A., & Herbig, P. (1999). *Cross-cultural business negotiation.* Westport, CT: Praeger.

Hofstede, G. (1980). *Culture's consequences: International differences in work-related values.* Newbury Park, CA: Sage.

Hofstede, G. (1998). *Masculinity and femininity: The taboo dimension of national cultures.* Thousand Oaks, CA: Sage.

Hofstede, G. (2001). *Culture's consequences: Comparing values, behaviors, institutions, and organizations across nations.* Thousand Oaks, CA: Sage.

Lee, Y.T. & Duenas, G. (1995). Stereotype accuracy in multicultural business. In Y.T. Lee, I.J. Jussim, & C.R. McCauley (Eds). *Stereotype accuracy: Towards appreciating group differences* (pp. 157–86). Washington, DC: American Psychological Association.

Levine, R. (1997). *A geography of time.* New York: Simon & Schuster.

Levine, R.A. & Bartlett, K. (1984). Pace of life, punctuality, and coronary heart disease in six countries. *Journal of Cross-Cultural Psychology*, 15, 233–55.

Lin, Z. (1997). Ambiguity with a purpose: The shadow of power in communication. In P.C. Earley & M. Erez (Eds). *New perspectives on international industrial/organizational psychology* (pp. 363–76). San Francisco: New Lexington Press.

Nisbett, R.E. (2003). *The geography of thought: Why we think the way we do.* New York: Free Press.

Riatu, I. (1983). Thinking internationally: A comparison of how international executives learn. *International Studies of Management and Organizations*, 13, 139–50.

Robinson, J.P. (1982). *How Americans use time: A social-psychological analysis of everyday behavior.* New York: Praeger.

Rosch, M. (1987). Communications: Focal point of culture. *Management International Review*, 27(4), 60–65.

Sussman, N.M. & Rosenfeld, H.M. (1982). Influence of culture, language and sex on conversational distance. *Journal of Personality & Social Psychology*, 42, 66–72.

Tannen, D. (2001). *You just don't understand: Men and women in conversation*. New York: Quill.

Ting-Toomey, S. (1985). *Japanese communication patterns: Insiders versus the outsider perspective*. Paper presented at the Annual Meeting of the Eastern Communication Association, 76th, Providence, RI, 2–5 May.

Ting-Toomey, S. (1988). Intercultural conflict styles: A face-negotiation theory. In Y. Kim & W. Gudykunst (Eds). *Theories in intercultural communication* (pp. 213–35). Newbury Park, CA: Sage.

Ting-Toomey, S. (1999). *Communicating across cultures*. New York: Guilford Press.

Ting-Toomey, S. & Korzenny, F. (1993). *Language, communication and culture*. Newbury Park, CA: Sage.

Ting-Toomey, S. & Oetzel, J.H. (2001). *Managing intercultural conflict effectively*. Thousand Oaks, CA: Sage.

Ting-Toomey, S., Gao, G., Trubinsky, P., Yang, Z., Kim, H.S., Lin, S.L., & Nishida, T. (1991). Culture, face maintenance and styles of handling interpersonal conflict: A study in five cultures. *International Journal of Conflict Management*, 2, 275–96.

Triandis, H.C. (1975). Cultural training, cognitive complexity, and interpersonal attitudes. In R.W. Brislin, S. Bochner, & W.J. Lonner (Eds). *Cross-cultural perspectives on learning* (pp. 4–39). New York: John Wiley & Sons.

Triandis, H.C. (1977). *Interpersonal behavior*. Los Angeles, CA: Brooks/Cole Publications.

Triandis, H.C. (1994). *Culture and social behavior*. New York: McGraw-Hill.

Triandis, H.C. & Albert, R.D. (1987). Cross-cultural perspectives. In F.M. Jablin, L.L. Putman, K.H. Roberts, & L.W. Porter (Eds). *Handbook of organizational communication: An interdisciplinary perspective* (pp. 264–95). Beverly Hills, CA: Sage.

Weldon, E. & Jehn, K.A. (1995). Examining cross-cultural differences in conflict management behavior: A strategy for future research. *International Journal of Conflict Management*, 6, 387–403.

5. Cultural variations in negotiation, conflict management, and decision-making

Negotiation between multinational and global corporations occur both as discrete and continuous events in the process of expanding business operations across nations and cultures.

Negotiations can take place at multiple levels—at the intra-organizational level, it takes place between senior managers between two or more global companies trying to reach a set of outcomes which are satisfying to both or all the parties concerned. Managers of global corporations must be proficient in negotiating with individuals from other countries and cultures. They need to do so for developing specific strategies for exporting their products and services, setting joint ventures and strategic alliances, and managing subsidiaries in dissimilar political contexts and cultures. The art of effective negotiation is difficult at best, and it can be a challenging, if not daunting, task for even the most experienced senior managers of multinational and global corporations. The art and science of effective negotiation require that one pays careful attention to the various elements of the negotiation process before, during, and after the negotiation.

DEFINITION OF NEGOTIATION

Negotiation can be defined as a set of processes in which two or more parties engage in order to achieve some mutually satisfying objectives. Negotiations occur when the allocation of gains between the two parties or among many parties is asymmetrical to begin with and is in need of adjustment by engaging in dialogue and exchange of meaningful information. It is a process that characterizes (1) labor–management relations such as those between General Motors and Ford Motor Company with United Automobile Works (UAW) and Teamsters; (2) contractual negotiations between business organizations such as the BP Petroleum Company of The Netherlands and Halliburton of Houston to drill the ocean floor for oil exploration purposes; (3) various types of sales agreements between supplier organizations and retailing operations—both in the domestic sphere and across nations; (4) the creation of joint venture and strategic alliance-based agreements, technology, and knowledge transfer; and (5) various types of international negotiations involving agencies of the United Nations as well as various government and non-governmental organizations.

The scientific investigation of negotiation occupied a central position in labor and industrial relations (Walton & McKersie, 1965; Kochan, 1980) and social psychology (Rubin & Brown, 1975; Rubin, 1980; Pruitt, 1981). During the past two decades, the study of negotiation, and especially the process of negotiation across nations and cultures in the context of expanding business operations of multinational and global corporations, has emerged as a major topic of research in international and cross-cultural management (Shapiro, Sheppard, & Cheraskin, 1992; Shapiro, Lewicki, & Devine, 1995; Herbig, 1997; Brett & Okumura, 1998; Thompson, 2001; Bazerman, Magliozzi, & Neal, 2003; Morris, Larrick, & Su, 2003).

In both theory and practice of international management, negotiation is understood as the process of discussion by which two or more parties attempt to reach a mutually acceptable agreement. For long-term positive outcomes, the goal should be to encourage the emergence of a win–win situation—that is, to bring about a settlement or a set of agreements that are clearly acceptable and beneficial to all parties concerned. The process of negotiation, it must be noted, is difficult enough when it takes place among people of similar socioeconomic and cultural backgrounds. It becomes more complex when negotiation takes place across nations and dissimilar cultures. Such negotiations routinely involve dissimilar expectations in goals and objectives, use of different styles of verbal and non-verbal exchanges, emphasis on formal versus informal procedures and problem-solving techniques and approaches, and last, but not least, differences in cultural values and orientations. The complexity increases when the number of stakeholders that are involved in the negotiation across borders increases. This is illustrated in Figure 5.1.

In preparing for negotiation across borders and cultures, it is important to start with the assumption that individuals on the other side of the fence do not necessarily think and feel the same way as those who are initiating the negotiation. In other words, the assumption of cognitive similarity— which supports the view that others are likely to perceive, think, and use rational methods in the same way as the initiators of the negotiation may not necessarily be correct. Differences in cultural values and related situational influences exercise profound effects on the outcome of negotiation. Negotiators who have been successful in the past have a much better sense of the often hidden significance of the agendas based on the cultural values

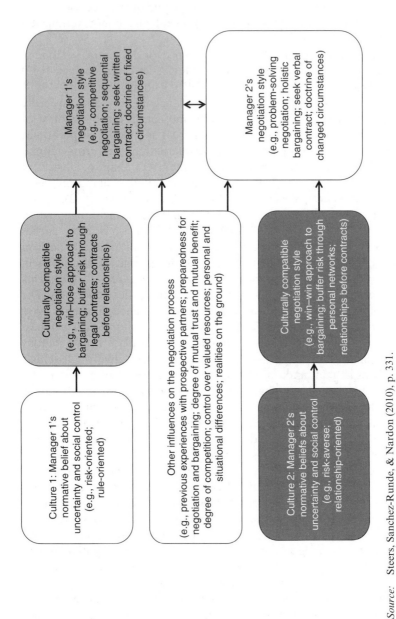

Source: Steers, Sanchez-Runde, & Nardon (2010), p. 331.

Figure 5.1 Competitive and problem-solving bargaining stages

of their counterparts. They are also comfortable in sharing their own views of the preferred outcomes without adopting an ethnocentric (feeling that one's perspective is superior to the other party) perspective.

THE NEGOTIATION PROCESS

The process of negotiation across borders and cultures consists of the four fundamental elements:

1. Two or more parties involved in real or perceived conflict over important goals and objectives.
2. Shared interest in resolving the conflict and reaching an agreeable solution.
3. Background information leading to the process of negotiation.
4. A goal, but not a certainty or confidence in reaching a mutual agreement.

Negotiation involves continuous communication and, as discussed in Chapter 4, involves face-to-face meetings and, now, teleconferencing and exchanges of information and data by means of computer-mediated communication. In the current era of globalization, the Internet is playing a much more significant role in accomplishing important negotiations across national borders and cultures. The results of empirical investigations (e.g. Dwyer, 2001) regarding the efficacy of Internet and computer-aided communication indicate growing satisfaction; however, we must underscore the need for maintaining face-to-face communication, especially when the cultures of the parties involved in negotiation are dissimilar.

The negotiation process involves five stages:

1. *Preparation* where two or more parties gather data, information, and knowledge regarding the motives, abilities, and willingness of the other party or parties to reach a mutual agreement.
2. *Relationship-building* this is an important stage in the sense that this is where the parties discuss their mutual interests in negotiation and get to know each other, not only at the formal level but also at the informal level.
3. *Information exchange* typically, this is a formal process in which each party presents an initial position and the discussion of both primary and secondary issues follows.
4. *Persuasion* during this stage, each party is concerned with changing the beliefs, the mindsets, preferences, structures, attitudes, and interests of the other party.

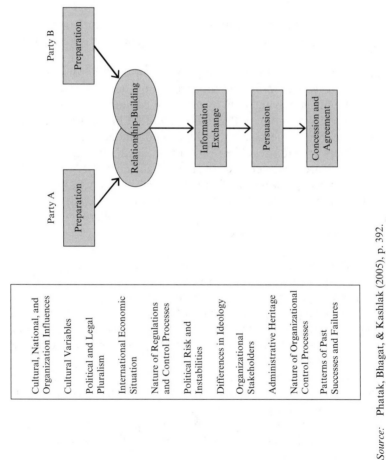

Source: Phatak, Bhagat, & Kashlak (2005), p. 392.

Figure 5.2   Stages of negotiation in international management

5. *Making concessions and reaching agreement* this is the final stage of negotiation in which the parties make appropriate concessions and reach agreements. Often these agreements are made binding by employing legal means and then validated by third parties.

Table 5.1   Competitive and problem-solving bargaining stages

Stages in negotiation	Competitive bargaining	Problem-solving bargaining
(1) Preparation	Identify current economic and other benefits your firm seeks from the deal. Prepare to defend your firm's position.	Define the long-term strategic interests of your firm. Prepare to overcome cross-cultural barriers to defining mutual interest.
(2) Relationship-building	Look for weaknesses in your opponent's position. Learn about your opponent, but reveal as little as possible.	Adapt to the other side's culture. Separate the people involved in negotiation from the problems and goals that need to be solved.
(3) Information exchange and first offer	Provide as little information as possible to your opponent. Make your position explicit. Make a hard offer that is more favorable to your side than you realistically expect to receive.	Give and demand to receive objective information that clarifies each party's interests. Accept cultural differences in speed of response and type of information needs. Make firm but reasonable first offer.
(4) Persuasion	Use dirty tricks and pressure tactics where appropriate to win.	Search for new creative options that benefit the interests of both parties.
(5) Concessions	Begin with high initial demands. Make concessions slowly and grudgingly.	Search for mutually acceptable criteria for reaching accord. Accept cultural differences in starting position and in how and when concessions are made.
(6) Agreement	Sign only if you win and then ensure that you sign an ironclad contract.	Sign when the interests of your firm are met. Adapt to cultural differences in contracts where necessary.

Source: Steers, Sanchez-Runde, & Nardon (2010).

Of the five stages mentioned above, the process of building relationships is most important. Executives from the home country should get to know their contacts or counterparts in the host country and also spend time in building mutual trust. Building of trust is crucial before embarking on business-related transactions. This process is given more importance in most parts of the developing world and also in Southern Europe and Latin America than is the case in the US, Western Europe, Canada, Australia, and New Zealand, that is, the Anglo-Saxon part of the G-20 countries. US managers by and large tend to be very well informed about the specific nature of the business transactions. They know the antecedents and the consequences of both success and failures of negotiations involving their companies and the companies with which they are transacting. They want to get to the specific issues during the initial stages of the negotiation process and are not inclined to spend time in getting down to the "brass tacks" of business transactions. They like to reach a quick decision which will be legally binding for both the parties and move on to other aspects of business. Such tendencies toward efficiencies are not particularly productive and can, in fact, be quite detrimental to developing long-term and mutually trusting relationships with managers of collectivistic countries, and particularly those from East, Southeast, and South Asia. The point is that development of a mutually trusting relationship is the very cornerstone of successful negotiation for Asian businesses.

The process of building trust usually involves participation in social events, rituals, and ceremonies. It may also involve taking the guests for tours of the company premises, including interesting sites in the surrounding areas. This process has been termed "nontask sounding" (*nemawashi*), which involves polite conversations and informal exchange of information regarding families, interests, hobbies, and so on. In most collectivistic cultures, it is important for the guests to get to know the host and wait for the host to initiate the actual business negotiation. It is also important to note that the relationship-building phase is in fact the first phase of negotiation and is quite important—unlike the situation in Western individualistic contexts.

Experienced negotiators recommend that managers get to use an intermediary or intermediaries who already have the trust and respect of the parties involved and who act as a bridge in maintaining the relationship. Managers of companies in the Middle East and in much of the Arabian Peninsula prefer to negotiate through a trusted intermediary, or what may be called a third party, who intervenes in the process of negotiation but does not dictate or have a major role in determining the shape or the outcome of the negotiation as time goes on. It is interesting to note that Arabs in particular like to do business with the person from the Western country or wherever he or she may be from. They are much less interested in knowing the dynamics and the financial health of the company with which they are dealing. Therefore, development of interpersonal trust between the parties is of paramount importance.

After this phase of relationship-building including various aspects of nontask sounding, both parties state their formal positions; this involves posturing to include general discussion regarding the tone of the meeting that is to follow. This phase normally results in a spirit of cooperation but is not guaranteed by any means, especially when strong cross-cultural differences of values and ideologies are involved. In order to obtain better results, it is important to respect the position of the other party or parties and emphasize the spirit of mutual benefit rather than use language that might reflect a sense of ethnocentrism, arrogance, or urgency.

In the stage of exchanging task-related information, each side makes a formal presentation and states its position. A question and answer session follows and the various alternatives for reaching the agreement are discussed. From an American or Western European perspective, this typically represents a straightforward, objective, efficient, and easily interpretable stage in the process of negotiation. However, negotiators from collectivistic and high power distance countries might adopt a more indirect approach and show an inclination for becoming suspicious. There might be little inclination on the part of these collectivists to present substantive details of the transactions that are at stake. Evasive conversations which are of peripheral significance to the process of negotiation are pursued at the expense of engaging in substantive aspects of negotiation. The Chinese have a tendency to ask many questions and typically are rather slow in coming to the crux of the issue at hand (Pye, 1982; Tung, 1982; Graham & Lam, 2003). One might get the impression that the Chinese are looking for complete clarity of issues involved. However, in their presentation, they tend to present relatively ambiguous and vague information regarding their preferences in both the short and long term. It has often been noted by John Graham and his colleagues (2003) that the key to success in negotiating with the managers of multinational and global corporations of the Far Eastern countries is to take a long-term perspective and not necessarily emphasize the need to succeed in the first round of negotiation. This is where the short-term perspective in US societal as well as organizational culture plays a not-so-helpful role. In their urge to seek immediate or relatively immediate results at the end of a discussion, US managers might be successful in the initial stages of the negotiation, but then regret having lost the more substantive outcomes that they could have had if only they had been willing to adopt a longer time horizon.

Research on the Russian style of negotiation reveals that they enter negotiations well prepared and tend to be knowledgeable in some of the specific details pertaining to the core aspects of the negotiation. Unless the Western managers are willing to take an intermediary with a superior technical knowledge regarding the objectives of the negotiation, it typically becomes difficult to tackle the various inquiries that the Russian managers might bring to the table. Russians also like to follow formal protocols and make it clear at the start of the negotiation that they prefer to deal with only the higher-level managers in the Western organizational charts. Nancy Adler (2002) suggests that negotiators from the Western European countries and the US should not just be concerned with presenting the objective data pertaining to the goals and preferred states, but also develop an isomorphic understanding (the point of view of the other party using similar types of attributions) of the other parties. Learning to focus on the entire range of issues that concern both parties, it becomes possible to assess the comparative advantages and disadvantages of a wider range of alternatives or solutions to the issues involved. Adler also strongly emphasizes that for one to be effective in the process of negotiation across borders and cultures, it is essential not to limit one's self to preconceived and rigidly held positions, no matter how ideologically grounded one ought to be. It is important to practice reversal of roles in one's own context before leaving for the host country and get to the actual process of negotiating on business transactions that are tricky and might involve major consequences for both parties.

In stage four (i.e., the stage of persuading the other party), the hard part of bargaining begins. Both parties attempt to persuade the other to be understanding of their positions and give up some of their own preferences in order to reach an agreement. More often than not, such persuasion might have taken place before the beginning of the nontask sounding stage of the negotiation and through a series of e-mail and other computer-mediated communication or through the use of intermediaries. The idea of *houmanui*—that is, arriving at some pre-negotiation outcomes that are acceptable to both the parties—is reasonably common among Japanese and Chinese negotiators (Rosch & Segler, 1987). It is not uncommon to find many Western managers that are thoroughly confused and frustrated with this process of bargaining and making concessions before engaging in task-related information regarding the substantive issues. Different uses of verbal and non-verbal communication (see Chapter 4), and selected interpretations of what is being said in contrast to what is being understood, can be quite difficult to deal with in the short term and tend to be rather frustrating in the long term.

To be sure, skillful negotiators recognize the pitfalls of conducting business transactions with managers of culturally dissimilar countries.

The process becomes even more complex when the size of the organizations (involving more formalization, standardization, and use of prior
protocols) tends to be large. Easterners do not like the idea of negotiating
with executives with whom they have not dealt before. The sense of relational continuity is very important in the Far Eastern countries as well
as in Southern European countries, Mexico, Latin American countries,
and a large number of countries from the African continent. Research
by John Graham (1985) comparing the use of various tactics (promises
for continuing new types of new business deals, threats to withdraw
from the business relationship, and a combination of the two) shows that
the Japanese and Americans tend to be similar in their propensities to
employ these tactics. On the other hand, the Japanese and Brazilians are
less similar in their preference for using such tactics. Brazilians use fewer
promises and are not as prone to making quick commitments as either
the Japanese or the Americans. They tend to follow the directives that are
given to them by their immediate organizational superiors, that is, there
is a display of power distance-related phenomena in the case of Brazilian
negotiators.

The use of "dirty tricks"—that is, deliberate attempts to mislead the
other party—is not uncommon in international business negotiation.
Some negotiators may give distorted information or use the excuse of
ambiguous authority (i.e., emphasize the locus of ultimate decision-
making and power in the hands of senior executives in the organizational
hierarchy when such is truly not the case) and conflicting views about
who is truly in charge in making decisions in their party. This can make
the process of conducting negotiation rather difficult and frustrating in
both the short and long term. In addition, some prudent managers might
employ some misleading cues and information before making decisions
based on their intuition or trusting someone based on past experiences.
Other rough tactics that might sometimes be employed include conducting negotiations in the very early hours of the morning when the guests
have not recovered from jet lag. Setting the time and date for arriving
at a final outcome just prior to the guests' planned return to their home
country is also used by members of some cultures. Other inappropriate
techniques include calculated delays in reaching a settlement, threats to
stop negotiating, escalating demands as initial stages of negotiations are
completed successfully, and use of a "take-it-or-leave-it attitude" with a
sense of strong ethnocentrism. In a survey of over 18 US–Korean joint
ventures, US executives reported the behavior of Korean counterparts
to involve "shouting matches, desk-pounding, and chest-beating" (Tung,
1991, p. 23). From the perspective of Western Europe-, Canada-, and
US-based managers, such behaviors are unacceptable, but in the context

of Korean organizations and political culture, they are not so unusual. We have seen on international television such as CNN instances of severe disagreements in political campaigns in the Korean parliament leading to shouting matches and desk-pounding.

SOME IMPORTANT ELEMENTS IN NEGOTIATING WITH THE CHINESE

A considerable amount of research on intercultural aspects of negotiation concerns negotiation between US managers and managers from the People's Republic of China. The reasons are obvious. China is going to be the largest economy in the world by 2020 (Jacques, 2009). In fact, Jacques' treatment of the evolution of Chinese global organizations has the important accompanying observation that the rise of the Chinese economy may signal the end of the Western world and the birth of a new global order. The same point is echoed by Zakaria (2008). Obviously, negotiation with the Chinese (as was the case with negotiation with the Japanese during the economic dominance of Japanese global organizations in the 1980s) is a topic of central interest in international and intercultural management. Graham & Lam (2003) note some of the important cultural elements that underlie the essence of the negotiation style of Chinese managers. They are:

1. *Quanxi* (establishment of personal relationships). While Americans place a great deal of importance on gathering information and authorizations about procedures, institutions, and so on to network, the Chinese put a premium on developing social capital with their immediate social circle and expect the same kinds of patterns to prevail in negotiating with managers from Western multinationals.
2. *Zhongjian Ren* (importance of third parties/intermediaries). During the initial phases of negotiation, Chinese managers are reluctant to trust the parties with whom they are negotiating. The use of a third party or intermediary is essential.
3. *Shehui Dengji* (importance of social status). The Chinese embrace Confucian values which emphasize the value of obedience and deference to others who are in positions of higher status. The role of status is crucial in negotiating with the Chinese; the informality of US and some Western European cultures (not all) may act as a hindrance. In other words, the casual nature of American negotiators may not work as well with their Chinese counterparts.

4. *Renji Hexie* (importance of maintaining interpersonal harmony). Chinese proverbs such as, "A man without a smile should not open a business" and "Sweet temperament and friendliness produce more money than ill-tempers and unfriendliness" highlight the extreme importance of maintaining harmony during the process of negotiation and even in its aftermath. One must remember that negotiation with the Chinese is not over unless they are totally satisfied with the process and the outcome of initial transactions. If the Western managers are able to maintain harmony, it is possible to re-negotiate on related transactions at future points.

5. *Zhengti Guannian* (holistic approach). Negotiators from the West usually break down the negotiation process into smaller issues, such as price, quantity, delivery terms, and so on, whereas negotiators from China think in terms of the whole process. The Chinese are prone to discuss the issues in terms of their total significance. To Westerners, it may appear that they like to jump around the various issues and are not likely to settle on anything in a reasonable period of time. Ideological concerns may enter into negotiations even though they are of peripheral importance.

6. *Jiejian* (importance of thrift). China's long history of economic and political instabilities has inoculated the values of frugality—a practice known as *jiejian*. Some elements of bargaining and haggling can result and, coupled with a tendency to save face, make the process of negotiation appear to go on for a long time. It has been noted that Chinese negotiators are likely to cushion their offers with more room to maneuver than most US negotiators. Concessions on price are likely to be made with great reluctance and only after discussing many aspects of the negotiation all over again.

7. *Mianzi* (importance of face). As in most Asian cultures, the importance of face and strategies for saving face are essential issues to consider. *Mianzi* typically involves an individual's identity in his or her collectives and in-groups. It is crucial for Western negotiators to realize the extreme importance of saving face for their Chinese counterparts. Actions that are likely to negatively affect *mianzi* can permanently ruin future expectations of re-negotiations.

8. *Chiku Nailo* (endurance and relentlessness in the negotiation process). Last, but not least, is the importance that the Chinese place on the process of endurance in tolerating the various shifts in expectations and results during the negotiation process. Stories abound as to how Westerners get frustrated in the process of reaching an agreement while their Chinese counterparts are still willing to carry on the "nitty-gritty" of negotiations.

CULTURAL DIFFERENCES, COGNITIVE DYNAMICS, AND BIASES

Morris & Gelfand (2004) suggest that public elements of cultures—such as cultural institutions, public discourses, and social structures and norms—affect the availability, accessibility, and activation of knowledge structures in the cognitive dynamics of individuals who must negotiate across cultures. Such interactions tend to be more crucial for intercultural negotiations as opposed to negotiations within a culture. These authors suggest that the cross-cultural challenge to negotiation is best developed by avoiding the pitfalls of *relativism* on the one hand and the strong emphasis on *universalism* on the other. A theory that addresses the role of culture in negotiators' cognitions should address the following issues:

- What kind of *biases* are likely to be more sensitive to cultural influences and what kind are likely to be invariant across nations and cultures?
- What kind of *causal pathways* are present in the role of cultural variations on the thought processes of negotiation?
- What are the *specific situational influences* that are likely to trigger the influence of cultural variations?

It is widely accepted by negotiation researchers that all biases on negotiation reflect learned ideas and responses (heuristic cues, cognitive schemas, etc.) more than hardwired mental rules and cognitive structures (Morris & Gelfand, 2004). Biases in social and interpersonal judgments—assessment of character, evaluation of fairness, expectations of others' reactions—are more prone to cultural influences than biases in numerical judgments.

Research in the area of social judgments clearly indicates that there are no solid bases for expecting cultural invariance in the way parties in a negotiation may judge each other. Negotiators are likely to vary in how they interpret social situations in which the negotiation is embedded and also attributions of various personality traits in the other party (e.g., an executive from a global company headquartered in New York may be comfortable in teasing his or her boss—however, to a Chinese or Japanese executive, this kind of interaction with one's boss is likely to be interpreted as lack of respect for someone who is his or her superior). Social judgments regarding how individuals may be categorized (e.g., along caste lines in the Hindu context of Indian global companies, but along class lines in the UK or France) are important considerations in negotiation across cultural divides. In addition, how one might assign meaning into relationships varies largely across cultures (e.g., one builds trust easily through *compadres* and *simpatico* in Mexico, but *guanaxi* in China, *chaebol* in Korea, and *ziabatsu* in Japan) (Bhagat, McDevitt, & McDevitt, 2010).

Conceptions of self are also a function of cultural variations (Triandis, 1989; Heine, Lehman, Markus, & Kitayama, 1999; Markus & Kitayama, 1991). So is the concept of other persons with whom one must engage in negotiations (Morris & Peng, 1994). All in all, social judgment biases arise from the negotiators' reliance on culture-specific knowledge structures such as conceptions of the negotiation situation, and conceptions of self and those of the other parties involved in intercultural transactions.

The concept of *limited good,* that is, fixed pie bias, falsely assumes that there is little room for integrative bargaining—that the interests of the parties are diametrically opposite (Thompson & Hastie, 1990). Research with US subjects suggests that the concept of fixed pie bias arises from conceptions of conflict (either based on historical factors, ethnic differences, or on differences due to administrative heritage of the negotiation involved). This bias is quite commonplace in competitive sports, such as a game with a winner and a loser like American football. A collaborative undertaking like solving a problem for a client in a joint venture type of situation does not evoke this fixed pie mindset (Pinkley, 1990). North American negotiators are more noted for their win–lose mentality even when they have been given complete information highlighting the fact that the interests of the parties involved in negotiation are not necessarily opposite (Pinkley & Northcraft, 1994). This illustrates the overriding importance of the fixed pie or limited good mentality in negotiation, and this is particularly strong in transactions across borders and cultures.

Another bias that clouds judgments of fairness concerns *egocentrism,* or the inclination to view one's own judgments and behaviors in negotiation situations to be more fair than those of the other parties (Thompson & Lowenstein, 1992). For example, parties in a dispute enter final offer arbitration with overly optimistic assessments of the likelihood that their own proposal will be judged as being fairer and therefore preferred by the other party. Self-serving fairness judgments also lead parties to take aggressive positions which may result in costly delays. They may also shrink the pie or the outcome of value that would ultimately be divided (Thompson & Lowenstein, 1992; Babcock & Lowenstein, 1997). The issue of self-concept enters in this equation in an interesting fashion. As we have already discussed in Chapter 2 and above in this chapter, self-concept has a different structure or scope in non-Western and particularly in East Asian cultures compared with the cultures of Western Europe, the US, Canada, Australia, and so on. There is evidence that East Asians think of themselves as being less isolated in terms of their relationships with others of their in-groups (e.g., their spouses, mentors, and members of kith and kin). Therefore, the role of egocentric bias and problems related to such biases are more pronounced in East Asian cultures. East Asians tend to process the arguments and concerns on both sides of the conflict through the construal of their interdependent concepts of self (Markus & Kitayama, 1991). Research by Gelfand et al. (2002) supports this line of thinking.

Finally, another set of errors in negotiations stems from incorrect attributions of traits of other parties. Negotiators often have false impressions of the characteristics of the others involved (e.g., inflexible attitudes, greed, and closed mindset). Failure to consider the significance of situational influences in negotiation processes results in false and rigid attributions of traits in others. And over time, such attributions tend to crystallize, making future attempts to negotiate difficult to initiate—that is, leading to maladaptive decisions. This is where the use of a third party arbitrator is helpful. The negotiators give up their sense of control, and the potential for creating value through the process of negotiation may be rekindled. Most Western negotiators are likely to ignore the role of situational or contextual forces even when they are aware of the importance of such factors in negotiating with members of other cultures. The disposition to attribute behaviors of others to personality traits and other dispositions (Nisbett & Ross, 1980) is strong on the part of negotiators from the West. That is, the dispositionist attribution error leads negotiators to interpret disagreements and conflicts as being rooted in differences in personalities and personal trait-based differences and not embedded in the situation. The East Asians, on the other hand, are more prone to attributing difficulties that arise in negotiation as stemming from contextual factors. More often than not, the truth lies somewhere in between. However, one can see how such differences in attribution error that are rooted in knowledge structures of respective cultures of the negotiators can cause significant obstacles in reaching agreements. This dispositionist bias, so salient in North American negotiators, is termed "fundamental attribution error," and such biases are much less prevalent among East Asians. For the latter group, the concept of the self of the individual person as *agentic* or causal is much less absolute. In other words, East Asians do not necessarily attribute difficulties in negotiation as being rooted in the personality structures or traits of the other party. Research by Nisbett and his colleagues at the University of Michigan (Nisbett & Ross, 1980) strongly bears out the importance of these cultural differences.

Summary

Social judgments routinely occur in negotiations across borders and cultures, and there are three kinds of biases: (1) in social judgment of other parties, (2) fixed pie or limited good assumptions, (3) egocentric biases in fairness judgments. Morris & Gelfand (2004) note that it is premature to develop a comprehensive taxonomy of social judgments that is likely to complicate negotiation across borders and cultures. A more fruitful direction for future research and practice would be to systematically investigate the role of cultural variations in biases that are linked to social knowledge structures such as conceptions of self or personhood, and of relationships that are involved in negotiations (the social perception bias and some cognitive and motivational biases). Adopting a more dynamic and constructivist approach is likely to provide a sounder basis for predicting the role of biases and how they might differ across cultures.

MANAGING CONFLICT RESOLUTION

As is clear by now, much of the negotiation process is fraught with conflict. Conflicts can be either explicit or implicit in character, and experience of conflict often leads to a freezing of respective positions and the development of a lose–lose mindset. This is not a positive outcome, not only because of its immediate impact on the outcomes that were perhaps achievable, but also because experience of conflicts (whether implicit or explicit) has adverse effects in terms of premature closure of future negotiations. Research in this area indicates that much of the conflict is rooted in cultural differences between the parties—in terms of the different expectations they bring to the negotiating context, their behaviors in the situation, and particularly in differences in terms of how and what they communicate in terms of substantive issues versus stylistic considerations. Negotiating with the Chinese is often fraught with numerous conflicts, but it is essential for many countries in the West in the global economy of the 21st century (Jacques, 2009, pp. 151–93).

Instrumental-oriented conflict occurs when there are strong differences in the negotiation process on the basis of factual information and logical analyses. In contrast, *expressive-oriented conflict* takes place when the negotiation situation is handled indirectly and implicitly without clear delineation of the roles and responsibilities of the parties who are involved. Such conflicts are more prevalent in high-context cultures (see Chapter 4). In such cultures, negotiators are not inclined to become involved in a confrontational situation because a lack of competence in handling confrontational situations is regarded as insulting. Such scenarios are also likely to cause a loss of face. Use of evasion and avoidance if members of high-context cultures are not able to reach agreement through emotional appeals results in expressive-oriented conflicts. Managers from Western multinationals and global organizations are especially encouraged to read cues and non-verbal signs that are present when parties experience such conflicts. The tendency to avoid discussions and either proceed very slowly or not at all leads to experience of discomfort on the part of managers from low-context cultures such as the Swiss, Germans, Americans, and British. Clearly, there is a difference in the way individuals from low- and high-context cultures approach negotiation (see Figure 4.3 for location of important countries on this dimension of low–high context).

There are no easy answers to how a manager from countries such as the US, UK, Canada, France, Japan, and Brazil can manage conflicts that are inevitable in negotiations across cultures. Whether the negotiations take place at the highest levels of the transacting multinational and global organizations, or at the level of heads of departments of special branches of production and operations, marketing, accounting, and so on, managers must be systematically coached in *culture-assimilator training* (Triandis, 1977; Triandis et al., 1975; Bhagat, 1979; Triandis & Bhawuk, 1997; Bhawuk, 2009). The ability to train managers to make correct attributions in negotiation situations involving people from dissimilar cultures is crucial in avoiding conflicts. The importance of this cannot be over-emphasized. Also, training pertaining to the expectations of the other parties with whom one must negotiate, and knowledge of various contextual factors inherent in the organizational, national, and macroeconomic contexts are also important (see Figure 5.1 for details). Knowledge concerning styles of communication (verbal versus non-verbal, relative emphasis on Internet and computer-mediated communication strategies) that are preferred by the other party and the tactics of negotiating (use of conciliatory tactics or threatening postures) that are more prevalent in the other party is vital. Senior managers who are ultimately responsible for the outcomes of the negotiation must calculate the cost–benefit of various offers to arrive at a win–win situation. It is only when a win–win situation is achieved that negotiations are deemed successful and lead to development of long-term relationships. Also, such relationships are free from conflicts, whether implicit or explicit. As we noted earlier, use of a host country advisor, or arbitrator or mediator, might facilitate the diffusion of issues that could otherwise escalate into a conflict situation.

DECISION-MAKING ACROSS CULTURES

The literature on antecedents and consequences of decision-making in organizations is vast (Miller & Wilson, 2006). In this section, our objective is to be concerned with the outcome of a series of small and large decisions that lead to successful negotiations between executives of two or more multinational organizations from dissimilar cultures. Decisions pertaining to the position that the initiating party to the negotiation will take and the fallback positions upon which it will rely are important. Some decisions are of an incremental type (i.e., they take place over time and as a series of steps). Decisions involving how to react to disagreeable stances, when and how to proceed, when to confront and concede, and on what issues agreements are possible and what issues are beyond the scope of negotiation are critical for the success of negotiations. The stand that the US government and the Department of State have taken with respect to curbing of international terrorism is that no negotiation involving US trade and business transactions will be conducted with nations whose governments actively or covertly sponsor terrorism. Iran, Libya, and North Korea are not the kinds of countries with which the US and its allies are likely to negotiate. This decision reflects the policy of the US government as a strong and sovereign nation and is also strongly rooted in the assumption that the US must act as the leader of the free world and should not succumb to terrorist tactics for initiating negotiations. Similar decisions are also adopted by the governments of Israel, India, the UK, and so on.

The role of decision-making in the conduct of international business transactions goes beyond the context of negotiating with global organizations from dissimilar nations and cultures. Decision-making is a daily ritual in the lives of managers (Mintzberg, 1973). Decisions are made on the shop floor, with first line production operators developing consensus before the decisions are moved up the organizational hierarchy. *Programmed decisions* (i.e., decisions that are routine and are conducted by various algorithms and computer-generated programs) require minimal time and effort compared with *non-programmed* decisions of far broader scope and importance. The decision to enter into a joint venture with an organization or strategic alliances with a group of companies (whether in the private or public sector) is a good case in point. Such decisions are totally non-programmatic and require a set of decisions by the senior managers such as senior vice-presidents which are then conveyed through a series of negotiations with the foreign counterparts. We must also note that an element of luck is involved in addition to all the careful planning and analyses in which managers might engage. Often, there is no recognition of situational events (i.e., favorable exchange rates, effective intervention by the respective governments or public sector officials, concessions made by labor unions) in the success of a negotiation across borders and cultures.

Non-programmed decisions involve the following seven basic steps (see Figure 5.3).

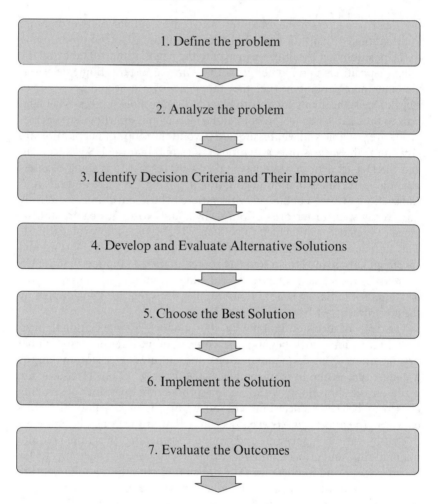

Source: Phatak, Bhagat, & Kashlak (2005), p. 406.

Figure 5.3 Steps in the decision-making process

1. *Defining the problem.* It is the first step in decision-making and is perhaps the most important one. A problem represents a state of affairs different from normal and desired functioning. If the problem is not well defined, or if it is defined incorrectly or without appropriate understanding, the solution arrived at will be sub-optimal. For example, if the problem in setting up a joint venture is rooted in the differences in administrative heritages and management philosophies

of the two global companies, but the parties begin to focus on cultural differences, the problem will not be properly defined, and the solution will not be correct.

2. *Analyzing the problem.* During this stage, the focus is on locating the major and minor factors that are responsible for the underlying issues or problems. These factors could be inherent in the past, in the nature of the people who are involved with the negotiation, or in the nature of the situation (i.e., whether the outcome of the negotiation is vitally important for the future survival of the company or only partially relevant for its overall effectiveness). In launching a new product in a dissimilar culture or in introducing significant innovations in services marketing, if the key factor happens to be the *demand* for the product or the service, but the manager identifies the *quality* of the product or the service as the most important factor, then he or she is analyzing the wrong set of causes for reaching an optimal decision.

3. *Identifying decision criteria and their importance.* During this third stage of decision-making, the criteria for arriving at a correct and optimal decision are determined. For example, in selecting a new site for establishing a manufacturing unit of the Toyota Corporation of Japan, the senior executives might be more interested to maximize the benefits of having a motivated and committed workforce and minimize the complications of dealing with labor unions. If these criteria are of crucial importance, then the decision to locate the future manufacturing plants in the southern states of the US is obviously more appropriate. States such as Alabama, Tennessee, Mississippi, and South Carolina are right-to-work states and labor unions such as the United Automobile Workers' Union and Teamsters do not have much influence in these situations.

4. *Developing and evaluating alternative solutions.* During the stage of decision-making, the focus is on comparing and contrasting different methods of solving problems. The method that is chosen is that which offers maximal opportunities for realizing organizational goals and objectives. Executives who have a broad range of experience both in the domestic and international contexts are likely to envision and contrast various alternative solutions and choose those which offer the best possible path for reaching the objectives. Once again, an element of luck is important and a fortunate encounter whereby a major obstacle is removed or lessened in its importance will obviously enhance the adoption of the most effective strategy.

5. *Choosing the best solution.* This is a crucial step of decision-making and is not necessarily an easy one. A manager may come up with a set

of scenarios or solutions that appear to be equally viable or attractive, but the one that will maximize the outcome may not always be clear. Such dilemmas are routinely encountered in conducting international negotiations. When confronted with political risks in countries of sub-Saharan Africa such as Nigeria and Zimbabwe, and Central America, some oil and gas exploration companies might select to pull out completely without recognizing the long-term benefits of continuing to work with the new political regimes which are likely to be less corrupt and more friendly to multinational companies (Blunt & Jones, 1992; Engholm & Grimes, 1997).

6. *Implementing the solution.* During this stage, the decision is implemented in the organizational context or in the network of the subsidiaries of the multinational and global corporations. Decisions are easily implemented in US organizations where group-based consensus is not sought. The lower participants in organizations are expected to follow the directives that are generated at the higher levels of the corporation. However, in Japanese, and to some extent in South Korean, multinational and global organizations, the decisions are implemented by examining the nature of their acceptance at the lower levels. There are no pressures from the senior echelons of the organization, and the acceptance evolves slowly from bottom to top of the organization (Abbeglen & Stalk, 1985; Steers, Sanchez-Runde, & Nardon, 2009).

7. *Evaluating the outcomes of an implemented decision.* This is the final stage. However, many multinational and global organizations do not appreciate the importance of evaluating the effectiveness of the implemented decision. The decision may be arrived at after a great deal of scientific analysis, scrutiny, and brain-storming sessions, with the best and brightest of the organization spending numerous hours and sleepless nights. However, when it comes to evaluating the effectiveness of the implemented decision, many senior managers avoid the task. This is because, if a decision is not found to be effective or has caused a backlash (whether major or minor), it can lead to loss of face for the managers of East Asian countries and loss of prestige and reputation, and also possible dislocation of career objectives on the part of managers of Western countries. We suggest that global managers need to pay special attention to this step because there are numerous conflicting factors that must be carefully considered in this final stage. This stage is becoming more important as the competition between multinational and global organizations intensifies in the global marketplace of the 21st century.

THE ROLE OF CULTURAL DIFFERENCES IN DECISION-MAKING

Just as understanding the role of cultural differences in the process of negotiation is important, so is the case here. Culture affects decision-making through the established value system of the national culture which emphasizes certain preferred modes of decision-making. Cultural variations also influence the process of selective perception or interpretation of the various issues that are inherent in a decision-making context. For example, immigrant professionals from collectivist contexts of China, India, Japan, and South Korea experience a great deal of discomfort in terminating the jobs of junior employees, especially during times of economic downturn. In many interviews conducted by the first author of this book with managers of Texas Instruments, Raytheon Corporation, City of Dallas, and Hilton Corporation, he was informed by many managers of Asian origin (both East and South Asia) that they did not like to make the decision, in fact they abhorred the decision, to lay off employees in their departments. Obviously, the role of collectivist culture has a strong influence in this context. On the other hand, US managers of Anglo- and Western European countries were not so troubled by the fact that they had to make decisions regarding laying off or terminating the jobs of junior engineers or employees in such high-tech corporations during times of economic distress.

Two managers might approach the same objective situation and each make a different decision because the elements of the situation that are perceived as being important by one manager may be accorded much less importance by his or her colleague. Hitt, Tyler, & Park (1990) found that a culturally more homogenizing influence exists in the minds of South Korean executives than in US executives. In other words, South Korean managers have a tendency to make decisions that are fairly identical. On the other hand, the individualistic values of US culture encourage US executives to arrive at different decisions. The willingness to conform to a modal pattern of decision is much less important, if it occurs at all, in the minds of US managers.

Cultural variations influence the following stages of decision-making more than other stages: (1) definition of the problem; (2) the process of gathering and analyzing relevant data; (3) considering alternative solutions; (4) deciding on the best solution; and finally (5) the process of implementing the decision. It is normally assumed, and perhaps rightly so, that Western managers from Anglo-Saxon countries are likely to adopt a more objective or rational approach in making decisions. However, this approach is not so common throughout the collectivistic and high uncertainty avoidance countries of Latin America, Africa, and Asia. Even among the member countries of the European community, managers from Belgium, Germany, and Austria have lower tolerance for risk than managers from Japan, the Netherlands, and India—with US managers having the highest tolerance for risks (Bass & Burger, 1979).

An important variable that is often overlooked in the process of decision-making is the perception of control or locus of control over the outcomes of a decision. Some managers feel confident that they can plan effectively in terms of arriving at certain desirable outcomes because they feel they are in control of events and they can exercise some direction over the future course of actions. In contrast, some other managers— particularly from the Arabian Peninsula (e.g., the UAE, Saudi Arabia, Yemen, and Oman), sub-Saharan Africa, and parts of South Asia (managers from rural parts of India where a fatalistic outlook is strongly encouraged)—feel that they have little control over the outcomes of their decisions and that "If God wills," then positive outcomes will result. US managers believe strongly in self-determination and are more prone to perceiving decision-making situations as something that they can control and manage to a great extent.

The inclination to try new and innovative approaches also varies a great deal across national borders and cultures. Many managers, particularly from the EU countries, are likely to value past successes in similar situations as being important in signaling the amount of confidence they can have in arriving at a successful decision. On the other hand, Americans are more oriented toward obtaining positive outcomes in the future and are quick to adopt new, innovative, and even novel (not yet proven) approaches to decision-making. In some European countries, particularly in France, US managers are regarded as being too quick to make their decisions. The French express considerable amazement at the willingness of American executives to try something new and innovative without experiencing a great deal of dissonance.

APPROACHES TO DECISION-MAKING

In addition to influencing the various stages of decision-making, cultural variations strongly influence the approaches that are preferred by decision-makers from different countries and cultures. The value of utilitarianism versus moral idealism affects the overall approach to decision-making in situations which are likely to have strong societal implications. Even though utilitarianism is a prime concern in decision-making in Western multinational and global corporations, there are interesting and important variations even in the EU countries of Western Europe and North America. Canadian managers are more influenced by short-term and cost–benefit approaches to decision-making than their Hong Kong counterparts. In addition, they are more utilitarian in their approach than executives from mainland China, who might approach some decision-making tasks associated with international negotiations from the stand-point of Communist Party-based and moral idealism. In other words, emphasizing the long-term benefits of a decision that will have a positive and lasting impact on a society, as opposed to the organization and the individuals involved, is important to Chinese managers.

The role of autocratic versus participative leadership is also important in the effectiveness in decisions that managers might make. In vertical collectivistic cultures such as India, China, Japan, Mexico, Brazil, and Argentina, authorization for decisions has to be passed through the upper echelons of management before final decisions and actions can be under-taken. The process is often laden with red tape and is bureaucratic and slow. However, as Gunnar Myrdal observed in his classic analysis *The Asian drama* (1966), such bureaucratic processes of arriving at decisions are major causes of economic backwardness of these countries—especially during the 1960s. Most employees in these countries, including the BRIC countries (recognized as the leading global economies of the 21st century), still have state-sponsored bureaucratic processes that make decision-making regarding adoption of foreign direct investment difficult and slow at best. In comparison, the locus of decision-making in the countries of Northern Europe, such as Sweden, Denmark, Norway, and Finland, is decentralized, and participative decision-making is the hallmark of German multinational and global companies. Arriving at decisions in these EU countries is not as cumbersome or complicated as is the case with the countries mentioned earlier. US managers emphasize the impor-tance of participative decision-making and leadership, but in practice the decision-making process in US multinational and global organizations lies between the autocratic and participative approaches.

As discussed earlier, the managers of the Arabian Peninsula are likely to be slow and refer to luck, that is, believe in fatalism and attribute the success of decisions to the will of God (i.e., Allah) more than managers from other Asian and Western countries. Business in these countries is best conducted through the use of a likeable intermediary, even though both parties are aware that the final decisions will be made by senior executives of the corporation.

One final issue that needs our attention concerns the relative speed of decision-making. While the bureaucratic processes and red tape in many of the bureaucratic cultures of the West and in Africa, Latin America, and

Asia affect the speed of decision-making, cultural issues are also important in this regard. The role of delegation is crucial. Many autocratic cultures do not encourage delegation of decision-making authority to junior managers on lower rungs of the organizational chart. In fact, it is often found that managers from these countries express a great deal of frustration in discussing the lack of speed in making decisions in their organizations—especially if they have been trained in Western educational systems (e.g., engineering, business, and medical schools). Immigration of highly talented professionals from these countries often stems from their frustrations in dealing with the bureaucratic processes regarding decision-making, including the fairness doctrine, of their home country-based organizations.

CONCLUDING THOUGHTS

It is clear that competitive positioning and successful operations of multinational and global organizations require more than a working knowledge of how negotiations are conducted across countries and cultures. Cultural variations influence these processes in a myriad of ways and this chapter has provided a comprehensive review of the important processes that are at play. Although managers may make decisions that do not necessarily involve country- and culture-based considerations in negotiation, the fact remains that they cannot negotiate effectively without understanding the causes and consequences of various decisions and approaches to various decisions in their organizational contexts. More importantly, they must understand the cultural and behavioral aspects of these processes so that they will feel more effective in dealing with people from dissimilar national contexts and cultures. As cultural diversity increases in the global workforce, a knowledge of negotiation, conflict management, and decision-making becomes increasingly important. With a more than adequate understanding of the environmental and cultural issues involved in these important organizational processes, multinational and global corporations are likely to achieve desirable results and achieve international competitiveness in the global marketplace.

REFERENCES

Abegglen, J. & Stalk, G. (1985). *The Japanese corporation*. New York: Basic Books.
Adler, Nancy (2002). *International dimensions of organizational behavior*. Cincinnati, OH: South-Western.

Babcock, L. & Lowenstein, G. (1997). Explaining bargaining impasse: The rule of self-serving biases. *Journal of Economic Perspectives*, 11(1), 109–25.

Bass, B.M. & Burger, P. (1979). *Assessment of managers: An international comparison*. New York: Free Press.

Bazerman, M.H., Magliozzi, T., & Neal, M.A. (2003). Integrative bargaining in a competitive market. In Leigh L. Thompson (Ed.). *The social psychology of organizational behavior* (pp. 294–313). New York: Psychology Press.

Bhagat, R.S., McDevitt, A.S., & McDevitt, I. (2010). On improving the robustness of Asian management theories: Theoretical anchors in the era of globalization. *Asia Pacific Journal of Management*, doi:10.1007/s10490-009-9158-z.

Bhagat, R.S. (1979). Black and white ethnic differences in identification with the work ethic: Some implications for organizational integration. *Academy of Management Review*, 4(3), 381–91.

Bhawuk, D.P.S. (2009). Intercultural training for the global workplace: Review, synthesis, and theoretical explanations. In R.S. Bhagat & R.M. Steers (Eds). *Cambridge handbook of culture, organizations, and work* (pp. 462–88). Cambridge: Cambridge University Press.

Blunt, P. & Jones, M.L. (1992). *Managing organizations in Africa*. New York: Walter de Gruyter.

Brett, J.A. & Okumura, T. (1998). Inter- and intracultural negotiations: U.S. and Japanese negotiators. *Academy of Management Review*, 31(5), 495–510.

Dwyer, T. (2001). Web globalization: Write once, deploy worldwide. In Lois Enos (Ed.). *English-only a mistake for US sites. E-Commerce Times*, 17 May. Available at: www.EcommerceTimes.com.

Engholm, C. & Grimes, S. (1997). *Doing business in Mexico*. Paramus, NJ: Prentice-Hall.

Fisher, R. & Ury, W. (1981). *Getting to yes*. Boston, MA: Houghton Mifflin.

Gelfand, M.J., Higgins, M., Nishii, L., Raver, J., Dominquez, A., Yamaguchi, S., Murakami, F., & Toyama, M. (2002). Culture and egocentric biases of fairness in conflict and negotiation. *Journal of Applied Psychology*, 87, 833–45.

Graham, J.L. (1985). The influence of culture on the process of business negotiations in an exploratory study. *Journal of International Business Studies*, Spring, 81–96.

Graham, J.L. & Lam, N.M. (2003). The Chinese negotiation. *Harvard Business Review*, 81(10), 1–11.

Heine, S.J., Lehman, D.R., Markus, H.R., & Kitayama, S. (1999). Is there a universal need for positive self-regard? *Psychological Review*, 106, 766–94.

Herbig, P. (1997). External influences in the cross-cultural negotiation process. *Industrial Management & Data Systems*. 97(3–4), 150–61.

Hitt, M.A., Tyler, B., & Park, D. (1990). A cross-cultural examination of strategic decision-models: A comparison of Korean and U.S. Executives. *Proceedings of the Academy of Management*, August, 111–15.

Jacques, M. (2009). *When China rules the world*. New York: Penguin.

Kochan, T.A. (1980). *Collective bargaining and industrial relations*. Homewood, IL: R.D. Irwin.

Markus, H. & Kitayama, S. (1991). Culture and the self: Implications for cognition, emotion, and motivation. *Psychological Review*, 98, 224–53.

Miller, S.J. & Wilson, D.C. (2006). Perspectives in organizational decision-making. In S.R. Clegg, C. Hardy, T.B. Lawrence, & W.R. Nord (Eds). *The Sage handbook of organization studies* (pp. 469–519). Los Angeles, CA: Sage.

Mintzberg, H. (1973). *The nature of managerial work*. New York: Harper & Row.

Morris, M.W. & Gelfand, M.J. (2004). Cultural differences and cognitive dynamics: Expanding the cognitive perspective on negotiation. In M.J. Gelmand & J.M. Brett (Eds). *The handbook of negotiation and culture* (pp. 45–70). Stanford, CA: Stanford Business Books.

Morris, M.W. & Peng, K. (1994). Culture and cause: American and Chinese attribution for social and physical events. *Journal of Personality and Social Psychology*, 67, 949–71.

Morris, M.W., Larrick, R.P., & Su, S.K. (2003). Misperceiving negotiation counterparts: When situationally determined bargaining behaviors are attributed to personality traits. In Leigh L. Thompson (Ed.). *The social psychology of organizational behavior* (pp. 141–62). New York: Psychology Press.

Myrdal, G. (1966). *The Asian drama*. New York: Knopf Doubleday Publishing.

Nisbett, R.E. & Ross, L. (1980). *Human inference: Strategies and shortcomings of social judgment*. Englewood Cliffs, NJ: Prentice-Hall.

Phatak, A.V., Bhagat, R.S., & Kashlak, R.J. (2005). *International management; managing in a diverse and dynamic environment*. Burr-Ridge, IL: McGraw-Hill Irvin.

Pinkley, R. (1990). Dimensions of conflict frame: Disputant interpretations of conflict. *Journal of Applied Psychology*, 75, 117–26.

Pinkley, R.L. & Northcraft, G.B. (1994). Cognitive interpretations of conflict: Implications for dispute processes and outcomes. *Academy of Management Journal*, 37(1), 193–205.

Pruitt, D.G. (1981). *Negotiation behavior*. New York: Academic Press.

Pye, L. (1982). *Chinese commercial negotiating style*. Cambridge, MA: Oelgeschlanger, Gunn, & Hain Publishers, Inc.

Rosch, M. & Segler, K.G. (1987). Communication with Japanese. *Management International Review*, 27(4), 56–67.

Rubin, J. (1980). Experimental research on third-party intervention in conflict: Toward some generalizations. *Psychological Bulletin*, 87, 379–91.

Rubin, J. & Brown, B. (1975). *The social psychology of bargaining and negotiation*. New York: Academic Press.

Shapiro, D.L., Lewicki, R.J., & Devine, P. (1995). When do employees choose deceptive tactics to stop unwanted change? A relational perspective. In R. Lewicki, B. Sheppark, & R. Bies (Eds). *Research on negotiation in organizations* (vol. 5, pp. 155–84). Greenwich, CT: JAI Press.

Shapiro, D., Sheppard, B.H., & Cheraskin, L. (1992). Business on a handshake. *Negotiation Journal*, 8, 365–77.

Steers, R.M., Sanchez-Runde, C.J, & Nardon, L. (2010). *Management across cultures: Challenges and strategies*. Cambridge: Cambridge University Press.

Thompson, L. (2001). *The mind and heart of the negotiator*. Upper Saddle River, NJ: Prentice-Hall.

Thompson, L. & Hastie, R. (1990). Social perception in negotiation. *Organizational Behavior and Human Decision Processes*, 47, 98–123.

Thompson, L. & Lowenstein, G. (1992). Egocentric interpretations of fairness and negotiation. *Organizational Behavior and Human Decision Processes*, 51, 176–97.

Triandis, H.C. (1975). Cultural training, cognitive complexity, and interpersonal attitudes. In R.W. Brislin, S. Bochner, & W.L. Lonner (Eds). *Cross-cultural perspectives on learning* (pp. 39–77). New York: John Wiley.

Triandis, H.C. (1977). Theoretical framework for evaluation of cross-cultural training effectiveness. *International Journal of Intercultural Relations*, 1, 19–45.

Triandis, H.C. (1989). Self and social behavior in differing cultural contexts. *Psychological Review*, 96, 269–89.

Triandis, H.C. & Bhawuk, D.P.S. (1997). Culture theory and the meaning of relatedness. In P.C. Earley & M. Erez (Eds). *New perspectives in international industrial/organizational psychology*. New York: Lexington Free Press.

Tung, R.L. (1982). US China trade negotiations: Practices, procedures and outcomes. *Journal of International Business Studies*, Fall, 25–37.

Tung, R.L. (1991). Handshakes across the sea. *Organizational Dynamics*, 3, 30–40.

Walton, R. & McKersie, R. (1965). *A behavioral theory of negotiation*. New York: McGraw-Hill.

Zakaria, F. (2008). *The post-American world*. New York: W.W. Norton & Company.

6. Cultural variations in work motivation, job satisfaction, and organizational commitment

People in work organizations come with a distinct set of abilities and skills, and vary in their demographics, educational accomplishments, and expectations of income from their labor. They are our colleagues, managers, supervisors, subordinates, advisors in technical and scientific laboratories, customers, clients, and even personal friends who are concerned with our work-related expectations and experiences. Multinational and global organizations employ people who speak different languages, approach issues of problem-solving in remarkably different ways, and often seek different kinds of rewards and outcomes for doing the same job. What most of these people have in common, though, is a collective need to make useful contributions to accomplish the goals and objectives of the organization. The majority of them would like to be known as "useful" employees and do not like to be labeled as "social loafers"—free-riders who do not make appropriate contributions and hope that their lack of effort will be masked under the collective contributions of their work groups. Research shows that people from individualist cultures are often social loafers, while people from collectivist cultures do not loaf when they work with in-group members (Earley & Gibson, 1998). Nevertheless, a large majority of individuals in all cultures feel motivated as well as committed to their work roles and to their employee organization.

To be effective, managers of multinational, global corporations must have first-hand knowledge and some instinctive sense of how cultural differences influence the way people feel when they work (i.e., perform a series of interrelated tasks assigned to them by their work group and work organization), including what energizes them (i.e., what motivates and sustains their levels of effort in performing their jobs). Also of significant concern to the global manager are issues related to why some individuals leave an organization (i.e., what makes them feel like withdrawing from performing their work roles in a sustained fashion and eventually leave or attempt to leave the organization; what makes them have either low or high values of commitment to the organization?). The motives for working vary widely across national borders and cultures—largely, but not completely, in accordance with the inherent values of their ethnic and national cultures. Before discussing the role of cultural and some personality-related variations on motivation, it is important to define motivation.

Two thousand years ago, Confucius noted that people are basically the same, but they are motivated to do different things at different stages of their lives. Recently, Honda Motor Company co-founder Takeo Fujisawa observed that while Japanese and American managers are 95 percent the same, they differ in some important ways (Earley, 1989). Even if the difference is exhibited in just 5 percent, if these 5 percent are of great importance, the implications for productivity and international competitiveness will be great.

In a detailed analysis of the philosophical themes and famous novels and novellas from countries such as Greece, Italy, Spain, Portugal (i.e., Southern European countries) and the UK, Ireland, France, Germany, US, and Canada (Western European and Anglo countries of North America), it has been observed that differences in cultural upbringing have significant implications for the kind of meaning that people attach to working and the meaning of working throughout their adult lives (England, 1987).

DEFINITION OF MOTIVATION, JOB SATISFACTION, JOB INVOLVEMENT, AND RELATED CONSTRUCTS

Motivation is concerned with the amount of effort that an individual is willing to exert or put into his or her work role to accomplish an organizationally valued objective. An instructor in a Japanese auto plant who likes to stay after his or her regular working hours and instruct new employees in various aspects of their work role is clearly more motivated than someone who leaves the plant at the end of their shift. Another example concerns the amount of effort that a new regulator in the US Department of Treasury or Securities and Exchange Commission applies to prevent future abuses of the sub-prime mortgage rates that triggered the major economic slowdown of 2008. Central to the topic of work motivation and organizational commitment are the persistence and perseverance displayed in order to perform a work role. Motivated workers feel good when working; they also come to work earlier, put in longer hours, and do not mind "walking the extra mile" to get the job done. Another way of looking at motivation is to interpret it as the *willingness* to exert high levels of effort to accomplish goals and objectives. Of course, there is usually a link between accomplishing the goals of an organization and obtaining both intrinsic (i.e., a sense of inner joy, fulfillment, and accomplishment) and extrinsic (i.e., better salaries, a promotion, transfer to a desirable location, better benefits including health care and retirement) rewards.

It is important to emphasize that managers cannot determine who is motivated in their immediate work group, or in the larger scale of the work organization, simply by observing the behavior of employees or work groups. An employee who produces 10 units an hour is probably twice as motivated as another who produces 5 units an hour, only if their situations are identical. If one has excellent equipment and the other does not that could be the explanation for the difference in their output. Motivation is not the only factor that affects job performance—but it is an important factor. Other important factors are job-related abilities (both native and trained skills), clear-cut and unambiguous job descriptions, supportive supervisors, and a good work environment. *Job-related abilities* are clearly the most important factors in performing a job. In fact, it has been suggested that for lower-level jobs, abilities are more important than work motivation in maintaining a decent level of performance over a considerable period of time. Next in importance is an accurate perception of the requirements of one's job.

New employees are unlikely to have a clear-cut sense or perception of the requirements of the job. The ability to understand the requirements of a role tends to increase over one's career; it doesn't happen overnight—that is. it takes a significant amount of introspection and experience to figure out or make sense of the *tangible* and *non-tangible* aspects of one's work role. Companies can create positive work environments (see Cameron et al., 2003, on positive organizational scholarship) that facilitate the productivity of managers at all levels of the organization. Global companies like Microsoft, Apple Computers, Hewlett-Packard, Toyota, Samsung, and Infosys of India have created work environments that facilitate superior performance on the job. For example, in the early 1980s, Apple Computers of Cuppertino, CA created a flexible-time work environment for programmers and hardware engineers. They could arrive at the R & D labs at almost any time and begin to design computers, including Apple I and Apple II. A work environment that facilitates positive interactions is very likely to create conditions that maximize motivation.

MEANING OF WORKING ACROSS NATIONS AND CULTURES

Research has shown that work has different meanings in different cultures. In cultures where the environment is challenging (i.e., people who work hard get rewarded) work is a "good" concept, but in cultures where no matter how hard one works there are few rewards, work is a "bad" concept and the ideal is to do as little as possible. When it is very hot, one desires to do as little as possible; when it is very cold one spends most available energy fighting the cold. In short, in very cold or very hot climates work is not as "good" as it is in temperate climates (Triandis, 1973).

While teaching graduate students in business schools in various parts of the world, we have heard many stories and examples, as well as complaints, from managers who have had the opportunity to work with or supervise a group of employees from dissimilar cultures. For example, one complaint was that Mexicans "do not take their responsibilities seriously" and are quick to quit their work after they have made enough money to go home for Christmas or other religious holidays. However, Mexico is very large, and those who live in very hot parts of that country just do not have the stamina to work hard. On the other hand, those from the temperate or cool parts of that country do work very hard. Also, there are stereotypes such as Germans are methodical and dedicated to their work while Brazilians do not value punctuality in performing their tasks. Again we must be careful, because the Germans who were raised in the East part of that country were not as motivated as those raised in the West part (Greenberg & Baron, 2003). Another stereotype is that Americans tend to be fair in assessing the potential for advancement of their subordinates compared with their counterparts in some collectivist countries. These statements contain a grain of truth, but there is so much variety within a country that they cannot be used as a dependable guide toward understanding another country. Think how absurd it is to say "all Americans eat pizza!" Nevertheless, the significance of working or the meaning of work varies greatly from country to country. Working is central to the self-concept and self-definition of many Americans and is also quite important in the UK, Germany, Canada, Australia, New Zealand, and to some extent in France. The Nordic countries of Europe are also high on emphasizing the overall significance of work and working. The East Asian countries (i.e., Japan, South Korea, China, Vietnam, etc.) are also known to emphasize the significance of work. South Asian countries, such as India and Thailand, also emphasize the importance of work in the lives of individuals regardless of gender differences. All in all, Americans work the longest number of hours in a year (about 2000 hours—according to estimates provided by Juliette Schor (1994) of Harvard University), followed by Japan, Germany, and South Korea, in that order.

In 1987, a group of international management researchers, led by George W. England of the University of Oklahoma, conducted a comparative study of the meaning of working and the centrality of work in the life of individuals, in eight countries. The Western countries were the US, Britain, Germany, the Netherlands, Belgium, and the former Yugoslavia. Data were also obtained from Japan (representing Asia) and Israel (representing the Middle East). The three key concepts used to assess the significance of the meaning of work were defined as follows:

1. *Work centrality.* The degree or scale of importance, meaning, and value attributed to one's work role throughout one's work life. Work centrality is supposed to decline after one retires from working.
2. *Societal norms about working.* Normative beliefs and expectations regarding specific rights such as *entitlement* and duties (*obligations*) which are attached to work. These beliefs imply that each individual has the right to have interesting and meaningful work, the proper training to continue such work, and the right to be an active participant in the work setting. From a societal point of view, these norms imply that everyone has the obligation to contribute to the well-being of a society by working and to save for their future.
3. *Work goals.* Outcomes which are work-related throughout the working life (i.e., interesting work, decent pay, job security, learning opportunities, and a good "fit" between the employee and the job). There are 11 possible work goals in Belgium, the Netherlands, Japan, and the UK.

The clear implications of the meaning of working study were that the higher the meaning for work centrality score, the more motivated and committed the workers are in that society. An implication for managers of multinational, global corporations is that the score provides specific reasons for valuing work. It also indicates how the need for work is satisfied in different societies. Figure 6.1 shows that in 1987 the mean centrality score was highest in Japan (7.78) and lowest in Britain (6.36). The relative importance of work goals is illustrated in Table 6.1, and it shows that in four countries, interesting work was ranked to be of the highest importance out of eleven possible work goals.

The importance of pay was highest in Britain (ranked two out of eleven) and in Germany, it ranked one out of eleven. The importance of achieving a good fit between the abilities and expectations of the worker and the job that he or she performs was of highest significance in Japan and lowest in Belgium. This study also found that the importance of work remained fairly constant in the United States from immediately after World War II until the early 1980s. In Britain, on the other hand, the centrality or importance of work declined after World War II until the early 1980s. The strong influence of British labor and trade unions was perhaps responsible

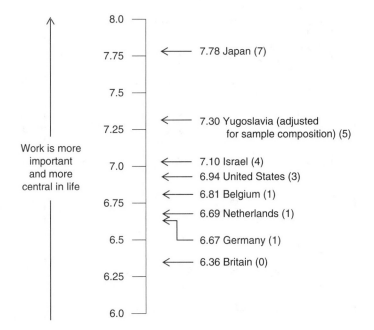

Figure 6.1   Work centrality scores

for the decline in the significance of work, but no statistical analyses were performed in the 1987 version of the study. While the results would probably be different today, multinational and global organizations experience consistent pressures to respond appropriately to the motivational contexts of different countries. The meaning of work study provided some insights into the question of what people regard as satisfying aspects of work in different countries.

Figure 6.1 provides the perceived importance of work goals. It is interesting to note that the need hierarchy theory of Maslow and Hertzberg's categories of motivators and maintenance factors are important to a different extent in different countries (Hertzberg, 1966, 1981). Maslow's (1954) theory of needs hierarchy has been a guiding framework in Western countries since the 1950s (see Bhagat, Kedia, Crawford, & Kapan, 1990 for details; Bhagat & McQuaid, 1982). It is likely that two or three steps in Maslow's need hierarchy are universal in terms of their significance in both collectivistic and individualistic countries of the world. However, the construct of self-actualization is a construct uniquely suited to Western

Table 6.1   The importance of work goals

Work goals	Belgium (N = 466)		Germany (N = 1248)		Israel (N = 772)		Japan (N = 2897)		Netherlands (N = 967)		United States (N = 988)		Yugoslavia (N = 512)*		Britain (N = 742)	
													COUNTRIES			
Interesting work	8.25	1	7.26	3	6.75	1	7.38	2	7.59	2	7.41	1	7.47	2	8.02	1
Good pay	7.13	2	7.73	1	6.60	3	6.56	5	6.27	5	6.82	2	6.73	3	7.80	2
Good interpersonal relations	6.34	5	6.43	4	6.67	2	6.39	6	7.19	3	6.08	7	7.52	1	6.33	4
Good job security	6.80	3	7.57	2	5.22	10	6.71	4	5.68	7	6.30	3	5.21	9	7.12	3
A good match between you and your job	5.77	8	6.09	5	5.61	6	7.83	1	6.17	6	6.19	4	6.49	5	5.63	6
A lot of autonomy	6.56	4	5.66	8	6.00	4	6.89	3	7.61	1	5.79	8	5.42	8	4.69	10
Opportunity to learn	5.80	7	4.97	9	5.83	5	6.26	7	5.38	9	6.16	5	6.61	4	5.55	8
A lot of variety	5.96	6	5.71	6	4.89	11	5.05	9	6.86	4	6.10	6	5.62	7	5.62	7
Convenient work hours	4.71	9	5.71	6	5.53	7	5.46	8	5.59	8	5.25	9	5.01	10	6.11	5
Good physical working conditions	4.19	11	4.39	11	5.28	9	4.18	10	5.03	10	4.84	11	5.94	6	4.87	9
Good opportunity for upgrading or promotion	4.49	10	4.48	10	5.29	8	3.33	11	3.31	11	5.08	10	4.00	11	4.27	11

Notes: Mean ranks. The rank of each work goal within given country. Rank 1 is the most important work goal for a country, while rank 11 is the least important work goal for a country. * Combined target group data were used for Yugoslavia.

Source: Reprinted from England (1987). Copyright © 1987, with permission from Elsevier.

countries, where centrality of work and achievement-oriented norms are highly salient. Yang (2000), in a detailed review of cross-cultural research on work motivation, found that self-actualization is not the highest level of need prized or valued by the collectivists in East Asia and in other developing countries of the world. Satisfaction of one's in-group with one's actions is more important in collectivistic countries. There is a strong individualistic and pro-Western bias in the development of theoretical frameworks that aim to provide explanations for the developments of different types of work motivation (intrinsic and extrinsic motivation) in the theories developed since the 1950s. However, recent cross-cultural research (see Erez, 1994, 1997; Erez & Gati, 2004 for a detailed review) shows that people in different cultures internalize the important values of their collectives in a fashion that serves appropriate anchors for enhancing their self-worth or for appropriate accommodation with the members of their in-groups. The motivation force of a given reward system, therefore, is likely to be determined by its congruence with the dominant cultural values of the society at any given point in time. If significant shifts in the underlying patterns of cultural values occur over time, then reward systems may be designed differently and sometimes in sharp contrast with what was the practice a few decades ago.

Western theories of motivation have emphasized the significance of a set of motives that are related to *independent self-expression*—including self-determination, personal choice, intrinsic motivation, and uniqueness—to be strong drivers of individual work behaviors and subjective well-being (Ryan & Deci, 2000; Gelfand, Erez, & Aycan, 2007). Extrinsic motivation—that is, motivation aroused by financial rewards and incentives, bonuses, opportunities for promotion, and so on—was not considered to be particularly significant for subjective well-being for workers and managers in the Western countries. In fact, Hertzberg and his colleagues (1965), based on their research in upper Midwestern states in the US, found that extrinsic rewards were equivalent to hygiene factors (the absence of which may cause irritation and poor health including physical discomfort) but that their presence did not necessarily enhance intrinsic motivation and satisfaction. However, lack of opportunities for learning and utilizing one's valued skills, abilities, and talents was responsible for adversely affecting and lowering the intrinsic motivation and job satisfaction experienced. Intrinsic motivation is often associated with subjective well-being of Anglo-Americans but not necessarily for Asian-Americans. Asian-Americans experience more intrinsic motivation when the choices to be performed in the context of one's job are made for them by a trusted senior colleague, someone at a higher managerial rank in the organization, or by their peers. Extrinsic rewards do serve as motivators in non-Western cultures. Romanians, for example, reported that financial rewards were important for energizing self-direction and were quite important for enhancing their subjective well-being (Frost & Frost, 2000).

In addition to differences that are found among countries within each category, it is interesting to note that the Israelis derive a higher level of interest and satisfaction from work as compared with the Germans—a finding that is somewhat counter-intuitive. Although income from one's job is clearly important in all of the countries, it has a far greater importance than any other work goal in Japan. In the Netherlands, the relative importance of different work goals is more evenly distributed. The broader implication of these country-wise comparisons is that the meaning one attaches to one's work and working life varies considerably across nations and cultures. The low importance of status and prestige derived from work, as rated by Japanese workers, suggests that these needs are perhaps more fully satisfied elsewhere it their lives, such as within the contexts of family, community, and other historically significant activities.

Perhaps the most interesting contrast is found in the Middle Eastern countries, where the role of religion in Islamic countries is of major importance. The Islamic work ethic expresses a commitment towards fulfillment in life that is consistent with Islam. Success in business activities is regarded as important but not at the expense of one's dedication and commitment to an Islamic way of life. In short, religion is the paramount factor in thinking about work. Muslims feel that work is a virtue and the obligation to establish a balance between work and personal life, especially one's obligation to one's family, is of crucial importance. Arabs, in particular, define themselves by their level of commitment to their in-groups and the outcomes of working are regarded as the prime determinants of the quality of personal life. Recent studies (e.g. Muna, 2003) have shown that while there is a commitment to the Islamic work ethic, the tendency toward individualistic ways of establishing contractual relationships with the organization is considerably weaker in such countries. A sense of benevolent paternalism permeates the work organization (for more about this see Chapter 9).

The economic well-being of a country and especially the level of per capita income are significant determinants of the perceived importance of work and working across virtually all nations and cultures. The spirit of economic globalization (see Chapter 1) carries with it a strong potential to socialize individuals and instill the value of a "good" work ethic. The importance of occupations, dual career families, and 24/7 work hours in all advanced globalized economies of the world clearly nurtures the importance of work and working in all societies (Inglehart & Baker, 2000). This study, using the World Values Survey, provides evidence of both massive cultural shifts and the persistence of traditional values during the last decades of the 20th century in many parts of the world. The meaning of work has become a "good" concept in those societies that have benefited from globalization. In some parts of the world there have been clashes concerning the values of work; it is unclear whether many developing countries will adopt the very positive view of the meaning of work found in Japan and the West. Doubts regarding the significance of working and the importance of working are expressed by Huntington (1996), who noted that while some people in Middle Eastern cultures are likely "to bite into the Big Mac," it is unlikely that they will embrace the Magna Charta.

The move from rural to industrial societies and to information societies typically brings a shift toward a much stronger universalistic orientation and away from particularistic concerns. Importance of trust, tolerance of different values, encouragement of subjective and objective well-being of one's colleagues, and post-materialistic values become important. One works not for the sake of the instrumental gains that working provides but also for the sake of expressing one's values, talents, and creative abilities. Often when individuals switch jobs or careers they experience greater personal fulfillment and intrinsic joy (see Inglehart & Baker, 2000 for details). Modernization does not necessarily follow a linear path. The rise of the service sector, especially in countries like China, India, and the Philippines, coupled with a transition to a knowledge-driven society, precipitates a different set of cultural changes from those that characterized the change from agricultural to industrial societies in the early 1800s.

To be sure, the importance of working, and especially working within strict temporal limits as imposed by the organization of an industrial society, was in some ways confining and created blue-collar "blues", and in some cases, white-collar "blues" (Heckscher, 1995). However, the move from an industrial society to an information society has generally created opportunities for working in jobs that are intrinsically rewarding and provide ample opportunities to utilize one's valued occupational skills. The world of work is much more specialized today than in the past; the *Dictionary of occupational titles* lists over 12,000 job categories. The shift from agricultural to industrial and to information societies is linked to major declines in the role of religious institutions such as churches, temples, synagogues, and mosques. It was this belief that led Karl Marx, and his colleague Frederick Engels, to postulate that the importance of working for the state, coupled with guarantees for life-time employment with a steady level of income, would be most important for all individuals in all societies. This ideology influenced the shift from Czarist Russia to the Soviet Union, which emphasized the importance of working for the state. However, the occupational structures that were created in massive public sector manufacturing organizations rarely provided any opportunities for the expression of one's valued skills and abilities. Those with superior talent were much more inclined to immigrate to societies where opportunities for utilizing valued skills and abilities were more easily available.

It is interesting that modern societies which emphasize the importance of motivation, organizational commitment, and job satisfaction tend to be largely secular. But interestingly, they do not de-emphasize the role of religion in any of the groups in society. In some parts of the world, especially in the US, there has been a growing tendency to find meaning and purpose in life through religious practices and rituals. It is hard to tell whether the importance and meaning that individuals and groups attach to work will shift in a significant way as a result of the religious beliefs and practices that are commonly found in industrial countries.

Having discussed the significance of work centrality and the meaning of work across borders and cultures, it is now important to present various theories of motivation that are applicable in the international and cross-cultural context. The question is, "what motivates workers in a country like China, India, Brazil or Russia?" As the importance of the BRIC economies has increased in the past decade, Western multinational, global organizations are becoming particularly interested in designing organizations and compensation systems that fulfill and indeed motivate workers in emerging economies. In the 1950s and 1960s when US-based multinationals were the primary agents of globalization in the world, their human resources department tended to rely, implicitly or explicitly, on Maslow's need hierarchy theory as a guide for understanding the structure of rewards that motivated workers in different cultures of the world. A classic study of 3641 people by Haire, Ghiselli, & Porter (1963) found that higher-order needs, as specified in Maslow's need hierarchy theory, are important in all countries. Maslow's theory was supported in this large-scale study. However, conducting large-scale studies in the 1960s was difficult and presented insurmountable challenges. Collaborators from different countries did not fully understand the need for collecting country-specific (emic) data on work motivation. In addition, both workers and managers were reluctant to express their preferences for the various types of intrinsic and extrinsic rewards that their organizations either provided or were supposed to provide. A study by Ronen (1986), which investigated the similarity of work values and work-related needs of individuals in several countries, found that occupationally well-trained males expressed similarities in Germany, Canada, France, the UK, and Japan. The cluster of similarities included:

- job goals, that is, work space, work hours, working conditions, benefits, and job security;
- relationships with superiors and co-workers;
- challenging work; opportunities to use one's skills.

Ronan concluded that these need-clusters tend to be of equal importance across nations. Thus the hierarchical pattern of needs suggested by Maslow (1954) is valid in both Western and non-Western countries.

How one's opinion influences the importance of needs and work-related outcomes also varies across cultures. China, Israel, and Korea give highest importance to achieving in the context of work. Individuals in these countries feel that achievement on the job is the best method for realizing one's self-actualization needs. On the other hand, in the more globalized countries of Germany, Holland, and the US, the opportunity to work on "intrinsically fulfilling jobs" was given higher importance (Steers, Sanchez-Runde, & Nardon, 2010). A clear conclusion is that managers around the world have a similar pattern of needs, but tend to depict different levels of satisfaction when these needs are fulfilled in the context of their working lives. As we discussed earlier, cultural factors may not be the only ones at play here—individuals in transition economies like Russia, South Africa, Mexico, and Brazil stress the need for job security and belongingness; they consider them more important than higher-order needs like intrinsically challenging work. What seems to be clear is that in highly globalized Western economies, the opportunity to work on *interesting* jobs clearly predominates over the need for job security and the need for making important social connections in the organization (Bhagat et al., 2010). The work of Bhagat et al. illustrates the importance of contextual factors and that extra-job-related behaviors and propensities—such as mentoring one's junior colleagues and walking the extra mile for improving satisfaction of the customers of the company—are more important in collectivist countries such as Japan, South Korea, and China than in individualistic countries such as the US, Canada, UK, and countries of Oceania. Even in India, where the professional working class has adopted some individualistic values, collectivist values are important. Another interesting point in this connection is the importance of various kinds of organizational rewards: recognition in the form of plaques, praise from one's seniors in the organizational hierarchy, applause, and recognition at annual meetings and company picnics, and so on is very important in Japanese manufacturing organizations, in both Japan itself and in other countries where there are Japanese subsidiaries and related business transactions. A great deal of emphasis on material rewards, that is, tangible financial rewards (often preferred in the US and other Western individualistic countries) is not necessarily the main reason for working in predominantly collectivistic countries like Japan, South Korea, Vietnam, Singapore, and Thailand. In these latter countries, as well as in former state-owned enterprises in China, *egalitarianism* is stressed in matters concerning the distribution of financial rewards or incentives. The rewards tend to be based on age, loyalty, seniority, and even gender—male workers and managers receive significantly higher salaries and incentives compared with females performing identical jobs—that is, rewards are distributed without any regard to demographic and other factors that are not related to objective indicators of performance.

However, a model that was introduced in the 1990s which emphasizes merit and achievement-related issues is gaining ground in collectivist cultures. Rewards based on occupational qualifications and skills, the level of training needed to perform tasks, level of responsibility, and objective indicators of performance are being recognized, as these multinational, global corporations from collectivistic countries are beginning to emerge as leaders in the global marketplace. Especially in the subsidiaries of these corporations located in countries such as Western Europe, the US, Canada, Australia, and New Zealand, the need for performance- as opposed to seniority-based reward systems is recognized. This is done to be consistent with the reward distribution policies of the individualistic contexts where these East Asian multinationals must now operate (see Steers, Sanchez-Runde, & Nardon, 2010, pp. 302–6 for a detailed discussion of this reward policy).

In Japan, however, attempts to introduce Western-style merit-based systems have often led to increases in overall labor costs. This happens because in Japan it is very important that people do not lose face and that harmony be preserved within the work group. Thus a merit-based system still requires companies to pay the less productive workers their current levels of pay. So, here we see a clear case where cultural factors can make it difficult to adopt innovations in employment relationships in line with the demands of the global marketplace. Similar results concerning the influence of cultural values, schemata, and scripts on reward systems, as well as human resource management practices, have begun to emerge from research in South Korean organizations (Nam, 1995; Steers, Sanchez-Runde, & Nardon, 2010, p. 316). Research by Nam has shown that employees in joint ventures of Korean banks which had agreements with Japanese banks were more productive and committed compared with the employees of joint ventures of Korean banks which had agreements with US banks and followed the Western style of reward distribution and personnel policies. In addition, the Korean banks which had agreements to follow a blend of Korean and Japanese human resource management practices demonstrated higher financial performance compared with those which followed predominantly US-style personnel policies. The clear message from this kind of cross-cultural research is that employees in different cultural contexts are not necessarily motivated by the same types of rewards and outcomes of job performance.

EXECUTIVE COMPENSATION

Since the 1980s, issues regarding the compensation of senior executives have been of major concern in business periodicals like *The Economist*, *Business Week*, *Fortune Magazine*, and the *Asian Wall Street Journal*. Particularly in the US, and to some extent in Western Europe, the compensation of senior executives has been regarded as key to hiring and retaining the best talent. While it is certainly true that in the individualistic countries, the role of financial compensation is of crucial significance in hiring and motivating senior managers who will be at the helms of companies, many columnists, senators, members of congress, and the public are asking "How much money is truly necessary to hire or motivate the necessary talents to run US corporations?" This is especially relevant to those in the financial sector. The collapse of the financial sector in the autumn of 2008 has made the US government, citizens, and other concerned stakeholders particularly wary of the "imperial CEOs and CFOs" running the financial institutions that almost brought the US economy to a standstill. In some instances the compensation of executives is tied to stock prices, and this has, in some instances, led to unethical or even illegal actions. Good examples of such ethical violations are found in the much publicized cases of Enron (1997), WorldCom, Tyco, AIG, and many others. About 20 years ago, the average CEO made roughly 40 times the salary of the lowest-paid blue-collar worker in his or her company. Today, the compensation of the average CEO is in the range of 100 to 400 times the salary of the lowest-paid worker. The world press has noted that in the majority of cases where excessive executive compensation has been an issue the executive was male not female. Two issues are at play here—even as we enter the second decade of the 21st century, the percentage of female CEOs in US and Western European multinational, global corporations is around 7 percent. There is a glass ceiling (more about this phenomenon in Chapter 9) that prevents the upward mobility of female executives. In addition, it may be that female executives are not as aggressive about financial compensation as their male counterparts (see Eagly, Johannesen-Schmidt, & van Engen's (2003) work on sex differences in leadership in the US). The average CEO compensation compared with the average worker in the manufacturing and services sectors in both the globalized and the

Table 6.2   Ratio of average CEO compensation to average employee compensation

Country	Pay ratio	Country	Pay ratio	Country	Pay ratio
United States	475	United Kingdom	24	Netherlands	16
Venezuela	50	Thailand	24	France	14
Brazil	49	Australia	23	New Zealand	13
Mexico	47	South Africa	22	Sweden	12
Singapore	44	Canada	20	Germany	12
Argentina	44	Italy	20	Switzerland	11
Malaysia	42	Belgium	18	Japan	11
Hong Kong	41	Spain	16	South Korea	8

Note: Numbers express the ratios between the average CEO compensation and the average compensation received by industrial and service workers in the same country.

Source: Based on Steers & Nardon (2006).

emergent economies of the world shows that CEOs in the US are paid much more than their counterparts in other countries (see Table 6.2).

Knowledge of comparative CEO compensation raises the issue of why such a disparity exists. Are US CEOs in some way special? Do they bring some special qualities and talents that are not found in other parts of the world? We suggest that as competition among the multinationals intensifies, there will be an accompanying change or decline in the compensation packages of US executives. This issue needs further investigation in terms of its cultural underpinnings. The US is a vertical individualist country, and competition is a very important value. In horizontal individualist countries, such as Sweden, it is not such a crucial value. An American executive's self-esteem depends more on how much he makes than on other qualities (say, how much he helps others). However, we also suggest that the employee–organization contract, in a highly individualistic country like the US, is a factor determining the reward system. In addition, the hedonistic overtone of individualism (see Chapter 2) contributes to the mounting pressure experienced by financial sector organizations to compensate their executives at an unprecedented rate.

GENDER DIFFERENCES IN COMPENSATION AND REWARD DISTRIBUTION

An interesting issue that arises at this time concerns the role of gender differences in compensation levels across national boundaries. Table 6.3

Table 6.3   Wage gaps between men and women across nations

Country	Wage gap (%)	Country	Wage gap (%)	Country	Wage gap (%)
New Zealand	6	Sweden	15	Finland	20
Belgium	9	Spain	17	United States	21
Poland	11	OECD average	18	Canada	22
Greece	12	Czech Republic	19	Switzerland	22
France	12	Portugal	19	Germany	24
Hungary	12	Ireland	20	Japan	32
Denmark	14	United Kingdom	20	Korea	40
Australia	15				

Note: Numbers are expressed as a percentage of the average wage gap between men and women by country.

Source: Data derived from OECD (2007), pp. 15–18.

shows that disparity between the sexes varies from about 6 percent in New Zealand (a horizontal individualistic country) to a high of 40 percent in South Korea (a vertical collectivistic country).

The data in Table 6.3 are derived from the OECD (2007, pp. 15–18) and mask the differences in executive compensation. From recent surveys (Evans, Pucik, & Barsoux, 2010) we have seen that the disparity between male and female executives across cultures is even more pronounced. In manufacturing industries, on average, female executives make considerably less than their male counterparts. While there is a tendency for the compensation to be roughly at the same level in service industries—especially involving call center operations, financial services, customer services, public relations, human resources management, and education—the point remains that male managers are paid at a higher level than their female counterparts. It is not clear how this trend will develop—it could go either way. As multinationals in all countries begin to experience a shortage of executive talent, the need to treat male and female executives in identical fashion will increase. In today's high technology-oriented service sector, the percentage of females in senior managerial roles is about 48 percent and is increasing. It is unwise to treat such a large portion of the labor force inequitably, as this is likely to affect the productivity of these organizations and in turn their global competitiveness.

In addition, as the number of female expatriates in the subsidiaries of multinational, global corporations increases, the need for equal financial and non-financial rewards and incentives will also increase. The cost of expatriate failure is very high (over 70 percent of the cost is for recruitment, then a major cost is finding jobs in a domestic context during the first year of their return from overseas assignments), and increasingly multinational organizations find that female expatriates are better able to manage with appropriate cultural sensitivities in international operations. Therefore, it goes without saying that these types of development in the global marketplace will lead to pressure to equalize the financial and non-financial rewards of male and female global managers. We expect the impact on motivation, organizational commitment, job satisfaction, and withdrawal tendencies to improve accordingly.

We turn now to the role of work-related attitudes (such as job satisfaction, organizational commitment, and job involvement) as important correlates of work motivation.

WORK-RELATED ATTITUDES

Positive work-related attitudes like high levels of job satisfaction and job involvement coupled with a strong sense of personal commitment are important intrinsic rewards, and are helpful in keeping managers abroad. Since the costs of early return to the corporate home base are enormous, these factors are very important. The significance of these outcomes has increased in a consistent fashion since the 1950s. At one time, during the heyday of US dominance in manufacturing industries, it was common for both blue-collar and white-collar workers to experience significant amounts of job-related tension and unhappiness (see Kornhauser, 1959; Heckscher, 1995 for a detailed review of blue-collar and white-collar "blues" in the US).

As mentioned previously, *job satisfaction* is defined as the degree to which a person's work is associated with positive emotions, such as joy, pleasure, and a sense of accomplishment. If work satisfies a person's needs then positive affect will be associated with the job. Job satisfaction is viewed as a multidimensional concept in that a person may be satisfied with certain aspects of his or her work ("I like my co-workers") while simultaneously being unhappy with other aspects of the work ("the pay and working conditions are not good"). Many implicit and explicit definitions of job satisfaction are found in the literature. This definition has been operationalized in comparative studies of job satisfaction in the international context. In the majority of these cases, the countries involved were from both collectivist and individualist as well as from high and low power distance cultures (see Bhagat & McQuaid, 1982; Bhagat, Kedia, Crawford, & Kapan, 1990; Sanchez-Runde, Lee, & Steers, 2009).

Locke (1976) proposed the definition that job satisfaction is an *emo-*

tional reaction that "results from the perception that one's job fulfills or allows the fulfillment of one's important job values, providing and to the degree that those values are congruent with one's needs" (p. 1307). Low levels of job satisfaction are called *job dissatisfaction.* In later definitions, the concept of emotion has been given greater importance (Weiss & Cropanzano, 1996). Weiss & Cropanzano's definition relies not only on an evaluative judgment about one's job but also on the *emotional experiences* at work. Some abstract beliefs about how a job is supposed to provide satisfaction of a series of needs during one's career are also important determinants of job satisfaction. Neither Locke (1976) nor Weiss & Cropanzano (1996) provided a list of specific emotions that are involved in the determination of job satisfaction. However, research in the past two decades (Barsade, Brief, & Spataro, 2003) has revealed the nature of emotions experienced in one's work to be a significant determinant of job satisfaction. What this means is that if an individual appraises his or her job to be fulfilling of specific needs that he or she values, that would certainly lead to job satisfaction. However, if he or she also notices many instances of employee harassment, such as sexual harassment, then his or her job satisfaction will be significantly diminished.

Job satisfaction is not the same concept as *morale.* Morale concerns the overall attitudes of a work group rather than the feelings of a single individual. Therefore, when one notes that the morale in the current financial services sector in the US is rather low, this implies that the average level of job satisfaction associated with a majority of the individuals at all levels of the financial services industry is low. It also indicates that perhaps the financial services industry has lower morale than other industries, such as high tech, food processing, biomedical or the health care industries.

Affective events theory (Weiss & Cropanzano, 1996) has provided important avenues of research concerning the role of cultural variations in job satisfaction and morale in the international context. High job satisfaction is not necessarily found in either affluent countries or emerging economies. Nor is it found in countries with a strong religious orientation. Diener, Diener, & Diener (1995) found that, after controlling for national wealth, individualism was the best predictor of subjective well-being at the national level. They explain the finding by noting that people in individualistic societies enjoy more freedom to do what they like to do and pursue individually satisfying goals whether they are congruent with societal goals or not. Most satisfied employees tend to be found in countries where the management practices are in consonance with the important values of local cultures—assuming of course that the local cultures are supportive of participative decision-making and do not endorse high power distance-related values in the functioning of the organizations. Perhaps the most important determinant of job dissatisfaction is concerned with the perception of equity versus inequity in the employee interpretation of the rewards that he or she receives. In addition, the perception of unfairness in the treatment of one's colleagues is also an important determinant of job dissatisfaction in tight collectivist cultures such as Japan.

Job satisfaction and related work attitudes are interpreted in the context of a *psychological contract* (Rousseau, 1995). Individuals expect certain outcomes (both intrinsic and extrinsic) in exchange for their efforts, performance, commitment, loyalty, and reputation. Especially in the case of job satisfaction, people tend to become satisfied to the extent they perceive that their rewards are fair. This seems to be the case in most individualistic countries of the world where transactional and contractual relationships are the guiding principles in employment contracts (Earley & Erez, 1997; Bhawuk, 2001; Erez & Earley, 2003; Bhagat et al., 2010). In collectivistic countries, the principle of equality in distribution of rewards is more important than the norm of equitable transactions. Employees from East Asian multinational, global corporations are pleased if the rewards are distributed equally to the members of the work group. They would be upset if one or a few select members received a high percentage of the rewards. The latter scenario is likely in individualistic countries, even during the current era of severe economic recession in the US and the countries of the European Union.

While this pattern is true if the countries or the organizations are uniformly individualistic or collectivistic, in reality that is rarely the case. Even in Japan, where the rewards are distributed based on seniority and equality has been a recent shift in their distribution, increasingly rewards are based on one's individual contribution. The cultural orientation of the Japanese work organization has shifted from being predominantly collectivist to having individualistic elements in some functional groups. Research scientists and directors of R & D labs, for example, in large Japanese global corporations, are less inclined to accept rewards based on equality; they like to have their unique and sustained contributions appreciated and explicitly recognized since they contribute to the effectiveness of their laboratories and organizations.

In individualistic countries as well, the desire for a better quality of work life and policies that sustain effective work–family integration (Kossek & Lambert, 2005) are slowly replacing the focus on higher pay. In a recent survey of US workers (Steers, Sanchez-Runde, & Nardon, 2010), it was found that, given a choice between two weeks of extra pay and two weeks of vacation, employees preferred, by an overwhelming margin of 50 percent, the extra vacation. In Europe, particularly in countries around the Mediterranean, preference for paid vacation time significantly outweighs the importance of overtime pay, bonuses, and related financial incentives. As pressures for increased productivity in global organizations increase with growing interdependence and interconnectiveness of work systems in dissimilar nations and cultures, it may become necessary for organizations, particularly production facilities, not to pay as much attention to working conditions that foster well-being (Bhagat, Segovis, & Nelson, 2012).

Earlier research has shown that positive job attitudes do not necessarily correlate or lead to higher levels of employee productivity (Greenberg & Baron, 2003). Individuals tend to exhibit high levels of performance when their co-workers or colleagues are also performing at high rates and are being fairly rewarded. This leads us to speculate that work productivity is going to be increasingly detached from the need for maintaining positive work climate and morale in highly competitive multinational and global organizations.

A second concept that has received a great deal of interest in US and Western European theories of organizational behavior falls under the general rubric of organizational commitment (recently being referred to as "employee attachment"). This concept is also presumed to be multidimensional and is concerned with the attachment or adherence of the individual to any of the following: to the concept of working for an organization indefinitely; to showing a strong degree of interest and passion in one's chosen occupation or profession; to one's actual day-to-day work-related duties and responsibilities (Hulin, 1991; Meyer & Allen, 1991; Mowday & Colwell, 2003).

The third construct that has been of strong interest in dealing with employee motivation and job satisfaction is concerned with the degree of devotion that individuals have to their jobs or work roles. Called *job involvement*, this construct is independent of the particular jobs that an individual has held in the past or the particular organization for which he or she may be working at a given time in his or her working life. A most important aspect of job involvement is the person's perception of the centrality of work in his or her life. As discussed earlier, an individual who does not see that work has a central role in his or her life is not likely to have a strong sense of job involvement. To be sure, the degree of intrinsic job satisfaction associated with the tasks performed by the individual and the opportunity for learning and growth associated with one's job are the primary determinants of job involvement. For example, if a person likes to work as a marketing analyst for his or her company and the company's marketing department provides the person with ample opportunities for developing his or her marketing or sales-related skills, then he or she will develop a strong sense of job involvement. Research has also shown that certain personality types are more inclined to be dedicated to their jobs to the point of developing not only a high degree of job involvement but also tendencies toward workaholism (Burke, 1995).

The fact that labor unions are becoming weaker in the US, Canada, and other Western European countries is well known. Roughly 15 percent of the US workforce is currently unionized. In these countries memberships of trade unions are declining both in the public and private sectors. Apparently, people are now generally happy with their levels of pay and other benefits. Traditional benefits of union membership—higher wages, job security, safe and pleasant working conditions, to name a few—are no longer sources of dissatisfaction for a very large majority of working people in both the US and Canada.

From a managerial and motivational standpoint, the declining role of labor unions is significant for managing multinational, global corporations, especially their subsidiaries in other cultures. Employee benefits are increasingly accounting for sizable percentages of overall labor costs in all countries of the world. There has been a general decline in the growth of personal income in the Western countries (the US, Canada, UK, France, Germany), and the pattern seems to occur in other countries as well (Japan, Singapore, Brazil, China, Russia, and India). The costs of employee benefits range from 33 to 50 percent of salaries. The important thing to remember is that there is a large variation in the type of benefits that are preferred by employees in different cultures and nations. US-based companies that offer stock options for expatriates as an important part of their compensation package may discover that the local tax structure can take a significant percentage of such benefits, thus reducing any motivational or incentive-related effects. It follows that human resources departments of multinationals should investigate the local culture-specific preferences for employee benefits and other compensation systems. The first author finds that in India the assignment of a chauffeur or domestic workers for the homes of expatriates from Western multinationals are welcome benefits. The lives of expatriates can become not only manageable but indeed quite comfortable when domestic workers carry out a significant part of the chores of maintaining a home, that are typically done by the couples themselves (more often than not by the wives in the West). Furthermore, the traffic in many developing countries is chaotic, and a chauffeur can reduce stress. It is money well spent for the corporation. These issues are important to consider when designing rewards systems that are motivational for multinationals working across nations and cultures.

ORGANIZATIONAL COMMITMENT AND JOB INVOLVEMENT

Earlier we discussed the concept of job satisfaction. One is satisfied with one's job if one's needs and values are satisfied by the job. It follows that higher levels of job satisfaction will lead the individual to experience a sense of attachment to the work organization. This sense of attachment, which can be measured accurately, is called *organizational commitment*. This concept is vital in the study of work motivation, job satisfaction, and organizational stress, and has attracted more attention among organizational researchers than any other type of work commitment. Porter, Steers, Mowday, & Boulin (1974), in one of the early formulations of organizational commitment, saw it as consisting of three interrelated (though not identical) attitudes and intentions: (1) a strong belief in and acceptance of the organization's mission, values, and goals; (2) a willingness to exert considerable effort on behalf of the organization in performing the job-related duties and responsibilities; (3) a definite plan to remain a member of the organization for an indefinite period of time. The Porter et al. approach has been the guiding force behind much research on organizational commitment for the past three decades. In recent assessments of this concept of commitment (Meyer & Allen, 1991, 1997, 2006), researchers noted that employees with a strong *affective commitment* like to continue their association and/or employment with the work organization.

A second component of organizational commitment is known as *normative commitment* (Meyer & Allen, 1991), which consists of the sum total of internalized normative pressures to act in a fashion that sustains the goals and interests of the organization. This type of commitment motivates individuals to behave in ways that they believe are morally right for the organization rather than in ways that are instrumental in advancing their own career or job-related goals. Religious practitioners in institutions such as churches, temples, synagogues, or mosques have high normative commitments. University professors, researchers in R & D labs, and even prison officials often have high levels of normative commitment. The point is that individuals who have high levels of normative commitment to their organizations: (1) are more inclined to make personal sacrifices and are willing to subordinate personal goals in favor of goals of their work groups or the organization; (2) remain occupied with the objectives of the organization and spend considerable time and energy in doing so.

The third aspect of organizational commitment is known as *calculative* or *continuance commitment* (Meyer et al., 1989; Meyer & Allen, 1997). Based on the concept of transactions, this form of organizational commitment is concerned with an individual's attachment to an organization by the calculation of cost–benefit analyses. If an individual feels that his or her continued association with the organization results in benefits (good levels of pay, other financial incentives, good employee benefits, including retirement benefits, etc.) that exceed the cost of not being associated (e.g., opportunity cost associated with not working for a more reputed organization, giving up the opportunity to move to another location where one's spouse can be gainfully employed), then he or she is more likely to continue working for the organization. According to this perspective, an employee is committed to the extent that benefits outweigh the costs. The attachment is not necessarily based on the experience of positive emotion, which was the case with normative commitment, but is primarily a function of sheer economic and pragmatic considerations. Under conditions of tight labor markets, one may not have the opportunities to engage in a cost–benefit analysis. However, when the opportunities for finding alternative jobs with better benefits (both in terms of extrinsic and intrinsic rewards) are high, organizational commitment tends to become anchored solely on calculative considerations. Some observations pertaining to the significance of organizational commitment are as follows:

1. It has generally been found that employee commitments are higher in Japanese than in Western work organizations. Japanese culture and tradition dictate that managers at various levels of the organization consult with their subordinates on many aspects of individual and departmental performance, and everyone is encouraged and socialized for a long period of time to contribute toward the overall effectiveness of the organization over the long term.
2. In Germany, employee participation in the form of co-determination (lower-level employees sit with managers in committees) is also helpful in maintaining high levels of work motivation and organizational commitment. Genuine patterns of work participation are significant determinants for sustaining organizational commitment, as discussed in Dachler & Wilpert (1978). Dachler & Wilpert found that the German system of employee participation and industrial democracy is more effective than the US, UK, or other Western countries' systems of encouraging organization commitment.
3. Organizational commitment also increases when individuals work in self-managing work teams. Self-managing work teams design the whole project and break down the tasks to be performed by a team of employees. That allows the team to design, perform, and implement the work routine. Self-managing work teams basically provide job enrichment at the group level. These groups require significant amounts of autonomy (as is the case of a group of R & D scientists

designing new types of computer systems or central processing units) and the support of management. Self-managing work teams are found in virtually all Japanese, South Korean, and other organizations in East and Southeast Asia. While this technique is increasingly being implemented in Western organizations, because it improves work motivation, organizational commitment, and job satisfaction, it is not clear that Western organizations are as effective in implementing these techniques as are the organizations of East Asia.

Job Involvement

This concept is concerned with an individual's devotion or dedication to work *per se.* It is independent of the organization in which he or she is working. Job involvement is strongly related to a person's intrinsic identification and compliance with the centrality of work in his or her life. For example, if a person enjoys being a computer operator, he or she will enjoy (i.e., be involved with) working in that role regardless of whether he or she is performing it in a private or public sector organization or in a domestic or multinational organization. Personality and cultural background are important determinants of job involvement (see Pinder, 2008). In general, automobile designers and engineers in Germany (regardless of whether they are working for Mercedes Benz or BMW or Audi) have higher levels of job involvement compared with Arab executives in petroleum industries in the Middle Eastern countries. To the extent that one's cultural values tend to de-emphasize the importance of one's occupational role, individuals might find it troublesome to develop strong identifications with their occupational roles. *Workaholism* as a phenomenon has been of interest in the study of organizational behavior for the past 30 years in countries such as the US, UK, Germany, Japan, and South Korea (see Bakker, Demerouti, & Burke, 2009). A survey of research in this area reveals that while research on this topic has been growing in the Western countries and also in select East Asian economies, there has been hardly any investigation of this phenomenon in countries of the Middle East, Latin and Central America, or Africa. In these countries, work is accorded less importance in the overall life space of the individual. In the Middle East religion is a very central concern, and work is less central. In Latin America and Africa social relations, including family obligations, take precedence over work. In many countries people think that Americans and Japanese live to work, while they work to live. Brazilians, in particular, feel that Americans work hard without appreciating the significance of other aspects of life (Levine, 1997).

Next, we will discuss the relationship among job satisfaction, organizational commitment, and withdrawal tendencies with particular attention to the generalizability of the US-based findings to other globalizing countries and emerging economies such as the BRIC countries (see Chapter 3).

JOB SATISFACTION, ORGANIZATIONAL COMMITMENT, AND WITHDRAWAL TENDENCIES

Managers have assumed, for over six decades since the end of World War II, that low levels of job satisfaction were the prime determinants of low levels of commitment to the organization. Furthermore, they assumed that low levels of organizational commitment led to withdrawal tendencies from the organization and actual turnover of staff under appropriate labor market conditions. Affective commitment is perhaps the best predictor of various forms of withdrawal tendencies (intention to withdraw when opportunities become available, absenteeism from the work role, and actual turnover). Normative commitment and continuance commitment do not seem to be related to such withdrawal tendencies. It is interesting to note that low levels of commitment do not necessarily result in actual turnover, and the relationship becomes weaker over time. Only when the opportunities in the external labor market are ripe, do lower levels of commitment lead to absenteeism and withdrawal. It is also interesting to note that one's organizational commitment is not necessarily predictive of job performance (Mathieu & Zajac, 1990). Organizational commitment is not necessarily correlated with lateness and lack of citizenship-related behaviors. This happens because lateness is an undesirable behavior in all organizations regardless of national and cultural variations. Also, those who do not come to work late as a matter of habit are not likely to exhibit lateness regardless of the levels of commitment they developed at different points in their careers. In a good summary of the link between commitment and withdrawal behavior, Meyer & Allen (1997) concluded the following:

1. An organization should try to develop a stable workforce which values continued membership that it can depend on. Any form of commitment is fine as long as the organization can depend on the employees to perform their work-related duties and responsibilities, not only during boom times, but also during lean years.
2. Organizations must emphasize the importance of high levels of performance on the part of their employees. If the policy requiring high levels of performance requires that the weak performers quit the organization, the organization should not consider it an undesir-

able outcome. In fact, some voluntary turnover is helpful rather than harmful to the organization. Voluntary resignations for employees who perform poorly or are disruptive can be beneficial to the organization, both in the short and long term. In other words, most organizations should want higher levels of performance from committed employees rather than continued membership on the part of employees who are poor performers or lack work centrality and work motivation.

Culture is an important factor in commitment. A personality factor that corresponds to collectivism called *allocentrism* is associated with people being less likely to leave the organization even when they are dissatisfied with their jobs. Wasti (2002) showed that allocentrics, whose continuance commitment was associated with higher levels of normative costs compared with idiocentrics (people whose personality corresponds to individualism), were less likely to contemplate quitting the organization when they were dissatisfied. Also, they were less likely to engage in withdrawal behaviors such as tardiness. In her study, affective commitment, which developed from positive work experiences and organizational collectivism, was related to positive outcomes such as lower levels of turnover intentions and withdrawal behaviors, as well as higher levels of citizenship behaviors and subjective well-being for both allocentrics and idiocentrics.

It must be noted that an individual is not only committed to perform the necessary duties and responsibilities on behalf of his or her organization. There are competing domains in one's life that one has commitments to: one's family and friends, one's hobbies, one's religion, one's community, and many others. More than three decades ago, Rotondi (1975) found that R & D engineers tended to be less creative and innovative if they were excessively committed to their research. Excessive involvement with one's job has also been found to correlate with marital dissatisfaction and work–family conflicts (Burke & Weir, 1978; Pitt-Catsouphes, Kossek, & Sweet, 2006). Ethnographic studies with Japanese managers during the 1970s and 1980s revealed that their personal lives were not happy and their wives were dissatisfied with the amount of time that their husbands spent within the family.

Reichers (1985) notes that allegiance to organizational goals, products, and services can often be in conflict with commitments to one's labor union, vendors and suppliers, customers, professional associations, and, last but not least, one's family and friends. The nature of commitment, and accompanying levels of stress and dissatisfaction, is a function of individual differences, that is, it varies from person to person. The ability to handle multiple and conflicting commitments emanating from different facets of one's work and personal life is an important issue to consider in the recruitment and placement of expatriates. One may be quite comfortable with the kind of role that one will be required to perform in an overseas assignment, and indeed depict high levels of commitment, but such commitments may be in strong conflict with commitments to maintain the peace and prosperity of one's family and other related concerns. In fact one of the most important factors in the early repatriation of executives is the inability of their spouse to live in the other culture. Bhagat (1983, 1985) and Bhagat, McQuaid, Lindholm, & Segovis (1985) advanced the concept of "total life stress," which is concerned with demands and stresses from the domain of one's work along with those from one's non-work activities. They showed that commitment to one's organization tends to be significantly lower when the total amount of life's stresses exceeds a manageable level. Consider the case of a US expatriate who is required to deal with the challenges of a new assignment in Saudi Arabia or Dubai. Adjustment to work roles in these countries requires considerable knowledge of cultural differences and one has to be culturally sensitive to handle the idiosyncrasies of the work ethic and the Islamic patterns of work orientation, which are quite different from the realities of US and Western European countries. In addition, if this individual also experiences significant difficulties with his or her spouse regarding a move to a new and culturally highly dissimilar country, then the total amount of stress that he or she experiences would be high. Commitment to one's work role and especially to one's work organization suffers in these situations and declines considerably as the experience of total life stress intensifies (Bhagat, Steverson, & Segovis, 2007b; Bhagat, McQuaid, Lindholm, & Segovis, 1985).

IMPLICATIONS FOR THE 21st CENTURY

Maintenance of adequate levels of motivation, job satisfaction, and morale in the workplace is important not only for domestic organizations but also for multinational, global organizations. Work motivation is a cognitive state that arouses an individual to put sustained effort in accomplishing job-related duties and responsibilities for the organization. US-based theories of need hierarchy (Maslow, 1954), Hertzberg's (1968) motivation-hygiene theory, McClelland's (1961) learned needs theory, goal-setting theory (Locke & Latham, 1990), expectancy theory (Vroom, 1972; Lawler, 1973), equity theory (Adams, 1963), and affective events theory (Weiss & Cropanzano, 1996) have provided much of the theoretical background for exploring the determinants of these cognitive and effective states of employees in various countries. Theories (Theory Z, GLOBE studies from the Wharton School) specifically generated for the understanding of Japanese management practices (Ouchi, 1981) and other organizational practices in 26 different societies (House, Hanges, Javidan, & Dorfman, 2004) provide new insights into the role of national and cultural differences and are important to consider in understanding the motivational dynamics of modern work organizations.

We have discussed the role of rewards as being most important in determining the motivation of employees. Selection and administration of rewards that are compatible with the cultural background of the large majority of workers are clearly the key to success in managing large-scale global organizations in the 21st century. The centrality of work research tradition pioneered by England and his colleagues (1987) has provided interesting insights into the meaning of working in some culturally dissimilar countries of the world. Managers of multinational and global corporations must realize that work is not necessarily the central focus of all employees in all countries. In countries where work, and especially the importance of various occupations, is emphasized, working becomes central to the life of most people. This is especially true for sustained work that is linked to desirable work outcomes.

Gender differences in preferences for work are increasingly disappearing in the globalized countries of the world. Gone are the days when women performed jobs that were largely at the clerical level and had peripheral significance for the organizations. Modern well-educated women in all societies regardless of their cultural predispositions prefer jobs that are well paying and provide opportunities for fulfillment of their intrinsic needs. Even though some countries (especially Japan, which is the most masculine country in the world according to Hofstede's 2001 rankings, and the Islamic countries) do not promote women to senior managerial ranks, opportunities for women in the majority of countries that are globalizing are increasing. China, in particular, has played an important role in this connection and the same pattern holds true for India, Brazil, and Russia—the other three members of the BRIC economies.

It will be interesting to see how the reward distributions in the majority of the Western countries of the EU, US, Canada, and Oceania change as the Chinese multinationals become the leading multinational organizations in the world (Jacques, 2009).

The concepts and frameworks presented in this chapter underscored the importance of work motivation and work-related attitudes, not only in the contexts of the US and Western countries, but also in various globalizing and culturally dissimilar parts of the world.

Our discussions have suggested that cultural variations influence the meaning of work and working in different parts of the world. Culture has a significant main effect on the motivating potential of intrinsic and extrinsic rewards in conjunction with intrapersonal and social satisfaction derived in the context of working. Cultural variations do not seem to affect the motivation potential of the contextual factors of work, the work group, and the organizational structure. Cultural variations do moderate the effect of differential rewards and situational factors on individuals' assessments of self-worth, well-being, and job performance (Bhagat, Van Scotter, Steverson, & Moustafa, 2007). It is important for managers of multinational and global organizations to be interested in reasons why the rewards that motivate individuals in one cultural context (e.g., the US or UK) do not have as much relevance or value in a different cultural context (e.g., China, Japan, South Korea, Singapore, Vietnam, Brazil, Indonesia, etc.). It is safe to assume that a large percentage of the world's working population is motivated by rewards that are concretely anchored in the context of the well-being of the in-group members of the job incumbent.

It is only in about less than 10 percent of the world's working population that working has led to intrinsic rewards as well as opportunities for fulfilling self-actualizing needs. A large majority of the world's population either go to work or work at home or in other social contexts without thinking about the intrinsic joys and pleasures of working. As levels of education increase in the countries that are globalizing, there will be slow movement toward emphasizing requirements for obtaining satisfaction of intrinsic needs in the context of one's work.

The first author has had unique encounters with this phenomenon. Many Indian immigrant professionals who have achieved considerable success in their careers and have also accumulated sufficient wealth long to go back to their mother land. Some of them go back and stay, but a large percentage go back but return to their host country within a period of two to five years. The reasons they give have almost nothing to do with satisfaction with pay or financial incentives. The cost of living in India is quite reasonable, given the wealth that these Indian professionals accumulate over their working lives. However, they find that the jobs in most Indian work organizations are managed by bureaucrats who are strong believers in the values of vertical collectivism. There is not much opportunity for working on enriched jobs leading to high levels of intrinsic motivation and satisfaction. Forget about opportunities for self-actualization! The major reason why some resettle in India has to do with the satisfaction they receive from reconnecting with the members of their family and in-groups. In other words, unlike the men and women of Western work organizations, social and interpersonal rewards can become the most important category of need whose satisfaction might become more important than satisfying self-actualizing needs.

In response to the processes of different types of motivational patterns emerging in the era of globalization, new forms of work arrangements and rewards systems are being designed by multinational and global corporations. Motivational needs during times of mergers and acquisitions, strategic alliances, and times of economic meltdown are important issues that should not escape our attention. This chapter was written with the hope of providing a broad but detailed survey of the various important theoretical perspectives in this area.

REFERENCES

Adams, J.S. (1963). Toward an understanding of inequity. *Journal of Abnormal Psychology*, 67, 442–36.

Bakker, A.B., Demerouti, E., & Burke, R. (2009). Workaholism and relationship quality: A spillover–cross-over perspective. *Journal of Occupational Health Psychology*, 14(1), 23–33.

Barsade, S.G., Brief, A.P., & Spataro, S.E. (2003). The affective revolution in organizational behavior: The emergence of a paradigm. In Jerald Greenberg (Ed.). *Organizational behavior: The state of the science* (pp. 3–52). Mahwah, NJ: Lawrence Erlbaum Associates, Publishers.

Bhagat, R.S. (1983). The effects of stressful life events on individual performance effectiveness and work adjustment processes within organizational settings: A research model. *Academy of Management Review*, 8(4), 660–71.

Bhagat, R.S. (1985). Acculturative stress in immigrants: A development perspective. In T.A. Beehr & R.S. Bhagat (Eds). *Human stress and cognition* (pp. 325–46). New York: John Wiley Interscience Publications.

Bhagat, R.S. & McQuaid, S.J. (1982). Role of subjective culture in organizations: A review and directions for future research. *Journal of Applied Psychology Monograph*, 67(5), 653–85.

Bhagat, R.S., McQuaid, S.J., Lindholm, H., & Segovis, J.C. (1985). Total life stress: A multi-method validation of the construct and its effects on organizationally valued outcomes and withdrawal behaviors. *Journal of Applied Psychology*, 70(1), 202–14.

Bhagat, R.S., Kedia, B.L., Crawford, S.E., & Kapan, M.R. (1990). Cross-cultural issues in organizational psychology: Emergent trends and directions for research in the 1990s. In C.L. Cooper and Ivan T. Robertson (Eds). *International Review of Industrial and Organizational Psychology* (vol. 5, pp. 59–99). New York: John Wiley & Sons.

Bhagat, R.S., Segovis, J.C., & Nelson, T.A. (2003). *Work stress and coping in the era of globalization*. New York: Routledge.

Bhagat, R.S., Steverson, P., & Segovis, J. (2007a). Cultural variations in employee assistance programs in an era of globalization. In D.L. Stone & E.F. Stone-Romero (Eds). *The influence of culture on human resource management processes and practices* (pp. 207–34). New York: Psychology Press.

Bhagat, R.S., Steverson, P.K., & Segovis, J.C. (2007b). International and cultural variations in employee assistance programs: implications for managerial health and effectiveness. *Journal of Management Studies*, 44(2), 222–42.

Bhagat, R.S., Van Scotter, J.C., Steverson, P., & Moustafa, K.S. (2007). Cultural variations in individual job performance: Implications for industrial and organizational psychology in the 21st century. In G.P. Hodgkinson & J.K. Ford (Eds). *International review of industrial and organizational psychology* (vol. 22, pp. 235–64). Chichester: John Wiley & Sons, Ltd.

Bhagat, R.S., Van Scotter, J., Bosco, F., Bhawuk, D.P.S., & Kanfer, R. (2010). Do individuals perform differently across cultures?: An integrative perspective. Manuscript submitted for publication, July 2012 (Working paper).

Bhawuk, D.P.S. (2001). Evolution of culture assimilators: Toward theory-based assimilators. *International Journal of Intercultural Relations*, 25(2), 141–63.

Burke, R.J. (1995). A longitudinal study of psychological burnout in teachers. *Human Relations*, 48(2), 187–202.

Burke, R.J. & Weir, T. (1978). *Sex differences in adolescent life stress, social support, and well-being*. New York: Taylor & Francis.

Cameron, K., Dutton, J.E., & Quinn, R.E. (2003). *Positive organizational scholarship: Foundations of a new discipline*. San Francisco, CA: Berrett-Koehler.

Chabris, C. & Simons, D. (2010). *The invisible gorilla*. New York: Crown.

Dachler, H.P. & Wilpert, B. (1978). Conceptual dimensions and boundaries of participation in organizations: A crucial evaluation. *Administrative Science Quarterly*, 23, 1–39.

Diener, E., Diener, M., & Diener, C. (1995). Factors predicting the subjective well-being of nations. *Journal of Personality and Social Psychology*, 58, 653–63.

Eagly, Alice H., Johannesen-Schmidt, Mary C., & van Engen, Marloes L. (2003). Transformational, transactional, and laissez-faire leadership styles: A meta-analysis comparing women and men. *Psychological Bulletin*, 129(4), 569–91. doi: 10.1037/0033-2909.129.4.569.

Earley, P.C. (1989). Social loafing and collectivism: A comparison of the United States with the People's Republic of China. *Administrative Science Quarterly*, 34(4), 565–81.

Earley, P.C. (1997). Doing an about-face: Social motivation and cross-cultural currents. In P.C. Earley & M. Erez (Eds). *New perspectives on international industrial/organizational psychology* (pp. 243–55). San Francisco, CA: New Lexington Press.

Earley, P.C. & Erez, M. (1997). *The transplanted executive*. New York: Oxford University Press.

Earley, P.C. & Gibson, C. (1998). Taking stock in our progress on individualism–collectivism: 100 years of solidarity and community. *Journal of Management*, 3(4), 265–304.

England, G.W. (1987). *Meaning of working: An international perspective*. MOW International Research Team. Amsterdam: Elsevier.

Erez, M. (1994). Toward a new model of cross-cultural I/O psychology. In H.C. Triandis, M.D. Dunnette, & L. Hough (Eds). *The handbook of industrial and organizational psychology* (2nd edn, vol. 4., pp. 569–607). Palo Alto, CA: Consulting Psychologists Press.

Erez, M. (1997). A culture-based model of work motivation. In P.C. Earley & M. Erez (Eds). *New perspectives on international industrial/organizational psychology* (pp. 193–242). Frontiers of Industrial and Organizational Psychology series. San Francisco, CA: New Lexington Press.

Erez, M. & Earley, P.C. (2003). *Culture, self-identity, and work*. New York: Oxford University Press.

Erez, M. & Gati, E. (2004). A dynamic, multi-level model of culture: From the micro-level of the individual to the macro-level of a global culture. *Applied Psychology: An International Review*, 53, 583–98.

Evans, P., Pucik, V., & Barsoux, J.-L. (2010). *The global challenge*. New York: McGraw-Hill Irwin.

Frost, K.M. & Frost, J.C. (2000). Romanian and American life aspirations in relation to psychological well-being. *Journal of Cross-Cultural Psychology*, 31, 726–51.

Gelfand, M., Erez, M., & Aycan, Z. (2007). Cross-cultural organizational behavior. *Annual Review of Psychology*, 58, 479–514.

Greenberg, J. & Baron, R.A. (2003). *Behavior in organizations*. Upper Saddle River, NJ: Prentice-Hall.

Haire, M., Ghiselli, E.E., & Porter, L.W. (1963). Cultural patterns in the role of managers. *Industrial Relations*, 12(2), 95–117.

Heckscher, C. (1995). *White-collar blues: Management loyalties in an age of corporate restructuring*. New York: Basic Books.

Hertzberg, F. (1968). One more time: How do you motivate employees? *Harvard Business Review*, 46, 53–62.

Hertzberg, F. (1966). *Work and the nature of man*. Cleveland, OH: World Publishing.

Hertzberg, F. (1981). Motivating people. In P. Mali (Ed.). *Management handbook*. New York: John Wiley & Sons.

Hofstede, G. (2001). *Culture's consequences*. Thousand Oaks, CA: Sage.

House, R., Hanges, P.J., Javidan, M., & Dorfman, P.W. (2004). *Culture, leadership and organizations: The GLOBE study of 62 societies*. Thousand Oaks, CA: Sage.

Hulin, C.L. (1991). Adaption, persistence, and commitment in organizations. In M.D. Dunnette & L.M. Hough (Eds). *Handbook of industrial and organizational psychology* (pp. 445–506). Palo Alto, CA: Consulting Psychologist Press, Inc.

Huntington, S. (1996). *The clash of civilizations and the remaking of world order*. New York: Simon & Schuster Publishing.

Inglehart, R. & Baker, W.E. (2000). Modernization, cultural change, and the persistence of traditional values. *American Sociological Review*, 65(1), 19–51.

Jacques, M. (2009). *When China rules the world*. New York: The Penguin Press.

Kornhauser, W. (1959). *The politics of mass society*. New York: The Free Press.

Kossek, E.E. & Lambert, S.J. (2005). *Work and life integration*. Mahwah, NJ: Lawrence Erlbaum Associates.

Lawler, E.E. (1973). *Motivation and work organizations*. Monterey, CA: Brooks/ Cole.

Levine, R. (1997). *The geography of time*. New York: One World Publications.

Locke, E. (1976). The nature and causes of job satisfaction. In M. Dunnette (Ed.). *Handbook of industrial and organizational psychology* (pp. 1297–1350). Chicago: Rand-McNally.

Locke, E.A. & Latham, G.P. (1990). *A theory of goal setting and task performance*. New York: Prentice-Hall.

Maslow, A. (1954). *Motivation and personality*. New York: Harper & Row.

Mathieu, J.E. & Zajac, D.M. (1990). A review and meta-analysis of the antecedents, correlates, and consequences of organizational commitment. *Pyschological Bulletin*, 108(2), 171–94.

McClelland, D.C. (1961). *The achieving society*. Princeton, NJ: Van Nostrand.

Meyer, J.P. & Allen, N.J. (1991). A three-component conceptualization of organizational commitment. *Human Resource Management Review*, 1(1), 61–89.

Meyer, J.P. & Allen, N.J. (1991). A three-component conceptualization of organizational commitment. *Human Resource Management Review*, 1, 61–89.

Meyer, J.P. & Allen, N.J. (1997). *Commitment in the workplace*. Thousand Oaks, CA: Sage.

Meyer, J.P. & Allen, N.J. (2006). Social identities and commitments at work: Toward an integrative model. *Journal of Organizational Behavior*, 27(5), 665–83.

Meyer, J.P., Paunonen, S.V., Gellatly, I.R., Goffin, R.D., & Jackson, D.N. (1989). Organizational commitment and job performance: It's the nature of the commitment that counts. *Journal of Applied Psychology*, 74(1), 152–6.

Mowday, R.T. & Colwell, K.A. (2003). Employee reactions to unfair outcomes in the workplace: The contribution of Adam's equity theory to understanding work motivation. In L.W. Porter, G.A. Bigley, & R.M. Steers (Eds). *Motivation and work behavior* (7th edn, pp. 65–87). Burr Ridge, IL: McGraw-Hill/Irwin.

Muna, F.A. (2003). Seven metaphors on management: Tools for managers in the Arab world. Burlington, VT: Gower.

Nam, S. (1995). Culture, control, and commitment in an international joint venture. *International Journal of Human Resource Management*, (6), 553–67.

OECD (2007). *Women and men in the OECD*. Paris: OECD.

Ouchi, W.G. (1981). *Theory Z: How American business can meet the Japanese challenge*. Reading, MA: Addison Wesley.

Pinder, C.C. (2008). *Work motivation in organizational behavior*. New York: Psychology Press.

Pitt-Catsouphes, M., Kossek, E.E., & Sweet, S. (2006). *Work and family handbook*. Mahwah, NJ: Lawrence Erlbaum Associates.

Porter, L.W., Steers, R.M., Mowday, R.T., & Boulin, P.V. (1974). Organization commitment, job satisfaction, and turnover among psychiatric technicians. *Journal of Applied Psychology*, 59(5), 603–609.

Reichers, A.E. (1985). A review and reconceptualization of organizational commitment. *Academy of Management Review*, 10(3), 465–76.

Ronen, S. (1986). *Comparative and multinational management*. New York: John Wiley & Sons.

Rotondi, T. (1975). Organizational identification: Issues and implications. *Organizational Behavior and Human Performance*, 13(1), 95–109.

Rousseau, D.M. (1995). *Psychological contracts in organizations: Understanding written and unwritten agreements*. Thousand Oaks, CA: Sage Publishing.

Ryan, R.M. & Deci, E.L. (2000). Self-determination theory and the facilitation of intrinsic motivation, social development, and well-being. *American Psychologist*, 55(1), 68–78.

Sanchez-Runde, C., Lee, S.M., & Steers, R.M. (2009). Cultural drivers of work behavior: Personal values, motivation, and job attitude. In Rabi. S. Bhagat & Richard M. Steers (Eds). *Management across cultures: Challenges and strategies* (pp. 305–34). Cambridge: Cambridge University Press.

Schor, J. (1994). *The overworked American: The unexpected decline in leisure*. New York: Basic Books.

Steers, R.M. & Nardon, L. (2006). *Managing in the global economy*. Armonk, NY: M.E. Sharpe.

Steers, R.M., Sanchez-Runde, C.J., & Nardon, L. (2010). *Management across cultures*. Cambridge: Cambridge University Press.

Triandis, H.C. (1973). Work and non-work: Intercultural perspectives. In M.D. Dunnette (Ed.). *Work and non-work in the year 2001* (pp. 29–52). Monterey, CA: Brooks/Cole.

Vroom, V.H. (1972). *Work and motivation*. New York: John Wiley & Sons.

Wasti, S.A. (2002). Affective and continuance commitment to the organization: Test of an integrated model in the Turkish context. *International Journal of Intercultural Relations*, 25, 525–50.

Weiss, H.M. & Cropanzano, R. (1996). Affective events theory: A theoretical discussion of the structure, causes, and consequences of affective experiences at work. In B.M. Straw & L.L. Cummings (Eds). *Research in organizational behavior* (vol. 18, pp. 1–74). Greenwich, CT: JAI Press.

Yang (2000). Nebraska Symposium on Motivation.

7. Cultural variations, work, and organizational stress and coping

Globalization, which has been a major trend during the past 30 years, has created considerable economic prosperity in both advanced and emergent countries. Globalization has two important facets: economic and socio-cultural. Economic globalization is primarily concerned with the spreading of economic activities and transactions across dissimilar nations and cultures. Social and cultural globalization tends to accompany economic globalization and sometimes follows it. A major consequence of the social aspect of globalization is the continuous pressure on multinational and global organizations to align their organizational structures, networks, and processes on a continuous basis in order to compete successfully in the global marketplace.

A recent survey of 11,000 companies in 13 countries by the Regus Management Group found an increase of 58 percent in work and organization stress from 2007–09. In particular, Chinese workers reported an 86 percent increase in work stress in this period (*The Economist*, 2009). Qualitative as well as anecdotal evidence from Indian call centers suggests that stress is due to long hours, excessive demands, and repetitive jobs, as well as low compensation. Turnover of female employees soared to 45–50 percent in 2005 (Bhagat, Segovis, & Nelson, 2012). Since that time, however, there has been some improvement in turnover, yet, because of increased competition globally, Indians firms have experienced elevated stress in the workplace. The phenomenon of *karoshi* (excessive overworking) is no longer limited to employees in Japan and has spread to other countries such as Singapore, Vietnam, China, South Korea, and India. *The Economist* (2009) reported an Indian software worker who died at his desk after working 13 hour days without a break.

Consider the following story from a Chinese manager of a global organization:

> "The pressure does not necessarily ease with different economic situations," said Sam Liu, a 21 year-old marketing strategy manager with a global company. "You have one kind of pressure in good times and another kind in bad times. I have to sleep. But I have to sacrifice my hobbies and the time I would like to spend with my friends." Among other reasons why some Chinese people work

so hard is the massive competition within the vast workforce. "There is always another guy who is willing to do 12 things when your boss has asked you to do 10 things. You deal with the pressure or you quit," Liu said. "It is up to you." (*The Economist*, 2009, pp. 1, 2)

Similar reports of increases in pressures experienced by multinational and global organizations are found in business periodicals such as the *Wall Street Journal, Business Week, Singapore Times*, and *Asian Wall Street Journal*. Global competition is creating new types of organizational realities (both in terms of internal as well as external environments) in both advanced and globalizing countries. The BRIC countries in particular and the MIST (Mexico, Indonesia, South Korea, and Turkey) countries are now important participants in the global marketplace. Gone are the days when long siestas were acceptable in the work cultures of Latin American countries. Longer days, coupled with excessive work demands, are becoming common in these countries. People, organizations, communities, and nations around the world are being affected by economic, technological, political, and environmental developments that take place in different geographical locales—some close and others far away. Increased global competition, fluctuating interest rates, rapid introduction of new technologies, and related economic, social, and cultural consequences lead to both positive and negative outcomes. One of the major negative consequences of operating in the global environment is an increase in the uncertainties which lead to more work and organizational stresses. Organizational consequences that lead to increases in work stress include:

- the phenomenal rate of growth in cross-border mergers and acquisitions;
- complexities in coordinating worldwide operations;
- relentless pressures to innovate;
- new workplace realities and organizational structures;
- evolution of new managerial roles;
- changing patterns of psychological contracts and employee attitudes;
- work–homelife imbalance.

Mergers and Acquisitions

International mergers and acquisitions have increased since the early 1980s. These mergers, acquisitions, and downsizing events generally create feelings of uncertainty, fear, suspicion, and cynicism at all levels of the organization. Mergers and acquisitions become even more difficult to deal with when they are accompanied by technological changes, business process re-engineering and reorganization efforts, governmental regulations, and the de-layering and flattening of the organization. Fear of job loss after a merger or acquisition was the number one factor among worries and anxieties reported by 54 percent of the senior managers in the 1000 largest US companies—many of which operate in the global marketplace (Robert Half International, 1991). The second most common factor, burnout, was reported by 26 percent of these executives (Shirom, 2011).

Stressful experiences do not occur only in the case of hostile takeovers but are common among managers of companies that experience all mergers and acquisitions, whether domestic or cross-border. Instead of managing the crises that arise during times of mergers and acquisitions, senior managers tend to experience threats, become less accessible to their colleagues and subordinates, and either cut off or limit lines of communication. Mergers and acquisitions induce considerable uncertainties because employees at most levels are uninformed about the nature of changes that might take place in the workplace. The nature of authority and lines of communication in the new organization tend to be different from the earlier era, requiring considerable psychological adjustments.

Complexities in Coordinating Worldwide Operations

The early 1990s were characterized by economic slowdown, planned closings, reduction of budgets, and layoffs. The last few years have been reminiscent of this era. Major austerity programs have affected the operation of both private and public organizations, resulting in an emphasis on balanced budgets and strong fiscal responsibilities. Organizations are becoming "leaner and meaner" (Levine, 1980; Gilmore & Hirshhorn, 1983) as they compete globally. While over one-third of *Fortune* global 1000 companies have downsized their workforces by about 10 percent each year starting in the 1980s, they did not do so because they were losing money. The key economic drivers were increased global competition and technological changes (i.e., robots, computers, and information-processing technologies) that lowered labor costs and increased productivity. These drivers have become increasingly salient in recent times.

Blue-collar workers in manufacturing have been downsized at a faster rate than managers and white-collar workers (accounting for about 50 percent of the job losses in the 1990s) (Quick et al., 2003). However, the downsizing that continued as a strategy to increase profitability and lower labor costs began to affect white-collar workers as well. In the past decade, white-collar workers have became as vulnerable as blue-collar workers, and good past performance is not necessarily a guarantee of continued employment. If a division or department is being downsized because of the future strategic objectives of the company, then both blue- and white-collar employees would be downsized, that is, be laid off or terminated. The stresses experienced by downsized workers tend to be severe and unsettling because of the loss of self-esteem and the pressures to find another job with comparable income.

Relentless Pressures to Innovate

Companies from the US, UK, Canada, and East Asia are confronted with increasing pressures from the global marketplace to innovate. Innovation can take place at the level of developing new products and services or in designing new forms of work arrangements (i.e., globally distributed work teams), both of which have major consequences for organizations. We live in the Information Age defined by the Internet. Thirty years ago, it was inconceivable to think of a manager working in Dallas corresponding daily with colleagues in Bangalore, Shanghai, and Dublin. Now this often happens in real time and continuously. Global organizations that survive the challenging realities of the marketplace do so by engaging in creative processes of technology and knowledge creation (Davenport & Prusak, 1998; Hamel, 1999).

Dealing with New Workplace Realities and Organizational Structures

Major restructuring of work and work organizations has been taking place on a scale not seen since the Industrial Revolution. With rapid innovations in technologies and global competition, modern workplaces are being transformed. Changes include the restructuring of managerial roles, modifications in the nature of the psychological contract between the employee and the organization, and in the number of working hours. Smaller, networked organizations are evolving not only in the Western world but also in the developing companies and emergent economies (Grantham, 2002). Research conducted in different parts of the world reports that the amount of work that managers are expected to perform has been increasing every decade. Individuals are required to do more without any expectation of increases in pay and other benefits. Moreover, a sense of job insecurity is a hallmark of 21st century work organizations, and it affects all employees regardless of their position in the organizational hierarchy. Gone are the days when "blue-collar blues" characterized only the workers at lower levels of the organization. "White-collar woes" are becoming common in all globalized economies due to sudden and turbulent changes in the nature of demands of the global marketplace (Heckscher, 1995).

Evolution of New Managerial Roles

As noted earlier, the nature of managerial work has been undergoing profound changes in the advanced and globalizing countries of the world. No doubt the nature and speed of these changes are more intense in the G-7 countries but they are spreading to other countries in the G-20 network. Cooper (1998), in a survey of managerial work, finds that the demands being placed on managers are increasing and that a majority had minimal training to cope with such pressures and changes. The major findings of the Cooper survey are:

- 82 percent of managers felt that they were suffering from excessive amounts of information overload;
- 76 percent reported that they were increasingly dependent on use of social and interpersonal skills rather than using the authority associated with their positions;
- 60 percent reported that they were spending far more time dealing with the various dilemmas associated with organizational politics and strategies of upward influence;
- 60 percent thought that their jobs were becoming increasingly fragmented and that they had less uninterrupted time to focus on and complete important tasks which may be of long-term significance.

Observations such as these and other reports published in various business and trade magazines clearly depict that *role overload* (too much work to do in a given span of time), *role conflict* (conflicting expectations in the performance of one's role), and *under-utilization of valued skills* (when one does not get to use one's important occupational skills in performing tasks associated with one's work role) have been increasing since the 1980s.

Changing Patterns of Psychological Contract and Employee Attitudes

Many multinational and global companies outsource key business functions to organizations located in low labor cost countries and employ individuals on contingent, short-term, or part-time contracts. The development of the contingent workforce, temporary personnel, and others on a part-time basis has profound implications for the nature of the psychological contract that employees have with their organizations (Rosseau, 1995). The number of part-time workers nearly doubled during the 1990s and this trend continues (Quick et al., 2003). The trend is to hire individuals on short-term contracts to do specific tasks or carry out specific projects for the company. Collectively, these developments leave little room for considering the role of the psychological contract in the employment equation. In the UK, for example, there are growing perceptions that more people are working on short-term contracts than are on permanent, full-time jobs.

The changing workplace in the current era of globalization precipitates a significant shift of employee attitudes, commitment, and related affective and behavioral intentions toward their work organization. This process of transformation is not limited to the organizations in North America. There have been significant changes in the attitudes, work norms, expectations, and work-related values of employees in countries of Southern Europe (e.g., Italy, Spain, Greece, and Portugal), Western Europe (e.g., Ireland, the UK, and France), South Asia (e.g., India and Sri Lanka), East Asia (e.g., China, South Korea, and Japan), and South America (e.g., Brazil, Chile, and Argentina).

When organizational changes induced by globalization-related demands are poorly managed, the stresses of managers and other employees increase. It is not surprising that there can be intense feelings of insecurity, powerlessness, and alienation during organizational restructuring. Patterns of organizational commitment can also be low and decrease as the sense of job insecurity increases because of organizational restructuring. Over 64 percent of employees felt lower levels of commitment during such times (Quick et al., 2003). It should be clear that the negative impact of restructuring on work stress, job satisfaction, and morale is high. It is becoming apparent that the changing nature of the workplace is responsible for inducing a variety of stressful reactions at all levels of the organization.

Managing Work–Life Balance

The impact of participation in the global marketplace is reflected in the increasing number of hours that individuals work. Working hours have been increasing since the 1980s, not only in Western countries but also in the context of East and Southeast Asian countries. Juliet Schor (1992) reported that Americans worked the most number of hours (1949 per year), followed by the Japanese, more than any other country among the G-20 nations. The trend continues and, in fact, it can be noted that the more globalized the country and work organization the longer the work days become. Countries which are becoming globalized (e.g., Bolivia, Ecuador, Mongolia, and countries in sub-Saharan Africa) are experiencing increases in per capita income and other material benefits for their citizens. However, in such countries the number of working hours tends to be much lower than those in the globalized and emerging economies (i.e., the BRIC countries). There is a strong disconnect between the number of hours that a manager has written in his or her employment contract and how much he or she really has to work, especially while coping with the pressures of the global marketplace.

Public sector organizations and government bureaucracies tend to have stable environments and tend to benefit from some level of protection from their national governments. Therefore, they do not require their managers to work as hard or as long as the private sector organizations.

Pressure to work long hours necessitates that one has to learn to manage the work–home life balance (the delicate relationship between work and non-work life). Issues concerning work–life balance have emerged as a major topic of research in the past two decades (see Pitt-Catsouphes, Kossek, & Sweet, 2006). The importance of work in relation to one's personal life has been increasing since the 1970s and it increases as one moves up the corporate ladder. In other words, the higher one advances in one's career and takes on more decision-making responsibility, the more work "looms large" in one's life. Even though individuals tend to be aware of the adverse effects of working long hours at the expense of developing nurturing relationships in their personal life, they feel they are not in a position to do so. Sixty-five percent of managers think that the amount of work they do has an adverse effect on their psychological, emotional, and physical health. About 70 percent of employees think that spending long hours on the job leads to poor relationships with their spouse or significant other (Quick et al., 2003).

HUMAN CONSEQUENCES

Along with organizational consequences, there are many human consequences of living in the globalized world. These consequences are directly related to the effects of globalization at the level of the organization and society; however, for providing clear theoretical distinction, we call them human consequences because they strongly manifest at a micro level, with implications for the individual and his or her family. They include:

- adapting to new patterns of culture at work and in the society;
- continuous upgrading of skills and abilities;
- working in cross-cultural work teams;
- dealing with new demographic realities.

Adapting to New Patterns of Culture at Work and in the Society

Globalization introduces rapid changes in patterns of consumption and the spread of global brand goods and services across dissimilar cultures. It leads to the growth of the consumer class in developing nations and emergent economies, creating similar patterns of material desires and lifestyles (Wolf, 2004) in most global societies. The new consumer class consists of individuals and families who use telephones, televisions, and the Internet, and are influenced by the culture and ideas that are transmitted via these media (Worldwatch Institute, 2004). There has been substantial growth in the consumer class in China, India, Brazil, Mexico, South Africa, and so on, and the patterns of consumption tend to converge with those of Western countries, such as the US, Canada, and UK. The supermarkets in the globalizing countries now carry many global brands (e.g., Coca-Cola, Sprite, Seven-Up), leading to "McDonaldization" of consumer cultures. Such changes in the patterns of consumption in non-Western countries lead to the slow transformation of cultural values and practices. In some sectors of the economy, the process tends to be slow whereas in others the transformation process is rapid. The worldwide spread of economic activities increases the tendency to emphasize rationality and reliance on science and technology. As developing countries and emerging nations take steps toward becoming more globalized, they begin to use Western countries as references not only in the governance of economic and political affairs, but also in the regulation of lives at work and non-work. The corporate cultures of organizations are becoming more results-oriented, driven more by profit as opposed to concern for employees. Values of consumerism, individualism, competition, and efficiency gradually replace traditional values of non-materialism, collectivism, and cooperation in the workplace. The human consequences of such changes are profound.

A curious new breed of professional workers, called the creative class (Florida, 2005), has emerged. In describing their work habits, Deborah Blumenthal wrote: "Tucked away discreetly in corners of living rooms, behind bedroom doors, in basements, attics, garages, and even bureau drawers, home offices have become the primary place of work for thousands" (Blumenthal, 1979, p. 3). Until around 1987, the type of work one could do at home was fairly limited. Today's creative classes, in order to cope with the changing pressures at work, are working continuously with iPhones/iPads, Blackberry phones, and Android smartphones/tablets connected to the Internet. The negatives of such work patterns have only intensified since Blumenthal's analysis in 1979. They are characterized by a complete lack of separation between work and non-work lives, a lack of face-to-face interaction with colleagues, and a dogged sense that work is expected to be done at all hours.

The need to work, work, work has penetrated our sense of collective well-being. Reports of executives buying expensive gifts for children but not having time to spend with them during the holidays are found in newspapers and business periodicals all over the world. A new era has evolved where one may enjoy working on a software problem for the company and find it more rewarding than helping children with schoolwork or a spouse with household chores. New computer-mediated technologies like Skype™ often substitute for personal interaction and allow one to rationalize staying in the office to complete projects. Numerous careers are being characterized by what Korman & Korman (1980) called the "career success/personal failure syndrome." This syndrome—which connotes high levels of accomplishment accompanied by divorce, marital conflict, and related symptoms of family strain—has become commonplace in the largest global economy of the world (the US) and is spreading to other emergent economies.

With more multinational and global organizations expanding their worldwide operations and using such management techniques as outsourcing, offshoring, and temporary work teams to improve efficiency, serious consequences for work stress and employee health have developed. Corporate and work cultures of rapidly globalizing companies are becoming less employee-centered, and psychological contracts, implied at the time of recruitment, rapidly lose significance (Cappelli, 1999). Fluctuating market demands of the global marketplace make it necessary for many organizations to develop new patterns of employment contracts that in our view are largely responsible for the evolution of stressful experiences for the employees and their families.

Job insecurity, higher work pace, long and fluctuating working hours, low control over job content and processes, and low wages add further stresses and occupational hazards (Smith & Carayon, 2011). Incompetent styles of management, sexual harassment of working women, poor working conditions, inappropriate and unfair labor relations practices, discrimination in hiring and advancement policies, and insufficient training are all negative aspects that can be found routinely in work environments in different countries. To be sure, working conditions are generally much better in advanced globalized countries of the West but not so in globalizing and emergent economies (such as the BRIC countries). In their rush to improve economic growth, national governments and work organizations of globalizing countries have paid insufficient attention to the occupational health psychology and physical well-being of workers who work in the sectors that are particularly vulnerable.

Continuous Upgrading of Skills and Abilities

In many countries we find relentless pressures to innovate and continuously upgrade occupational skills and abilities at all levels of the organization. This severely weakens the participation and earnings potential of older workers. Massive restructuring processes in both economic and occupational structures of globalizing countries create discrepancies between those who have the right kinds of skills and talents needed in the marketplace and those who do not. More often than not, those who do not have the right skills suffer because they work in roles that are underpaid, do not get access to appropriate forms of training, and continue to lag behind in terms of their economic success and psychological well-being (see Grantham, 2002; Hofacker, 2010). Upgrading political skills in managing relationships at work has also been found to relate to work effectiveness (Ferris, Davidson, & Perrewe, 2005). The issue of making sense of the political reality in one's work group and organization was almost never raised and discussed in the organizational literature in the 1970s but now it has become an important topic and many researchers claim that a lack of political skills and abilities can create a stressful experience in one's work life (Ferris, Davidson, & Perrewe, 2005).

Working in Cross-Cultural Work Teams

Geographically distributed work teams are composed of members of the same organization (or sometimes different organizations) from different countries of the world. More often than not, they differ in terms of their national and cultural origins and in terms of their work habits and work ethics. It is not easy to work with the members of a geographically distributed work team (Stanko & Gibson, 2009). Consider the case of a financial services manager of American Express in the New York City headquarters who has to correspond with his Japanese or Chinese counterpart both by using the telephone and with computer-mediated communication. This manager has to wake up in the early hours of the morning to coordinate his or her work with those located in the Asian time zones (i.e., typically 9 to 15 hours ahead of US Eastern Standard time). Along with difficulties of coordinating across temporal zones, one has to make sense of working in the context of multicultural work teams (Burke et al., 2008) and manage the challenges of dealing with the cultural diversities that characterize virtual work teams (Stanko & Gibson, 2009).

Dealing with New Demographic Realities

The economic and cultural realities of the rapid growth of global linkages lead to significant changes in the composition of not only the working population, but the population of globalizing societies as a whole. Huntington (2004) provides a detailed portrayal of the new demographic realities in US society. Similar developments also characterize the population distributions of Western Europe, Australia, and New Zealand. In particular, the large cities of the world, which are the global headquarters of large multinational and global organizations, are getting larger. The working population in multinational, global companies is increasingly composed of immigrants and culturally dissimilar individuals from different nations. Global cities such as London, Paris, Sydney, and Sao Paolo have become highly heterogenous in terms of the composition of workers, who come from distinct national, ethnic, racial, and religious groups. Consider the current demographic situation in New York City: it has over 30 percent foreign-born workers. Given the nature of cultural diversity that characterizes cities like Toronto and New York it is quite conceivable that a native New Yorker might feel more comfortable working in another global city like Sydney or Berlin, compared with working in Memphis, Tennessee or Paris, Texas, which have remained relatively static in terms of cultural composition.

There is growing evidence that immigrant workers from the former Communist bloc countries, like Poland, Hungary, and Romania, have distinct patterns of work motivation and ethics that are difficult for Western colleagues and supervisors to understand and work with (Bhagat, McDevitt, & Segovis, 2011). Global organizations must learn to deal with the challenges of growing heterogeneity in their workforce in terms of ethnic and cultural background. This is the case because different ethnic and cultural groups appraise and cope with work stress and stressful events in accordance with the values of their cultures.

WORK STRESS AND COPING: A CULTURAL CONSEQUENCE OF PERSPECTIVE

Globalization involves increasingly frequent encounters with organizations, individuals, and situations whose national and cultural backgrounds differ considerably. Learning to appreciate the exact nature and consequences of globalization at the level of the organization and the individual necessarily involves a comprehensive understanding of cultural differences. We define *culture* as a multifaceted construct that comprises the totality of knowledge, beliefs, attitudes, norms, and values of a group

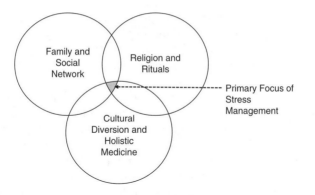

Figure 7.1   Primary focus of stress management in non-Western cultures

of people who speak the same language and are located in the same geo-graphical region of the world. Culture is a collection of habits, beliefs, practices, arguments, and values that regulates and guides human life. Cultures evolve distinctly in response to ecological and social demands in different parts of the world. Culture transmits practical solutions to everyday problems—like how to avoid painful interpersonal and social interactions and how to form successful family structures. Perhaps one of the most important roles that culture plays is to educate and train our emotions such as feelings of joy, pride, pain, accomplishment, grief, shame, guilt, and so on.

Different cultures of the world emphasize distinctive narratives, holi-days, symbols, and works of art that contain implicit and explicit mes-sages about how we ought to feel, respond, and make sense of our social environment. Social support from one's immediate family and significant social networks is also important in the appraisal and management of work stress. Last, but not least, is the role of religion and religious rituals in making sense of and coping with stressful work experiences. Ritualistic practices associated with Hinduism, Confucianism, Buddhism, and Taoism are regarded as crucial for managing stressful experiences in Eastern and South Asian cultures. Reliance on traditional holistic medi-cine supposedly helps control one's fate through adoption of healthy life-styles. Culturally sanctioned diversions such as the use of humor, playing various games with members of one's in-group, and eating as a community are also regarded as significant in the appraisal of and coping with work stress. Figure 7.1 shows the importance of these three sources of influence in the way people perceive, appraise, and cope with stressful experiences.

Consider the following examples (see Brooks, 2011 for details) of sus-tained cultural differences that exist across national and ethnic borders:

1. Plays and movies produced in Germany are three times as likely to have unhappy and tragic endings as plays from the US and India.
2. Members of Western societies are surprised that in India love is not a precondition for marriage (where over half of marriages are arranged).
3. Sixty-five percent of Japanese, compared to just 25 percent of Americans, are afraid of saying the wrong thing in a social situation.
4. In the UK couples rarely touch each other in public, whereas in France more physical touching is common—in Paris over 110 touches were observed in coffee houses in an hour of having coffee (Keltner, 2009). In the Latino culture of San Juan, Puerto Rico, the number of touches between a couple during an hour of coffee was close to 180 (Keltner, 2009).
5. Cultural differences are also observed in the various regions of the US. In the American South, where a culture of honor is dominant, words like "gun" are found in the names of cities (e.g., Gun Point, FL); however, in the northern states words like "joy" and "ville" are common (e.g., Joy, IL; Louisville, KY; Danville, IN).
6. Religion and various religious rituals play important roles in managing work stress in East Asian, South Asian, and Latin American countries. The overwhelming importance of religion in dealing with stressful events and traumatic experiences is found in much of Africa. The importance of rituals including exercising regimens such as *chi gong*, *tai chi*, and *falun gong* have increased in China as Chinese multinationals fiercely compete in the global marketplace. It is believed these rituals help one control the mood and physical tension occurring during intense stressful experiences at work.
7. Religion, just like in the East and South Asian and other contexts, also plays an important role in coping with stress in Turkey. Turkey has been experiencing rapid rates of growth in the past few years. It is a country whose population is predominantly Muslim. It is interesting to note that it has been most successful in blending its emphasis on Islamic beliefs and practices with the organizational and human consequences of rapid globalization. Because of the influence of Kemal Atatürk in the 1920s, the practice of Islam as a religion is less overt in Turkey compared with other Middle Eastern countries. However, the importance of Islam and Islamic rituals in managing stresses and strains is crucial. Similarly, religion and ritualistic practices help a large majority of the working population in Mexico to escape the pressures and stresses of life by encouraging participation in various intense spiritual rituals.

The culture of a country or a region of the world (e.g., Japan, East Asia) is not a recipe that creates uniformity in human behavior. Each culture has its own internal debates, unresolved issues, and persistent tensions. Culture-specific beliefs, attitudes, and values often work in conjunction with religious beliefs, practices, and rituals in guiding the appraisal of and in coping with work stress.

Cultures do not exist simply as static influences. Instead, cultures compete with one another for establishing better and worse ways of getting things done and accomplishing cherished goals for future generations. They pursue the objectives of social, economic, and technological growth at the organizational and societal levels, not from the standpoint of some objective observers but from the standpoint of people within the culture who act as guides in developing practices and value systems.

Certain cultures are better adapted at absorbing technological advances and becoming modern. Harrison (2006) reports that people in *progress-prone* cultures start with the assumption that they can play major roles in shaping their destiny while people in *progress-resistant* cultures believe that they are not able to control events that occur in their lives and are largely fatalistic in their outlook. He found that people in progress-prone cultures live to work, whereas those in progress-resistant cultures work to live. People in progress-prone cultures are likely to trust others, are more competitive and optimistic, emphasize education, and value punctuality. The social mechanism for controlling people in these cultures is to make them internalize guilt so that they are more likely to hold themselves responsible. In contrast, people in progress-resistant cultures are likely to be distrustful of others, externalize guilt, and blame others for their failures and misfortunes.

Progress-prone cultures are likely to be more effective in dealing with the organizational and human consequences of globalization. They deal with work stress better than progress-resistant cultures. Scandinavian cultures (e.g., Sweden, Denmark, and Norway) and Western European countries (e.g., the Netherlands, UK, and Germany) are good examples of progress-prone cultures. While they have experienced considerable difficulties in dealing with many of the dilemmas that are associated with globalization, they are largely successful; however, countries of the Middle East, North Africa, sub-Saharan Africa, and much of Central America and certain parts of West Asia (e.g., Afghanistan) have not benefitted much from globalization. Admittedly, these countries lack adequate infrastructures, institutions, and educational systems that can make their citizens able to adapt to various facets of globalization. Citizens of progress-resistant cultures do not differentiate the positive consequences of globalization from the dysfunctional ones. The point is that stressful consequences of globalization are more widely experienced in progress-resistant cultures than in progress-prone cultures. In the next section, we will deal with the role of cultural variations that are important in understanding the effects of work and organizational stress on individuals, work groups, and organizations.

The concept of *cultural syndromes* is helpful in understanding work stress and coping patterns from a multicultural perspective. A cultural syndrome is a pattern of shared beliefs, attitudes, categorizations, self-definitions, norms, role definitions, and values that is organized around a theme which can be identified by those who speak a particular language and reside in a given geographical locale, during a specific historic period. Thus, if a given operation in a specific geographical region of the world is high on a given dimension of cultural variation, the theory will take one form; however, if the population is low on that dimension, then the theory might take a different form (Kitayama, Markus, & Lieberman, 1995; Kitayama, Markus, & Matsumoto, 1995; Kitayama, Duffy, & Uchida, 2007). Important dimensions of cultural syndromes include:

- *Tightness.* In some cultures, there are many norms and expected patterns of behavior that apply across many social and organizational situations; minor deviations from these norms are often criticized and punished. In other cultures, there are few norms and only minor deviations from norms are criticized and may often be tolerated. The United States, for example, at this time is a rather loose culture in most domains of life, whereas Japan is a much tighter culture. However, it is important to pay attention to the domain. The United States is tight when it comes to behaviors at a bank, such as passing a bad check. In short, the United States is loose on average across many domains, but tight in some domains. Japan is tight across many domains, and loose in only a few. Thus in Japan there are many rules governing social and organizational behaviors and people are extremely concerned about not breaking them (Iwao, 1993; Triandis, 1996).
- *Cultural complexity.* The number of different social and cultural elements that are present in a society can be either large or small. Cultural complexity is higher when the number of elements that people of a given region have to deal with, on a regular basis, is large. For example, New York City is much more complex than a rural village. The complexity and multiplicity of religious, economic, political, social, and other forms of institutions in a large city like New York directly contribute to increases in its cultural complexity. One of the best measures of complexity is the number of people in a given culture.

- *Active–passive.* This dimension was first described by Diaz-Guerrero (1967) and includes a number of active and passive elements. A society that is high on this dimension encourages ongoing competition among its members, action, and self-fulfillment. On the other hand, societies that are passive encourage engagement in reflective thoughts, leaving the initiative to others and fostering cooperation among their members.

- *Individualism–collectivism.* Individualism is defined as a social pattern that consists of loosely linked individuals who view themselves as largely independent of collectives (e.g., family, work groups, community, and related social networks) and are motivated by their own preferences, needs, rights, and contracts. Collectivism, on the other hand, is a social pattern that consists of closely linked individuals that see themselves as belonging to one or more collectives (e.g., family, tribes or clans, co-workers, in-groups, and work organizations) and are largely motivated by the expectations, norms, duties, and obligations associated with these groups. While individualists think of self-reliance as "being free and able to do my own thing", collectivists think of self-reliance as "not being an unnecessary burden to my family or in-groups." The four defining attributes of individualism and collectivism that are essential to understanding how these individuals and groups appraise work stresses and cope with them are as follows:

1. *Definition of the self.* Individualists view their "selves" as independent and autonomous from the groups to which they belong. They construe themselves in an independent mode (Markus & Kitayama, 1991; Reykowski, 1994) and largely rely on their own efforts for coping with difficult situations that occur in both work and non-work contexts. Collectivists, on the other hand, view themselves as interdependent with the members of their collectives and appraise and cope with stressful events in a manner that is highly isomorphic with the views of their in-groups. They feel much less constrained in sharing stories of their stressful experiences with members of their family, in-groups, and other important collectives.

2. *Structure of goals.* Individualists pursue goals in work and life that reflect their personal desires and objectives. These goals need not necessarily be compatible with the goals of their in-groups or collectives. Collectivists, on the other hand, are socialized to pursue goals that are usually compatible with the goals of their in-groups (Schwartz, 1992, 1994; Triandis, 1994, 1995, 1998). In cases of conflict between individual and collective goals, collectivists are more comfortable giving

priority to in-group goals. However, individualists are unlikely to abandon their personal goals in favor of the goals of their collectives.

3. *Emphases on norms versus attitudes.* The drivers of social and organizational behaviors for individualists are primarily their own attitudes, personal needs, perceived rights, and contracts (Davidson et al., 1976; Bontempo & Rivero, 1992; Miller, 1994; Triandis, 1998; Bhawuk, 2001), whereas for collectivists they are norms, duties, and obligations. Social norms and expectations regarding how one ought to deal with a stressful experience are more important for collectivists whereas personal attitudes, preferences, and inclinations are more important for individualists. The link between personal attitudes, behavioral intention, and behavior is more ambiguous in describing collectivists than individualists. In other words, collectivists may behave in accordance with the expected norms and mores that are preferred by members of their in-group, even in situations where their personal attitudes do not correspond to their behavior.

4. *Emphases on relatedness versus rationality.* In dealing with members of their collectives, collectivists emphasize unconditional relatedness whereas individualists emphasize rationality and rational calculations. Relatedness means that one gives priority to relationships and is diligent about taking into account the needs of one's in-group, even when such relationships are not necessarily advantageous and may even be costly in the long term. Rationality, on the other hand, emphasizes careful calculation of the cost and benefits of engaging in a relationship (whether within individual, work groups, or organizations).

Vertical and Horizontal Relationships

In some societies, hierarchy is very important and in-group authorities determine most of the preferred patterns of social and organizational behavior. In other societies, however, social and organizational behavior is more egalitarian and much less concerned with hierarchical relationships. Vertical societies assume that people are different from each other and that a social hierarchy is essential for effective functioning and coordination of human action. Vertical relations are common in societies that are high in Hofstede's (1980, 2001) power distance. Horizontal relations are found in societies that are low in power distance. The traditional cultures of China, Japan, India, South Korea, and much of Latin America and Africa reflect vertical patterns of relationships. In contrast, horizontal cultures strongly emphasize a tradition of equality, as is found in the Israeli kibbutz. The cultures of Australia, New Zealand, Sweden, and other Scandinavian countries are largely horizontal. Integrating horizontal (i.e., same self) and vertical (i.e., different self) dimensions of self with interdependent and independent self results in four distinct types of individualism and collectivism:

- horizontal collectivism (e.g., found in Israeli kibbutz);
- horizontal individualism (e.g., Sweden, Denmark, Australia, New Zealand);
- vertical collectivism (e.g., traditional India, China, Japan, South Korea, Brazil);
- vertical individualism (e.g., France, US, UK).

The Role of Cultural Syndromes

Cultural syndromes are essential for developing insights into the appraisal and management of stressful work experiences in different countries. Perhaps the two most important cultural syndromes relevant for understanding the process of coping with work stress and seeking social support are individualism, collectivism, and cultural complexity. Individualists tend to pursue their own personal goals and objectives, and use rational and calculated exchanges with supervisors, co-workers, and other significant members of their work group and organizations. This is especially true of vertical individualists. Collectivists, on the other hand, are largely motivated by the expectations and norms of their in-groups and are more likely to abandon their personal goals and objectives in favor of collective goals—which often include members of their work groups and organizations. Members of societies which emphasize the value of institutional collectivism (e.g., Japan) are likely to experience less stress when confronted with various destabilizing influences in the workplace due to advances in globalization and related multinational activities. Vertical individualists are likely to be comfortable with those advances that are congruent with their personal goals and objectives.

Coping refers to cognitive and behavioral efforts that one employs in order to manage internal and external demands in a stressful situation. The stress can be ongoing or episodic. Globalization results in ongoing stress because of the long work hours, whereas an episodic event is concerned with the temporary increases in work pressures due to increased competition. We suggest that coping with such stressful experiences tends to be different for individualists and collectivists. Collectivists are likely to sample pertinent information relevant to coping from members of their in-groups and families. Individualists, on the other hand, are more likely to appraise, manage, and cope with stressful experiences at work (and in non-work situations as well) based largely on their personal experiences and resources. This is not to say that individualists do not seek appropriate counsel and guidance from members of their work groups, family, and so on, but that they prefer relying on their own resources before engaging the assistance of their social support network.

Coping can be classified in various ways. *Problem-focused* coping involves activities that are primarily directed at changing the stressful situation, whereas *emotion-focused* coping involves activities that are primarily directed at ameliorating negative emotions caused by psychological strain and distress (Lazarus & Folkman, 1984; Folkman & Moskowitz, 2004). Coping is a dynamic process that involves transactions between individuals and their stressful environment. Assessment of coping necessarily involves asking individuals to indicate the extent to which they use either problem-focused, emotion-focused, or a combination of these strategies.

It is important for people in multinational and global organizations to understand the fundamental issues that underlie the work stress and coping-related processes. Culture affects the experience of work stress and coping effectiveness in four ways. First, the cultural contexts (e.g., national, ethnic, racial, occupational, organizational) have a major role in shaping the types of stresses that an individual or work group is likely to experience. As discussed earlier, a person is exposed to several types of cultural influence, all acting simultaneously. Influences from one's national culture, coupled with the culture of the work organization, the ethnic or racial culture to which one belongs, and the culture of the occupation to which one belongs are important to consider. Second, cultural influences strongly affect the appraisal of the stressfulness of a given event. Third, cultures play a large role in the choice of coping strategies that an individual may utilize. Fourth, cultural contexts also provide different institutional mechanisms that are likely to be present in both the organizational and national contexts. In Figure 7.2, we present a model based on the socio-cultural model of stress, coping, and adaptation (Aldwin, 2007). This model shows that cultural beliefs and values, in conjunction with religion-specific practices and rituals, not only influence the nature of beliefs and values that the individual holds but also the reactions of significant others (i.e., co-workers, supervisors, family) in the situation. Appraisal of stress and the experience of psychological strain are a function of individual beliefs, cultural beliefs, the specific nature of work stress, and the relevant cultural demands and resources. Appraisal is also a function of the reactions of significant others and coping resources of the individual. The effectiveness of coping is affected by four factors: appraisal

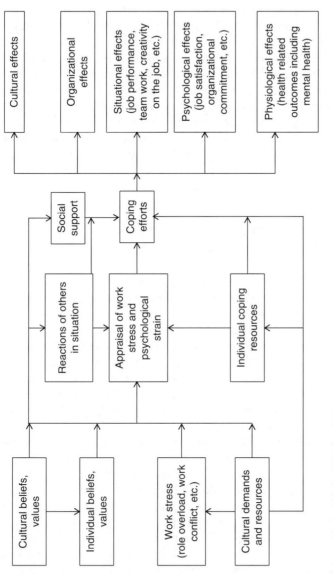

Source: Adapted from Aldwin (2007), p. 247.

Figure 7.2   A theoretical model of work stress, coping, and adaptation applicable to both Western and non-Western contexts

of the stressful situation, the person's coping style and resources, insights and resources provided by the culture including social support, and the reactions of significant others (Aldwin, 2007).

Outcomes of coping (both effective and ineffective patterns of coping) have effects on important psychological, physiological, organizational, and cultural outcomes. For example, if members of a global organization are not able to cope with the stressful consequences of increased workloads, role conflicts, and new types of organizational structures and cultures due to increases in cross-border mergers and acquisitions, then the organization will be less effective. The cumulative effects of individuals coping with stressful experiences at various levels of the organization are important for multinational and global organizations to consider. When stressful experiences in the work context are not coped with effectively and result in loss of creativity and innovativeness, then the economic benefits of globalization are not likely to be realized.

IMPLICATIONS FOR MULTINATIONAL AND GLOBAL ORGANIZATIONS

Global competition has created a new type of organizational reality for work organizations in both developed and developing countries. There has been a significant increase in work and organizational stress experienced by employees of multinational and global organizations. Increased competition in the global marketplace results in individuals experiencing the risk of occupational obsolescence, job stress, and adverse health consequences. These are in addition to experiencing the organizational and human consequences of globalization discussed earlier. There is a need to deal with the ongoing pressure to perform at a higher rate and to innovate, resulting in work stresses of all kinds.

We have argued that distinctive national and cultural contexts provide unique types of demands as well as resources for both appraising and coping with these pressures. A socio-cultural model based on the work of Aldwin (2007) is advanced in order to delineate the role of cultural differences and cultural syndromes on the stress and coping process. It has been suggested that the efficacy of an individual's coping with work stress is largely dependent on the role of the cultural contexts in which he or she is immersed and their relevance in providing appropriate cues and guidance. Multinational and global organizations should attempt to provide culture-specific employee assistance programs and counseling in various subsidiaries. Bhagat, Steverson, & Segovis (2007) provide a detailed culture-specific analysis of the evolution and effectiveness of employee assistance programs in various regions of the world. Members of Western cultures are more comfortable with individual-specific therapy and counseling, whereas members from collectivistic cultures are more oriented toward seeking guidance from in-groups and religion-based practices and rituals. The point is that in our attempts to make employees of multinational and global organizations effective in dealing with the stressful consequences of work, it is imperative to examine the role of the contextual factors as discussed in this chapter.

REFERENCES

Aldwin, C.N. (2007). *Stress, coping, and development: An integrative perspective.* New York: Guilford Press.

Bhagat, R.S., Steverson, P.K., & Segovis, J.C. (2007). Cultural variations in employee assistance programs in an era of globalization. In D.L. Stone & E.F. Stone-Romero (Eds). *The influence of culture on human resource management processes and practices* (pp. 207–33). New York: LEA Press.

Bhagat, R.S., McDevitt, A.M., & Segovis, J.C. (2011). Immigration as an adaptive challenge: Implications for lifelong learning. In M. London (Ed.). *Oxford handbook of lifelong learning* (pp. 402–21). Oxford: Oxford University Press.

Bhagat, R.S., Segovis, J.C., & Nelson, T.A. (2012). *Work stress and coping in the era of globalization.* New York: Routledge.

Bhawuk, D.P.S. (2001). Cross-cultural training: A review. *Applied Psychology*, 49, 162–91.

Blumenthal, D. (1979). At work they are at home. *New York Times*, 15 July.

Bontempo, R. & Rivero, J.C. (1992). Cultural variation in cognition: The role of self-concept in the attitude–behavior link. Paper presented at the meeting of the American Academy of Management, Las Vegas, NV, July.

Brooks, D. (2011). *The social animal.* New York: Random House.

Burke, C.S., Priest, H.A., Upshaw, C.L., Salas, E., & Pierce, L. (2008). A sense-making approach to understanding multicultural teams: An initial framework. In D.L. Stone & E.F. Stone-Romero (Eds). *The influence of culture on human resource management processes and practices* (pp. 269–306). New York: Taylor & Francis.

Cappelli, P. (1999). *Employment practices and business strategies.* New York: Oxford University Press.

Cooper, C.L. (1998). *Theories of organizational stress.* New York: Oxford University Press.

Davenport, T.H. & Lawrence Prusak, L. (1998). *Working knowledge: How organizations manage what they know.* Cambridge, MA: Harvard Business School Press.

Davidson, A.R., Jaccard, J.J., Triandis, H.C., Morales, M.L., & Diaz-Guerrero, R. (1976). Cross-cultural model testing: Toward a solution of the etic–emic dilemma. *International Journal of Psychology*, 11, 1–13.

Diaz-Guerrero, R. (1967). *Psychology of the Mexican culture and personality.* Austin, TX: University of Texas Press.

Ferris, G.R., Davidson, S.L., & Perrewe, P.L. (2005). *Political skill at work: Impact on work effectiveness.* Mountain View, CA: Davies-Black Publishing.

Florida, R. (2005). *The rise of the creative class.* New York: Basic Books.

Folkman, S. & Moskowitz, J.T. (2004). Coping: Pitfalls and promises. *Annual Review of Psychology,* 55, 745–74.

Gilmore, T. & Hirshhorn, L. (1983). Management challenges under conditions of retrenchment. *Human Resource Management,* 22, 341–57.

Grantham, C. (2002). *The future of work: The promise of the new digital work society.* New York: McGraw-Hill.

Hamel, G. (1999). Strategy as revolution. *Harvard Business Review,* 74, 69–82.

Harrison, L. (2006). *The central liberal truth.* Oxford: Oxford University Press.

Heckscher, C. (1995). *White collar blues: Management loyalties in an age of corporate restructuring.* New York: Basic Books.

Hofacker, D. (2010). *Older workers in a globalizing world.* Cheltenham, UK: Edward Elgar.

Hofstede, G. (1980). *Culture's consequences: International differences in work-related values.* Beverly Hills, CA: Sage.

Hofstede, G. (2001). *Culture's consequences.* Thousand Oaks, CA: Sage.

Huntington, S. (2004). *The clash of civilization and the remaking of world order.* New York: Simon and Schuster.

Iwao, S. (1993). *The Japanese woman: Traditional image and changing reality.* New York: Free Press.

Keltner, D. (2009). *Born to be good: The science of a meaningful life.* New York: W.W. Norton & Co.

Kitayama, S., Markus, H., & Lieberman, C. (1995). The collective construction of self-esteem. In J.A. Russell (Ed.). *Everyday conceptions of emotion* (pp. 523–50). Dordrecht: Kluwer Academic Publishers.

Kitayama, S., Markus, H., & Matsumoto, H. (1995). Individual and collective processes in the construction of self: Self-enhancement in the United States and self-criticism in Japan. *Journal of Personality and Social Psychology,* 72(6), 1245–67.

Kitayama, S., Duffy, S., & Uchida, Y. (2007). Self as cultural mode of being. In S. Kitayama & D. Cohen (Eds). *Handbook of cultural psychology* (pp. 136–74). New York: Guilford Press.

Korman, A. & Korman, R. (1980). *Career success, personal failure.* Englewood Cliffs, NJ: Prentice-Hall.

Lazarus, R.S. & Folkman, S. (1984). *Stress, appraisal, and coping.* New York: Springer Publishing.

Levine, C.H. (Ed.) (1980). *Managing fiscal stress: The crisis in the public sector.* Chatham, NJ: Chatham House Publishing, Inc.

Markus, H., & Kitayama, S. (1991). Culture and the self: Implications for cognition, emotion, and motivation. *Psychological Review,* 98, 224–53.

Miller, J.G. (1994). Cultural diversity in the morality of caring: Individually-oriented versus duty-oriented interpersonal codes. *Cross-Cultural Research,* 28, 3–39.

Pitt-Catsouphes, M., Kossek, E., & Sweet, W. (2006). *The work and family handbook: Multi-disciplinary perspective, methods, and approaches.* New York: Lawrence Erbaum.

Quick, J.C., Cooper, C.L., Nelson, D.L., Quick, J.D., & Gavin, J.H. (2003). Stress, health, and well-being at work. In J. Greenberg (Ed.). *Organizational behavior: The state of the science* (2nd edn). Mahwah, NJ: Lawrence Erbaum Associates.

Reykowski, J. (1994). Collectivism and individualism as dimension of social change. In U.Kim, H.C. Triandis, C. Kagitcibasi, S.-C. Choi, & G. Yoon (Eds). *Individualism and collectivism: Theory, method and application* (pp. 276–92). Newbury Park, NJ: Sage.

Robert Half International (1991). *A survey of executives' greatest anxieties.* New York: Robert Half International.

Rousseau, D.M. (1995). *Psychological contracts in organizations: Understanding written and unwritten agreements.* Thousand Oaks, CA: Sage.

Schor, J. (1992). *The overworked American: The unexpected decline of leisure.* New York: Basic Books.

Schwartz, S.H. (1992). Universals in the structure and content of value: Theoretical advances and empirical tests in 20 countries. In M.P. Zanna (Ed.). *Advances in experimental social psychology* (vol. 25, pp. 1–65). Orlando, FL: Academic Press.

Schwartz, S.H. (1994). Beyond individualism and collectivism: New cultural dimensions of values. In U. Kim, H.C. Triandis, C. Kagitcibasi, S.-C. Choi, & G. Yoon (Eds). *Individualism and collectivism: Theory and method and applications* (pp. 85–119). Newbury Park, NJ: Sage.

Shirom, A. (2011). Job-related burnout: A review of the major research foci and challenges. In J.C. Quick & L.E. Tetrick (Eds). *Handbook of occupational health psychology* (pp. 245–65). Washington, DC: American Psychological Association.

Smith, M.J. & Carayon, P. (2011). Controlling occupational safety and health hazards. In J.C. Quick & L. Tetrick (Eds). *Handbook of occupational health psychology.* Washington, DC: American Psychological Association.

Stanko, T.L. & Gibson, C.B. (2009). The role of cultural elements in virtual teams. In R.S. Bhagat & R.M. Steers (Eds). *Cambridge handbook of culture, organizations, and work* (pp. 272–304). Cambridge: Cambridge University Press.

Triandis, H.C. (1994). *Culture and social behavior.* New York: McGraw-Hill.

Triandis, H.C. (1995). *Individualism and collectivism.* Boulder, CO: Westview Press.

Triandis, H.C. (1996). The psychological measurement of cultural syndrome. *American Psychologist,* 51, 407–15.

Triandis, H.C. (1998). Vertical and horizontal individualism and collectivism: Theory and research implication for international comparative management. *Advances in International Comparative Management,* 12, 7–35.

Wolf, M. (2004). *Why globalization works.* New Haven, CT: Yale University Press.

Worldwatch Institute (2004). *Annual report.* Washington, DC, p. 9. Available at: http://www.worldwatch.org/taxonomy/term/34.

8. Cultural variations in group processes and work teams

Work groups are vital to organizations—whether they function in the monocultural or multicultural context. Various types of groups are created for accomplishing different goals and objectives of the organization and at different levels. They are called *task groups*, *teams*, and *special purpose groups*. Groups are necessary because contributions from individual members are more than the sum total of each individual contributing toward the group goal in his or her unique way. When people work together to perform a task and accomplish an important organizational objective, cultural differences between them become more salient. The reality of managing work teams (especially virtual teams) that are composed of culturally dissimilar members who are located in geographically distant locales (i.e., subsidiaries of large global corporations like General Motors, Toyota, Microsoft, General Electric, and Siemens) poses significant challenges.

As we have noted in earlier chapters, globalization makes geographic boundaries unimportant in international business transactions, and managers increasingly find themselves managing virtual work groups and multicultural teams that function with minimal to no face-to-face interactions. In this chapter we take a closer look at the cultural issues involved in the functioning of work groups and teams in the context of multinational and global organizations of the 21st century.

WORK GROUPS

Humans are social animals, and they join groups for various reasons. Members of a marketing research team in a global company such as Federal Express Corporation contribute to the organizational goals in a formal sense, whereas members of a local bridge club may gather on a weekly basis to enhance the quality of social interactions. "Group" is defined as a collection of three or more individuals who engage in ongoing interactions in the context of a stable pattern of relationships in order to accomplish a goal or a mission. Goals may be assigned by supervisors of the groups or may be generated by the group itself as it engages in accomplishing the formal objectives. Members of work groups must perceive themselves as belonging to a group. It is also essential that other members of the organization who work with the group perceive the collection as a group having stable patterns of ongoing interaction. In order to understand the functioning of groups—whether in monocultural or multicultural contexts—it is necessary that we understand the following four properties (Greenberg & Baron, 2008).

1. *Common goals and objectives.*   The most important characteristic of groups is that the members share common interests or goals. There has to be a reasonable degree of convergence or overlap of beliefs, values, and practices regarding how the group members interact in the process of accomplishing the assigned and generated goals. If a large number of individuals are either not aware of or do not share the objectives of the group, then the group will not function effectively and may cease to exist.

2. *Stability.*   Work groups must have a stable structure. Composition of groups can change over time and it often does as a result of long-term members leaving the group due to transfer, other assignments, or retirement. However, there must be a pattern of stable relationships that keeps the group members communicating with each other in a systemic fashion so that functioning as a social unit is possible. To be considered a work group, a greater level of stability is necessary.

3. *Social interaction.*   One of the most important characteristics of groups is that they are composed of three or more people in social interaction. In other words, members of groups are influenced by each other—the collective problem-solving and decision-making abilities of a group determine the quality of group processes and effectiveness. Methods for sustaining social interaction can be both non-verbal (such as exchanging pleasant gestures to convey good feelings to a co-worker) and verbal (such as discussing strategies for designing a better marketing plan). Members of geographically dispersed teams do not have the opportunity for face-to-face interaction including the exchange of verbal and non-verbal messages. However, the members of such teams must also believe that there is a pattern of social interaction that connects the members in meaningful ways for teams to be effective.

4. *Recognition of being a group.*   To be recognized as a work group, the individuals involved must perceive themselves as belonging to a group. The existence of formal organizational structure facilitates the creation of groups throughout the entire organization, but some

members of groups more than others strongly identify themselves with the objectives and day-to-day function of the group. The more strongly members of a group identify themselves as belonging to a group, the more cohesive the group becomes.

ATTRIBUTES OF TASK-DRIVEN GROUPS

There has been a significant growth of new forms of groups in work organizations and particularly in work organizations that function across borders and cultures. Some of these groups may have only partial-to-moderate resemblance to those that have historically been studied in small group research conducted in the 1960s and 1970s. Due to some of these recent developments, including the proliferation of groups of different types located in geographically dispersed areas, it becomes difficult to generalize from past research on small group behavior to the current type of groups that exist in a globalized environment. Four attributes should be used to distinguish among different types of groups (see Table 8.1):

1. The degree to which the responsibility of accomplishing the group tasks lies primarily with the group as a whole versus with individual members.
2. The degree to which members interact synchronously in real time versus asynchronously at their own discretion.
3. The level of authority groups have to manage their own processes.
4. The nature of work that the group is performing or assigned.

The first two attributes, taken together, lead to the development of four distinct types of task-driven groups. Work groups that function in a face-to-face fashion (identified in the upper right quadrant of the table) are what people have in mind when they talk about groups and teams in

Table 8.1   Four types of groups

	Responsibility for achieving group purposes	
	Individual members	Group as a whole
Levels of synchronicity		
Real time interactions	"Surgical" teams	Face-to-face groups
Asynchronous interactions	Co-acting groups	Virtual teams

Source: Adapted From Hackman & Wageman (2005), p. 40.

the context of work organizations. There is much research literature on group behavior and performance about these groups, including the role of cultural variations. Members of such groups are co-located and work interdependently in real time to accomplish organizational tasks for which they are collectively responsible. These groups require coordinated contributions in real time from a variety of members who have complementary expertise, experience, and perspectives (Mathieu et al., 2000). In the lower right quadrant of the table are virtual teams, sometimes called geographically distributed or dispersed work groups. Members of virtual teams share responsibility and accountability for accomplishing the collective goals that are entrusted with them but are not necessarily co-located and do not necessarily interact with one another in synchronous and real time. Rapid and recent innovation in information and communication technologies make it possible for multinational and global organizations to create virtual teams whose members are able to interact with other members of the team in an exclusive fashion using electronic means and to their own schedules, that is, asynchronously. Virtual teams of multinational and global organizations of the 21st century are larger, more diverse, and collectively more knowledgeable than those whose members interact face to face.

When virtual teams are designed well, they are able to assimilate widely dispersed information, data, and knowledge to improve the quality of the group product, that is, the effectiveness of the group. Virtual teams are most frequently used when interdependent work is necessary, but it would be difficult, if not impossible, to bring together all the members of the team to perform the activity in a face-to-face context. Development of a new pharmaceutical product by select members of R & D laboratories of large global firms such as Pfizer, Inc. and Merck requires that members combine their collective insights from different locales of the organization and in an asynchronous fashion.

Groups in the upper left quadrant are what have been called *surgical teams* (Brooks, 1995). These groups function by entrusting responsibility and accountability for achieving the outcomes to one person (called the surgeon), but accomplishing that work requires coordinated interaction among all members in real time, and that he or she has all the necessary information and assistance that members can provide. Teams that develop complex software tend to function like surgical teams with members working together closely, but one individual, that is, the lead programmer, has the primary responsibility for the quality of the output. These kinds of teams have emerged in recent years where the expertise of an individual with advanced skills and insights is required, along with the complementary assistance of other team members.

Groups in the lower left quadrant are known as *co-acting groups*, and the performance of these groups is determined by collective contributions of the individual members. Any given member's work does not necessarily depend on what others do—it is simply an aggregate of the individual members' contributions. A great deal of work of multinational and global organizations is performed by groups of people who are called members of work teams but are actually members of co-acting groups. Co-acting groups do not generate synergistic products, but they can benefit from social interactions with others. The members often work in parallel and observe others performing some well-learned tasks from which they can benefit.

LEVEL OF AUTHORITY

Four types of basic functions must be performed when a group engages in accomplishing its goals and objectives. First, groups must choose to engage either completely or partially in accomplishing the tasks that are assigned. Secondly, the group must engage in a series of interactions to facilitate the process of executing the formal tasks. Thirdly, groups must monitor and manage work processes, collecting and interpreting data about how the group is operating, and then making necessary corrections. Fourthly, groups have to design mechanisms for securing necessary support and resources for executing the tasks that are assigned. The amount of authority that groups have in fulfilling these four functions varies. The decision-making latitude of some work groups is highly restricted—that is, delegated primarily from the management—whereas other groups may have autonomy in controlling all aspects of the four processes just mentioned.

WORK GROUP EFFECTIVENESS

A fundamental reason for studying the basic processes underlying the functioning of groups is to give better insights into group effectiveness, that is, how well the group uses its resources to accomplish its assigned tasks or mission. Not all groups located at various organizational levels have clearly assigned tasks or have developed correct strategies for accomplishing their objectives. The long-term effectiveness of a work group or team, such as a virtual team, cannot be adequately assessed by considering its effectiveness at any given point in time. A broader perspective of work group effectiveness is necessary in the context of today's highly interdependent and culturally diverse work environment. Three essential aspects of group effectiveness focus on the following:

- First, the output of the group must meet or exceed the standards of quantity and quality as expected by the organization. In addition, the group output should be available on time and as prescribed in accordance with organizational routines.
- Secondly, the processes engaged in by the group should contribute to both task-relevant and interpersonal abilities and skills of members.
- Thirdly, the experience of belonging to a group should contribute to the personal growth and professional well-being of the members so that they can become more effective members of the organization.

This definition (Hackman, 1990) suggests that group effectiveness is best understood by adopting a long-term view. Sometimes work groups are created quickly without adequate consideration being given to the composition of the group or the kinds of resources that it needs for its effective functioning, and the experience of difficulties on the part of work groups during the early stages of their functioning may not necessarily be due to any faulty processes adopted by the group. Many groups fail due to inadequate planning during the early stages of group formation.

A model that helps explain the role of six sets of variables in determining the group process and effectiveness is depicted in Figure 8.1. These variables are:

1. The nature of the task that the group has been assigned or has chosen to perform.
2. The external context of the group, that is, the nature of immediate work and social environment that have direct relevance for functioning of the group.
3. Resources of the group, including occupational skills and abilities of the members.
4. The nature of the group structure, that is, the nature of authority invested in the group (e.g., face-to-face versus virtual groups).
5. The group process—mechanisms (i.e., communication patterns, decision processes, and conflict resolution techniques) for focusing group effort in the accomplishment of the task.
6. Composition of the group in terms of diversity of skills and cultural background of the members.

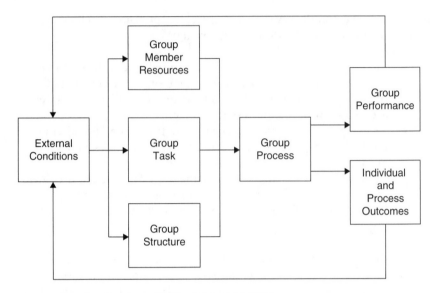

Source: Based on Goodman, Ravlin, & Schminke (1987).

Figure 8.1 Group Process Model

The role of cultural variations is better understood in the context of the model, which includes cultural composition of the members as it relates to the other factors. The roles of the six sets of variables that affect group process and performance are discussed as follows:

External Context

Groups do not function in isolation, that is, they are very much embedded in the social fabric of the work organization (Campion, Medskar, & Higgs, 1993). If an organization has had leadership orientation that is largely authoritarian, the leaders of the various groups are likely to reflect a similar style in their process of managing. The strategy of the organization and the various rules and regulations to implement the strategy are all important contextual factors that are relevant for functioning of work groups, teams, and virtual teams in multinational and global organizations. Successful multinational corporations are able to provide adequate resources for the various types of groups that they might create in the accomplishment of their goals. In addition, virtual teams of such organizations are likely to become composed of members who are highly skilled and motivated to accomplish the necessary tasks.

The ability to facilitate asynchronous interaction among geographically dispersed members of virtual teams is generally much better in multinationals which already possess or have developed a body of knowledge in this area.

Member Resources

Members of groups bring two distinct types of resources as they perform the assigned tasks and duties: personal attributes—including their cognitive style, beliefs, attitudes, and values—and their job-relevant abilities and skills. Both technical and social skills are necessary in the execution of group tasks in all multinational and global organizations. Highly skilled members of all types of teams as presented in Table 8.1 make significant contributions to group performance. Culture-specific beliefs and values of group members affect the quality and quantity of group performance as well.

Group Structure

Depending on the nature of tasks that the groups perform, they can be classified as task forces, teams, or crews (such as the members of a flight team in a commercial airline). As discussed earlier, different structures have a different set of expectations from the members, not only in terms of valuable skills and ability, but also in terms of the kind of norms, expectations, and status relationships that they must adhere to. Group norms are crucial in the functioning of groups; they specify the nature of procedures that the members must follow and the level of effort that each member contributes to the group task. There are many determinants of group norms. The most important among them is the nature of prior experiences of the members—either in the context of the same group or groups of a similar nature in a different organization. Critical incidents in the development of the group and the type of early patterns of behavior that emerge and are important. Cultural variations regarding beliefs about how groups may initiate performance strategies relevant to a group task are also important. Differentiation among the various roles should also fit the nature of the tasks that the group is performing—the type of roles that a face-to-face group might be comfortable with may be quite unsuitable for a virtual team entrusted with the responsibility for a new product or a selected segment of the global market. Role ambiguities and role conflicts created due to insufficient attention being paid to the design of work groups can have adverse effects on group effectiveness.

Group Processes

As mentioned earlier, group processes are concerned with how groups go about achieving their goals and objectives. They involve such processes as focusing collective efforts of the group on the performance of the task by breaking it into manageable segments, facilitating the nature of social exchanges during the various phases of group functioning, and enhancing the positive effects of group structure on members. A group may be said to work effectively if the processes adopted and developed by the members contribute to the effectiveness of each member such that the group product is enhanced and clearly better than the sum of the individual members' contributions. Group-related processes such as establishing a network of communication among the members, developing a method of making decisions, and resolving conflicts are essential for groups in order to enhance their effectiveness. A loss of time, resources, and energy on the part of the members creates what is known as a *process loss*. When the collective effort of a group exceeds the contribution of even the most valued or skilled member, a *process gain* is said to occur. Groups with members with distinctive cultural orientations and strong personal beliefs and values may either facilitate or hinder this phenomenon. When cultural variations create conflicts among members, a process loss is likely to result. It might take more time to resolve the underlying cultural issues before normal group activities and processes can operate.

A phenomenon called *group-think* occurs when the consensus of the group endorses a chosen course of action by ignoring cues and information which suggest a different course of action generated by minority members. It can be quite detrimental for the functioning of groups—especially in the context of multinational and global organizations. Group-think may be easily prevented in groups with members with dissimilar values and orientations. Another phenomenon called *social loafing* also leads to impairment of group effectiveness. Social loafing happens when members choose to reduce their personal efforts on group tasks in situations when they are aware that performance will be measured on a group basis and they will remain anonymous. Earley (1989) found that there is significant cultural difference between Chinese workers (largely collectivistic) and US workers (largely individualistic). Chinese workers performed best when told that their performances would be measured in groups of ten and that their contributions would be assessed on a collective basis. In contrast, the American workers performed best when they were made aware that their performances would be measured individually. In addition, American workers performed poorly when working on a group task, knowing that their performances would be anonymous, that is, that they would not get credit or rewards for superior performance on an individual basis. These kinds of process losses cause significant impairments in the effectiveness of virtual teams. Without the benefit of face-to-face interactions where contributions of a member may be assessed by the group, the asynchronous nature of coordination of the members who may be located in different countries causes social loafing and group-think to emerge.

Group Task

The nature of task which the work group performs strongly influences the process underlying their interactions and the group effectiveness. The nature of task that the group is assigned to perform or chooses to perform determines the nature of group process to a large extent. The kind of group processes that are required in the execution of a clearly defined production task is different in terms of the group processes that are initiated compared with tasks that require collective cognitive inputs from the members of the work group. Performance on production tasks requires motor skills, and performance on these types of tasks may be easily measured. In contrast, performance on problem-solving and complex decision-making tasks (such as the launch of an innovative customer service plan on a global scale) is difficult to measure, at least in the initial stages. It is important to distinguish among the five distinct types of tasks that groups perform in the context of work organization.

1. *Disjunctive tasks.* The performance of the group in these kinds of tasks is a direct function of the performance of its most skilled or talented member. For example, the effectiveness of international business negotiations is determined by the skills and experience of the lead negotiator. The absence of the lead negotiator may significantly hinder the outcome of an international negotiation.
2. *Conjunctive tasks.* In these groups, the performance of the least competent member determines the effectiveness of the group.
3. *Additive tasks.* In these groups, the group performance is the sum of the members' contributions. For example, the successful development of a pharmaceutical product in a global firm is a function of the sum total of the contributions made by the members of an R & D group who may be located in different countries.
4. *Compensatory tasks.* Similar to additive tasks, the performance of groups working on compensatory tasks is a function of each member's contribution. The expectation is that individual errors are compensated for by others' performance in the right direction.

5. *Complementary tasks.* Groups divide these tasks into sub-tasks that are assigned to members with complementary skills. For example, a global R & D team in charge of developing a new product or service by integrating dissimilar but valuable ideas from members in different subsidiaries is performing a complementary task. A not-so-good idea may be replaced by a superior contribution by another member, resulting in an optimal level of performance.

It is important to note that some of these tasks are likely to be characterized by a high degree of process losses due to dysfunctional behaviors such as group-think, social loafing, and inflexible work styles on the part of some members due to cultural biases or other factors. Unless these issues are resolved, it is difficult to expect these groups to perform effectively on an ongoing basis.

Group Composition

The composition of the members is crucial as groups are formed with the objective of performing complex tasks. Members of work groups may be similar or different on a number of demographic factors (e.g., gender, age, education, experience, nationality). Such differences do not make large differences in the performance of group tasks that are routine and simple, that is, production tasks and other tasks performed at lower levels of the organization. However, as multinational and global organizations begin to form groups and teams to solve complex issues, it becomes necessary to examine the dynamics of group composition in terms of its effectiveness on group process and structure. Gone are the days when homogenous teams were found at higher levels of the hierarchy. In today's multinational organizations, heterogenous and multicultural work groups and teams are commonplace. In multicultural teams, members represent three or more ethnic and cultural backgrounds. An increasing number of organizational task forces are members of globally distributed teams who differ on a number of important dimensions, including language, race, religion, occupation, and lifestyle. It is naively assumed that these differences do not matter much in the way the group will engage in problem-solving and decision-making. However, research (Stanko & Gibson, 2009) shows that multicultural groups, while being productive on complex tasks, have their unique problems.

Cultural diversity makes functioning of international work teams more challenging because the team members may find it more difficult to appreciate and act in a fashion that is consonant with culturally dissimilar members. Misperception (including strong tendencies to stereotype culturally dissimilar members), miscommunication, and inappropriate evaluation of contributions of others occur. In a later section, we discuss the advantages and disadvantages of employing multicultural teams in the context of global organizations. However, it is important to note that group heterogeneity on task-related abilities and skills has positive effects on group tasks that are additive, compensatory, and complementary. However, group heterogeneity in terms of skills, tenure in the organization, and ethnic composition may be responsible for creating process losses, resulting in reduced effectiveness.

Cultural Variations in Work Groups and Teams

Cultural variations are reflected in terms of the composition of the group members. A group composed of a large number of culturally dissimilar members is likely to be influenced by a variety of cultural perspectives compared with a group which is homogenous. However, the nature of the group task, group structure, and the cultural context of the work organization (i.e., employee-centered versus task-centered) are also important in this regard. Cultural variations influence the following processes:

1. *The nature of group norms.* Norms are ideas about correct and appropriate behavior for members of a group. Norms about punctuality, type of contribution expected from members located in dissimilar geographical locales of the multinational corporation, and so on are important. Such norms may be influenced by specific orientations of the cultures of the members. A group composed of only Japanese managers may develop working norms from which a member may not easily deviate. In contrast, a work team of a global company in New York City composed of culturally dissimilar members may have norms from which one may deviate without sanction.

2. *Preference for rewards for group performance.* As a general rule, members of collectivistic cultures are more comfortable in accepting rewards based on the *principle of equality*, that is, each member gets the same reward regardless of his or her contribution. Individualists are uncomfortable with the idea that a member who does not contribute as much as others gets the same level of reward. The *principle of equity* is a much stronger norm governing the preference of individualists for group performance. Cultures with belief systems saying, "God wants everyone to have the same" emphasize an equality norm which stands in stark contrast to the equity norm. Conflicts among group members may emerge due to differences in the preferences for how rewards ought to be distributed for group performance.

3. *Unique preferences in the methods of working.* Cultural variations play a strong role in the preference for styles and methods of working. Members of some cultures may not choose to work on religious and other national holidays, causing slowdown in the process of coordinating contributions that are necessary for completing the assigned group task. This issue can influence effectiveness of virtual global teams. Not all members of a virtual work team feel comfortable using computer-mediated communication in accomplishing a task that needs contributions from different subsidiaries of the corporation. As a general rule, collectivist members of a virtual work team may feel less comfortable with instructions via electronic media and related computer-mediated technologies. While these cultural differences are slowly disappearing, the fact remains that not all cultures react to technological advances that may be incorporated to coordinate group activities. Electronic technologies change the way group work is organized. Members of virtual work teams in this era of globalization need to understand the interplay of new ways of working and accomplishing group objectives.

4. *In-group/out-group distinction.* Individualists expect their work to be organized in such a way that it facilitates self-expression and also matching of personal interests (economic and others) with the employer's interests. The relationship between an employee and the organization is largely contractual in nature. Individualists are socialized to work with members who may not be a part of their in-groups, that is, family, community, and so on. In a collectivistic culture, an employer hires more than just an individual—the in-group to which an individual belongs is also given its due consideration. If an individual is hired into a group which may become his or her in-group at a later stage, then the contribution of that individual will be higher. The ability of collectivists to work in a harmonious fashion with the members of in-groups is well supported (Triandis, 1994). Confrontations that arise in the group as it settles on a suitable method of working are avoided by collectivists but not necessarily by the individualist. These differences can affect the performance of a work group composed of collectivists and individualists. Collectivists, in contrast to individualists, emphasize a particularly strict mode of thinking and acting while working in groups. Establishment of interpersonal trust is crucial before collectivists can be expected to perform their best in enhancing the effectiveness of the work group. In order to work with collectivist members of a work group, it is important to spend some time with them and get to know their personal preferences regarding work styles and so on. Since it is not feasible to take time to develop trusting relationships in the context of today's fast-paced society, it might be

the case that some collectivist members of an international work team may not be engaged to the extent necessary for sustaining high levels of effectiveness.

5. *Psychological contracts.* In addition to formal contracts specifying terms of economic rewards for working, psychological contracts are important, especially at the higher levels of organizations. Individuals work for today's multinational and global corporations not only for economic rewards but also for a number of intrinsic rewards that contribute to the quality of working lives. Cultures differ to the extent that psychological contract with the employing work organization is assumed. High levels of occupational obsolescence and the need to replace managers at all levels by new recruits are growing in all globalized countries. Psychological contracts which have been found to be valuable are being violated in many cases—particularly in organizations that are located in individualistic cultures such as the US, UK, and Australia. Collectivistic members of such organizations often feel disenchanted when their culture-specific psychological contracts are not recognized as being legitimate or worthy of rewards.

Cultural Diversity and Work Teams

Heterogeneity of members has both positive and negative effects on a team's functioning and productivity. Multiple perspectives from different members of the group enhance creativity by countering dysfunctional processes such as group-think, stereotyping, and rigid mindsets. Multicultural teams have the potential to achieve higher productivity than homogenous teams, but they also experience greater process losses that are associated with the difficulties of bringing multiple perspectives together. Cultural diversity makes functioning of work teams (face-to-face and virtual) more challenging because team members need to learn the value of divergent perspectives while acting in similar ways to enhance group effectiveness. Team members with similar cultural predispositions find it easier to communicate with one another and trust each other easily. In culturally diverse teams (especially in virtual work teams), issues of misperception, miscommunication, and faulty attributions arise. Trusting a member from a dissimilar culture in the context of group functioning takes time, and norms of reciprocity among members that can enhance group effectiveness are relatively more difficult to develop. Members of multicultural and heterogenous teams often tend to disagree on the nature of strategies for performing the group task and the expectations associated with the quality of performance. They experience higher levels of work stress compared with members of homogenous teams. Cohesiveness

Table 8.2 Diversity in multicultural teams: advantages and disadvantages

Advantages	Disadvantages

Diversity permits increased creativity
  Wider range of perspectives
  More and better ideas
  Less groupthink
	Diversity causes a lack of cohesion
	
	Mistrust
	  Lower interpersonal attractiveness
	  Inaccurate stereotyping
	  More within-culture conversations

Diversity forces enhanced
  concentration to understand others'
  Ideas
  Perspectives
  Meanings
  Arguments
	Miscommunication
	  Slower speech: non-native speakers
	    and translation problems
	  Less accuracy
	
	Stress
	  More counterproductive behavior
	  Less disagreement on content
	  Tension

Increased creativity can lead to
  generating
  Better problem definitions
  More alternatives
  Better solutions
  Better decisions
	Lack of cohesion causes an inability to
	  Validate ideas and people
	  Agree when agreement is needed
	  Gain consensus on decisions
	  Take concerted action

Teams can become
  More effective
  More productive
	Teams can become
	  Less efficient
	  Less effective
	  Less productive

Source: Adler (2008), p. 135.

tends to be low in heterogenous groups. While this is not a major factor in affecting performance in complex work teams that are geographically dispersed, it can affect group productivity in co-acting, face-to-face, and surgical teams. Advantages and disadvantages of cultural diversity in the functioning of multicultural teams are presented in Table 8.2.

A group can affect the level of psychological arousal experienced by members. The mere presence of other group members can either enhance arousal, leading to higher efforts toward individual contributions of the group task, or lower it. The nature of the group task is the major determinant of how group-originated signals and messages can affect arousal and productivity. Arousal created in the group context generally facilitates the *dominant task-related responses* of the individual. Performance on well-learned tasks is typically facilitated by dominant task responses. On the other hand, performance on unfamiliar (complex or learning) tasks is affected adversely by dominant response. As a general rule, when a group becomes increasingly evaluative and threatening, performance of members on complex tasks decreases, but performance on well-learned tasks may not necessarily suffer. When experience of working in the group context is perceived as being supportive, comforting, and almost unconditionally accepting, effectiveness should increase for complex (i.e., learning) tasks. Individuals in organizations are known to use their group memberships as a means of achieving comfortable levels of arousal in order to sustain daily pressures for productivity and managing stress. Individuals in high-pressure managerial jobs, for example, often find the need to gather as a group (i.e., with few associates) who can and do provide comfort and acceptance, especially when confronted with difficult problem-solving and decision-making situations.

Virtual Work Teams

Functioning of virtual work teams and especially their effectiveness is of growing interest in multinational and global organizations. Virtual work teams are defined as a group of individuals with complementary skills in locations that are geographically dispersed from central offices or production facilities of the organization. The members have no personal contact with each other and must carry on the process of communication, decision-making, and problem-solving by extensive use of computer-mediated communication (Stanko & Gibson, 2009). Virtual teams in the context of multinational and global organizations are those that cut across national, functional, or organizational boundaries and are connected by a complex web of information technologies. The nature of interaction and the effectiveness of the virtual work team are largely a function of the following three factors:

1. Synchronicity of the team members' interaction (i.e., the ability to bring widely dispersed information and expertise to the team's attention in a coordinated fashion).
2. The extent to which members are comfortable with using complex information technologies.
3. The amount of task-related information and knowledge that these technologies make available for each of the members to enhance their contribution to the performance of the group product.

As discussed earlier, virtual teams are most frequently used when interdependent work is required but—due to the nature of organizational arrangements (i.e., networks) across dissimilar nations and cultures—it is impossible for team members to perform on the task face to face. There is not a great deal of research on the role of arousal in enhancing performance on tasks that virtual teams are assigned or undertake. What is clear is that achieving the group's purpose requires coordinated contributions from members in a complementary and coordinated fashion so that synchronicity is maintained (Stewart & Barrick, 2000; Mathieu et al., 2000). Global virtual work teams have been conceptualized as being composed of members who function in a technology-mediated, globally distributed, and culturally diverse environment (Hardin, Fuller, & Davison, 2007). In a survey of 243 members of universities in the US and Hong Kong, during which the members participated in a series of virtual team projects, Hardin et al. found that, regardless of cultural background, members tended to report less confidence in their ability to work in virtual team environments compared with traditional face-to-face work teams. However, the role of cultural differences became more salient in examining the role of self-efficacy in the performance of group tasks. Team members from the US universities tended to report higher levels of efficacy, both at the individual and group levels, in the performance of the task, which was not the case with members from Hong Kong universities.

The cultural composition of a virtual work team is a significant predictor of its performance on high-technology projects such as programming tasks (Swigger et al., 2004; Stanko & Gibson, 2009). Cultural beliefs and attitudes about organizational hierarchy, the nature of harmony present in the organizational culture, and beliefs about how much influence one has over one's work environment are strongly correlated with group performance. Team members who have stronger beliefs regarding the importance of hierarchy, that is, power distance-related cultural values, perform poorly in terms of their contribution to group effectiveness compared with those who do not have such beliefs. Stanko & Gibson (2009) provide a detailed review of the role of cultural differences in the functioning and effectiveness of virtual work teams.

Individualism–Collectivism and Work Groups

Collectivists are socialized to view themselves by using groups as appropriate units of analysis or a social lens; individualists use individuals and socially significant others for this purpose. The definition and function of self in collectivistic cultures is rooted in the groups (i.e., primary, secondary, occupational) to which one belongs. Collectivists are much more comfortable in functioning in the context of work groups and do not become terribly concerned if their individual contributions are not appropriately rewarded. Their selves are rooted in viewing the collective well-being of the group as taking precedence over their own well-being. They view their relationship with the group as an organic one as opposed to a contractual one; that is, they expect to contribute meaningfully to the group process and tasks on an ongoing basis and in a complementary fashion.

Given the above predisposition, collectivists function better in the context of work groups, are comfortable with norms of equality in the expectation and distribution of rewards, and are comfortable in developing harmonious relationships with other group members, especially if they are culturally similar (i.e., are members of an in-group). Individualists, in contrast, may function better while working alone than in groups. Hackman (1990) identified characteristics of groups in US cultures that do and do not work harmoniously. Individualists are more comfortable with principles of equity in the expectation and distribution of organizational rewards, expect and manage conflicts within the group, and do not have their identities embedded in the group.

Collectivists like to pursue those goals that are compatible with the goals of the in-groups. When the in-groups of collectivists largely overlap with their work groups, then higher levels of contributions are expected. If there is a discrepancy between personal goals and the goals of the in-groups, chances are that collectivists will abandon the individual goals in favor of group goals. Individualists use accomplishment of individual goals as one of the primary goals of their lives. In cases of discrepancy between individual goals and the goals of the work group, individualists are likely to pursue their own goals unless there are major sanctions against such tendencies. It is safe to say that individualists who have achieved a great deal of recognition in the work context for their past contributions may choose to deviate from the expected patterns of behavior in a group context. The nature of the group tasks determines whether such deviations are productive for enhancing team effectiveness.

Groups composed of collectivists are more productive for routine, repetitive tasks found in the context of manufacturing organizations. Conflicts are easily resolved, and there is a greater overlap between goals of the individual and the goals of the work group. Collectivists do not like to challenge the legitimacy of the assigned goals and are comfortable with following instructions from their supervisors or group leader. Groups composed of individualists may or may not be productive on routine and repetitive tasks. However, the tendency of individualists to pursue their personal goals may enhance the effectiveness of their groups in that innovative and creative tasks are better accomplished by individuals who pay attention to their own views regarding the nature of task performance.

The contribution of a group member is a function of their personal attitudes (i.e, work ethic, centrality of work), work norms, and working conditions. Across a large number of group situations, collectivists give more importance to social norms than to their personal attitudes and predispositions in determining the amount of contribution or effort that they might apply. Individualists, on the other hand, are more likely to be influenced by the importance of their personal orientations (such as the intrinsic significance of the work and their commitment to the work).

It is necessary to change the work norms that exist in a given group situation in order to make a large number of collectivists conform to the new patterns. Such cannot necessarily be expected of individualists. Some of them may change their orientation in order to contribute in a sustained fashion, whereas others may leave the organization. To put it simply, collectivists are more sensitive to work-related norms in the performance of their duties and responsibilities, whether they occur in the context of individual performance or group performance.

IMPLICATIONS FOR THE FUNCTIONING OF MULTICULTURAL TEAMS

Multicultural work teams are becoming commonplace in those multinational and global organizations which are launching global high-technology products in different countries of the world at the same time. Consider the launch of a new type of mobile phone, for example a new model of I-Phone. While the nature of technology going into the production of these phones is the same in different manufacturing facilities of the Apple Corporation, the fact is that for the phones to work effectively in the distinctive telecommunications environments of different countries, it must incorporate national differences in switching mechanisms of telecommunications towers. This is where design engineers from different countries can contribute their knowledge and experience in the design and launch of the product, which is essentially a totally global product. Gone are the days when creation and launch of a new product or service did not require the collective inputs of a group of culturally dissimilar individuals. As noted earlier, these multicultural teams may meet face to face once in a while, but the typical mode of working is through electronic mail.

Different culture-specific expectations regarding how effective team work can be developed in the context of little or no face-to-face contact is a significant problem for these teams (Earley & Gibson, 2002). It is not clear whether homogenous teams are more effective than heterogenous ones. Watson, Kumar, & Michaelson (1993) found that cultural heterogeneity leads to better problem-solving strategies in groups that have worked for a reasonable period. Cumulative knowledge from diverse team membership and flexibility on the part of individual members contribute to group effectiveness. Multicultural teams are likely to be more successful if they can develop an effective team culture on their own. Earley & Mosakowski (2000) confirmed this hypothesis in four-person teams in British business schools. The members of these teams came from different cultures and nations. However, their results also suggest that when culturally derived fault lines begin to emerge in such multicultural teams, effectiveness is impaired.

The role of leadership in the management of multicultural teams has not been studied in great depth. It is generally accepted that leaders are not necessary to coordinate and provide guidance in unstructured and temporarily multicultural teams that are formed for a relatively short period of time. It is interesting to note that members of culturally diverse teams may feel less satisfied with their own levels of contribution to the group product despite the fact that their teams were more effective than monocultural or homogenous teams.

The role of trust among the members of dissimilar cultures is also of crucial importance in the effectiveness of multicultural teams. Trust in the context of multicultural teams is defined as the expectation of beneficent treatment from others in the group in uncertain or risky situations (Kashima & Foddy, 2002). It reflects a belief that team members are prepared to act in a way so as to benefit (or not harm oneself before one can be made aware of the intentions and outcomes of others' actions). Trust is an essential element in those multicultural situations where a member has the potential to gain at the expense of another member but chooses not to engage in such actions (Yamagishi & Takahashi, 1994). When multicultural teams are created by emphasizing directly or indirectly mutual friendships and professional connections, opportunity for developing trust is present. We advance the notion that members of multicultural teams who belong to the same type of professional organization (e.g., International Association of Electronic and Electrical Engineers) are likely to develop trusting relationships in a relatively short period of time. Therefore, the level of professionalism in any multicultural team is a significant predictor of group effectiveness in the short term. Unless conflicts based on self- interest and culture-specific beliefs and attitudes develop among members, it is safe to say that groups composed of accomplished professionals are likely to be more effective in a multicultural and virtual team context.

REFERENCES

Adler, N.J. (2008). *International dimensions of organizational behavior.* 5th edn. South-Western Cengage Learning.

Brooks, F.P. (1995). *The mythical man-month.* 2nd edn. Reading, MA: Addison-Wesley.

Brooks, D. (2011). *The social animal.* New York: Random House.

Campion, M.A., Medskar, G.J., & Higgs, A.C. (2006). Relationships between work group characteristics and effectiveness: Implications for designing effective work groups. *Personnel Psychology*, 46(4), 823–47.

Earley, P.C. (1989). Social loafing and collectivism: A comparison of the United States and People's Republic of China. *Administrative Science Quarterly*, 34(4), 565–81.

Earley, P.C. & Gibson, C.B. (2002). *Multinational work teams: A new perspective.* Mahwah, NJ: Lawrence Erlbaum.

Earley, P.C. & Mosakowski, E. (2000). Creating hybrid team cultures: An empirical test of transnational team functioning. *Academy of Management Journal*, 43, 26–49.

Earley, P.C. & Gibson, C.B. (2002). *Multinational work teams: A new perspective.* Mahwah, NJ: Lawrence Erlbaum.

Goodman, P.S., Ravlin, E., & Schminke, M. (1987). Understanding groups in organizations. *Research in Organizational Behavior*, 9, 121–73.

Greenberg, J. & Baron, R.A. (2008). *Behavior in organizations.* Englewood Cliffs, NJ: Prentice-Hall.

Hackman, J.R. (Ed.) (1990). *Groups that work (and those that don't).* San Francisco, CA: Jossey-Bass.

Hackman, J.R. & Wageman, R. (2005). When and how team leaders matter. *Research in Organizational Behavior*, 26, 37–74.

Hardin, A.M., Fuller, M.A., & Davison, R.M. (2007). I know I can but can we? Culture and efficacy beliefs in global virtual teams. *Small Group Research*, 38, 130–55.

Kashima, Y. & Foddy, M. (2002). Time and self: The historical construction of the self. In Y. Kashima, M. Foddy, & M.J. Platow (Eds). *Self and identity: Personal, social and symbolic* (pp. 181–206). Mahwah, NJ: Lawrence Erlbaum Associates.

Mathieu, J.E., Heffner, T.S., Goodwin, G.F., Salas, E., & Cannon-Bowers, J.A. (2000). The influence of shared mental models on team process and performance. *Journal of Applied Psychology*, 85, 273–283.

Stanko, T.L. & Gibson, C. (2009). The role of cultural elements in virtual teams. In R.S. Bhagat & R.M. Steers (Eds). *Cambridge handbook of culture, organizations and work* (pp. 272–304). Cambridge: Cambridge University Press.

Stewart, G.L. & Barrick, M.R. (2000). Team structure and performance: Assessing the mediating role of intrateam process and the moderating role of task type. *Academy of Management Journal*, 43, 135–48.

Swigger, K., Alpaslan, G., Brazile, R., & Monticino, M. (2004). Effects of culture on computer-supported international collaborators. *International Journal of Human-Computer Studies*, 60(3), 365–80.

Thomas, D.C. (2008). *Cross-cultural management.* Thousand Oaks, CA: Sage.

Triandis, H.C. (1994). *Culture and social behavior.* New York: McGraw-Hill.

Watson, W.E., Kumar, K., & Michaelson, L.K. (1993). Cultural diversity's impact on interaction process and performance comparing homogenous and diverse task groups. *Academy of Management Journal*, 36, 590–602.

Yamagishi, T. and Takahashi, N. (1994). Evolution of norms without metanorms. In U. Shulz, W. Albers, & U. Mueller (Eds). *Social dilemmas and cooperation* (pp. 311–26). Berlin: Springer.

9. Cultural variations and leadership

Recent reports suggest that Vladimir Putin, the former president of the Russian Federation and now the prime minister, has continued to maintain high levels of popularity (70 percent) even in the face of recent terrorist attacks in Moscow (July 2010). North Americans and Western Europeans do not quite understand why Putin, who is quite authoritarian in his policies and in his administration of the Russian Federation, remains popular (Pew Research Center, 2007). In a parallel vein, presidential election campaigns in the US are quite heavily influenced by the religious beliefs and values of the candidates; religion does not play a major role in either Western or Eastern Europe. Whether a candidate is married or supports gay marriage is not considered as relevant in running for the presidency of France, Spain, or the Netherlands as it is in the US. In the US, presidential candidates who support gay marriage in an explicit fashion would have little chance of being elected.

In each of these cases, cultural differences among societies, and in particular how individuals construe images and prototypes of leaders, are strongly reflected in which issues leaders choose to emphasize.

Few topics within the field of organizational behavior have drawn as much anecdotal as well as research interest as that of leadership. Besides the field of organizational behavior, the study of leadership, evolution of leadership, determinants of leadership, and outcomes of both effective and ineffective leadership have long captured the imagination of philosophers, historians, and theologians. Stories concerning the great acts of sacrifice and heroism of particular individuals are abundant in the folk and classical literature of all societies. Mahatma Gandhi (the great soul), who led India's independence from the British in 1947, is revered as the father of post-independence India even today, and his image appears on all the tenders produced by the central bank of India. At the time of his death, it was estimated that his net financial assets were about $12, but the resources dedicated to the study of his method of influencing followers have consumed millions of dollars, in universities, all over the world. Even today, the political leaders of India swear by the Gandhian principles of leadership as the best method for governing a country as diverse and complex as India.

Leadership expert Warren Bennis of the University of Southern California captures the essence of leadership by noting that, "Leadership is like beauty; it is hard to define, but you know it when you see it" (Bennis, 1989). We suggest that how leadership is perceived is highly dependent on the cultural context of the society or country in which it evolves. Some cultures value leaders who are prepared to take charge, are visible, and assertive; other cultures value leaders who are less visible, choosing to get things done by working behind the scenes. Some cultures like leaders to stand out from the crowd and demand respect, even at the risk of physical harm. Consider the case of Boris Yeltsin in August 1991, at the beginning of the dissolution of the Soviet Union, when he stood over the Soviet tanks and challenged the Communists to take over the Kremlin. It was Yeltsin's great courage that helped Mikhail Gorbachev to gain freedom and declare the dissolution of the USSR into 15 independent republics. These republics constitute the Council of Independent States (CIS). Gorbachev also emphasized principles of governance that went against the grain of Communist thinking at that time, and had been widely accepted in the USSR since 1917. It is doubtful that a Gandhian style of leadership, emphasizing the fundamental importance of non-violent, non-cooperation would have been of any value in bringing about the fundamental changes in the Soviet system that took place in the early 1990s by the actions of these two bold leaders. Variations in the acts of leadership are too common to mention at this stage—what is important to note is that the best-known leaders of the world, whether from the domain of business or from other domains, tend to mirror the essential cultural fabric of the society in which they find themselves.

WHAT IS LEADERSHIP?

One of the most challenging tasks that international and global managers face is the need to work with and lead people of dissimilar national and cultural backgrounds. The process of leading others to accomplish tasks effectively is one of the most complex yet least understood areas in the management of global organizations. In this chapter, we examine the concepts and theories of leadership as they have evolved in Western countries, particularly in the United States, and analyze their suitability in other nations and cultures.

To be sure, managers of multinational and global corporations are confronted with the urgent need to understand the nature of cultural context that enables one to become an effective leader, not only in one's own situation but also in dissimilar situations. In the previous section, we provided examples of leadership that reflected indigenous and cultural values that were essential in the evolution of leaders. Leadership has existed as a concept since the beginning of recorded history. In fact, a great portion of world history can be summarized as the study of leadership of the various kings, queens, princes and princesses, and their various ministers in the process of governing. Powerful and influential leaders have moved masses and accomplished objectives that ordinary men and women conceive to be impossible to accomplish. George Washington, Abraham Lincoln, Franklin D. Roosevelt, Eleanor Roosevelt, Winston Churchill, Andrew Carnegie, Mahatma Gandhi, Nelson Mandela, Golda Meir, Anwar Sadat, and Margaret Thatcher, for example, came from different parts of the world and have been powerful forces in leading major changes in their countries. Sir Winston Churchill is probably singularly responsible among the leaders of Western Europe in perceiving the danger of a Nazi Europe and took appropriate military action even in the face of insurmountable odds. He is clearly one of the greatest leaders of the 20th century. The history of mankind, as recorded in the 20th century, would be incomplete without a detailed account of his broad and insightful vision, including his understanding of the course of European and world events in the face of the emergence of Nazism.

No generally accepted definition of leadership has emerged during the past 50 years of research on this topic. However, scholars agree that *leadership* may be defined as the process of influencing people and providing a work environment so that they can accomplish their group or organizational objectives. Effective leaders create appropriate conditions to help groups of people define their goals and find appropriate ways of achieving them.

The definition given by researchers in the West tends to focus on the ability of individuals to influence their followers toward goal accomplishment (Yukl, 1994). This definition is accepted in different parts of the world; however, as we have already noted, cultural differences rooted in beliefs, attitudes, values, norms, standards, and social axioms present important challenges for understanding the importance and execution of leadership in different nations and cultures. Terms for leaders include boss, administrator, supervisor, director, manager, coach, head, chief, chair, master, and so on. In the United States, distinctions among titles such as assistant vice-president, managing director, division head, senior vice-president, and president have a great deal of meaning.

The differentiation among corporate ranks found in the US is not found in all countries. It is also important to pay attention to the difference between being a leader that everyone accepts and respects and the act of assuming formal organizational roles like division vice-president.

In the former case we see the exercise of both substantial and subtle influence over followers to perform actions that go beyond simple compliance and routine job descriptions. In other words, while Person A may be the formal organizational leader of a group (say the department of sales and marketing), Person B may actually be the true leader in terms of being able to exercise substantial and subtle influences over the members of the group which the formal leader (Person A) may not be able to. Administrators and managers can get routine tasks accomplished without appropriate acts of leadership, but it is only leaders that can enable as well as empower subordinates to go beyond the normal requirements of their duties and responsibilities. This is the essence of the difference between managers and leaders: managers are able to accomplish the tasks that are assigned to them and to the groups that they are responsible for or supervise. However, it is only the leaders of the work groups who are able to move the group beyond its normal duties and responsibilities and accomplish tasks and goals that are not required to be performed in the normal course of duties. In a sense, these individuals are able to transform the expectations that the subordinates have of themselves, and they are often charismatic and transformational in nature. In many cases the "informal leader" is the one who gets people to work hard, while the "formal leader" only gets them to do the minimum required. We discuss this issue more completely in a later section.

Effective transformational leaders are able to achieve higher levels of group and organizational performance by emphasizing the creativity inherent in each of the followers and empowering them to achieve higher levels of accomplishment by their superior vision. However, as we will see later, the significance of their vision has a distinct set of cultural underpinnings. A vision that is appropriate for a given organizational situation in a society may not be appropriate in another organizational context in another society.

No matter how leadership is defined around the world, only about 8 percent of executives in large global organizations think that their firms employ a sufficient number of leaders who are likely to be effective in different national and cultural contexts (Govindarajan & Gupta, 2008). Programs for enhancing leadership skills of managers and supervisors exist in both small and large corporations that have business transactions across different cultures. Universities and numerous consulting firms have developed programs to train leaders for both profit (Microsoft, Ford, Toyota, etc.) and non-profit (Peace Corps, Red Cross, various agencies of the United Nations such as UNESCO, etc.). Although individuals in global organizations are likely to say, "Oh, I'm not a leader—I just happen to get the job done with the help of my team"—the fact is that when one is accomplishing tasks by exercising judgment and taking appropriate actions that are culturally isomorphic with the beliefs, expectations, and values of the work group, one is exercising leadership and, indeed, culturally sanctioned leadership.

PERSPECTIVES ON LEADERSHIP

Research on the role of leadership has been conducted primarily in the United States after World War II. Five distinct perspectives are present in US studies, with distinctive theoretical underpinnings. They are the: *trait-based perspective, behavioral perspective, contingency perspective, implicit perspective*, and *transformational perspective.*

Trait-Based Perspective

Bill Gates, the chairman of the largest software company in the world— Microsoft—, who dropped out of Harvard in the 1970s and started his software company, is generally viewed as one of the great leaders of US business. He had a long-term vision of the future role of the software industry in the world; he was also able to assemble a team of highly talented individuals in spearheading a company that became the industry leader and has maintained that status since the 1980s. Similarly, Louis Gerstner, Jr., who was recruited by IBM as its chairman and chief executive in 1993, was instrumental in changing this major industry. He transformed IBM into a business solutions company as opposed to a company that focused primarily on hardware and mainframes. Gerstner had no previous experience in the computer industry, having been a management consultant for McKinsey & Company. His experience from the food-processing industry was not particularly relevant but his keen analytical abilities in identifying major strengths and weaknesses of IBM were instrumental in transforming and restoring it to its previous glory. Another example is that of Lee Iacocca of Chrysler Corporation, who was successful in transforming an unsuccessful company into a profitable one in the early 1980s. Lee Iacocca is regarded as a leader who had the right kinds of traits and skills—primarily his vision and his sustained energy.

From these examples, it appears that the individuals who possess important personal traits or personal characteristics or competencies are sometimes successful in making important changes in an organization. These changes can be observed at various levels of the organization. Leadership competencies include natural and learned abilities, values,

Table 9.1   Characteristics of in-group collectivism

HIGH IN-GROUP COLLECTIVISM societies have characteristics such as. . .
- Duties and obligations are important determinants of social behavior.
- A strong distinction is made between in-groups and out-groups.
- People emphasize relatedness with groups.
- The pace of life is slower.
- Love is assigned little weight in marriage.

LOW IN-GROUP COLLECTIVISM societies have characteristics such as. . .
- Personal needs and attitudes are important determinants of social behavior.
- Little distinction is made between in-groups and out-groups.
- People emphasize rationality in behavior.
- The pace of life is faster.
- Love is assigned great weight in marriage.

Source: Grove (2005a, b).

personality traits such as drive, ability to forecast the future, and other characteristics that create favorable environments for positive changes and growth.

During the first part of the 20th century, management scholars used scientific methods to discern the nature of personality traits and physical characteristics of leaders. The "great men" theories of the early 1900s, however, failed to identify traits that are both necessary and sufficient for widely accepted leadership. It became clear in the 1960s that certain behaviors are associated with good leadership. Surveys and laboratory studies conducted primarily at the universities of Michigan and Ohio State indicated that certain traits are important in all situations of leadership. These are depicted in Table 9.1.

Behavioral Perspective

Behavioral perspectives of leadership consider specific behaviors that are predictive of effective leadership. Two clusters of leadership behaviors have been identified—these two categories are *consideration* and *initiation of structure*. The consideration cluster includes behaviors that are people-oriented and is based on the notion of trust, respect, and a general concern for others. Leaders who rate high in this cluster are those who are supportive and respectful of their employees. On the other hand, behaviors associated with the cluster of initiation of structure develop well-defined work roles. Leaders who rank high in this cluster are usually concerned with the assignment of specific tasks and clarification of duties and procedures which result in compliance with company policy and procedures, as well as maximum performance of the employee.

In general, a leader who rates high on *both* of these clusters tends to achieve higher performance levels from subordinates within their organizations. From a cross-cultural perspective, research on these two clusters has demonstrated that individuals who are relationship-oriented (i.e., such as those in Japan, Korea, and China) generally are able to improve employee satisfaction. On the other hand, the influence of structure (i.e., task orientation) is a complex construct in a cross-cultural setting, and it is not clearly understood (Phatak, Bhagat, & Kashlak, 2009). In the dynamic environment of multinational corporations and global organizations, effective leaders must be able to deal with the situation at hand and understand the needs of their employees while at the same time doing whatever it takes to get the job done and achieve the objectives of the organization. The Japanese psychologist Misumi (1985) developed a theory that is parallel to the point of view just described. It will be presented later.

Contingency Perspective

As mentioned previously, a global manager must adjust to an ever-changing environment. The adaptability or flexibility of a leader to respond to situations or conditions is a competitive edge for any organization. In the contingency framework, the situation moderates the relationship between a leader's style and the effectiveness of the group. In this perspective, the nature of the situation is determined by the leader's position power, the quality of the relationship between the leader and his or her subordinates, and the degree of task structure. This framework suggests that leaders who are liked by their subordinates and are in a strong position of power tend to improve group performance, particularly in situations where the task-related responsibilities and duties are clearly stated and there are no ambiguities inherent in the performance of roles of the followers. Conversely, leaders who are more relationship-oriented are able to motivate their employees to achieve optimal levels of performance, when the task is less structured and when the leader's position of power is less clear. A number of cross-cultural studies have been conducted using this approach (see Hoppe & Bhagat, 2007). Filipino managers who were task-oriented were better at creating and sustaining high-performance groups, but Chinese managers who were relationship-oriented were more effective in achieving goals in somewhat ambiguous situations. Research with Japanese managers and workers has not supported contingency theory, and in Mexico, where self-monitoring (being sensitive about the impact of one's behavior on others and incorporating the responses of others in the conduct of leadership) is used as a characteristic of the leader, the support for the contingency perspective was mixed.

The *path-goal theory* developed by Robert House and his colleagues (2002) identified four leader behaviors and a number of situational and follower characteristics which influence the relationship between leader style and follower satisfaction and performance. This theory of leadership effectiveness has been supported in the US but has not been adequately tested in other cultures. Cultural differences, which are often the major situational characteristics as we examined in Chapters 1 and 2, may intervene in explicit and subtle ways in the exercise of leadership.

Substitutes for leadership
Substitutes for leadership are various situational characteristics that moderate the influence of leadership on group performance and member satisfaction. The characteristics of subordinates, such as the degree of intrinsic interest in performing the task, their occupational interests and skills, and their degree of professionalism can act as substitutes for leadership and exercise strong moderating influences on leader behavior. In other words, situations characterized by strong substitutes for leadership are much less likely to be influenced by the acts and strategies of the leader. This tends to be true across cultures. For example, work groups in high-technology companies in India do not require the kind of nurturing leadership styles that are found to be more suitable and effective in other Indian industry contexts. Professionals and managers working for the majority of high-tech companies are well trained, have high levels of skill, and are highly motivated. Such individuals will perform well even when there is no leader. Groups composed of such individuals do not require the actions of a leader and the leader's style is irrelevant.

Implicit Perspective

Implicit theories of leadership were developed in the United States and focus on the way subordinates perceive a leader. According to one of these theories, followers develop prototypes or mental representations of leaders through their life experiences and interactions with others. Specific behaviors on the part of a leader do not necessarily make that person be perceived as a leader unless the followers perceive him or her according to their prototypes of a leader. The idea that different cultures have different prototypes for leader behaviors has received strong support in international studies. Leaders who meet the expectations of their followers gain their trust and are effective in some cultures (Thomas & Ravlin, 1995). A major tenet of the implicit leadership theory (ILT) is that leadership is in the eye of the beholder. That is, leadership is a social level given to individuals if either: (1) their personality attributes, traits, and behaviors match reasonably well with the followers' beliefs about what leaders do and ought to do in various situations in work organizations; or (2) the observers attribute group success or failure to the activities of the perceived leader (Lord & Maher, 1991; House, 2004, pp. 3–9).

Despite some of the ongoing debates about the nature of the cognitive prototypes that subordinates hold or tend to value in accordance with the cultural stereotypes of leaders, it is widely accepted that ILT is a valued perspective that can be applied to understand the functioning of leaders in work organizations across cultures (Yukl, 2002). An important issue for leaders to think about is whether it is more important for a leader to exhibit behaviors consistent with culture-specific expectations of his or her cultural context or for a leader to exhibit behavior consistent with universally held leadership expectations (Dorfman, Hanges, & Brodbeck, 2004). In other words, how do we conceptualize the effectiveness of a leader who violates culturally sanctioned or endorsed norms regarding appropriate leader behavior but is still effective in the long term because of using some of the universally endorsed actions of leaders? This is particularly relevant in examining patterns of leadership in many of the Arabic countries of the Middle East. Leaders who were perceived to be effective in creating appropriate conditions for modernizing the country and improving its economy are not necessarily perceived to be effective from the point of view of their followers. In fact, in the context of Middle Eastern countries it is difficult to be both a leader of the country and an organization, since the culturally endorsed beliefs regarding what leaders should do and perform are not necessarily sanctioned by the world at large.

The GLOBE Studies of Leadership and Organizations (House, 2004; Chhokar, Brodbeck, & House, 2007) present interesting data that are valid for specifying the content of culturally endorsed implicit leadership effectiveness.

Transformational Perspective

The transformational perspective is concerned with the process of a leader using his or her charisma to inspire followers to go beyond their immediate self-interests for the good of the work group and the organization. *Charisma* is a special quality of interpersonal influence that some individuals possess more than others. Charismatic individuals are particularly successful in eliciting a strong sense of trust and respect toward themselves from their followers. As noted earlier, charismatic leaders are to be found in all nations and cultures. Franklin D. Roosevelt, John F. Kennedy, Ronald Reagan, and Bill Clinton from the US; Winston Churchill, Margaret Thatcher, and Tony Blair from the UK; Mikail Gorbachav from the former USSR; Mahatma Gandhi and Netaji Subhas C. Bose from India; Ben-Gurion and Golda Mair from Israel; Anwar Sadat from Egypt; Eva Peron from Argentina; and Nelson Mandela from South Africa have all been charismatic leaders. From the perspective of industry and work organizations, Lee Iococca of the Chrysler Corporation, Henry Ford of the Ford Motor Company, Bill Gates of Microsoft, Akio Morita of the Sony Corporation, and the late Steve Jobs of Apple, Inc. are good examples of charismatic leaders.

Charismatic leaders are self-confident, have an ideal vision, and are deeply committed to their goals. They are able to communicate the importance of their vision in a highly effective fashion—a good example being Ronald Reagan of the US, who was known as the "great communicator." Despite his limited understanding of the dynamics of the US economy, Ronald Reagan was uniquely successful in winning the trust and respect of a large segment of the US population during his presidency in the 1980s.

Charismatic leaders are perceived as being somewhat unconventional and radical thinkers who are quite fearless in the face of difficult challenges and still succeed in motivating their followers, whether the followers are from the larger society or the work organization. We might hasten to add that it is an energizing experience to work under charismatic leaders regardless of the cultural contexts to which the leaders and followers belong. The notion that charismatic leaders are more effective than non-charismatic leaders regardless of national and cultural differences is supported in research across cultures (Dorfman, 1996; House, 2004; Hoppe & Bhagat, 2007). There is little doubt that the transformational leadership style in which leaders use charisma as a natural mechanism for eliciting trust and respect from their followers is effective in very different countries, such as the Netherlands, Singapore, and the Dominican Republic. It is interesting that transformational leaders have had relatively little influence in Japan compared with other countries. Perhaps when a culture is tight it does not allow room for the leader to be creative. Charismatic leadership has been found to be more effective in the US than in Mexico (Clugston, Howell, & Dorfman, 2000).

The interest in the processes that leaders adopt is of greater importance to scholars studying the cross-cultural generalizability of leadership. This perspective has the best potential for being applicable across different cultures. However, more research is needed to fully understand the nature of interactions between charisma and cultural differences and how they affect the development of effective leadership.

THEORIES OF LEADERSHIP DEVELOPED IN NON-WESTERN COUNTRIES

In our discussions thus far, we have described the significance of five different perspectives to understand the determinants and consequences of leadership. All of these theories have their roots in the US. There is clearly a remarkable interest in the United States in the phenomenon of leadership. The phenomenon has been explored in a social and political context as well as in industrial and business organizations. It is safe to say that scholars in Western Europe and in other parts of the globe have relied on the insights gained by US researchers into the dynamics of leadership and leadership-related processes. That is not to say that perspectives developed in non-Western countries are less important. The non-Western theories of leadership that we will now discuss are: (1) the performance–maintenance (PM) leadership theory developed by Misumi (1985) in Japan; and (2) the nurturance–task (NT) leadership theory developed by Sinha (1980, 1995) in India. Ayman & Chemers (1991) also analyzed the cultural parameters of the major US theory of leadership (i.e., the contingency theory). His extension of US-based contingency theory to dissimilar cultural contexts is known as contingency theory in the cultural perspective.

Performance–Maintenance Theory of Leadership

PM leadership theory identifies two functions on which leaders in any situation rely: the performance function (P), which has to do with emphasizing task accomplishment, and the maintenance function (M), which is concerned with maintaining good relations among members of the work group working interdependently to perform the task.

Typical P behaviors include scheduling, defining goals, telling people how to attain goals, and making sure that people do what is expected of them. Typical M behaviors include paying attention to the needs of people, making people feel important, helping people learn new skills, and inspiring people to find the work stimulating. There are four kinds of leaders designated according to whether they do many or few of these behaviors: MP, mP, pM, and mp. The best leaders are PM, the worst pm. However, in some settings an mP leader might be excellent; in other settings a pM leader might be. The meaning of P depends on the context: P in the presence of M means "planning" and "expertise," while P in the context of m means "pressure for production." The meaning of P and M also depends on culture. For example, "to criticize a subordinate directly in one's office" is M in the United States but m in Japan, where one is not supposed to criticize directly, but indirectly, by using the services of a friend of the employee to convey the criticism.

Misumi postulated that P and M functions are not independent of each other but are highly complementary. This implies that effectiveness of a leader who places considerable importance on both the P and M functions is likely to be greater than the leader who is high on either P or M (Smith, Peterson, & Schwartz, 2002). This theory of leadership is highly consistent with the harmonious and context-embedded nature of leadership effectiveness in Japan. One does not become a leader by encouraging one's followers to perform at a higher level of effectiveness or by focusing excessively on maintaining cordial relationships within the group. One becomes a leader by displaying equal amounts of emphasis on performance and maintenance functions (P and M functions) and doing so in a holistic and interwoven fashion consistent with the harmonious and highly contextual nature of Japanese society. As we have just noted, this theory of leadership is largely a reflection of the dominant cultural ethos of Japan, in the sense that individuals are perceived as leaders who reflect the culturally sanctioned and endorsed values.

PM theory also suggests that leadership functions differ from situation to situation, depending on the context in which the leadership takes place. The specific contextual properties of the organization and the tasks that the leaders face are also quite important in the exercise of appropriate leadership. The PM theory of leadership has received most empirical support from research conducted in Japanese organizations—with leaders who are simultaneously high on P and M functions being rated more effective than those who are high on either P or M. Research in Hong Kong, the United Kingdom, and the United States also lends support to this theory, providing some evidence for its generalizability across nations and cultures (Smith et al., 1989). The largest differences between P and M functions were found to be in the US context, signifying that in US work organizations, an individual can be perceived to be a leader if he or she is high on either the P or M functions, depending on the unique demands of the situation. Smith et al. (1989) noted that even though the fundamental tenets of Misumi's theory reflect the deeply held values of Japanese culture, research from other cultures also endorses Misumi's view that leader behaviors tend to have no objective or generalized underpinnings. Leader behaviors acquire meaning through the context in which they occur.

Nurturance–Task Theory of Leadership

Sinha's NT theory (1980, 1994, 1995) was developed in India and focuses on two dimensions of effective leader behavior: nurturance (N) and task (T) performance. Sinha noted that in the relatively hierarchical context of India (India being relatively high in power distance) leaders often emphasize appropriate task performance from their subordinates even at the expense of supportive behaviors. In fact, some studies (Sinha, 1994) have shown that autocratic methods of supervision are preferred by subordinates in Indian work organizations. However, Sinha's research revealed that leaders, in a wide range of work organizations in India, were in fact more effective when they emphasized greater participation in decision-making by their subordinates while simultaneously demanding and emphasizing task performance. He noted that Indian subordinates perceive a person to be a leader if the person engages in a series of nurturant behaviors towards his or her subordinates.

The preferred leadership style in India, according to Sinha, is concerned with simultaneous emphasis on tasks and nurturant behaviors. From the Western perspective, it reflects a distinctive style of paternalistic leadership. This theory has received some support from research in work groups from highly collectivistic and hierarchically organized societies in different parts of the world. Ayman & Chemers (1991) extended Fiedler's contingency theory of leadership developed in the US context to collectivistic cultures such as Iran, Mexico, and Japan. They proposed that if leadership match is conceptualized in subjective terms, then leaders who have a good fit between their psychological orientation and their perception of the objective situation are likely to experience more positive emotional outcomes (i.e., confidence, enthusiasm, and an upbeat mood). These, in turn, create work climates that sustain high levels of productivity and satisfaction on the part of followers. Some empirical support for this cultural version of Fiedler's contingency theory exists (see Chemers, 1997).

Another approach to leadership effectiveness in a cultural perspective has been proposed by Triandis (1993). He related Alan Fiske's relational orientations to leadership patterns that are likely to evolve and be effective in different cultural contexts. Fiske's relational orientations reflect the assumptions that underlie the way people construe their social relationships in various contexts in different cultures. The first relational orientation is that of *community-sharing*, which emphasizes principles of association by underscoring collectivistic values of cooperation and in-group harmony. Societies which are high on this orientation are characterized by strong in-groups with significant amounts of generosity and concern for others who are not necessarily members of the in-groups. Important social decisions are made by consensus. The second relationship orientation is *authority-ranking*. This orientation emphasizes asymmetrical power relationships. Subordinates in societies that emphasize this relationship orientation are expected to show deference, respect, obedience, and loyalty to their superiors. The third orientation, called *equality-matching*, emphasizes norms of reciprocity, equality, equal distribution of rewards, and importance of social justice. Interpersonal relations are characterized by a much lower level of status differentiation. The fourth orientation, called *market-pricing*, refers to a form of relationship that emphasizes the value of calculativeness and rational consideration in social exchanges. Important values underlying this relationship orientation are fairness and equality, individual achievement, rational decision-making, and individualism.

According to Triandis (1993), the ideal leader in the social context that emphasizes community-sharing would be a nurturant leader who says, "We will work together until the work gets done then each takes what is needed." In contexts that emphasize authority-ranking, a leader who is charismatic and understands the inner significance of status difference is likely to be most effective. In contexts emphasizing equality-matching, the group members work together and expect rewards to be shared equally and without emphasizing principles of equity. In contexts emphasizing market-pricing, the person who emerges as the best leader is the one who provides most rewards to the biggest contributor to the objectives of the group. While this theory has not been tested empirically across cultures, anecdotal evidence in support of the traditions is found in the literature and in popular business publications.

An Appraisal of Non-Western Perspectives on Leadership

A closer look at both of these theories of leadership—that is, that developed for the Japanese context by Misumi (1985) and that for the Indian context by Sinha (1994, 1995, 1980)—shows they are quite similar to the behavioral perspective of leadership developed in the US by scholars from the University of Michigan and Ohio State University. The major difference between these two theories developed in East and South Asia and those developed in the US is concerned with the immediate underpinnings of the leaders' behaviors in terms of culturally endorsed values and expectations. To put it simply: a person cannot be perceived as a leader regardless of his or her job-relevant abilities and charismatic qualities if he or she does not perform the behaviors that are culturally appropriate in the context of the work organization.

US-based theories of leadership do not explicitly take into account the role of cultural variations. Since these theories were developed before the GLOBE studies conducted by Robert House and his associates at the University of Pennsylvania in the mid 1990s (see below), the role of cultural variations was implicitly assumed to be rooted in the individualistic context of US society. In addition, these theories were developed to serve as guiding frameworks for training supervisors and junior managers in leading work groups primarily in US organizations. Concern for collectivistic orientations began to emerge in the 1980s when US organizations were confronted with the Japanese challenge (Ouchi, 1981). Similarly, the need for understanding Japanese and other Eastern culture-based styles of leadership began to emerge in the 1980s. The work of Misumi on PM theory and Sinha on NT theory provided useful culture-specific insights. However, it was again a US-based organizational researcher, Robert House, who used data from 62 cultures to develop the GLOBE theory of leadership. *Culture and leadership across the world* (Chhokar, Brodbeck, & House, 2007) provides detailed insights into the role of cultural variations in many nations.

Hoppe & Bhagat (2007) discussed leadership in the US. They argued that the profile of the leader, as a cultural hero, must reflect the values of vertical individualism in order to fit US culture. The point is that the values associated with the cultural dimensions of individualism and low power distance are essential for the successful exercise of leadership in the US, as depicted in Figure 9.1. A different picture emerges in examining the East Asian countries of China and Singapore (called the Confucian Asia Cluster by House et al., 2007). Values of both institutional and in-group collectivism are evident in the exercise of effective leadership in these countries. The importance of in-group collectivism is of crucial significance in both Japan and China—both cultures are largely rooted in the Confucian tradition. The Chinese tend to score lower on future needs to emphasize both institutional and in-group collectivism compared with their Japanese counterparts. In providing a detailed analysis of the role of Chinese culture in the exercise of effective leadership, Fu et al. (2007) observed that since the Tiananmen Square incident in 1989, there has been a growing spirit of "Chinese-style" individualism. The young Chinese consider themselves to be less under the influence of their parents and other elders found in their in-group, and feel that they are becoming increasingly independent of their work organizations. Many are only-children and such children are usually individualists (Falbo, 1992). Suffice it to say that unless this situation becomes clearer in the future, leaders who emphasize the values of both in-group and institutional collectivism are regarded as being more effective. In this connection, it is important to note that the notion of *harmony* in terms of equal emphases of P and M functions in the Japanese context and the notion of *nurturance* in the Indian context are important.

As discussed earlier, there are some apparent similarities of the theories developed by Misumi (i.e., the PM theory) in Japan and Sinha (i.e., the NT theory) in India with the behavioral perspectives developed in the US. However, we must note that just like the limited applicability of US

Characteristic of a hero		Characteristic of admired US leader
Called to adventure, to distinguish himself, as to do what is right, to redeem himself	←→	has a vision, attempts something new pursues a "dream," has sense of purpose
Transcends community, resists pull of conformity, is different	←→	is unconventional, unique, time to himself and his convictions
Leaves community, enters "wilderness" by himself	←→	is individualistic, is determined, sticks to his vision, leads by example
Acts in and on the world, is active and action oriented, seeks control over environment	←→	is active and action oriented, has sense of urgency, exerts control, is a doer
Takes great risks, encounters novel and difficult situations, faces significant enemy, shows courage	←→	takes risks, is catalyst, breaks through convention, faces great odds, shows courage, takes on big challenges
Possesses extraordinary gifts, talents, strengths, has experience	←→	has a good track record, is outstanding, executes well, has some special talents
Gets help from "protective" figure, wizard, special magic	←→	takes advantage of opportunities, has a "mentor", is optimistic
Stands tall, faces death, overcomes defeat, is victorious, rescues those in distress	←→	overcomes all odds, learns from mistakes, turns things around, works hard, is forceful, asserts himself, perseveres
Can move and/or save lesser people, carries their hopes	←→	is inspirational, galvanizes people, is transformational
Faces own demons, comes into his own, reintegrates into community	←→	is positive, shows honesty and integrity, makes changes for good

Source: Hoppe & Bhagat (2007), p. 497.

Figure 9.1   The leader as a hero ("warrior") in US culture

theories of leadership in non-Western contexts, the non-Western theories have limited usefulness in the Western context.

GLOBE STUDIES OF LEADERSHIP

Important leadership studies were pioneered by Robert House of the Wharton School at the University of Pennsylvania. It might be recalled that he was the primary theorist behind the path-goal theory of leadership developed in 1974. The GLOBE study is the most ambitious research on leadership effectiveness that explicitly takes into account the role of cultural variations (see House, 2004; Chhokar, Brodbeck, & House, 2007). A global network of more than 170 management scholars and social scientists from 62 countries collaborated in order to understand how societal and industry culture influences the evolution and practice of leadership in organizations. A total of 875 organizations in the financial services, food services, and telecommunications industries participated in the GLOBE study. The researchers used both quantitative and qualitative methods to collect data from over 18,000 managers representing a majority of the cultures of the world. The goal of the GLOBE project was to understand the patterns of leadership that were universally accepted and those which were subject to unique influences by the cultural context in which managers operated.

Findings showed that specific leader behaviors—being trustworthy, encouraging, an effective communicator, a good bargainer, and a team-builder, for example—are accepted in many cultures of the world. In a related vein, negative behaviors such as being uncooperative, egocentric, ruthless, and dictatorial are disliked in all parts of the world. Interestingly, behaviors that are culture-dependent (i.e., are desirable in one culture but not in another) are group orientation, self-protectiveness, participative skills, humanness, autonomy, and charisma.

The fundamental research questions (House, Javidan, Hanges, & Dorfman, 2002) were:

- Are there certain types of leader behaviors, attributes, and organizational practices that are accepted as being preferable and effective across nations and cultures?
- Are there some leader behaviors, attributes, and organizational practices that are accepted and found to be effective in some cultural contexts but not necessarily in others?
- How do attributes of societal and organizational cultures affect the kinds of leader behaviors and organizational practices that are accepted and effective?
- What are some of the effects of violating or not paying attention to cultural norms and values relevant to leadership and organizational practices in various cultures of the world?
- What is the relative standing or position of all 62 cultures on the 9 core dimensions of culture identified in the GLOBE study?
- Can the specific as well as universal attributes of leader behaviors and practices be explained in terms of an overarching and underlying theory that meaningfully accounts for the systematic differences found across cultures?

The definition of leadership that guided the GLOBE researchers was: "Leadership is the ability of an individual to influence, motivate, and enable others to contribute toward the effectiveness and success of the organizations of which they are members" (House, 2004). Starting with 23 leadership styles, these researchers identified the following 6 global leader behavioral dimensions:

- *Transformational–charismatic leader behavior.* In expressing this behavior, the leader acts in a decisive, performance-oriented, and visionary fashion. He or she provides inspiration to subordinates and is willing to make personal sacrifices for the organization on a sustained basis.
- *Team-oriented leader behavior.* In expressing this behavior, the leader acts in an integrative, diplomatic, and benevolent fashion with a strong spirit of collaboration. Even though US leadership studies in the 1960s and 70s were not particularly concerned with team-orientedness on the part of leaders in work organizations, the GLOBE researchers conceived of this dimension of leader behavior because of the international and cross-cultural nature of the project.
- *Self-protective leader behavior.* In this type of leader behavior, the leader acts in a self-centered, procedural, status-conscious, conflictual, and face-saving manner. Once again, the previous US and Western European studies of leader behaviors in work organizations did not focus on this kind of leader behavior because of some of the immediate dysfunctional consequences that might be precipitated. However, given the nature of the study involving 62 countries, the GLOBE team found it necessary to include this behavioral pattern in their research design.
- *Participative leader behavior.* In the participative style of behavior, a leader acts as a delegator and encourages participation of the subordinates in both important and not so important decisions affecting the various aspects of their work activities in the organization.
- *Human leadership-style behavior.* In this behavior, a leader shows modesty and compassion in dealing with the needs and feelings of his or her subordinates in the organization.
- *Autonomous leadership-style behavior.* In this behavior, leaders act in a relatively individualistic, independent, autonomous, and unique fashion.

Two of the leader behaviors (transformational/charismatic and team-oriented) were strongly endorsed by all of the regional country clusters in the study. However, the magnitude of the endorsement varied across country clusters. For example, both transformational/charismatic and team-oriented leadership styles were more strongly endorsed and valued in the Anglo cluster (US, UK, Ireland, New Zealand, South Africa, and Australia), Asian cluster (China, India, Hong Kong, and Singapore), and Latin America cluster (Argentina, Colombia, and Mexico). To be sure, these leader behaviors were endorsed in other cultural clusters of the world but with much less enthusiasm.

The leadership styles that were found to be more dependent on the cultural contexts were humane leadership and autonomous leadership. Leaders who were more humane in their orientation, as perceived by their followers, were more valued in the Asian, sub-Saharan Africa (Nigeria, Zambia, Namibia, Zimbabwe, and South Africa), and Anglo clusters. Interestingly, humane leaders were less highly endorsed in the cultural context of Latin America and Nordic Europe (Sweden, Denmark, and Finland). We suggest that since the Latin American countries were largely ruled by military dictators during the latter part of the 20th century, it is possible that the citizens of these countries did not have opportunities to become acquainted with a humane style of leadership. Future research involving the countries of Latin America will provide more insights into this phenomenon.

Autonomous style was not considered to either facilitate or hinder the effectiveness of a leader, although in Eastern Europe (Hungary, Poland, Albania, Slovenia, Kazakhstan, Georgia, Greece, and Russia) this style of leadership was considered highly effective. However, it was not perceived in the same fashion in other country clusters.

The self-protective and participative leadership behaviors had a great deal of variation across the country clusters. Therefore, it is difficult to draw a definite conclusion regarding their desirability in any one of the clusters.

Taken together, the GLOBE leadership studies provide evidence regarding the kind of managerial and leader behaviors that are likely to be enthusiastically endorsed in most of the country clusters of the world. They tell us also that the kind of behaviors that a leader may feel free to display in one cultural context may be either ineffective or dysfunctional in another country cluster.

Regarding the expectations about the role and pervasiveness of managerial authority in making decisions versus involving subordinates in participative decision-making, Americans and Germans clearly prefer more participation than do the Japanese or Italians. Indonesians are comfortable with a relatively autocratic style of decision-making, but managers in the UK, Denmark, and Sweden are highly uncomfortable with an autocratic mode of making decisions. Table 9.2 depicts the styles of leadership (as found in the GLOBE studies) that are most endorsed

Table 9.2   Endorsement of leadership styles in various geographical regions of the globe

Globe leadership dimensions	Characteristics of dimensions	Regions where leadership dimensions are most preferred and endorsed
Autonomous leadership	Highly individualistic, independent, and unique	• Strongly endorsed in Eastern European countries • Weakly endorsed in Latin American countries
Value-based/ charismatic leadership	Inspirational, visionary, self-sacrificing, decisive, and goal-oriented	• Endorsed in almost all countries of the world, but particularly so in Anglo, Asian, and Latin American countries • Weaker endorsement in Arab countries
Humane leadership	Modest, tolerant, sensitive	• Highly preferred in Anglo, Asian, and sub-Saharan African countries
Participative leadership	Active listening, non-autocratic mode of decision-making, flexible	• Wide variations exist in the endorsement of this style of leadership • Least preferred in Arabic and Latin American countries
Self-protective leadership	Self-centered, procedural, status conscious, and excessive concern for face-saving	• Wide variations in endorsement across all geographical regions of the GLOBE studies
Team-oriented leadership	Collaborative, integrating, and diplomatic	• Endorsed in all regions • Most strongly in Anglo, Asian, and Latin American cultures • Less so in Arab cultures

Source: Adapted from House (2004).

in various geographical regions of the world—the underlying notion is that the leadership style that is most preferred is strongly reflective of the important cultural variations that are embedded in that region.

The cross-cultural literature on societal values indicates that emphasis on a given value is typically correlated highly with the intensity of practices that are derived from it. However, in the GLOBE studies they were negatively correlated. In short, the managers indicated that "the way we do things" is negatively related to "what would be the ideal way of doing things." This was especially strong in the case of power distance. In most cultures the managers said there was a lot of power distance and they would like there to be much less. When uncertainty avoidance was high the managers indicated that they would have liked less of it. In most cultures there was male orientation, and again many respondents would have liked less of it. In most cultures there was much collectivism and not enough emphasis on high performance.

The data suggest that for economic development the managers are correct in wanting less power distance, less male domination, and more high performance, because that is the pattern found in countries with high gross national product per capita. The results suggest that movements toward economic and gender equality, as seen in Scandinavia, for instance, can be recommended.

For high prosperity one needs high performance orientation, institutional collectivism, and uncertainty avoidance, and little power distance and in-group collectivism. For human development, such as good health, the culture should be low in in-group collectivism and power distance. Life expectancy was positively correlated with uncertainty avoidance practices but negatively correlated with uncertainty avoidance values.

A major focus of the studies was the identification of leadership styles associated with different cultural patterns. Here we find attributes that facilitate (e.g., decisiveness) and inhibit (e.g., irritability) outstanding leadership. Charismatic/value-based leadership (leader is visionary, inspirational, self-sacrificing, performance-oriented) is seen as most desirable everywhere. Team-oriented (leader is collaborative, team integrator, diplomatic) and participative (leader is not autocratic) leadership are generally desirable, but in some cultures they are not. In most cultures autonomous and humane (modest, humane) leadership are neither desirable nor undesirable. Self-protective (leader is self-centered, status-conscious, conflict inducer) leadership is undesirable. We find that charismatic leadership is particularly high in the Anglo cluster of countries and low in the Middle East. Team-oriented is high in Latin America and low in the Middle East. Humane is high in South Asia and low in Nordic Europe. Autonomous is high in Eastern Europe and low in Latin America. Self-protective is high in South Asia and the Middle East and low in Nordic Europe.

Performance orientation is related to all culturally implied theories of leadership, except the self-protective. It is linked especially to charismatic leadership. Charismatic leadership is high also where there is gender equality, future orientation, and humane orientation. In-group collectivism values are positively related to the charismatic and negatively related to the self-protective leadership style.

The Middle East is interesting because the self-protective kind of leadership is seen as less of a problem than in other parts of the world. In the Middle East also the charismatic and team-oriented leaderships were not given the high endorsement they received in other regions. It is interesting that the humane style of leadership was emphasized somewhat more in the Middle East than in many other regions of the world. Finally, in the Middle East there was a local cluster of desirable attributes, such as familial, humble, and faithful. This last point makes one wonder if, in the rush to maximize economic development, many cultures no longer emphasize the humane attributes of warm hospitality and empathy that one finds in that part of the world.

LEADERSHIP STYLES AROUND THE WORLD: CONVERGENCE OR DIVERGENCE?

Given the rapid growth of globalization and interconnectedness among the various economies of the world, it is natural for managers of multinational and global organizations to ask: "Are the employees of various subsidiaries of these companies beginning to value the exercise of leadership in similar fashions in various parts of the world, or are they preferring to stick to the kind of leadership behaviors that were particularly valued or enshrined in their own cultures?" Consider the case of Indian employees in call center operations located in the southern cities of India such as Hyderabad, Bangalore, Chennai, and Calcutta. Do these call center employees expect their Western (US, UK, Canada, etc.) supervisors to be as nurturant in leading and managing the work groups in these centers as their Indian counterparts? In other words, is it possible for multinational and global organizations in both public and private sectors to create expectations regarding effective leader behaviors in uniform fashion around the world? There is a distinct tendency to endorse those styles of leadership that are highly valued in Western countries. However, can we expect the employees of the various multinational and global organizations to accept and be enthusiastic about those leaders who are keen on maintaining and enhancing group effectiveness by using the behaviors which are effective in Western countries?

Factors that Facilitate the Convergence of Leadership Styles

As the GLOBE studies depict, there is a universal preference for leadership that is charismatic and transformational. What they found is that, regardless of the stage of economic development of a country and its cultural characteristics, employees preferred leaders who functioned by emphasizing a charismatic and transformational style. This reflects a strong universal human tendency to prefer to have those individuals in positions of leadership who have these qualities. Admittedly, not all leaders—in fact, not even 10 percent of the leaders of work groups and large or small multinational and global organizations—are capable of displaying significant patterns of sustained charismatic and transformational leadership styles (House, 2004). The case of Jack Welch, a transformational leader of General Electric (GE) Corporation, and his style of initiating extensive organizational changes around the world is a good example. GE's approach in the 1980s was to eliminate supervisory positions and give employees more autonomy to manage their work role-related responsibilities and duties. This new way of managing was considered incompatible with the cultural expectations of many of the countries where GE had facilities and operations. However, as Tichy & Sherman (1994) noted, the strategy of GE worked well as pioneered and institutionalized by a charismatic leader like Jack Welch. Jack Welch's strategy for developing leadership in GE's various subsidiaries was to develop managers who functioned with a strong global orientation and had the ability to appreciate and respect the national and ethnic biases of people anywhere in the world. In the process, they were encouraged to feel comfortable in exercising a style of leadership that was charismatic and transformational, but at the same time more responsive to the culturally specific demands of the nations where GE operated.

Factors that Encourage Divergence in Styles of Leadership

As the GLOBE studies show, there are distinct preferences for leader behaviors in different regions of the world. Some countries are more focused on maintaining harmonious relationships in the work group and one of the main functions of the leader is to be relationship-focused. In contrast, there are other countries where rules and rationality are highly emphasized, and leaders are not necessarily devalued if they are less interested in relationships (as would be demonstrated by leaders who are highly humane and participative in their styles of leadership). The countries of South America strongly reflect a style of leadership where leaders are judged by the quality of relationships that they are able to develop and sustain with their subordinates. However, countries such as Germany and the countries of Nordic Europe are more rule-oriented, and leaders are judged for their ability to get things done in an orderly and timely fashion. Effectiveness in accomplishing tasks is more valued than maintaining harmony by investing a great deal of energy in relationships. It is unlikely that leadership styles that are valued and emphasized in the Nordic European context will be regarded as effective in the Latin American cluster of countries.

As we discussed in Chapters 1 and 2, the cultures of the countries in different geographical regions of the world are enduring, and despite forces of standardization that accompany the process of economic globalization, work organizations and the people who work in them are not open to accepting changes in the ways things are done. Transformations do take place, but they take generations to accomplish. For example, the young managers of India and Japan are likely to be more predisposed toward exacting leadership styles that are focused on tasks as opposed to nurturance. The young managers of India are better educated and do not necessarily have the kind of emotional dependence on their work organizations as was the case about three decades ago. Japan, which is more of a tight culture (Triandis, 1998), is also undergoing a transformation in the way leaders in organizations are supposed to manage and accomplish goals. However, Japan now has a very large number of applications for patents, which suggests much creativity, which was not present in previous generations. Tightness tends to be negatively related to creativity, so this indicates that Japan is now less tight than it was in the past.

While there are clear forces toward the evolution of a uniform and universal style of leadership, there are important cultural factors that are embedded in the national context of the various countries which make a universal leadership style less likely.

LEADING IN AN INCREASINGLY INTERDEPENDENT WORLD

There is no doubt that a great deal of energy and resources have been spent in identifying the styles of leadership that are effective in different countries and regional clusters. We seem to know a great deal about managing work groups, teams, subsidiaries, and work organizations in different parts of the world. The GLOBE studies in particular (House, 2004; Chhokar, Brodbeck, & House, 2007) provided a systematic set of insights that are most useful in the new era of globalization that has unfolded at the dawn of the 21st century. However, that is not to say that we know enough about managing work groups and teams who are located in geographically distinct and culturally dispersed areas of the world.

The meaning of leadership in some of the organizations where flexibility, fluidity, and a fast pace of change are the cornerstones of effectiveness is different from that in the organizations of yesterday which were characterized by some stability. Leading in e-businesses and virtual organizations is different from leading in traditional manufacturing organizations, where the pattern of hierarchy is well established and the chain of command is clearly understood. The main differences between leadership in traditional organizations and e-businesses such as e-commerce and virtual organizations are the speed at which decisions must be made, the importance of flexibility, and the need to create an ongoing vision of the future—one that continues to be simultaneously innovative, highly competitive, and effective. While the data may be available to make rapid decisions, the base of knowledge that is required to make informed judgments may be increasingly harder to obtain. These situations require flexibility in the sense that the traditional hierarchical system of decision-making needs to be de-emphasized in favor of a network-based learning organization. Leaders in these organizations must align the flow of activities in line with what works in the present and must anticipate the future as opposed to emphasizing the behaviors, rules, and procedures that have worked in the past.

Continuous focus on maintaining an informed and strategically well-grounded vision is indeed difficult. Business books are replete with information about how leaders of various multinational and global organizations appreciate and sense the changes in organizational environments and create new types of visions as necessary. In this era of the Internet and globalization, employees and clients of organizations expect more from the leaders of multinational and global firms than was the case in the past. The rules, policies, and regulations that used to be emphasized in traditional organizational structures and contexts, to reduce uncertainty for both leaders and their followers, often need to be set aside in favor of new policies and regulations that can capture the nature of the complexities and discontinuities that characterize the new world of global businesses.

Cairncross (2001) provides a detailed description of the various scenarios that are likely to evolve in organizational, governmental, and nation-states of the world in the era of the "death of distance." Formal guidelines that are typically valid in traditional organizations have limited utilities in digital and virtual organizations. It is the leader or the leaders of multinational and global organizations who must assume the responsibility of providing continuous directions for the evolution and competitiveness of the organization, no matter how complex the various situations might appear to be from one geographical and cultural region of the world to another. Whether the leaders of the various subsidiaries of the multinational and global organizations need to consult regarding the kinds of leadership that are going to be valued in various situations, it is necessary that they also pay some attention to the cultural context of the countries and the regions in which they operate.

CHARACTERISTICS OF GLOBAL LEADERSHIP

An inquiring mind, an impeccable sense of integrity, the ability to manage uncertainty and tension, and the need for emotional interconnectedness with people and employees in different parts of the world are clearly the hallmark of an effective global leader. These leaders should also be cognitively complex and have an acute sense of the scope and complexities of their business transactions in the global community. They must be quick to recognize market opportunities around the world and have the organizational know-how to harness the unique capabilities of their business units. Obviously, these leaders should have the skills and abilities to interact and integrate contributions of employees from diverse cultural backgrounds who work in different parts of the world and in dissimilar cultural contexts. Some of the important traits of the global manager are as follows:

- A combination of the skills of strategic thinking with those of the builder of organizational architectures and systems—and the ability to integrate these activities in a seamless fashion.
- A strong cosmopolitan orientation encompassing the ability to operate flexibly and in a sensitive fashion by integrating the distinctive demands of the different nations and cultures in which the global corporation operates.
- Being highly competent in communicating across nations and cultures—as we discussed in earlier chapters, the role of effective communication cannot be overemphasized. It is critical for a leader to develop appropriate skills in order to communicate face to face as well as through video-conferencing, e-mails, and other computer-mediated channels of communication in the current era of the Internet and globalization.
- The ability to remain non-judgmental in situations that are ambiguous and do not necessarily provide clear culturally sanctioned cues and signals to act in a decisive fashion. In addition, the capacity to acculturate into the dominant cultural milieu without necessarily de-emphasizing the anchors provided by one's native cultural background.
- Last, but not least, the eagerness to learn on an ongoing basis, how economic, institutional, political, and cultural influences interact. He or she must also understand how multinational and global organizations function in different parts of the world. Furthermore, it is critical to be aware of the changes that are occurring continuously and rapidly in the current era of globalization.

IMPLICATIONS FOR THE PRACTICE OF LEADERSHIP IN GLOBAL ORGANIZATIONS

Leadership involves continuous interaction with others—subordinates and other colleagues—in the organization to accomplish tasks at different levels of the organization—at the group level, at the organizational level, and at the interorganizational level. In a recent survey of 500 global firms, 85 percent of CEOs believed that they do not have a sufficient number of personnel who can be called effective global leaders (Govindarajan & Gupta, 2008). Sixty-five percent believed that their existing leaders managing the various multinational and global operations need to acquire additional skills and knowledge before they can deal effectively with the challenges of the global marketplace.

The need to understand the attributes of individuals who can be called global leaders and be trusted with managing operations of multinational and global firms has emerged with the increasing internationalization and globalization of businesses. Today's multinational and global organizations conduct business transactions with employees, vendors, customers, and stakeholders from countries that are quite different from those of their headquarters, in their economic, social, historical, and cultural contexts. The management of employees in outsourced operations is also emerging as a critical function of multinational firms.

It is not easy for leaders of global corporations to be knowledgeable about the idiosyncrasies of the cultural context of each of the countries in which they operate. Therefore, it is important that these leaders have specific personal characteristics, predispositions, and skills. Osland, Taylor, & Mendenhall (2009), in their analysis of global leadership, termed these kinds of characteristics as *mega skills*. These skills are overarching in nature and go beyond those required of managers who run domestic operations or function in expatriate capacities. A simple way to grasp the significance of the above characteristics is to note that individuals who find themselves in the roles of leaders in managing operations of multinational and global organizations must conform enough to the demands of the new economic and cultural milieu in which they find themselves. It is also important that they gain acceptance in the new environment and make necessary connections to make appropriate changes. Leaders who succeed in changing what needs to change in multinational and global organizations must challenge the current norms and practices—but not all of them and not all at once. Effective leaders should endeavor to understand the facets of culture that can be changed and those which cannot be changed and operate within those constraints. Carlos Ghosn, as one of the most successful global managers, did just that. In becoming the CEO of the second largest Japanese automobile company, Nissan, he studied the idiosyncrasies of Japanese culture and was successful in implementing the changes that were at odds with some cultural practices without creating significant upheavals or disturbances at Nissan.

Leading across national borders and cultures can indeed be challenging and often frustrating. Just when one expects the effectiveness of the organization to increase, the reverse can happen, leading to considerable frustration and pain on the part of the senior management and leadership team. Dorfman, Hanges, & Broderick (2004) note that while academic researchers have had difficulty developing a consensus regarding the definition and operationalization of leadership since the early 1950s, lay people do not seem to experience much difficulty with this term "leadership." Most individuals in all cultures have their own ideas about the nature of leaders and the constellation of behaviors that such leaders must exhibit in order to be perceived as leaders. People have implicit ideas about the kinds of behaviors that effective leaders must emit in the societal context of business, governmental, and other contexts, as well as why such behaviors are necessary. These naive or idiosyncratic leadership theories have been studied under the rubric of "leader categorization theory" (Lord, Foti, & DeVader, 1984). According to this theory, individuals have certain definite beliefs about the attributes and behaviors of leaders and such belief systems help them interpret and recognize new social information regarding the behavior of leaders in order to categorize them according to previous schemas. A major assertion of this theory is that the perception of leadership lies in the "eye of the beholder"—that is, leadership is a social level given to some individuals if their personality, attributes, and behaviors closely match the beliefs of the observer's or follower's concerning what leaders should and must do.

Integrating the findings of implicit leadership theories (ILT theories by Dickson, Hanges, & Lord, 2001) with cross-cultural research in the tradition of the themes discussed in Chhokar, Brodbeck, & House (2007) will be most valuable in developing firmly grounded insights into developing leaders who are capable of managing global organizations.

REFERENCES

Ayman, R. & Chemers, M.M. (1991). The effect of leadership match on subordinate satisfaction in Mexican organizations: Some moderating influences of self-monitoring. *International Review of Applied Psychology*, 40(3), 299–314.

Bennis, W. (1989). *On becoming a leader*. Reading, MA: Addison-Wesley.

Cairncross, F. (2001). *The death of distance: How the communications revolution is changing our lives.* Boston, MA: Harvard Business School Press.

Chemers, M.M. (1997). *An integrative theory of leadership.* Mahwah, NJ: Lawrence Erlbaum Associates.

Chhokar, J.S., Brodbeck, F.C., & House, R.J. (Eds) (2007). *Culture and leadership across the world: The GLOBE book of in-depth studies of 25 societies.* Mahwah, NJ: Lawrence Erlbaum Associates.

Clugston, M., Howell, J.P., & Dorfman, P.W. (2000). Does cultural socialization predict multiple bases and foci on commitment? *Journal of Management, 26,* 5–30.

Dickson, M.W., Hanges, P.J., & Lord, R.G. (2001). Trends, developments and gaps in cross-cultural research on leadership. 2, 75–100.

Dorfman, P.W. (1996). International and cross-cultural leadership. In J. Punnitt & O. Shenkar (Eds). *Handbook of international management research* (pp. 276–349). Cambridge, MA: Blackwell.

Dorfman, P.W., Hanges, P.J., & Brodbeck, F.C. (2004). Leadership and cultural variations: The identification of culturally endorsed leadership profiles. In R.J. House, P.J. Hanges, M. Javidan, P.W. Dorfman, & V. Gupta (Eds). *Culture, leadership and organizations* (pp. 669–720). Thousand Oaks, CA: Sage.

Falbo, T. (1992). Social norms and the one-child family. In F. Boer & J. Dunn (Eds). *Children's sibling relationship: Developmental and clinical issues* (pp. 71–82). Hillsdale, NJ: Erlbaum.

Fieldler, G.E. (1967). A theory of leadership and cultural heterogeneity on group performance: A test of the contingency theory model. *Journal of Experimental Social Psychology, 2,* 237–64.

Fu, J.H., Morris, M.W., Lee, S., Chao, M., Chiu, C., & Hong, Y. (2007). Epistemic motives and cultural conformity: Need for closure, culture, and context as determinants of conflict judgments. *Journal of Personality and Social Psychology, 92*(2), 191–207. doi: 10.1037/0022-3514.92.2.191.

Govindarajan, V. & Gupta, A. (2008). *In search of global dominance.* San Francisco, CA: Jossey-Bass.

Grove, C.N. (2005a). Introduction to the GLOBE Research Project on leadership worldwide. Available at: http://www.grovewell.com/pub-GLOBE-intro.html (accessed 13 April 2012).

Grove, C.N. (2005b). Worldwide differences in business values and practices: Overview of GLOBE research findings. Available at: http://www.grovewell.com/pub-GLOBE-dimensions.html (accessed 13 April 2012).

Groves, M. (1998). Cream rises to the top, but from a small crop. *Los Angeles Times,* 8 June.

Hoppe, M.H. & Bhagat, R.S. (2007). Leadership in the United States of America: The leader as cultural hero. In J.G. Chhokar, F.C. Brodbeck, & R.J. House (Eds). *Culture and leadership across the world* (pp. 475–544). New York: Taylor & Francis.

House, R.J. (2004). Introduction to the GLOBE studies. In R.J. House, P. Hanges, M. Javidan, P.W. Dorfman, & V. Gupta (Eds). *Culture, leadership, and organizations: The GLOBE study of 62 societies* (pp. 3–9). Thousand Oaks, CA: Sage.

House, R.J., Javidan, M., Hanges, P., & Dorfman, P. (2002). Understanding cultures and implicit leadership theories across the globe: An introduction of project GLOBE. *Journal of World Business, 37*(1), 3–10.

Lord, R. & Maher, K.J. (1991). *Leadership and information processing: Linking perceptions and performance.* Boston, MA: Unwin-Everyman.

Lord, R.D., Foti, R.J., & DeVader, C.L. (1984). A test of leadership categorization theory: Internal structure, information processing, and leadership perceptions. *Organizational Behavior and Human Performance*, 34, 343–78.

Misumi, J. (1985). *The behavioral science of leadership: An interdisciplinary Japanese research program.* Ann Arbor, MI: University of Michigan Press.

Osland, J., Taylor, S., & Mendenhall, M.E. (2009). Global leadership: Progress and challenges. In R.S. Bhagat & R.M. Steers (Eds). *Cambridge handbook of culture, organizations, and work* (pp. 242–71). Cambridge: Cambridge University Press.

Ouchi, W.G. (1981). *Theory Z.* Cambridge: Addison-Wesley Publishing.

Pew Research Center (2007). *Rising environmental concern, in 47 nation survey: Global unease with major world powers.* Washington, DC: Pew Research Center.

Phatak, A.V., Bhagat, R.S., & Kashlak, R.J. (2009). *International management: Managing in a diverse and dynamic global environment.* Boston, MA: McGraw-Hill.

Sinha, J.B.P. (1980). *The natural task leader.* New Delhi: Concept.

Sinha, J.B.P. (1984). A model of effective leadership styles in India. *International Studies of Management and Organizations*, 14(3), 86–98.

Sinha, J.B.P. (1994). Cultural embeddedness and the developmental role of industrial organizations in India. In H.C. Triandis, M.D. Dunnett, & L.M. Hough (Eds). *Handbook of industrial and organizational psychology* (2nd edn, vol. 4, pp. 727–64). Palo Alto, CA: Consulting Psychology Press.

Sinha, J.B.P. (1995). *The cultural context of leadership and power.* Thousand Oaks, CA: Sage.

Smith, P.B., Peterson, M.F., & Schwartz, S. (2002). Cultural values: Sources of guidance and their relevance to managerial behavior: A 47-country study. *Journal of Cross-Cultural Psychology*. 33(2), 188–208.

Smith, P.B., Misumi, J., Tayeb, M., Peterson, M., & Bond, M. (1989). On the generality of leadership styles across cultures. *Journal of Occupational Psychology*, 62, 97–109.

Thomas, D.C. & Ravlin, E.C. (1995). Responses of employees to cultural adaptation by a foreign manager. *Journal of Applied Psychology*, 80(1), 133–46.

Tichy, N. & Sherman, S. (1994). *Control your own destiny or someone else will: Lessons in mastering change – The principles Jack Welch is using to revolutionize General Electric.* New York: HarperBusiness.

Triandis, H.C. (1993). *The contingency model in cross-cultural perspective.* In M.M. Chemers & R. Ayman (Eds). *Leadership theory and research: Perspectives and directions* (pp. 167–88). San Diego, CA: Academic Press.

Triandis, H.C. (1998). Vertical and horizontal individualism and collectivism: Theory and research implications for international comparative management. *Advances in International Comparative Management*, 12, 7–35.

Yukl, G. (1994). *Leadership in organizations* (3rd edn). Upper Saddle River, NJ: Prentice-Hall.

Yukl, G. (2002). *Leadership in organizations.* Thousand Oaks, CA: Sage.

10. Cultural variations and organizational design

The success of a multinational and global organization depends on more than the collective skills, knowledge, and experience of its members and the selection of an appropriate strategy to match the demands of the global marketplace. An effective framework of organizing collective skills, knowledge, and experience is needed to operate across national borders and cultures. Organizational structure is such a framework. It is defined as:

> Organization structure defines lines of authority, coordinates flows of resources and establishes mechanisms of accountability. Structures define how the different functional and geographical units that operate under the scope of common governance of the firm are linked together. (UNCTAD, 1993, pp. 113–14)

In this chapter, we examine how culture influences organizational structure and design. The extent to which organizational structures and processes are influenced by cultural contexts depends on the state of globalization existing in a country. Globalization introduces a uniform logic regarding such processes as the size of the organization, formalization, and centralization—the basic elements of organizational structure. Organizational structures must facilitate the protection of the basic mission and the strategic core of the firm. Much of the economic activities that take place in the globalized world occur in societies (i.e., the US, UK, Germany, China, Japan, India, etc.), and these societies are inhabited by both large and small organizations whose structural properties differ not only in the domestic context but also internationally. For example, a domestic unit of Microsoft located in Dallas might have an organizational structure in terms of its size, formalization, and centralization different from another domestic unit located in Minneapolis. While these differences are noticeable and evolve due to distinct economic-, task-, and market-related demands found in these distinct regions, the differences in structures found among the subsidiaries of a global organization can be substantial. People working in factories and offices in both advanced and emerging economies are members of organizational societies (Presthus, 1978). Their work and life experiences are qualitatively different from those of people living in more traditional societies dominated primarily by domestic systems of production. Modern office and factory workers and managers share basic expectations and have necessary occupational skills and abilities that allow their organizations to operate on a day-to-day basis. The process of organizing their contributions in a fashion so as to make them both more efficient and effective is the essence of structuring of organizations. Cultural variations come into play in the way they affect the process of structuring. For example, can you expect the same type of bureaucratic organization in the French postal system as in the US?

An examination of the economic history of the world after World War II reveals many variations in national cultural characteristics, including the expected role of business organizations. The economic miracle that characterizes Japanese industrial growth and tremendous success in international business began to focus our attention on the distinctive cultural characteristics of Japan, which are different from those prevailing in the West. The Japanese organizations that were highly successful in the global marketplace in the 1980s and continue to be successful today are characterized by the collaborative spirit of a traditional Japanese village, or commune. Work relations are not viewed as contractual but more as relationships of interdependence, shared concern, and mutual help, much like what is found in traditional Japanese villages. Authority relations are often paternalistic, highly traditional, and differential. Strong links are developed between the long-term commitment and well-being of the individual employee, the organization, and the nation of Japan. Matsushita, one of the largest and most successful and global corporations from Japan, reflects these values in its corporate charter.

In order to understand the role of cultural variations in organizational structures, systems, and processes, it is important to examine the differences that are found across countries (e.g., between Japan and the US, or Brazil and Sweden) in cultural terms.

CULTURAL VARIATIONS AND ORGANIZATIONAL STRUCTURES

A study conducted by Stevens (1991) at the European Institute of Business Administration (INSEAD) shows that cultural variations influence the process of evolution of organizational structures in different parts of the world. When presented with an organizational problem (such as dealing with conflict between two departments or division heads within a company) MBA students at INSEAD from Britain, France, and Germany preferred remarkably different approaches. For the French, the problem

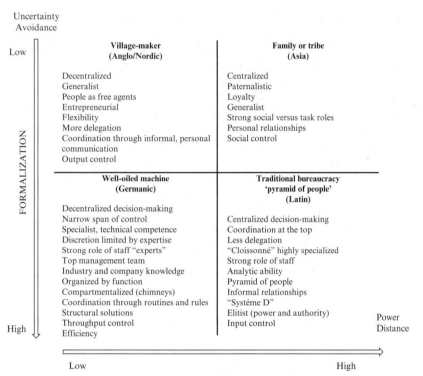

Source: Schneider (2003).

Figure 10.1 Emerging cultural profiles

is best resolved by referring it to the next level up and then eventually to the head of the organization as the case may be. Germans, on the other hand, argued strongly in favor of a better organizational structure that differentiates among roles, responsibilities, and expertise of individuals. Their implicit approach largely focused on highlighting the possible lack of clear role definitions of the two department heads. The British saw it as a problem of interpersonal communication between two department heads which should be resolved by engaging them in better interpersonal communication-related skills. In Figure 10.1, we present the implicit model of the process of effective organizing and organizational structures held by members of each of these nations.

For the French, an effective organization is constructed like a "pyramid of people", that is, explicitly formalized and logically centralized. For the

Germans, an effective organization should be constructed like a "well-oiled machine" (formalized but not too centralized). Intervention by senior members of management is not necessary except in certain perplexing situations. Rules and regulations should resolve problems. For the British, an effective organization should function like a "village market" (neither formalized nor centralized). Processes of formalization and centralization are not necessarily as important as the distinct demands of the situation, which are largely interpersonal and social in nature.

Comparative studies of organizational structure in France, Germany, and Britain (Brossard & Maurice, 1976) demonstrate that French organizations, as a general rule, tend to be more centralized with much less power delegated to lower levels of the hierarchy when compared with either German or British firms. The role of the CEO is to make key decisions and provide coordination at the top. It is necessary to have strong conceptual and analytic skills but not necessarily specific to the organization or the industry. The staff personnel provide the much needed organizational-specific expertise for decision-making.

German organizations, in contrast, tend to be decentralized, specialized, and formalized. They are structured according to functions they are supposed to perform, and coordination among these units is accomplished through rules, routines, and strictly prescribed procedures. Even though many multinational and global organizations working in the German context tend to be flatter and have a broader span of controlled when compared with the French (which are generally taller and emphasize hierarchy), middle managers tend to have less decision-making authority and are less empowered compared with their British counterparts. Germans put strong emphasis on specific technical expertise required to perform specialized tasks. Unlike the French situation, the senior managers in German organizations are expected to have not only high-level technical skills and competence but also organization- and industry-specific knowledge and expertise. Also unlike the French context, the top management is composed of a managing board called *Vostrand* whose role is to integrate and amplify the specialized knowledge of the various top managers and functional units. The decisions made by this board are most important, and in this respect German organizations are clearly different from their French and British counterparts.

In contrast to the strong emphasis on efficiency in the context of a structure that functions like a well-oiled machine, British (and US) organizations tend to function by highlighting the mechanisms of a village market. There is more concern for flexibility in these structures. Decision-making processes can be quickly decentralized and less formalized in order to incorporate the unique demands of the tasks or situation. There is no

central committee or *Vostrand* in either the British or American organization. The need for communicating and negotiating with colleagues, clients,
and senior members is emphasized more than formal bureaucratic rules
and regulations, as is the case with German organizations. Organizational
structures including the degree of formalization, the amount of authority
invested in the roles, and the extent of centralization or decentralization
needed to perform the task may be modified according to the unique
demands of the situation. Structures are not regarded as unchangeable
entities but may be reorganized or reshuffled to improve the efficiencies
as per the demands of both the internal and external contingencies in the
environment. Top managers may perceive suitable opportunities in the
global markets, but they cannot assume that important personnel necessary to seize the opportunity would be willing to cooperate easily. There
is a need to articulate a strategic view and to communicate and negotiate
with the stakeholders in a robust fashion.

Organizations in the Asian context fit the picture of the "family model"
as depicted in Figure 10.1. They tend to be more hierarchical, less formalized, and more centralized. The organizational structure of Japanese firms
tends to be different from the majority of those from East and Southeast
Asian countries. There is less emphasis on written manuals regarding how
to organize and execute work in different functional areas. Autocratic and
paternalistic decision-making tend to characterize the nature of organizing. A study of 39 multinational banks operating in Hong Kong (Steers,
Sanchez-Runde, & Nardon, 2010) found that, compared with banks from
other countries, Hong Kong-based banks had the greatest number of hierarchical levels (11). Other banks following the pattern of a large number
of hierarchies and centralized decision-making were from Singapore, the
Philippines, and India. The Confucian tradition of respect for patriar-
chal authority is remarkably persistent in Chinese and other East Asian
organizations. Control is exercised through authority which should not be
questioned, unlike the case with Scandinavian organizations. While globalization is beginning to introduce a move toward de-emphasis of hierarchy in East Asian organizations today, the fact remains that a powerful
founder or CEO is often at the center of all important decision-making
(Kao, 1993; Bartlett & Beamish, 2011).

Organizational structures of Russian organizations are also found to be
highly autocratic. The role of politics as opposed to pure merit is often at
play. Russian managers tend to value job security and also are risk-averse
in accordance with high levels of uncertainty avoidance in their country
context. However, there has been a recent trend toward encouraging
exchanges between employees and their organizations based on rational
calculations as opposed to institutional hierarchy.

What begins to emerge from the various studies of the role of cultural differences on organizational structure is that structures of highly competitive multinational and global organizations are converging despite their locations in dissimilar cultures. However, cultural factors should be taken into account. Cultural differences, as reflected in the evolution and structuring of organizations, reflect distinctly different conceptions of the organization (Laurent, 1983).

From a survey (see sample questions in Table 10.1), Andre Laurent found that cultural variations of power distance and uncertainty avoidance are two fundamental dimensions that are responsible for the evolution of distinctly different types of organizational structures across dissimilar nations. Workers and managers from dissimilar cultures respond in distinctively different ways in thinking about the importance of hierarchy, authority, role formalization, leadership, and political influence-related processes in their organizations. There was a time when a purely hierarchical and centralized organizational structure was the normal order of the day, particularly in the French context in the 1950s and 1960s. However, as the countries of Western Europe have globalized rapidly, the need for quick coordination and decision-making in response to the global marketplace has led to a progressive de-emphasis on hierarchical and centralized modes of structuring the organization. The boss is not expected to have all the precise and correct answers. However, in many organizations in the Asian, Latin American, and African contexts, there is a distinct emphasis on managers having more expertise than their subordinates. Scandinavian, British, and US managers have learned to function well by selectively ignoring the organizational hierarchy, especially in situations where reliance on hierarchy is a clear liability. Compared with Asian cultures, some of which are quite "tight" (strong adherence to established norms are expected and sanctions for deviation are severe), it is much easier to rely less on hierarchical processes in Nordic and Anglo cultures. In Latin American cultures, the importance of hierarchical decision-making persists, and managers in these contexts begin to view organizational decision-making as a political issue. Latin managers are quick to learn the importance of political processes in their societies. The political skills that are involved in negotiating with one's colleagues and clients are valued more in these contexts. These managers believe that it is next to impossible to execute an important task, such as launching a new product in the global marketplace or valuing a new joint venture with an Anglo organization, without adequate and appropriate access to those who have the power but not necessarily the knowledge or expertise.

Figure 10.2 depicts our approach to the role of cultural differences along with other relevant factors in the prediction of organizational

Table 10.1   Management questionnaire

	A = Strongly agree
	B = Tend to agree
	C = Neither agree, nor disagree
	D = Tend to disagree
	E = Strongly disagree

1. When the respective roles of the members of a department become complex, detailed job descriptions are a useful way of clarifying.   A B C D E

2. In order to have efficient work relationships, it is often necessary to bypass the hierarchical line.   A B C D E

8. An organizational structure in which certain subordinates have two direct bosses should be avoided at all costs.   A B C D E

13. The more complex a department's activities, the more important it is for each individual's functions to be well defined.   A B C D E

14. The main reason for having a hierarchical structure is so that everyone knows who has authority over whom.   A B C D E

19. Most organizations would be better off if conflict could be eliminated forever.   A B C D E

24. It is important for a manager to have at hand precise answers to most of the questions that his/her subordinates may raise about their work.   A B C D E

33. Most managers have a clear notion of what we call an organizational structure.   A B C D E

38. Most managers would achieve better results if their roles were less precisely defined.   A B C D E

40. Through their professional activity, managers play an important role in society.   A B C D E

43. The manager of tomorrow will be, primarily, a negotiator.   A B C D E

49. Most managers seem to be more motivated by obtaining power than by achieving objectives.   A B C D E

52. Today there seems to be an authority crisis in organizations.   A B C D E

Source: Laurent (1983).

structures of multinational and global firms. The nature of strategy adopted by an international company is the most important determinant of structure. Typically, a multinational and global organization considers the best strategic option that it must adopt in locating its R & D

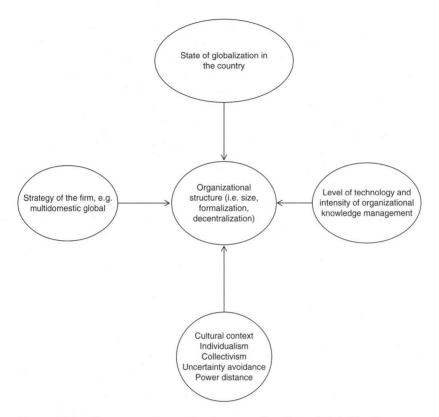

Figure 10.2   Structure of organizations as a function of globalization, technological complexity, organizational strategy, and societal culture

operations, production, marketing, and related functions. Collectively, the strategies reflected in organizing these operations help determine the nature of structure that the firm must adopt. For example, it is difficult, if not impossible, to adopt a strict hierarchical structure while developing a high-technology product (e.g., high-definition television) for the global market. Development of high-tech products needs integration of information and knowledge from various R & D operations of the global firm. An organizing principle emphasizing horizontal coordination of product and geographical divisions is more appropriate.

The state of technology that the firm utilizes and the complexity of organizational knowledge management are other major determinants of organizational structure. Perrow (1965, 1967) discussed the important role of technology as the determinant of organizational structure.

Organizational technologies that are directed toward production of simple products (e.g., running shoes in the South Korean subsidiary of Nike) create structures that emphasize high risk avoidance, greater instability, and high levels of formalization and standardization in structures. Contrast with the organizational structure of the Boeing Aircraft company in Redmond, Washington. The division of labor is complex: jobs are characterized by high levels of formalization at the lower levels but not at the higher levels of the organizational hierarchy. While procedures for assembly of the aircraft are fairly formalized, the processes may undergo rapid changes with continuous innovation and discontinuous shifts in the global marketplace.

How organizations differ in their structure depends on the factors depicted in Figure 10.2. While complexity of the technology employed by the organization is a major determinant of structure in organizations in the high-tech sector (e.g., software companies, aerospace, biotechnology, computers), its role diminishes as we examine the structures of organizations employing simple technologies (e.g., producing umbrellas in China, bicycles for the masses in China, food-processing in the US or India, production of liquor in France). Two important dimensions that are more closely related to structure are: *differentiation* and *integration.* The process of differentiation is concerned with effective division of labor among different subunits, functional areas, and work roles. Excessive differentiation may act as a centrifugal force (Aldrich & Marsden, 1988) that can have an adverse affect on the coherence of organizational units. Integration, on the other hand, is concerned with developing procedures which increase coherence and effective coordination among the various divisions (e.g., Cadillac versus the Chevrolet division of General Motors), functional areas, and diverse work roles. It is in the process of developing effective links and coordinating rules among the diverse functional areas of an organization that integration is achieved. A good example of an integrative process includes holding an annual meeting of the board of directors, internal trade shows (as happens on an annual basis in Japanese global organizations such as Toyota, Sony, and Matsushita). A simple example is holding weekly departmental meetings or circulating inter-office memoranda.

The structural dimension of differentiation tells us about the kind of *complexity* that is embedded in the organizational context. Structural complexity increases when the number of horizontal tasks (spread over many roles or units at the same or relatively similar organizational level) along with vertical tasks (spread over many levels in the organizational hierarchy of authority) increases over time. It increases even more when the organization has many operating sites (as is the case with General Motors or Toyota Corporation) or a large number of subsidiaries in the global context. Multinational and global organizations tend to be structured.

Along with the demands of the environment (i.e., various facets of the global marketplace), comparative studies of organizations have revealed the importance of heterogeneity, munificence, and uncertainty of the environment as another three determinants of structure. For example, the level of specialization of employment agencies is related to the heterogeneity of occupations and people in the local population (Blau & Shoenherr, 1971). Later studies (Dubick, 1978; Pfeffer, 1997) show that the structures of organizations are related to the degree of diversity and the rate of discontinuities in the environment. The roles of munificence and scarcity as determinants of structure have also been established. In fact, the institutional elements of the environment have been found to be more important than economic elements as determinants of structure in many cross-national studies of organizations. As an example of how cultural and these environmental elements influence the structure and design of Chinese organizations, we provide an analysis of the Chinese *quanxi*

THE CHINESE *QUANXI*

We discussed in Chapter 2 that values enshrined in Confucianism depict the essentials of Chinese culture. A Chinese emperor, Kong Qui, developed five codes of principles as essential guides for living in Chinese society in the 6th century. Called the *Five Cardinal Virtues*, these principles emphasize the value of filial piety, absolute loyalty to one's family and superiors, strict adherence to the seniority principle in work and non-work contexts, subordination of women to men, and mutual trust and harmony between members of in-groups, close friends, and co-workers. Kong Qui and his followers saw the social universe as a hierarchical system that is ruled by an educated aristocratic class. There was little emphasis on principles of equality between the sexes or social classes, or on the importance of making decisions on a participative basis. The essential nature of human relationships, according to the principles of the Cardinal Virtues, was to highlight the importance of interactions among un-equals and not among equals in societal as well as work contexts. Vertical relationships were emphasized more than horizontal ones. Socially appropriate patterns of interpersonal and other forms of exchange were largely determined by one's age (i.e., seniority), gender (males were to have more power and decision-making authority in both work and non-work domains), and ascribed status due to *quanxi* (see Figure 10.3). Particularistic exchanges were valued more than universalistic exchanges—an aspect of Chinese

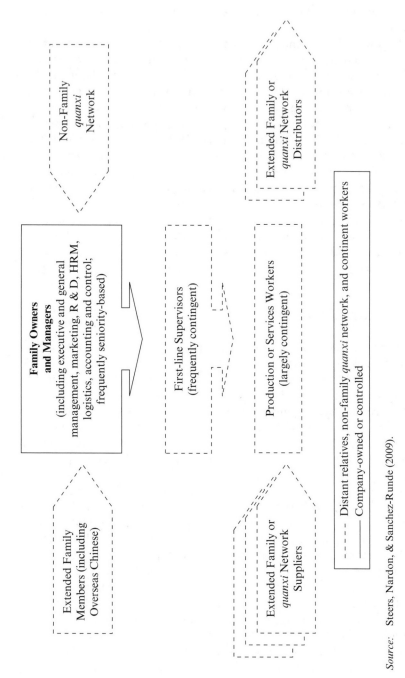

Family Owners and Managers
(including executive and general management, marketing, R & D, HRM, logistics, accounting and control; frequently seniority-based)

Non-Family *quanxi* Network

Extended Family Members (including Overseas Chinese)

First-line Supervisors (frequently contingent)

Production or Services Workers (largely contingent)

Extended Family or *quanxi* Network Distributors

Extended Family or *quanxi* Network Suppliers

- - - - Distant relatives, non-family *quanxi* network, and continent workers
——— Company-owned or controlled

Source: Steers, Nardon, & Sanchez-Runde (2009).

Figure 10.3 Organization design of a typical Chinese family-owned quanxi

248

culture that should be interpreted in the right spirit in order to understand structural idiosyncrasies. These types of relationships are key to
understanding the nature of cultural influences on structure in the Chinese
context. It is to be noted that these types of relationships continue to be
important as China emerges as the second largest economy in the world.

Another important cultural phenomenon that has a role in the development of structural properties of Chinese organizations is *mianzi*, or face
(i.e., dignity, self-respect, and prestige). Maintenance of interpersonal and
social harmony in the long term is an essential value of Confucianism. This
is generally accomplished by emphasizing both verbal and contextual cues
so that one does not lose face in a given situation (work or non-work).
Face can be classified into two types: *lian* and *mianzi*. *Lian* is reflected by
personal behavior, whereas *mianzi* is something valuable which can be
achieved. These two dimensions of face determine who has face, who can
gain face, and who can lose face. Face is defined as one's social identity
which reflects one's moral character. Losing face makes it difficult, if not
impossible, for an individual to function within a society. If an individual
fails to meet certain societal expectations, loss of face occurs as a result of
his or her actions or actions of those close to him or her. Face can also be
lost when an individual is not treated with the respect that is usually associated with an individual's position in a society. Loss of face makes it difficult
for an employee to function effectively in his or her work context as well as
in the community. This can happen when an individual, through negligence
of his or her actions, fails to meet the essential requirements of his or her
work role. It implies that when an individual at a senior level loses his or her
face, it becomes difficult for him or her to function effectively. Note that
loss of face is a relatively permanent phenomenon in the Chinese context,
particularly in rural China where the emphasis on Confucianism is strong.
In modern China, and especially organizations in a large affluent metropo-
lis like Shanghai, Hong Kong, Beijing, or Canton, one might be able to
gain one's lost "face" over time. Past *quanxi* relationships are critical in
the way Chinese organizations develop emphases on structural properties
such as formalization, centralization, participation in decision-making,
and hiring and promotion. Steers, Nardon, & Sanchez-Runde (2009) note
that requirements for behaving in a socially appropriate fashion differ
according to who is involved in the relationship of the transaction.

In view of China's strong cultural emphasis (it has a relatively tight
culture with respect with conduct of social behavior), both small and
large companies reflect the above cultural emphases in China, Singapore,
Taiwan, Malaysia, and in other overseas contexts where Chinese family
businesses have grown and prospered. Small Chinese businesses feel culturally bound to hire members of both nuclear and extended families and

others who are present in the *quanxi* network. Knowing that one can be trusted is key to hiring, promotion, and development-related decisions in Chinese organizations. Formal organizational processes tend to be overlooked, if not ignored in the development of structures—the Chinese prefer to work with structures that are consistent with the Confucian and Five Cardinal Virtues of the Chinese culture. For details on how cultural values have affected the design of organizational structures and evolution of capitalistic thoughts in modern China and Hong Kong, see Redding, 1990; Bond, 1996; and Smith, Bond, & Kagitcibasi, 2006.

STRUCTURE OF BRAZILIAN ORGANIZATIONS

Next, we consider the structure of Brazilian organizations. Brazil is an emergent economy which has experienced a growth rate of around 6 percent during the last decade under the charismatic President Lula. Brazilian managers face considerable uncertainties in day-to-day business transactions over which they have relatively little control. They function with a finely developed sense of intuition, having learned to trust their tacit knowledge regarding what works and what does not in their organizational contexts. The notion of *Jeitinho* is an important one which emphasizes the importance of going around a formal and established organizational process in order to get things done for an important client or customer. Flexibility and adaptability are byproducts of this process and the formal organizational structure becomes relatively unimportant.

Imagine a joint venture involving the cultures of Brazil, US, and China. One would expect that the firms involved in the joint venture would make every attempt to resolve their cultural differences on many fronts and emphasize the common mission of the project. However, the clash of cultures regarding how to run the operation would be high between the US and Chinese managers. The US managers would show much less concern for power and status and high perceived control over the demands of the global marketplace. The Chinese, on the other hand, would be concerned with maintaining face—especially for those at the higher echelons of the joint venture—and would regard the need to maintain differentiation of roles according to power to be of greater importance. The Brazilian managers would prefer a mode of structuring which would reflect a hybrid orientation. Unlike the US and Chinese managers, the Brazilians are likely to be less inclined to stress pragmatic concerns. However, the importance of getting things done without being constrained by the organization structure would be a major concern.

The organizational charts of various countries along with the structure

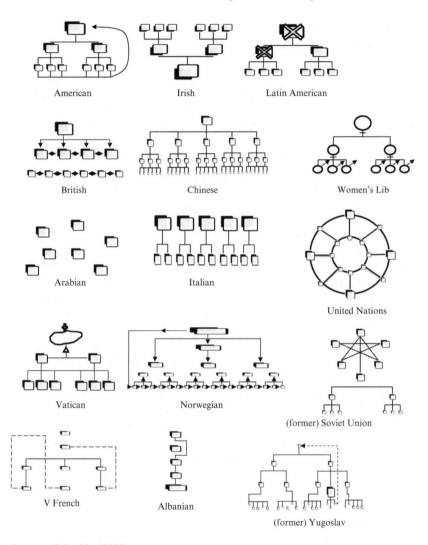

American

Irish

Latin American

British

Chinese

Women's Lib

Arabian

Italian

United Nations

Vatican

Norwegian

(former) Soviet Union

V French

Albanian

(former) Yugoslav

Source: Schneider (2008).

Figure 10.4 The organization chart

of the United Nations are depicted in Figure 10.4. The figure shows considerable variations in the way organizations are structured across nations and cultures. A contrast of the valued principles of working between US managers and Russian managers in their respective organizational constraints is presented in Table 10.2.

Table 10.2   Contrasting styles of Western and Russian managers

Western managers	Russian managers
Take initiative	Obey rules, do what is expected
Learn from mistakes, don't repeat	Don't make mistakes, punished for mistakes
Have a long-term, future orientation	Stay in the here and now, don't forget the past
Think of a company as a whole (integration)	Stick to job description, don't interfere

Source: Schneider (2003), p. 112.

The role of participative decision-making and empowering of lower-level employees have been increasing in the new structural arrangements in the US and Western European countries. The point is—the role of authority and the extent to which it needs to be necessarily located at the center or at the apex of the organization are being debated on an ongoing basis. The current role model of a supervisor or department leader is that of a "coach." As opposed to directly controlling the activities of subordinates and centralizing decision-making, the new role of leader in the flexible structures being emphasized in the US and Western European contexts emphasizes the process of facilitating and developing appropriate channels of communication to engage one's followers in participative decision-making. Notions of empowering subordinates and having leaders not as persons with a greater legitimate power are Western concepts. There is considerable difficulty in transferring these notions for management and developing structural arrangements suitable for competing in the global marketplace in Russia (and in Eastern European countries which belonged to the Soviet bloc).

Researchers and practitioners accept the notion that environmental, technological, and strategy-related variables determine organizational structures across all nations and cultures. The differences that are observed are due to the cultural significance of the role of organizations in different societies. Multinational and global organizations in the high-technology sector have to be more sensitive to ongoing fluctuations in customer demand along with intense pressures to incorporate the latest innovations. The role of cultural variables is somewhat lessened in these organizations compared with manufacturing organizations (i.e., producing machine tools, auto parts, heavy equipment, etc.) which function in a relatively less turbulent environment. Cultural influences affect the choice of modes of communication, decision-making, distribution of power and authority, and so on. Top management is not necessarily aware of the subconscious influences of culture and makes intuitive choices about how structures should evolve and function (Thomas, 2008). For example, the emphasis on hierarchies in German and Austrian multinational and global organizations reflect the significance of law and order as imposed from higher authorities in the cultural context of Germany and Central Europe. Child & Kieser (1979) and Ruedi & Lawrence (1970) note that inflexibility of organizational structures in German organizations is consistent with the dominant cultural values. In a seminal vein, the flat structure of Swedish automobile companies can be largely attributed to the egalitarian norms and values of Scandinavia (Ellegard et al., 1992).

Cultural influences are carried over in the design of subsidiaries in overseas locations. It is interesting to note that Japanese transplants in the US (Nissan in Tennessee, Honda in Ohio, Toyota in Mississippi and Kentucky, etc.) tend to mirror organizational structures that are largely reflective of what is preferred in the native Japanese context. Lincoln, Olson, & Hanada (1978) found that Japanese subsidiaries tended to resemble their headquarters in structure (especially with respect to specialization and formalization) in international work contexts as more Japanese worked in top management positions. Japanese organizations do not value task specialization as much as Western organizations, especially US companies. With more Japanese managers at the helm of the organization, subsidiaries in the US context tend to de-emphasize the significance of the structural property. We have already noted that environmental pressures from the demands of the global marketplace have the strongest influence in shaping organizational structures of multinational and global corporations regardless of their location. However, some distinctive properties of structures do undergo modifications when institutional, legal, and market-related pressures work in conjunction with the dominant cultural orientation of the society. In Figure 10.5, we depict a framework for examining the role of cultural variations in organizational structure and design across nations.

We have provided examples of differences in organizational structures (Figure 10.1) as direct consequences of cultural differences in these countries. The Chinese business emphasizes the role of *quanxi* and *paternalism* and these two cultural practices are observed widely in small business operations in various countries where the Chinese diaspora is present, such as San Francisco, Vancouver, and Melbourne. In the Japanese context, organizational structures reflect the dominant values enshrined in *keiretsu* (a complex interorganizational network across a large number of different industries including a trading company and a major bank). A similar mechanism is at work in South Korea, where *chaebol* dictates the design of organizational forms regardless of the industry. Companies like

Managing global organizations

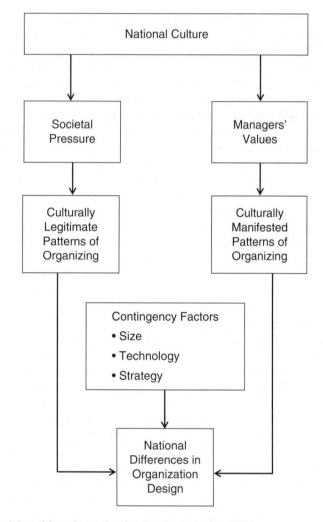

Source: Adapted from Steers, Sanchez-Runde, & Nardon (2010).

Figure 10.5   Cultural influence on organizational design

Nissan, Honda, and Toyota tend to align their organizational structure so as to be consistent with the principles of *keiretsu* in Japan. And, in the South Korean context, multi-industry conglomerates such as Hyundai, Samsung, Lucky Gold Star, and Daewoo are heavily influenced by principles enshrined in *chaebol*. *Chaebol* differs from *zaibatsu* in respect to employment of members of in-groups and close family, particularly at the senior management level. There have been several demonstrations against this practice in South Korea during the past two decades, but we have not yet noticed any major shifts toward making the organizational structures more like those in the West. Conformity to rules and regulations (however archaic they may be) is much easier to obtain from members of in-groups and close families. Korean multinationals and global companies tend to be large in size, partly because of this cultural practice and also because of governmental policies of low interest loans.

The nature of cultural influences on organizational design is depicted in Figure 10.6. Figure 10.7 presents the essence of this idea in the form of a non-overlapping figure of four major G-8 countries and Mexico which traditionally have had a family-oriented organizational structure. It should also be noted that no organizing framework in the context of any country exists forever. As globalization-related pressures increase, many of the collectivistic tendencies of organizational structures get slowly replaced by individualistic patterns. Market-related forces begin to determine the ultimate shape and size of organizations which compete in the global marketplace. The issue of convergence and divergence of organizational structures and forms is a topic of long-standing interest among organizational sociologists and international management scholars. Multinational and global organizations which are US-based and in Germany are strongly influenced by individualistic values. In fact, the system of incentives and rewards that makes structures thrive is strongly individualistic in the US and a little bit less so in the German context. In sharp contrast, multinational and global organizations from Japan, China, and Mexico are largely collectivistic in the way they operate and design their structural arrangements. For a detailed description of these culture-specific patterns of organizational design, see Steers, Sanchez-Runde, & Nardon (2010).

IMPLICATIONS FOR THE DESIGN OF MULTINATIONAL AND GLOBAL ORGANIZATIONS

Since the early studies by Udy (1970), who carried out comparative studies of organizational structure over a wide range of pre-industrial societies, we have come a long way in discerning the role of cultural variations in organizational structure. Later, in the 1970s and early 1980s, there was an emphasis on the role of political processes on the development of organizational structures. In particular, the role of Marxist ideologies on the development of structures in the Soviet bloc countries was examined and then contrasted with the patterns that exist in the US and other Western European countries. There was a widespread assumption among scholars

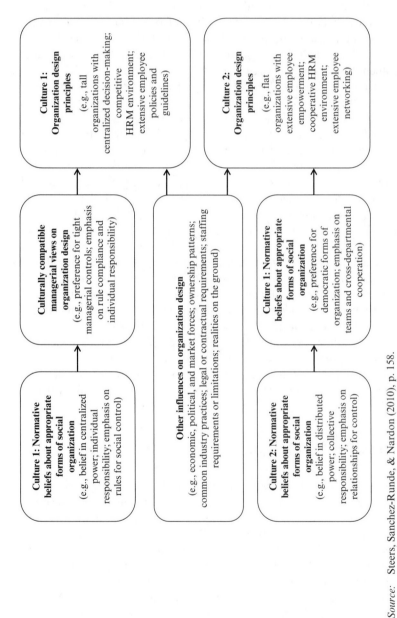

Source: Steers, Sanchez-Runde, & Nardon (2010), p. 158.

Figure 10.6   Cultural influences on organization design

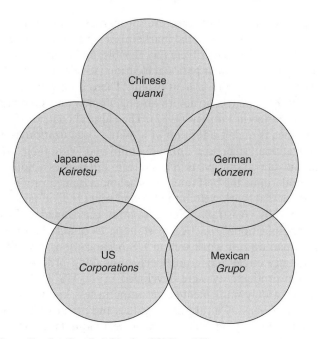

Source: Steers, Sanchez-Runde & Nardon (2010), p. 159.

Figure 10.7   Culture and organizational design: country examples

that in private enterprises of the West, the role of hierarchy and exploitation of workers was evident.

The notion that organizational structure is a function of size, technological complexity, history of the organization, the amount of resources it has at its command, and demands of the marketplace (e.g., the environment) was established in the 1980s and early 1990s. After the classic studies of Hofstede in 1980 and later, the role of cultural variations in the development and functioning of organizational structures began to be emphasized. There is an ongoing debate regarding the relative importance of technology and culture in shaping the organizational structure of firms in different geographical locales. The issues of convergence and divergence of organizational structure and design were being examined in the 1980s and 1990s. We have come a long way since then in understanding the role of environmental factors, strategic issues, technology, and culture on the development of organizational structures. The implications for effective design of multinational and global organizations are noted below:

1. It is safe to assume that structural properties of firms functioning in the highly competitive global marketplace and with complex technologies are likely to be relatively flat, flexible, and fluid. These organizations, regardless of their national location, are also going to be relying on matrix structure to a great extent. There is deep resistance to the adoption of a matrix structure among French and German managers, as reported in Laurent (1983). The cultural context of the French and Germans makes adoption of a matrix organization as a suitable organizational structure difficult compared with their Anglo and Scandinavian counterparts. The cultural differences among countries often undermine the best intentions behind assumed rationality of the structures that work well in the US and other individualistic contexts (e.g., the UK, Australia, New Zealand, and Canada). In a related vein, organizational practices pertaining to quality control methods from Japan do not work well in US organizations. Despite the fact that quality circle and group decision-making processes pertaining to group productivity were developed in the US in the 1950s, they were not widely implemented, resulting in less knowledge regarding their effectiveness. Culture-based values and practices may sometimes succeed in modifying a management technique (such as the quality circle approach to productivity) and organizational design (e.g., emphasis on matrix design); however, such examples are relatively rare. Effective transfer of management structure and processes from the US and Western European contexts to East and South Asian, and Latin American contexts depends on the ability of top management to recognize their merit and the nature of potential gain by applying these techniques. With the evolution of global organizational cultures, it is also becoming necessary for Western organizations to import management techniques (i.e., strategies for creating and diffusion of organizational knowledge) from East Asian multinationals (see Nonaka & Takeuchi, 1995). As noted earlier, there is a tendency toward convergence of organizational structure and forms, especially in high-technology-driven industries which also have to be highly responsive to the changing demands of the global marketplace.

2. Indigenous cultural values such as Confucian dynamism, emphasis on thrift, persistence, and a long-term perspective emphasize the evolution of organizational forms where hierarchical decision-making is the norm. Indeed, organizations in the banking and financial sectors in Hong Kong, Japan, and Singapore have outperformed their Western counterparts even though their structures are more hierarchical and participative decision-making is rarely practiced. Virtual teams and network organizations function well in the hierarchical context of

Asian and Latin American high-tech organizations, but much less effectively in Africa. Efforts to empower employees in Russia have not been successful. As discussed earlier, Russian managers expect a highly authoritarian style of decision-making, having been socialized in the values of Socialism which were dominant in the Russian context from 1917–99.

3. Issues concerning how to structure joint venture operations become important when the cultural distance between the countries is considered to be large. Consider a Swedish–Indonesian joint venture: there are going to be a large number of misunderstandings and clashes regarding the importance of hierarchy in decision-making. The Swedes would emphasize flat structures and would be more task-oriented compared with the Indonesians, who are less likely to bypass the legitimate authority (despite their boss's incompetence in some situations) in the organization to get the job done. The Indonesian firms are much more relationship-oriented, whereas the Swedish firms are more driven by rules and task specialization (Hooker, 2003). Cultural differences along this dimension are responsible for many clashes and failures in the operation of joint ventures. Relatively fewer cultural differences between the countries involved would ensure success of the operation, especially if there is congruence of mission, the type of technology employed, and a high level of professionalism.

We have suggested that environmental factors, including the nature of product (or service) diversity and the geographical spread of the multinational corporation, are crucial for the development of appropriate structures and designs. Cultural differences introduce significant gaps in the interpretation of the significance of various structural properties (i.e., tall versus flat, matrix versus traditional, centralized versus decentralized). Even with strong pressures to create organizational forms which converge over time, it is unlikely that multinational and global organizations functioning in relatively static (i.e., not turbulent) environments are going to create organizational structures which are relatively free from culture-specific values and expectations of the society in which they are embedded.

REFERENCES

Aldrich, H.E. & Marsden, P.V. (1988). Environments and organizations. In N.J. Smelser (Ed.). *Handbook of Sociology.* Newbury Park, CA: Sage.
Bartlett, C.A. & Beamish, P.W. (2011). *Transnational management.* Burr-Ridge, IL: McGraw-Hill/Irwin.

Blau, P.M. & Schoenherr, R.A. (1971). *The structure of organizations*. New York: Basic Books.

Bond, M.H. (1996). *The handbook of Chinese psychology*. Oxford: Oxford University Press.

Brossard, A. & Maurice, M. (1976). Is there a universal model of organization structure? *International Studies of Management and Organizations*, 6, 11–45.

Child, J. & Kieser, A. (1979). Organizational and managerial roles in British and West German companies: An examination of the culture-free thesis. In C.J. Lammers & D.J. Hickson (Eds). *Organizations alike and unalike: International and inter-institutional studies in the society of organizations* (pp. 251–71). London: Routledge & Kegan Paul.

Dubick, M.A. (1978). The organizational structure of newspapers in relation to their metropolitan environments. *Administrative Science Quarterly*, 23(3), 418–33.

Ellegard, K., Jonsson, D., Enstrom, T., Johansson, M., Medbo, L., & Johansson, B. (1992). Reflective production in the final assembly of motor vehicles: An emerging Swedish challenge. *International Journal of Operations and Production Management*, 12(7–8), 117–33.

Hofstede, G. (1980). *Culture's consequences*. Thousand Oaks, CA: Sage Publications.

Hooker, J. (2003). *Working across cultures*. Stanford, CA: Stanford University Press.

Kao, J. (1993). The world wide web of Chinese business. *Harvard Business Review*, March–April, 24–35.

Laurent, A. (1983). The cultural diversity of Western conceptions of management. *International Studies of Management and Organizations*, 13(1–2), 75–6.

Lincoln, J.R., Olson, J., & Hanada, M. (1978). Cultural effects on organizational structures: The case of Japanese firms in the United States. *American Sociological Review*, 43, 829–47.

Nonaka, I. (1995). *The knowledge-creating company: How Japanese companies create the dynamics of innovation*. Oxford: Oxford University Press.

Nonaka, I. & Takeuchi, H. (1995). *The knowledge creating company*. New York: Oxford University Press.

Perrow, C. (1965). Hospitals, technology, structures and goals. In J.G. March (Ed.). *Handbook of organizations* (pp. 910–71). Chicago: Rand-McNally.

Perrow, C. (1967). A framework for the comparative analysis of organizations. *American Sociological Review*, 32, 194–208.

Pfeffer, J. (1997). *New directions for organizations theory: Problems and prospects*. Stanford, CA: Stanford University Press.

Presthus, R. (1978). *The organizational society*. New York: St. Martin's.

Redding, S.G. (1990). *The spirit of Chinese capitalism*. Berlin: Walter de Gruyter.

Ruedi, A. & Lawrence, P.R. (1970). Organizations in two cultures. In J.W. Lorsch & P.R. Lawrence (Eds). *Studies in organizational design* (pp. 54–83). Homewood, IL: Irwin & Dorsey.

Schneider, S.C. (2003). *Managing across cultures*. Englewood Cliffs, NJ: Prentice-Hall.

Schneider, S. (2008). Culture and organizations. In C.A. Bartlett & Peter Beamish (Eds). *Transnational management* (p. 192). Burr Ridge, IL: McGraw-Hill/Irwin.

Smith, P.B., Bond, M.H., & Kagitcibasi, C. (2006). *Understanding social psychology across cultures: Living in a changing world*. Thousand Oaks, CA: Sage.

Steers, R.M., Nardon, L., & Sanchez-Runde, C. (2009). Culture and organizational design: Strategy, structure, and decision-making. In R.S. Bhagat and R.M. Steers (Eds). *Cambridge handbook of culture, organizations, and work* (p. 93). Cambridge: Cambridge University Press.

Steers, R.M., Sanchez-Runde, C.J., & Nardon, L. (2010). *Management across cultures: Challenges and strategies.* Cambridge: Cambridge University Press.

Stevens, O.J. (1991). *Cultures and organizations.* London: McGraw-Hill.

Thomas, D.C. (2008). *Cross-cultural management: Essential concepts.* Thousand Oaks, CA: Sage.

Udy, S.H. (1970). *Work in traditional and modern society.* Englewood Cliffs, NJ: Prentice-Hall.

United Nations Conference on Trade and Development Standing Committee on Economic Cooperation among Developing Countries (UNCTAD) (1993). *Report of the standing committee on Economic Cooperation among developing countries on its first session.* Palais des Nations, Geneva: UNCTAD.

11. Cultural variations in technology transfer and knowledge management

Written in collaboration with Ian McDevitt

Consider the case of the largest automobile company in the world, that is, Toyota, Incorporated of Japan, located near Tokyo. As a truly global company (that is the way they like to be known and promote themselves) it has major manufacturing units in Georgetown and Kentucky in the US, Sao Paulo in Brazil, and in India and France. It has sales offices and R & D centers in numerous countries of the WTO. As we discussed in Chapter 1, managing a global organization of the complexity of Toyota, Inc. is no easy task. Among many operations involved in the management of multinational–global organizations, the management of transferring various types of technologies and organizational knowledge across nations and cultures is of crucial importance. Global companies such as Toyota, Sony, Samsung, Microsoft, Siemens, and Pfizer, Inc. are routinely confronted with questions such as: "How do we create new forms of technologies that are needed in manufacturing subsidiaries in emerging economies like the BRIC countries?" "How do we successfully transfer knowledge created in the central R & D location in Toyota to other subsidiaries located in various countries and continents?" "How do we transfer effective marketing and sales strategies developed in the headquarter country to other growth-oriented markets like India, Brazil, and so on?"

The concept of technology transfer is not new, but the concepts and practices associated with the transfer of both organization-specific (i.e., systemic) and other forms of knowledge (explicit and implicit—or tacit) are relatively new. The complexities surrounding the process of technology transfer and organizational knowledge management have been growing in importance during the past four decades as competition in the global marketplace has intensified. Consider the case of the second largest automobile company, Ford Motor Company of the US, from the 1960s. In its move to become a truly global company and compete head-on with Toyota, Nissan, and Honda from Japan, it moved its design center where new technology and knowledge are created to its Central European subsidiary in Germany. The senior managers of Ford decided that moving the R & D center from Detroit to Germany would strengthen the transfer of new technologies to its worldwide manufacturing facilities. While the US is still the number one automobile market in the world, growth of this market in the Pacific Rim countries including India and China, and in the Middle East, has been considerable during the past three decades, and all global automobile companies must pay attention to the unique demands of the customers in these markets. During the 1970s, Americans had two cars for every three people, whereas in India and China, one out of 60 individuals had access to a car (Greider, 1997). It is interesting to note that one of the largest automobile manufacturing companies in India, the Tata Motor Company, plans to market a small sub-compact car called Nano in the US market. To the first author of this book, this news is hard to grasp. The world has indeed changed in terms of the shifting of manufacturing excellence from the Western countries to those in the developing countries and emerging economies. And this has happened, primarily, because of the efficient and relatively seamless transfer of technologies and organizational knowledge management across nations and cultures.

Along with the above development, the growing trend in a large majority of the G-20 countries has been to move away from emphasizing manufacturing to services, and especially managing knowledge-producing activities. Increasingly, only a small percentage of the world's working population is engaged in agriculture and manufacturing. The complexities associated with managing the creation, diffusion, and transfer of technological skills and organization-specific knowledge increase as globalization intensifies in all sectors of the economy. Peter Drucker noted as early as 1969 that the dominant emphasis in the US economy was moving from manufacturing to services. This forecast was ahead of its time, but now the concepts of "knowledge worker" and "knowledge-creating companies" (Nonaka & Takeuchi, 1995) have become commonplace in the current theoretical and applied literature on managing global companies.

The purpose of this chapter is to examine the significance of managing the process of technology transfer and organizational knowledge management across nations and cultures. In keeping with the central concern of this book, we put primary emphasis on the role of cultural variations in the creation, diffusion, and transfer of various types of technologies and organizational-specific forms of knowledge.

DEFINITIONS AND RELATED ISSUES

Most people have an intuitive sense of what technology is about, but they find it difficult to articulate the exact components of technology in a theoretically meaningful way.

Technology comprises systematically developed sets of information, skills, and processes needed to create, develop, and innovate products and services. New forms of technologies (e.g., development of electric/hybrid cars as opposed to petrol-driven cars) are developed to launch new products that markets and customers demand.

Technology transfer is concerned with movement of technology, knowledge, and skills from one company to another, from one unit to another, and from one person to another. Multinational–global organizations transfer technologies to other similar organizations as well as to their worldwide subsidiaries on a routine and sometimes not so routine basis. The tremendous growth of cell phones/mobile phones and Internet use in various countries of the world is a good example. Nokia of Finland and Microsoft of the US are routinely transferring their technologies to mobile phone companies in India, Hong Kong, China, and the Middle East. In fact, the countries which are reporting the highest growth rates in the use of mobile phone technologies are the BRIC countries, with India and China being the leading examples.

Selling heavy earth-moving equipment from companies such as Caterpillar of Peoria in the US and Komatsu of Japan to oil-rich countries in the Middle East provides a good example of technology transfer. However, this kind of transfer is vastly different from the transfer of mobile phone technology from Nokia, Motorola, Samsung, and Sony-Eriksson to other mobile phone manufacturers like Bharati Tel of India and Vodafone of the UK. Selling and transferring technological products like bulldozers, cranes, tractors, and heavy transportation trucks are examples of *product-embodied transfer*. Transferring *product-embodied technologies* is routine in the era of 21st century globalization. A large number of transfers that involve product-embodied technologies originate in Japan, South Korea, and the BRIC economies, while the receiving countries are Argentina, Nigeria, Mexico, and other developing countries.

Another type is the transfer of process-embedded technologies that include information. Transferring of blueprints or patent rights of scientific processes and engineering details are examples of these kinds of technology transfers. Examples include transfer of chemical technologies for the manufacturing of synthetic fibers and offshore oil exploration technology from large petroleum companies like Exxon-Mobil and

British Petroleum to Petrobar of Brazil, and so on. Technical details that are involved in oil-refining processes or the manufacturing of pharmaceutical products can be easily transmitted over the Internet or by video conferencing.

While complicated to transfer, transferring such technologies is much easier than transferring *person-embodied technologies* which involve continuous dialogue between the supplier and the recipient organizations pertaining to the intrinsic nature of the technology, and the best processes related to its diffusion, transfer, and absorption. The complex nature of person-embodied technologies makes the one-shot or quick transfer difficult. The effectiveness of these kinds of transfers involves a systemic consideration of the various strategic, technological, administrative, and cultural issues (see Figure 11.1). Consider the case of Bechel of San Francisco, an organization that transfers nuclear technologies to Indian organizations in the public sector. Transfer of complex surgical and medical techniques is also accomplished by sending teams of experts to the recipient organizations located in developing countries. An advanced scientific and technological infrastructure and a trained workforce at the receiving end are needed before such person-embodied technologies can be successfully transferred.

Bhagat and his colleagues (Bhagat & Kedia, 1988; Kedia & Bhagat, 1988; Bhagat, McDevitt, & McDevitt, 2010) reviewed the literature in this area and concluded that person-specific technologies are the most difficult types to transfer across nations and cultures. While there are good examples of transfers of pure product-embodied technologies, almost all recent transfers from developed and rich economies in the G-20 countries to developing and emerging economies necessarily involve some form of product, process, and person-embodied technologies. The competition for creating innovative forms of process and person-embodied technologies is increasingly fierce in various sectors, especially in high-tech, consumer electronics and products, and medical diagnostics. In order to take advantage of global talent and increasingly sophisticated scientific skills in countries such as India, South Korea, Singapore, and Poland, many Western global companies (such as GE, Microsoft, and Siemens) are finding it necessary to set up R & D operations in these countries and then engage in the continuous process of technology and knowledge transfer. Some of the typical problems that arise in the transfer of process and product-embodied technologies are mainly due to differences in the legal, administrative, and economic systems of the countries in which the organizations are located. Cultural differences also play important roles and will be considered below. Among the factors that influence technology transfers are:

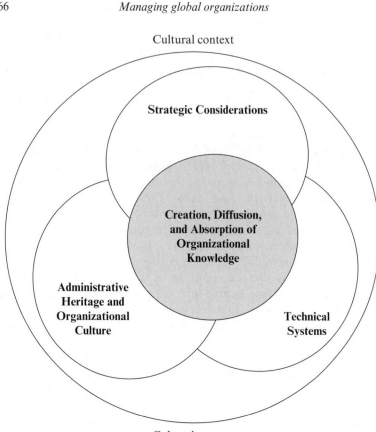

Source: Bhagat, Englis, & Kedia (2007), p. 107.

Figure 11.1   Creation, absorption, and diffusion of organizational knowledge

- *Similar language.*   Transfer of technology from an English-speaking country such as the United States to another English-speaking country like Australia or India is easier than transferring it to a country like China, where only a very small minority speaks English.
- *Common ancestry and shared history.*   Similarities in ancestry and historical background facilitate technology transfer. For example, Japanese high-tech organizations have been most successful in transferring technological know-how to countries such as South Korea, Taiwan, and Singapore which share a common Confucian background and in some cases similar historical developments.

- *Physical proximity.* US companies have been most effective in transferring technologies to their Canadian subsidiaries. General Motors' transfer of various forms of innovative automobile technologies from its Detroit headquarters to its Canadian subsidiaries located across the border in Ontario is a good case in point. In a related vein, German high-tech companies are effective in transferring technologies to Russian companies and to ex-Soviet bloc countries. While the US and Japanese high-tech companies might have some superior technologies, the mere fact that Germany is closer to Russia and the former Soviet republics facilitates the process of technology transfer.

- *Technical competence of the workforce.* This issue is more significant for newly emerging high-tech industries including the medical imaging and pharmaceutical sectors. Transferring various types of high-tech technologies from the US, Germany, and Japan to India and South Korea is easier due to the high level of occupational specialization and sophistication on the part of the workforce in the recipient organizations.

- *Complexity of technology involved.* It should not be surprising that complex technologies are more difficult to transfer compared with less complex technologies. Medical technologies involving neurosurgery and thoracic surgery, technologies involved in medical imaging processes, nuclear power plant technologies, and bullet (fast) train technologies from Japan and France are difficult to transfer regardless of where the recipient organizations are located. The sophistication of the workforce will facilitate the process of absorption of the complex technology, but it will nevertheless be a slow process.

- *Number of successful prior transfers.* If two organizations have been successful in the transfer of technologies in the past, the chances are that they will be successful in the future as well. The level of confidence on the part of both the sender and recipient organizations increases with each incidence of successful transfer. In addition, the organizational inertia and other structural barriers to successful transfer are likely to have been successfully dealt with when prior transfers were effective. A case in point is GE Medical Systems in Bangalore, India: established by the legendary CEO Jack Welch, GE Medical Systems in India has been reported to have been most successful in absorbing and diffusing technologies. In addition, it has also been successful in producing innovative medical imaging and other needed technologies due to its ability to successfully deal with prior technological transfers.

THE ROLE OF CULTURAL VARIATIONS

When we examine the history of technology and organizational knowledge management-related transfers, one factor stands out immediately. During the past 100 years, most of these transfers took place among Western nations and among subsidiaries of Western companies. Complexities arise when the sending and recipient organizations are located in two or more very different cultures. Consider two organizations located in two dissimilar societies like the US and Bulgaria. The US is moderate in uncertainty avoidance, and Bulgaria ranks rather high on this cultural dimension. Managers of Bulgarian organizations are less willing to absorb those technologies that might precipitate higher levels of uncertainties in the various organizational processes. In addition, the individualistic orientation of US managers who are transferring the technology are likely to be in conflict with the collectivistic orientation of their Bulgarian counterparts. R & D managers in individualistic cultures such as the US, UK, France, and Sweden are willing to take necessary risks (financial and other) in order to create more innovative technologies and also in their propensities to absorb and experiment with technologies from elsewhere.

Since the end of World War II, the rate of creation of new technologies has been high in the United States, United Kingdom, Germany, and Japan. With the exception of Japan, the other three countries are high on Hofstede's cultural dimension of individualism. While past history with technological experimentation and affluence exercised major influences in the creation of technologies, one cannot ignore the role of individualism as another major determinant. In the past three decades, starting with the 1980s, the rate of technological and organizational knowledge-based innovation has been growing at a much faster rate in countries that are collectivistic—the prime examples being South Korea, China, and India. *The Economist* (2011) in its lead coverage of intelligent forms of technologies reported that such technologies are being created in East and Southeast Asian countries at a faster rate than in the West.

The role of an activist state and higher professional skills on the part of engineers and scientists are clearly important, but cultural emphases on the virtues of long and sustained hours of work and adopting a long- versus short-term orientation toward results are also significant.

Figure 11.2 depicts a framework developed by Bhagat, Englis, & Kedia (2007) that shows the role of cultural differences at both the societal and organizational levels as determinants and moderators of the effectiveness of technology transfer across dissimilar nations. Along with the role of cultural variations, characteristics of the technologies (i.e., product, process, and person-embodied) and the absorptive capacity of

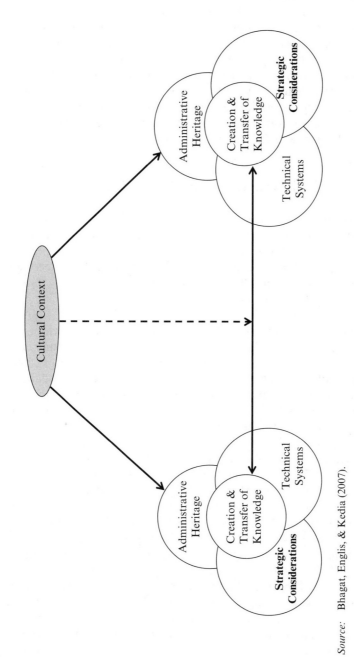

Source: Bhagat, Englis, & Kedia (2007).

Figure 11.2 Societal culture and other organization-based variables influencing the cross-border transfer of organizational knowledge

269

the recipient organization are also presented. Bhagat, Englis, & Kedia (2007) argue that product-embodied technologies are relatively easy to transfer across cultures, transfer of process-embodied technology is more difficult, and person-embodied technologies are the most difficult. The figure also shows the importance of strategic considerations, technical skills of people involved, organizational culture, and societal culture as important determinants in the effective transfer of technology across nations. Cultural considerations are particularly important when two dissimilar cultures engage in transferring technology—especially when they have not had much experience in doing so in the past.

MANAGING ORGANIZATIONAL KNOWLEDGE

Like technology, knowledge is an important commodity for multinational–global organizations. Effective management of organizational knowledge is crucial to creating and maintaining international competitiveness for high-technology and knowledge-intensive firms. Consider the operation of global management consulting firm McKenzie and Company located in San Francisco. Its mission and guiding principles involve making positive and lasting improvements in the effectiveness of its clients. In order to maintain its competitiveness, the firm seeks to attract, develop, and retain exceptional people. Being a member of the global consulting team involves seeking superior knowledge on a continuous basis and contributing to a spirit of partnership through effective teamwork and collaboration. McKenzie and Company has 15 centers of competence including developing institutional skills, outsourcing, integrative logistics, corporate finance, marketing, manufacturing, and strategic management (Bartlett, 1996). Its clients include multinational–global companies in automotive, banking, electronics, energy, healthcare, and related activities. To help develop a shared body of knowledge, the leadership of each of the 15 centers of competence initiates knowledge-sharing activities involving the core group and the practice network. Starting in 1978, the company launched the McKinsey Staff Papers series which was designed to actively encourage consultants to publish the key findings from their experiences in order to disseminate both technical and organization-specific knowledge. In 1987, the senior management designed a knowledge management project which focused on the following three objectives. First, the company had to make a major commitment to build a common database of knowledge accumulated through years of consulting with clients in various sectors in different countries and emerging economies. Secondly, it had to ensure that the databases were maintained and used in each of the 15 centers of competence. Thirdly, hiring and promotion practices were designed to emphasize the recruitment of specialists with in-depth technical knowledge.

The strategic significance of creating, diffusing, transferring, and absorbing organizational knowledge has increased exponentially since the publication of *The knowledge-creating company* (Nonaka & Takeuchi, 1995). In his endorsement of this book, Karl Weick noted that the process of creating and managing organizational knowledge had become essential in the 1990s. Similar to the pursuit of excellence in the 1980s, effective management of organizational knowledge in multinational–global organizations had become of paramount importance.

Knowledge has been defined in numerous ways and most people, regardless of whether they work for multinational and global organizations, have an intuitive sense of what knowledge is all about. Knowledge is broader, deeper, and richer than either data or information. *Data*, which are related to the concept of knowledge, reflect discrete and objective facts about events. Think of a large restaurant which keeps count of the kinds of meals customers order before Thanksgiving. Without any details, these transactions regarding the kinds of meals by themselves constitute what we may call "raw data." However, when the restaurant owners also know what type of customers are likely to order what kind of meals (i.e., steaks, seafood, or Italian specialities), then they have what is called *information.* Information is meant to change the cognitive frames a receiver may use to perceive something—that is, it makes an impact on the judgment and behavior of the decision-maker. The word inform means "to give shape to," and important information created in organizational contexts makes some difference in the outlook of the receiver (i.e., the restaurant owners in the present example). Whether a message is information or not is determined by the receiver and not by the sender. Multinational–global organizations keep huge amounts of quantitative as well as qualitative forms of data without necessarily analyzing the degree of connectivity that exists in these data banks. A caveat is in order: having a large amount of sophisticated information-processing equipment does not necessarily enhance the quality of information in a global organization.

Information can lead to the development of knowledge—the kind of systematic body of information that creates beliefs and commitments, and guides actions. Knowledge is created to meet some objectives or to "some end." Most importantly, organizational knowledge like organization-specific information is context-specific and largely relational in character.

The *intellectual capital* of a global corporation is the sum total of the stock of knowledge which is explicitly described in procedures and manuals as well as is systemically embedded in an organization's unique culture

and processes. Key individuals of the organization are largely responsible for creating and sustaining the kind of talent that it needs to have in
order to maintain international competitiveness. For example, knowledge
regarding the preferences and actions of clients in various countries that
are held in the mental and organizational processes of giant global financial companies like American Express is critical to their success and may
be referred to as their intellectual capital. Senior managers in charge of
creating and diffusing important strategic knowledge in the organization
note that there is no shortage of talented people in the world. But there is
a shortage of the right people in the right places. Management of talent
is becoming key to effective organizational knowledge management and
is becoming vital for multinational–global organizations. Knowledge can
be created from strands of information through the following processes:

- *Comparison.* When a given piece of information about an organizational event such as sales transactions in a subsidiary is compared
  with sales transactions in another subsidiary located in a dissimilar economy and culture, knowledge can be created. If the senior
  managers begin to sense that the new piece of information is more
  indicative of a trend that is taking place in the global marketplace,
  then this new information becomes knowledge of some strategic
  relevance. Consider the case of mobile phone use in the world. The
  number of mobile phones sold in India and China (two of the most
  populous countries in the world) is estimated to be growing at an
  exponential rate. Comparison of sales data from global companies
  such as AT&T and Nokia with the domestic mobile companies
  in India such as Tata Communication, Bharati-Tel, and Reliance
  Communication can reveal the preferences of customers in India.
- *Consequences.* If a strand of information can signal the development of a significant course of action that the company must initiate,
  then that information is clearly knowledge. Reliable information
  about a possible crash on Wall Street has important consequences
  for a manufacturing company from China that might plan to open
  a large factory in the American Midwest. Senior managers of multinational–global companies keep themselves informed regarding the
  latest trends which might precipitate new directions in developing
  products, services, and so on. Senior managers of multinational and
  global corporations are sensitive to all types of related and unrelated
  strands of information which (if interpreted meaningfully) may have
  important consequences for the organization.
- *Connections.* When a piece of information is related to other bits of
  information that the organization has in its inventory and working

manuals, then it becomes knowledge. Medical diagnostic equipment looks for all types of possible connections among various images of human organs. If a connection appears to result in important findings, then that connection becomes useful knowledge.

- *Conversation.* Related and unrelated pieces of information have the potential to become knowledge when managers discuss various aspects of such information and interpret it to arrive at meaningful and clear decisions. FBI professionals in the US use this process in detecting criminal behavior. Seemingly unrelated pieces of information eventually may lead to significant amounts of knowledge about hidden motives of a criminal and clues regarding his or her whereabouts. In the case of global corporations, various unrelated acts taking place in a developing country when a new product is introduced may, on reflection by a group of senior product development managers, yield valuable information regarding future marketing strategies.

CULTURE AND KNOWLEDGE TRANSFER

Knowledge is an intangible asset in a multinational and global organization composed of the skills and knowledge of senior managers, patents, databases, and networks, as well as information regarding relationships with customers, suppliers, and regulatory agencies, such as governmental agencies. Companies like General Electric, Microsoft, Canon, Inc. of Japan, and Siemens of Germany have been effective in converting various types of knowledge in creating systematic patterns of organizational learning which are essential for enhancing organizational effectiveness. A majority of the multinational and global corporations have chief knowledge or information officers who oversee the process of knowledge creation, transfer, diffusion, and absorption in the various subsidiaries of the company. Knowledge in organizations is created, accumulated, and held collectively in the working memories of the key individuals in the context of their work lives. The breadth and depth of experiences that key managers have in their specialized roles are developed over time. Chief knowledge management officers and their staff must find appropriate ways of articulating such knowledge in developing new products and improving processes.

Knowledge is of two kinds: *tacit* and *explicit*. Tacit knowledge is highly personal, difficult to communicate, and highly specialized. Processing and transferring it is difficult because it is part of the historical and cultural contexts in which the organization exists. Tacit knowledge reflects the collective body of interconnected information that results from a long-term process of continual knowing. It consists of specific information and know-how that are obtained through the experience of having "lived" in the environment or having performed a particular task many times over—like driving a car, flying a plane, or operating the basic system of a lap top computer. Tacit knowledge is difficult to transfer. For instance, you cannot teach people to drive a car without the experience of actually driving it. One must absorb tacit knowledge by repetition and trial and error. It cannot be easily codified and is highly sensitive to the cultural context (Bhagat, Kedia, Harveston, & Triandis, 2002; Bhagat, McDevitt, & McDevitt, 2010).

Explicit knowledge, on the other hand, is knowledge that can be written down and translated. It is discrete, or digital, and is usually stored in repositories such as libraries and company databases. As a general rule, explicit knowledge that is not classified by national governments can be accessed without difficulty. For example, blueprints for the construction of a hydroelectric or nuclear power plant can be transferred from one organization to another.

Tacit knowledge is becoming increasingly recognized as an important source of knowledge that can be leveraged for creating new ideas, products, services, and so on. It is particularly valued in the collectivistic cultures such as Japan, South Korea, China, India, and Brazil. Its importance was revealed and discussed in detail by Nonaka & Takuchi (1995) and also by Davenport and Prusak (1998). The development of the bread-making machine by Canon, Inc. of Japan is a good example of how tacit knowledge was converted into explicit knowledge and then harnessed for commercial gain. A team of computer programmers led by Ms. Tanaka of Canon, Inc. was able to simulate the movements of fingers of the bakers of the Osaka International Hotel as they kneaded dough for making bread (see related examples in Bartlett & Beamish, 2011).

While the technical expertise of the programmers certainly played an important role in this example, the fact is that people in some cultures are better able to transform knowledge of one form into another without a great deal of effort. Holden (2002) observed that one of the major problems that global organizations face is the diversity of countries in terms of language, culture, and ethnic backgrounds that come into play in the process of creating, transforming, diffusing, and transferring knowledge. Japanese global organizations are particularly effective in transferring knowledge from their headquarters when country managers of the subsidiaries are Japanese.

Examples of knowledge disavowal when subsidiary managers choose not to implement a particular form of technology or organizational knowledge management by noting that "people here will not buy into these foreign practices" happen due to sharp cultural differences in the way knowledge and innovation are appraised, valued, and implemented. The role of trust between the subsidiary and the headquarters and among the subsidiaries is most important—in fact, complete distortion of knowledge management-based practices may take place due to the lack of a shared history of success and trust. Interorganizational collaborations (e.g., joint ventures, strategic alliances, cross-border project teams) that global organizations must undertake on a routine basis increase the power of knowledge workers and chief knowledge information officers in different industries. Lack of inter-personal, inter-group, and interorganizational transactions based on trust is often a function of deeply held cultural differences, including prejudices, and can create insurmountable difficulties in collaborative projects (e.g., high-speed knowledge-sharing among R & D labs in culturally dissimilar locales) (Bhagat, McDevitt, & McDevitt, 2010).

We have noted that culture is to a society what memory is to an individual (Triandis, 1994, 1995, 1998). Several dimensions of cultural variations (see Chapter 2) are important in examining the process of creation, diffusion, absorption, and transfer of technologies and organizational knowledge management techniques. In this book, we have focused on the role of individualism–collectivism due to its significance in reflecting the deep structure of cultural differences among societies (Triandis, 1995; Greenfield, 1999; Hofstede, 2001; Bhagat, Kedia, Harveston, & Triandis, 2002). Research evidence presented in Markus & Kitayama (1991) and Kitayama, Duffy, & Uchida (2007) indicates that people in individualistic cultures think of their "selves" as independent of the immediate social or work environment and tend to evaluate each piece of information as being independent from the context in which it is found. Collectivists, on the other hand, view their "selves" as functioning interdependently with significant others (e.g., in-groups, co-workers) in the social or work environment and search for contextually relevant cues in interpreting and using each piece of information (Triandis, 1995, 1998; Bhagat, Kedia, Harveston, & Triandis, 2002; Bhagat, McDevitt, & McDevitt, 2010). An examination of successful instances of organizational knowledge management practices reveals the significance of past histories of success, norms of doing things in a specific fashion as preferred by the members of trans-acting groups, and so on; it also shows that collectivists are much more sensitive to receiving, interpreting, and implementing context-specific and tacit information. Systemic and tacit knowledge are likely to be more valued and implemented more effortlessly by collectivists compared with individualists (see Table 11.1). On the other hand, when organizational knowledge management activities emphasize seeing connections between various types of environmental events and processes, individualists are better at interpreting and incorporating them. Rational and abstractive

Table 11.1   Relative emphasis of different types of knowledge in individualistic and collectivistic cultures

Dimensions of knowledge	Individualistic cultures	Collectivistic cultures
Simple versus complex	No distinct preference for handling either type	
Tacit versus explicit	Explicit	Tacit
Independent versus systemic	Independent	Systemic
Mode of conversion	Externalization combination	Socialization internalization

Source: Bhagat, Kedia, Harveston, & Triandis (2002), p. 209.

connections are more valued by individualists as a causal chain of events in the cycle of knowledge management in organizations.

In Table 11.1, we depict the relative emphases of individualistic–collectivistic cultures in dealing with various dimensions of knowledge. The figure shows that individuals working in multinational and global organizations in individualistic countries (e.g., the US, Canada, Australia, UK, Germany) do not differ from individuals working in multinational corporations in collectivistic cultures (e.g., China, Japan, South Korea, Brazil, India) in terms of their preferences for "simple versus complex" types of knowledge. Complex knowledge involves a larger number of causal uncertainties when compared with simple knowledge (e.g., the technology involved in creating i-Phones is more complex than the technology involved in refining crude petroleum). However, members of individualistic cultures are more strongly predisposed toward processing explicit as opposed to tacit forms of knowledge. Also, individualists prefer knowledge that is relatively independent of the organizational system, and they also prefer to develop knowledge management systems that involve transactions between explicit forms of knowledge. A case in point is developing blueprints for lap tops based on blueprints from desk-top computers and accomplishing this technological feat regardless of the organizational context (i.e., it doesn't matter whether the individualists are working in the context of Dell Computers of Austin, Texas or Hewlett-Packard of San Francisco). Collectivists take more pride in designing technologies in accordance with the "Toyota way" or "Samsung way," and emphasize the superior relevance of the "invented here" perspective in organizational knowledge management. Bhagat, Kedia, Harveston, & Triandis (2002) and Bhagat, McDevitt, & McDevitt et al. (2010) have argued that collectivists are more adept in creation, absorption, diffusion, and transfer of

Table 11.2   Four modes of knowledge creation

Mode 1: Combination	Mode 2: Internationalization
Explicit ———→ Explicit Is much easier to codify and convey to significant parties and recipients in the transnational and global organizations.	Explicit ———→ Tacit Cannot be easily codified, cannot be easily conveyed and transmitted into significant parties and recipients.
Mode 3: Externalizations	Mode 4: Socialization
Tacit ———→ Explicit Cannot be easily codified and conveyed to those who might need this kind of knowledge.	Tacit ———→ Tacit Most difficult to codify; the process of such knowledge creation essentially focused on developing shared mental models among the important members and others who need this kind of knowledge.

Source: Based on Nonaka and Takeuchi's scheme; I.Nonaka and H.Takeuchi (1995), p. 58.

tacit forms of knowledge than individualists. Therefore, to the extent that a larger portion of knowledge management activities in the multinational–global organizations of tomorrow involves developing knowledge management systems that are largely dependent on tacit forms of knowledge, collectivists and their global organizations are likely to be more effective.

Individualists are strongly inclined to create knowledge that relies heavily on *externalization* (i.e., conversion of knowledge from tacit to explicit forms) and *combination* (i.e., conversion of knowledge from explicit to explicit forms). Two other modes of knowledge creation are *internalization* (conversion of knowledge from explicit to tacit) and *socialization* (conversion of knowledge from tacit to tacit). These four modes, as depicted in Table 11.2, are utilized by both domestic and global organizations. The effectiveness of organizational knowledge management lies to a great extent in the collective sense-making processes and abilities of senior managers to know which mode to employ, when to employ it, and in what situations (Bhagat, Englis, & Kedia, 2007). Some modes of knowledge creation are more effective in the context of some multinational and global organizations due to past history of successes, superior administrative heritages and technical systems, and appropriate cultural contexts (including interventions by activist governmental agencies in countries such as China, India, and Brazil). Individualists prefer knowledge that can be coded, calibrated, and made applicable in designing new types of products and services. There is also an emphasis on speed of innovation— preferred more by individualists than collectivists; however, recent evidence tends to show that the Japanese (strongly collectivistic culture) are much faster than Western cultures in bringing new products to the global marketplace (Tushman & Nelson, 1990). The effectiveness of creation, diffusion, absorption, and transfer of organizational knowledge lies at the intersection of strategic considerations, administrative heritage and organizational culture, and the technological system of the organization(s) involved (Figure 11.2). The role of societal culture and other organizational variables influencing cross-border transfer of organizational knowledge is depicted in Figure 11.3. This figure depicts the current state of thinking regarding the role of individualism–collectivism and the cross-border transfer of organizational knowledge. Bhagat, Kedia, Harveston, & Triandis (2002) and Bhagat, McDevitt, & McDevitt (2010) advance the idea that the transfer of knowledge is more effective when it involves two nations with identical cultural patterns of vertical individualism, vertical collectivism, horizontal individualism, and horizontal collectivism.

Individualists believe that knowledge can be articulated in a given domain of inquiry no matter how long it might take at times. In addition, they believe that knowledge can be organized (i.e., codified in a systematic form) and created from theoretical analyses and experimentation. Collectivists, on the other hand, are inclined to emphasize the salience of context (Nisbett, Peng, Choi, & Norenzayan, 2001; Chiu & Hong, 2006). This tendency leads collectivists to favor socialization and internalization as modes of knowledge creation in the organizational context.

The Role of Other Cultural Variations

Along with the important role of individualism versus collectivism, cultural variations of power distance (Hofstede, 2001), openness to change versus tendencies toward conservatism (Eckstein & Gurr, 1975; Haire, Ghiselli, & Porter, 1996; Smith & Schwartz, 1997), past, present, and future orientation (Kluckhohn & Strodbeck, 1961), cosmopolitan versus local orientation (Merton, 1968; Rogers & Shoemaker, 1971; Kedia & Bhagat, 1988), Confucian dynamism (Chinese Culture Connection, 1987), universalism versus particularism (Glenn & Glenn, 1981), and holistic versus linear orientation (Redding, 1980; Maruyama, 1994) have important implications for the way knowledge is generated, diffused, transformed, absorbed, and transferred in multinational and global organizations.

The role of cultural variations is ever present and influences each of these three intersecting and embedded systems (see Table 11.3).

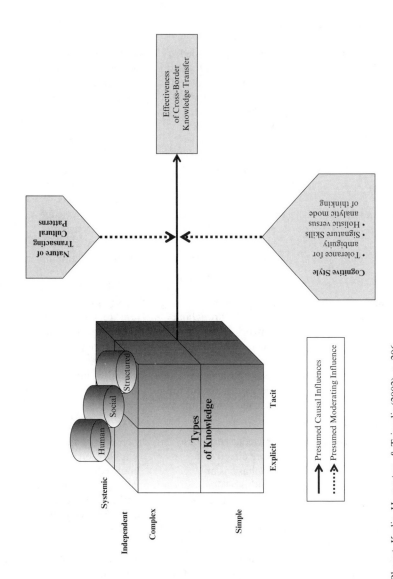

Source: Bhagat, Kedia, Harveston, & Triandis (2002), p. 206.

Figure 11.3   A model of knowledge transfer in a cross-border context

*Table 11.3   Factors affecting the creation of knowledge in transnational
              and global organizations*

Similar	Within	Across
Strategic Considerations		
Strategic intent for knowledge creation	Transferring knowledge in subsidiaries located in distinctive cultural contexts such as GM in US and Glaxco Wellcome in UK. Strategic intent generally facilitates such processes.	Transferring knowledge between two global organizations (i.e., IBM in the US with Fujutsu in Japan), differences in strategic intent generally prevents effective transfer in subsidiaries located in distinctive cultural contexts.
Emphasis on innovation	Transfer of knowledge generally emphasizes creation of new knowledge at the point of absorption.	Transfer of knowledge to fulfill licensing requirements and enhance functioning of recipient organization.
Tangible and administrative support for innovation	Making resources available throughout network to facilitate knowledge transfer is easier to accomplish when there is significant top management support.	Differs in available resources to facilitate knowledge transfer process may lead to selective absorption, retention, and diffusion.
Administrative Heritage		
Historical emphasis on knowledge creation	Knowledge transfer is more effective if emphasis is on continuous innovation throughout network.	Differences in historical emphasis on knowledge management may lead to ineffective knowledge transfer.
Values and practices of founders and senior managers	Likely consistency in managerial practices throughout network might aid knowledge transfer across subsidiaries.	Differences in managerial values and practices infused throughout distinct organizations likely to inhibit successful knowledge transfer.

Table 11.3   (continued)

Similar	Within	Across
Administrative Heritage Nature of organizational communication and quality of professional interaction	Processes, systems, and support infrastructure to facilitate creation of knowledge.	Processes, systems, and support infrastructure to facilitate creation of knowledge.
Technical Systems Research and development (R & D) systems	Likely compatibility of R & D systems throughout the world facilitates knowledge transfer.	Differences in compatibility and sophistication of R & D systems throughout the world inhibits effective knowledge transfer.
Sophistication of management information system	Continuous investment in MIS to facilitate knowledge transfer.	Differences in MIS systems inhibit effective transfer of knowledge.
Quality and competence of technical and administrative staff	Competent technical and administrative staff facilitate knowledge transfer.	Differences in skill levels of technical and administrative staff inhibit knowledge transfer.
Cultural Differences Individualism–Collectivism	Transferring implicit knowledge from a collectivistic context to an individualistic context, even though difficult, could still be accomplished with relative ease due to similarities in strategic considerations, administrative heritage and technical systems. Transferring explicit knowledge from a collectivistic context to an individualistic context, even though	Transferring implicit knowledge from a collectivistic context to an individualistic context will be more difficult due to differences similarities in strategic considerations, administrative heritage, and technical systems. Transferring explicit knowledge from collectivistic context to an individualistic context will be

Table 11.3 (continued)

Similar	Within	Across
Cultural Differences		
	difficult, could still be accomplished with relative ease due to similarities in strategic considerations, administrative heritage, and technical systems.	more difficult due to differences similarities in strategic considerations, administrative heritage, and technical systems.
Power Distance	Transferring implicit knowledge from a high power distance context to a low power distance context and visa versa, while difficult, could still be accomplished with relative ease due to above-mentioned similarities.	Transferring implicit knowledge from a high power distance context to a low power distance context and visa versa, will be more difficult due to differences similarities in strategic considerations, administrative heritages, and technical systems.
	Transferring explicit knowledge from a high power distance context to a low power distant context and visa versa, while difficult, could still be accomplished with relative ease due to above mentioned similarities.	Transferring explicit knowledge from a high power distant context to a low power distant context and visa versa, will be more difficult due to differences similarities in strategic considerations, administrative heritages, and technical systems.

Source: Bhagat et al. (2007), p. 111.

Multinational–global organizations must engage in creating and transforming tacit and explicit forms of knowledge. Numerous studies discuss the critical importance of many forms of knowledge that are essentially tacit (Kogut & Zander, 1993; Zander & Kogut, 1995). "Tacitness" is often associated with Polanyi's (1966) observation that "we know more than we can tell." Intuitive understanding that is not necessarily systematically coded can be effective in introducing innovative changes to products and services offered by multinational–global organizations. If such under-standing on the part of qualified technical personnel and senior manag-ers can be transmitted to those in charge of implementing innovations, then major advantages are obtained by the corporation. Such types of knowledge when they are systemically embedded often become "sticky" in character (Suzlanski, 1996) and cannot easily be transferred to other sub-sidiaries or organizations. There is no doubt that quantifiable technologies and processes have their foundations in bodies of explicit knowledge and can be easily transferred across dissimilar nations and cultures (Teagarden et al., 1995; Bhagat et al., 2002; Bhagat, McDevitt, & McDevitt, 2010).

While a vast majority of the knowledge management processes that are being designed and transferred across dissimilar cultures are explicit in character and use combinations as the mode of creation, there are impor-tant forms of tacit knowledge that emerge on a routine and non-routine basis in the context of multinational–global organizations. Rotation of technical personnel among various divisions is a common practice in Japanese, South Korean, Chinese, and Indian multinationals. Such tech-niques prevent the hoarding of knowledge in any given division and indeed can facilitate the process of sharing both explicit (e.g., important rules for executing processes) and tacit (e.g., recognition of cues that might lead to the development of new products or services) forms of knowledge.

The New Role of R & D Centers

The internal R & D organization acts as the backbone for innovation in multinational and global organizations. Some companies make a dis-tinction between those R & D units that focus primarily on developing new technologies and improving existing ones and those whose primary objective is the development of new products. Nokia of Finland and Shell of the Netherlands make this distinction. Shell has three central technical centers focusing on innovation and technology development, two in the Netherlands and one in Houston, Texas. There are in addition other technical centers that focus on product development, marketing support, and other specific assistance for regional operations located in countries such as the UK, France, Canada, India, Qatar, and Singapore. Shell has invested in developing a 3-D virtual reality suite (built within its second life virtual world) to enhance ongoing collaboration among these geographically dispersed units.

Just as the advent of railways, steamships, and the telephone stimulated a new era of internationalization in the 1900s, so has the digital revolution including the Internet contributed to globalization in the 21st century. E-mail, video-conferencing, computerized databases, and electronic forums have completely removed barriers for effective collaboration and interaction among key R & D personnel located in dissimilar nations and cultures. Despite some significant advantages of digital technologies in facilitating the process of sharing information and knowledge, giant companies Microsoft and Cisco are locating thousands of R & D and technical personnel in company headquarters in Redmond, Seattle, and San Jose, California, respectively. The R & D centers of large global companies are also located near research universities such as the University of California–Berkeley, Stanford University, MIT, Cambridge University, National Seoul University in South Korea, Fudan University in Shanghai, China, Indian Institute of Science, Bangalore and the Indian Institute of Technology in New Delhi. Perhaps the major objective of locating R & D units near universities is concerned with sharing of tacit knowledge, which requires extensive personal interaction (including attending brainstorming sessions, seminars, presentations, etc.) between the inventor and the R & D personnel of the organization. Innovation is above all a social process and, despite all developments in creating sophisticated forms of communication across R & D laboratories, the fact is that distance is detrimental. The management of R & D organizations is complex, and is discussed in Jain, Triandis, & Weick (2010). Linking important R & D personnel through travel and then clustering people who work together on similar projects is important for the precise reason that it helps facilitate sharing of tacit information and knowledge—regardless of cultural differences that might exist in R & D laboratories.

Most large global corporations carry out extensive R & D activities outside their home countries. A 1996 study by the management consultation firm of McKinsey & Company found that 80 top US-based R & D investors spent over $80 billion out of a total of $146 billion in R & D activities abroad. Similarly, the top 43 Japanese global firms invested $40 billion out of $72 billion in overseas R & D activities. The top 50 European multinationals spent $51 billion out of $117 billion in R & D activities outside the European continent. In the past three decades China, India, Eastern Europe, and Singapore have become favorite destinations for R & D investments. It is remarkable to note that over 83 percent of new R & D operations are being established in India and China, fueling much of their growth in creating new technologies in medical systems, high-tech products, pharmaceuticals, and other consumer goods. The Booz, Allen report concludes that global companies that take a worldwide view of developing R & D in different parts of the world, with a strong concentration at the headquarters, perform better than other companies in sustaining their long-term competitiveness.

WHERE DO WE GO FROM HERE?

At the outset of this chapter, we alluded to the growing importance of transferring technologies and managing organizational knowledge for multinational–global companies. The process is a challenging one involving managing conflicting cultural priorities, organizational goals and objectives, and related issues of integrating different strands of information into meaningful patterns with practical consequences. The process of managing technologies and organizational knowledge systems involves alternating cycles of divergent and convergent patterns of behaviors— exploring new directions some of the time with focused pursuit in a given direction at other times. Building new relationships across cultures and establishing effective channels of communication for the distortion-free flow of communication is no easy task. We have presented conceptual schemes to understand the basic processes of managing technologies and organizational knowledge management processes. Sustaining cycles of innovation is the key to the future success and growth of Western economies (*Time Magazine*, 2011; Zakaria, 2012). Effective management of organizational knowledge provides the foundation of this process.

REFERENCES

Bartlett, C.A. & Beamish, P.W. (2011). *Transnational management*. Burr-Ridge, IL: McGraw-Hill/Irwin.

Bartlett, C., Ghoshal, S., & Beamish, P. (2008). *Transnational management*. Boston, MA: McGraw-Hill.

Bhagat, R.S. & Kedia, B.L. (1988). Cultural constraints on the transfer of technology across nations: Implications for research in international and comparative management. *Academy of Management Review*, 13(4), 559–71.

Bhagat, R.S., Ford, D.L., Jones, C.A., & Taylor, R.R. (2002). Knowledge management in global organizations: Implications for international human resource management. In G.R. Ferris & J.J. Martocchio (Eds). *Research in Personnel and Human Resource Management* (Vol. 21, pp. 243–274). New York: JAI Press.

Bhagat, R.S., Kedia, B.L., Harveston, P., & Triandis, H.C. (2002). Cultural variations in the cross-border transfer of organizational knowledge: An integrative framework. *Academy of Management Review*, 27(2), 204–21.

Bhagat, R.S., Englis, P., & Kedia, B.L. (2007). Creation, diffusion, and transfer of organizational knowledge in transnational and global organizations: Where do we go from here? In L.L. Neider & C.A. Schriescheim (Eds).

Research in management: International perspectives (pp.118–26). Charlotte, NC: Information Age Publishing.

Bhagat, R.S., McDevitt, A.S., & McDevitt, I. (2010). On improving the robustness of Asian management theories: Theoretical anchors in the era of globalization. *Asia Pacific Journal of Management*, 27(2), 179–92.

Bhagat, R.S., McDevitt, A.S., & McDevitt, I. (2011). Cultural variations in the creation, diffusion, and transfer of organizational knowledge. In Rabi S. Bhagat & Richard M. Steers (Eds). *Cambridge handbook of culture, organizations, and work* (pp. 174–96). Cambridge: Cambridge University Press.

Chinese Culture Connection (1987). Chinese values and the search for culture-free dimension of culture. *Journal of Cross-Cultural Psychology*, 18, 143–64.

Chiu, C.-Y. & Hong, Y. (2006). *The social psychology of culture*. New York: Psychology Press.

Davenport, T.H. & Prusak, L. (1998). *Working knowledge: How organizations manage what they know*. Boston, MA: Harvard Business School Press.

Drucker, P. (1969). *The age of discontinuity*. New York: Harper & Row.

Eckstein, H. & Gurr, T.R. (1975). *Patterns of authority*. New York: John Wiley.

Glenn, E. & Glenn, P. (1981). *Man and mankind: Conflicts and communication between cultures*. Norwood, NJ: Ablex Co.

Greenfield, P. (1999). Three approaches to the psychology of culture: Where do they come from? Paper presented at the Third Conference of the Asian Association of Social Psychology, Taiwan, China (August).

Greider, W. (1997). *One world, ready or not*. New York: Simon & Schuster.

Haire, M., Ghiselli, E., & Porter, L.W. (1966). *Managerial thinking: An international study*. New York: John Wiley.

Hofstede, G. (2001). *Culture's consequences: Comparing values, behaviors, institutions, and organizations across nations*. Thousand Oaks, CA: Sage.

Holden, R. (2002). *Cross-cultural management: A knowledge management perspective*. Harlow: Financial Times/Prentice-Hall.

Jain, R., Triandis, H.C., & Weick, C.W. (2010). *Managing research, development and innovation: Managing the unmanageable*. 3rd edn. New York: Wiley.

Kedia, B.L. & Bhagat, R.S. (1988). Cultural constraints of transfer of technology across nations: Implications for research in international and comparative management. *Academy of Management Review*, 13(4), 559–71.

Kitayama, S., Duffy, S., & Uchida, Y. (2007). Self as cultural mode of being. In S. Kitayama and D. Cohen (Eds). *Handbook of cultural psychology* (pp. 136–74). New York: The Guilford Press.

Kluckhohn, F. & Strodbeck, G. (1961). *Variations in value orientations*. Evanston, IL: Row Peterson.

Kogut, B. & Zander, U. (1993). Knowledge of the firm and the evolutionary theory of the multinational corporation. *Journal of International Business Studies*, 24, 25–64.

Markus, H.R. & Kitayama, S. (1991). Culture and the self: Implications for cognitions, emotions, and motivation. *Psychology Review*, 98, 224–53.

Maruyama, M. (1994). *Mindscapes in management: Use of individual differences in multicultural management*. Aldershot: Dartmouth.

McKinsey & Company (1996). *Harvard Business School Case No. 9 357–396*, 1996. Cambridge, MA: Harvard Business School Press.

Merton, J. (1968). *Social theory and social structure*. New York: The Free Press–Glencoe.

Nisbett, R.E., Peng, K., & Norenzayan, A. (2001). Culture and systems of thought: Holistic versus analytic cognition. *Psychology Review*, 108, 291–310.

Nonaka, I. & Takeuchi, H. (1995). *The knowledge-creating company: How Japanese companies create the dynamics of innovation*. New York: Oxford University Press.

Peng, K., Choi, I., & Norenzayan, A. (2001). Culture and systems of thought: Holistic versus analytic cognitions. *Psychology Review*, 108, 291–310.

Polanyi, M. (1966). *The tacit dimension*. Garden City, NY: Doubleday.

Redding, S.G. (1980). Cognition as an aspect of culture and its reaction to management processes: An exploratory view of the Chinese case. *Journal of Management Studies*, 17, 127–48.

Rogers, E.M. & Shoemaker, F.F. (1971). *Communication of innovations: A cross-cultural approach*. New York: The Free Press.

Smith, P. & Schwartz, S. (1997). Values. In J.W. Berry, M.H. Segall, & C. Kagitcibasi (Eds). *Handbook of cross-cultural psychology: Social behavior and applications* (vol. 3, pp. 77–118). Boston, MA: Allyn & Bacon.

Suzlanski, G. (1996). Exploring internal stickiness: Impediment to the transferring best practice within the firm. *Strategic Management Journal*, 17 (Special Issue: *Knowledge and the firm worker*), 27–43.

Teagarden, M., von Glinow, M., Bowen, D., Frayne, C.A., Nason, S., et al. (1995). Toward building a theory of comparative research: An idiographic case study of the best international human resources management project. *Academy of Management Journal*, 38(5), 1261–87.

The Economist (2011), October.

Time Magazine (2011), 29 May.

Triandis, H.C. (1994). *Culture and social behavior*. New York: McGraw-Hill.

Triandis, H.C. (1995). *Individualism and collectivism*. Boulder, CO: Westview Press.

Triandis, H.C. (1998). Vertical and horizontal collectivism: Theory and research implications for international comparative management. In J.L. Cheng & R.B. Peterson (Eds). *Advances in international comparative management* (vol. 12, pp. 7–36). Stamford, CT: JAI Press.

Tushman, M. & Nelson, R.R. (1990). Introduction: Technology, organizations, and innovation. *Administrative Science Quarterly*, 35(1), 1–8.

Zakaria, F. (2012). *The post American world 2.0*. New York: W.W. Norton.

Zander, U. & Kogut, B. (1995). Knowledge and the speed of transfer and imitation of organizational capabilities: An empirical test. *Organizational Science*, 6, 76–92.

12. Cultural variations in international human resources management

During the 1980s, the idea of international human resources management (IHRM) began to evolve. In its current forms, human resources management including its international aspects is relatively recent. "Personnel management" provided the foundation of selecting, appraising, rewarding, and developing people in work organizations for much of the 20th century. However, as a concept in its own right, human resources management started emerging in the US during the late 1960s and early 1980s and personnel management as a branch of management began to diminish in importance. Books providing specific frameworks (Beer, Spector, Lawrence, Mills, & Walton, 1985; Fombrun, Tichy, & Devanna, 1984) urged a shift away from personnel management to managing people as human resources.

The idea of people as human resources who can be utilized like capital, raw materials, or other factors of production which can be bought or sold in the labor market and whose value must be maximized and exploited was seen to be an American idea. Indeed, as Schneider & Barsoux (2003) note, HRM practices of the type that are found in America are essentially culture-bound. Many question the applicability of US-based HRM principles and practices to other national and cultural contexts. In other words, HRM as envisioned in the context of US work organizations can be interpreted as a manifestation of the American dream of exchanging one's labor for a fair price. It has been noted that the essence of human resources management in the US context strongly emphasizes the notion of rationality and calculativeness, and the psychological contract surrounding the employment relationship is a "hard" as opposed to "soft" one. The US approach takes an instrumental (task-oriented) view of work organizations and is likely to cause genuine difficulties in national contexts which favor a more expressive, collaborative, and benevolent approach to employment relationships.

The development of human resource principles and practices in the US is rooted in the discipline of psychology, with its prime concern being the enhancement of work motivation and job satisfaction. In contrast, HRM in Europe has evolved from a sociological perspective. This perspective pays more attention to the idiosyncratic needs of the social system, the economic and political context, and the nature of relationships between key actors, including societal institutions such as government, unions, and management. In the US, the focus on the individual leads to analyzing jobs to match with employee needs and preferences and designing reward systems to improve motivation in the context of the ongoing emphasis on "performance management." In Western Europe (particularly in Germany), the promotion of industrial democracy (workers deciding their terms of contract in employment relationships) and industrial policy (the government decides the direction of economic policies) has clearly been more important since the end of World War II. This emphasis has led to legislation for working representation on the board of directors in West Germany (and now in unified Germany), quality of work–life councils in Sweden and other Scandinavian countries, and the *Code du Travaill* in France. These issues regarding employment relationships are widely debated in various councils of the European Union, with differing concerns and views regarding the role of national government and the welfare of workers. As a result of these macroeconomic and societal concerns, the nature of the employment contract as reflected in various HRM practices in Europe differs from the US approach. The legal contract between workers as represented by unions has been more important in the UK, France, Spain, Greece, and Italy—the legal contract determines what can be regulated and to what degree.

In the US, the relationship is considered "contractual," based on notions of fair exchange such that both parties, for example, guard their rights and make every attempt to preserve their autonomies and rights of self-determination. Many HRM practices such as performance appraisal, equal employment opportunity-based recruitment and promotion, training programs, and career development programs are often designed to avoid potential law suits.

GUIDING PRINCIPLES OF MODERN INTERNATIONAL HUMAN RESOURCES MANAGEMENT

There are three principles that are at the foundation of human resource management in multinational and global corporations today (Evans, Pucik, & Bjorkman, 2011). They are:

- Internal consistency
- Differentiation
- Balancing dualities

These principles are meant to be complementary, although most multinationals and global companies approach their implementation in a gradual manner, starting with maintaining consistency, then developing a more differentiated strategy (i.e., one that is sensitive to changing demands in different sectors and environments, including culture), and finally crafting a set of strategies to respond to the dualities that are embedded in cross-border management of organizations.

Internal Consistency

Internal consistency refers to the way in which a firm's HR policies and practices fit with each other and with other important structural features of the organization. The degree of task specialization and the emphasis on teamwork versus individuals working separately are important issues that are considered in maintaining the principle of internal consistency. For example, if a multinational firm (e.g., Microsoft of Seattle, US, GE of the US) uses a large number of cross-border and cross-cultural teams to accomplish important tasks, the HR policies should also reflect leadership practices that promote consensual decision-making as required in cross-border contexts. In a different vein, if a multinational firm finds it necessary to engage in ongoing skills development of its senior managers, it should emphasize employee retention through constructive feedback, competitive compensation, and effective career paths.

Empowering managers to contribute to the organization and rewarding them for the initiative are essential for sustaining skills development on an ongoing basis. The challenges of achieving a good fit that is internally consistent with IHRM policies are particularly difficult in multinational–global corporations because they operate in different nations, cultures, and institutional contexts. While the firm may espouse a worldwide and consistent view of IHRM at the corporate level, the actual practices evolve in response to local cultural and institutional contexts and therefore vary across cultures. Local managers (e.g., the country manager of Mittal Steel of the UK) are fond of saying, "Great idea at the corporate level, but unfortunately it doesn't apply in Hungary."

Differentiation

There are good reasons for emphasizing internal consistencies in the design of IHRM in multinational and global corporations. However, companies that spend too much time building and optimizing a well-integrated set of consistent IHRM practices that are non-isomorphic (i.e., do not match the demands and the idiosyncrasies of the changing environment and cultures)

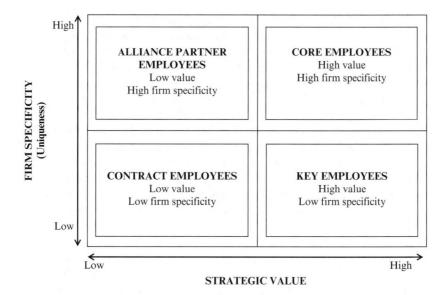

Source: Evans, Pucik, & Bjorkman (2011).

Figure 12.1   Classification of employees as a function of their strategic importance and firm characteristics

with the contexts run the risk of increasing financial costs and are ineffective in the long term.

Differentiation in IHRM practices due to differences in geographic and national locations has received most attention in the literature. A scheme that helps differentiate among employee groups in developing strategic aspects of IHRM is presented in Figure 12.1. This framework (Lepak & Snell, 1999, 2002, 2007) is arrived at by juxtaposing two dimensions: *strategic value* of the employees for sustaining the global operations, and *uniqueness*, which denotes their core significance to the firm. The *core employees* as depicted in Figure 12.1 are those whose skills are highly firm-specific and whose strategic importance is high. In contrast, the *contract employees* are of low strategic value to the multinational, and their skills are not necessarily specifically embedded in the organization. Finally, employees who work in joint venture operations or strategic alliances are of low strategic value but their skills are highly specific to the firm that they represent.

Some configuration of high-performance/commitment-based IRHM practices is the natural way to manage the employees who belong to the core group. This core group typically includes senior managers, heads of R & D groups, and high-potential recruits in important divisions such as global marketing, production, strategic planning groups, and so on. The employees in the quadrant of high strategic value but low uniqueness to the firm can be employed on a long-term basis. However, since their human capital is not unique to the firm, they can easily be replaced. Therefore, it makes less sense to invest heavily in the development of this group. The pilots of global air cargo companies like Fed-Ex and UPS fall into this category (Lepak & Snell, 2007). However, in some situations, sales professionals, for example, may be easy to replace, but those who have close relationships with unique customer groups become more valuable and therefore are harder to replace. Some multinationals choose to recruit employees who may have firm-specific knowledge but are of low strategic significance through long-term partnerships with service providers or outsourcing operations. The goal is not to employ them long term or on a full-time basis. A good case in point is Nokia, Inc. of Finland, which uses Price Waterhouse Coopers for issues related to international transfer of personnel and IBM for many of its information technology-related functions. Finally, there are certain tasks that are neither of high value nor require a unique set of skills or knowledge. These tasks can be carried out by temporary employees or outsourced on a relatively short-term competitive basis to countries such as India, Singapore, and the Philippines. Examples include business process outsourcing including routine accounting work, payroll services, and maintenance tasks of various kinds that are loosely coupled with the core mission of the multinational.

Lepak & Snell's (2007) arguments in favor of differentiating HR practices among different employee groups, as presented in Figure 12.1, are compelling and reflect the current realities that are found in many of the multinational–global companies from different parts of the world. A study of Spanish firms (Melian-Gonzalez & Verano-Tacarante, 2004) found that 70 percent utilized all four types of HR practices, whereas another study (Lepac & Snell, 2002) showed that multinationals used different combinations of HR practices to manage employee groups that differ in terms of their strategic differences and uniqueness to the core mission. What is important to note here is that multinational companies need to differentiate HR practices more across subunits and subsidiaries in addition to differentiating across employee groups. As would be expected, they are under considerable institutional and cultural pressures to adopt their HR practices to the societal needs and concerns that prevail at a given point in time.

Balancing Dualities

The third guiding principle of balancing dualities is concerned with how far to focus on one particular goal or objective at the expense of another.

In the case of multinational companies, there are no simple answers to the questions of how much to adopt HR practices in line with the societal and institutional requirements abroad. While differentiation across locations can help the multinational achieve a better fit with various national and cultural environments in which it operates, too close an alignment of HR practices to each distinct societal context gives rise to a loss of integration, leading to global inefficiencies, lack of learning across units, and problems of coordination and control. Transfer of tacit technologies and systemic organizational knowledge also becomes difficult, if not impossible, when too much differentiation is encouraged at the expense of global integration. The tension between differentiation on the one hand and consistency and integration on the other is generally attempted to be resolved through logical choices in structural- and design-related considerations. To put it simply, learning to manage differentiation and integration is the essence of the fundamental principle of designing structures of multinational and global organization (see Chapter 10 for details).

MAJOR FUNCTIONS OF INTERNATIONAL HUMAN RESOURCES MANAGEMENT

With the above three guiding principles, multinational corporations develop major international human resource functions. The objective is to cope with important IHRM tasks such as selecting talented personnel for managing subsidiaries in emergent economies, and attracting, motivating, developing, and retaining employees who are key to the strategic mission of the organization. Table 12.1 depicts the key international human resource functions that are employed in multinational and global organizations—some of the more important ones are discussed in terms of their functions and implications for IHRM.

Recruitment and Selection

Multinational and global companies worldwide face the challenge of meeting their needs for human capital and attracting new employees with valuable skills and competences. Without an appealing and differentiated IHRM system that potential employees will find attractive, it is difficult for the multinational corporation to win the race for global talent that characterizes the employment situation in many of the emerging growing economies in the 21st century. Just like global firms which need to build global brands (i.e., Microsoft, Coca-Cola, Toyota, etc.), contemporary IHRM practices are designed to reflect company-specific values. A variety

Table 12.1   Key human resource practices

Recruitment and selection
- Workforce planning
- Employer branding
- Recruitment
- Induction and socialization
- Selection
- International transfers
- Termination and outplacement

Development and training
- Training (on-the-job and off-the-job)
- Talent assessment and reviews
- Succession planning
- Career management
- Coaching and mentoring
- Leadership development

Performance management and rewards
- Job evaluation
- Goal-/standard-setting
- Performance measurement
- Appraisal and feedback
- Compensation and benefits
- Rewards and recognition

Communication

Labor and industrial relations

Source: Schneider & Barsoux (2003), p. 96.

of selection and assessment methods may be used to choose between internal and external candidates for jobs, but with big differences in how they may be employed across nations and cultures. All large multinational and global organizations recognize the importance of diversity in their workforces in different countries; however, they still like to fill the top executive positions with men (and sometimes women) from their home countries. One of the biggest challenges that a global organization faces in the 21st century is that of increasing cultural diversity in the upper echelons of management.

Another question that IHRM directors must address is whether to develop the talents they need from internal sources or by increasing their reliance on recruiting from other competing organizations and leading universities. In Chapter 11 we discussed the importance to knowledge-intensive companies of locating their R & D laboratories near world-class universities and research institutions like Stanford University in California, the Indian Institute of Science in Bangalore, India, Fudan University in Shanghai, China, and Osaka University in Japan. In their rush to recruit talented engineers from leading Indian technical institutes, global companies like GE, Microsoft, and Cisco Systems are offering compensation that is much higher than that considered normal for the area. This creates tensions in the regional labor market and talent pools which should also be addressed by the subsidiaries.

Development and Training

Developing effective trans-cultural managers is a high priority for the multinational and global firm. In fact, one of the major strategic preoccupations of senior executives is focused on developing a global mindset in all operations and in distinct geographic locales. Developing competent managers and leaders who can work with people from diverse cultures and in distinct locations is difficult (Earley & Soon, 2003). The criteria for developing such individuals are necessarily complex and can be fraught with competing objectives and political overtones. As discussed in Chapter 9, what constitutes effective leadership differs greatly across cultures, and the skills needed at the upper echelons of management are different from those at the lower levels.

International human resources managers have known for a long time that people learn most by accepting and learning from challenges—some difficult and others more manageable. For international managers, this implies managing assignments of technically competent people in different locations and being able to work effectively across their unique functional and geographical expertise. For example, if a senior manager at the headquarters of the Coca-Cola Company is able to assign technically competent personnel in charge of producing different brands of Coke and other soft-drink products, and at the same time can understand and relate effectively to other functional managers in different countries, then he or she has come a long way toward becoming a global manager. A majority of new recruits or promoted employees do not necessarily possess the appropriate skills needed for functioning effectively in their work roles in different cultures. Therefore, they must be trained and developed through on-the-job coaching, mentoring, and other forms of formal training through university-sponsored programs (e.g., internships and visiting assignments with R & D laboratories in universities or other companies).

It is important to remember that the greater the complexity of challenges that people take on, the higher the likelihood that they will make significant costly mistakes. Training, coaching, mentoring, and related career development processes are therefore designed to be an integral part of strategic human resources management undertaken on a worldwide basis. Leadership development has typically been conducted by managing the process top-down, with the senior managers focusing on developing a select group of high-potential junior individuals. This process can then be complemented by globalizing human resource management practices and using Internet-related training and technologies to facilitate the cross-border diffusion of knowledge. When managed successfully, these processes contribute greatly to the competitive advantage of the firm. However, making managers sophisticated, with a global mindset, may also inadvertently increase the chances of staff turnover. Skills that the international human resources management function aims at developing in recruits and recently promoted managers include:

- *People-management skills.* easier said than done. Managing people, especially at the higher levels, tends to be a demanding task and is often fraught with political overtones and clashes of powerful positions and personalities. Project managers tend to spend around 20–30 percent of their time managing people-related activities including such tasks as communicating, leading without exerting authority and power, negotiating, and defining boundaries (Evans, Pucik, & Bjorkman, 2011). Getting the right people into the right places and the right jobs means managing well across nations and cultures. In addition, if one knows how to negotiate with difficult people and coach demanding subordinates, then one would have been trained most effectively.
- *Managing teams.* As discussed in Chapter 8 on group processes and team effectiveness, managing teams is becoming vital in organizations that function by adopting a matrix structure. A manager must be skillful in building respect and trust across functional boundaries, manage conflicts, and negotiate clear goals for complex and ambiguous tasks. Learning to develop cohesive teams, whether they function in a mono-cultural setting or across cultures, is crucial. Increasingly, as we have noted in earlier chapters, much of the work of multinational and global organizations is conducted in the virtual environment. Training project and team leaders to translate their knowledge of developing teams in face-to-face situations to the virtual context—which has its own rhythm in integrating distributed patterns of work in dissimilar cultures—is indeed an important IHRM function. One of the major problems that IHRM manag-

ers must learn to deal with is to prevent the naturally occurring obstacles and difficulties in virtual team situations from becoming "self-fulfilling prophecies."

- *Divergent thinking (and developing a global mindset).* As multinational and global organizations confront conflicting challenges and diversities in the global marketplace and deal with ambiguous situations with innovative technologies on a routine basis, it becomes critical to learn to think by adopting a divergent mode of thinking. The objectives of the various well-printed brochures and programs sponsored by international human resources management departments may not spell it out explicitly, but the fact remains that a large number of these programs are being designed to help develop the cognitively complex manager of the 21st century.

- *Learning to manage risks.* Training individuals to minimize the risks associated with costly mistakes is preferred by global organizations of all types. The best way of training in this area is to closely link the training designed to enhance knowledge and information that the trainee may need in managing risks at the same time that he or she is assigned to the project. Evans, Pucik, & Bjorkman (2011) note that, more often than not, training is conducted on the basis of when people are available for the training, even though that time may be least beneficial. Simply put, if a group of executives receive appropriate training long before their departure for an overseas assignment (where such knowledge would be useful), the effectiveness of the training greatly diminishes.

- *Action learning.* Training to facilitate action learning essentially is concerned with coupling work on important strategic issues with programmed support and training for the team. Action learning helps improve the ability to function across boundaries and develop leadership skills in high-potential individuals in multinational–global organizations. IHRM managers must endeavor to make it clear that action learning activities are designed to enhance advanced forms of learning, leading to the development of cognitive complexities in different domains as opposed to improving immediate task-related performance. Training providers aiming to facilitate action learning often have sophisticated skills in program design and in blending classroom experiences with action learning. In addition, they should be able to coordinate learning activities with other learning methods for leadership development, such as 360° assessment, evaluation, and coaching. When conducted competently, action learning activities facilitate the exchange and merger of different perspectives that are relevant to effective transnational management—the essence of managing multinational–global organizations. Action learning tends to be holistic, and develops second-order learning skills (i.e., skills that develop by combining simple pieces of information to form a complex scenario that is more isomorphic to the requirements of a given context) and a tendency to view problems in the appropriate context. Action learning can alter the way managers think regarding investments in uncertain but emerging economies. A study by Arora, Jaju, Kelefas, & Merenich (2004) found that this is also the case in the US textile and apparel industry. General Electric, Nokia, and Apple, Inc. are well-known examples of global companies which facilitate action learning in high-potential executives with coaching and training activities supported by the corporate IHRM functions.

- *Coaching and mentoring.* It is well known in the traditional HRM literature that one of the important sources of training managers is by helping them develop relationships with other people—bosses who can play the roles of coaches, mentors, and both positive and negative role models. This role-playing involving coaching can help an individual or a cross-functional team in both professional and personal development. It is carried out in a non-directive fashion, often in connection with a formal training program. In recent years, coaching of junior executives has become a potent method for providing all kinds of important training that is needed to facilitate learning to manage situations of ambiguity, uncertainty, and risk. As various training programs in leading management development programs in world-class business schools have demonstrated repeatedly, the competence of professional coaches is almost always based on their abilities to integrate the experience of years of on-the-job training with knowledge of psychological processes, personal insight, and cross-border experiences. The term "coaching" is being used today to denote a management style that facilitates the taking of risks in situations that are uncertain. The performance culture of GE that evolved after Jack Welch took over as CEO in the early 1980s was designed to actively challenge managers to confront goals and objectives that often stretched their limits. The GE senior managers were encouraged to adopt the stance, "How can I help you achieve these difficult targets? What can I do to support you so that I may remove any major obstacles from your path?"

Mentoring has often been grouped with coaching but it is conceptually distinct. When an experienced senior manager or professional is paired with a high-potential employee in the context of a long-term relationship in a functional area, then mentoring is said to occur. This is especially the case when a senior manager takes a junior manager under his or her wing and helps facilitate the development of skills for the long-term success of the junior manager. Unlike universities and other non-profit organizations, mentoring can be a difficult training function to implement in the context of today's highly competitive global organizations. First, mentoring relationships are difficult to formalize, partly because of the personal and emotional nature of such relationships, but also because the values and personalities of the two managers must be compatible. If there is no match in values and personalities the mentoring may fail. Profit-driven multinational–global organizations, unlike their non-profit-oriented counterparts, do not necessarily have the kind of climates that facilitate the ongoing trust that is necessary in the context of developing productive mentoring relationships. Competition for both tangible and intangible rewards makes it difficult to sustain high-quality mentoring relationships in these profit-oriented multinational–global organizations.

CULTURAL DETERMINANTS OF INTERNATIONAL HUMAN RESOURCE MANAGEMENT FUNCTION

Cultural variations influence various aspects of international human resource management practices in all multinational and global companies. It was mentioned earlier that the instrumental and contractual aspects of employment relationships are emphasized more in the context of US multinationals as opposed to European and Asian multinationals. In Europe and Asia, unlike the US, international human resource management practices are designed to pay attention to the economic and political context of both the host and home countries of the multinational, and the nature of the relationships among the national government, workers unions, and management. A primary focus of a large majority of human resource management programs is concerned with who has the power to decide as well as who should have the power to decide the nature of reward distribution at the collective (e.g., union negotiation) and at the individual level (e.g., merit pay and stock options). Cultural differences at the country level have led to legislation for worker representation on the board of directors in Germany (e.g., work councils), quality of work–life councils in Scandinavian countries, and so on. And in Socialist and former Communist bloc countries, the role of the activist government is most important and works to develop work cultures where centrality of work is in question. In addition to societal culture, multinationals have their own organizational cultures (i.e., unique patterns of practices reflecting administrative heritages and history). IKEA, the Swedish home furnishing company, strongly emphasizes selecting those people whose values reflect those of the organization. IKEA emphasizes the value of being straight-forward, not arrogant, and not status-conscious (i.e., more egalitarian). *Odmjukhet*—a Swedish word that emphasizes modesty and politeness and humility toward one's fellow beings—is strongly desired in the individuals it selects.

Cultural variations reflecting individualism–collectivism, power dis-tance, uncertainty avoidance, task versus relationship orientation, high versus low context, masculinity versus femininity, and so on, that are likely to have an important influence on the development and implementation of various HRM processes are depicted in Table 12.2. The role of individual-ism versus collectivism seems to be most important, followed by the role of task (also rule) orientation versus relationship orientation. IHRM issues dealing with selection and recruitment, socialization (including coaching and mentoring), training (including action learning and global mindset development), performance appraisal, compensation and rewards, and career development are also influenced by cultural values. This is to be expected. Recent research examining the influence of culture on human resource management processes and practices (Stone & Stone-Romero, 2007) is being reported. Emergent issues dealing with the art and science of providing suitable types of feedback, employee assistance programs, work–family balance, and human resources in multicultural and globally dispersed teams are being addressed. For a detailed theoretical analysis and applied perspectives, see *The influence of culture on human resource management processes and practices* (Stone & Stone-Romero, 2007).

UNRESOLVED ISSUES

A careful look at the theories and concepts developed to address the various functions of HRM in the global context leads to identification of some unresolved issues. First, despite pressures toward convergence of HRM practices across nations and borders, and despite developing some commonalities in industries and in global companies with similar organizational cultures, the fact is that HRM practices tend to differ across countries, cultures, and world regions. Cultural and institutional theories provide sufficient explanations for this status of distinctive prac-tices in different countries, but more effort in both theory-building and gathering of anecdotal evidence-based knowledge is needed. Why is it that, despite strong pressures toward convergence of HRM practices due

Table 12.2   HRM menu: cultural determinants

HRM issues	Cultural determinants
Selection	
Who to hire? How to hire?	
● Desired behaviors—focus on skills/personality?	Doing versus being
● Specialists versus generalists?	Uncertainty avoidance
● Necessary qualifications?	Power/hierarchy
Level, discipline, or preferred institutions?	Individual versus collective
● How important is "what you know" versus "who you know"?	Task versus relationship
Socialization	
● What kind of "initiation rites" are acceptable? Team-building?	Task versus relationship Individual versus collective
● What are the messages being sent? Competition versus cooperation? Individual versus team effort?	Private versus professional life
● To what extent will people engage in/reject social events?	High versus low context
● To what extent should efforts be made to ensure "corporate culture" is shared?	
● To what extent should the corporate culture be made explicit (badges, posters, slogans, etc.)?	
Training	
For what purpose?	
● Develop generalist versus specialist perspective?	Uncertainty avoidance Individual versus collective
● Acquire company versus skill-specific (technical) knowledge?	Hierarchy Task versus relationship
● Extent of job rotation?	
● Role of mentorship?	
● Competences versus networking?	
How are training needs determined?	
● By company? By individual?	
● Who is sent for training? "High-flyers" versus "rank and file"?	
What training methods are most effective?	
● Case approach?	
● Reading and lecture?	
● Experiential exercise?	
● Professor- versus student-driven?	
● Group work?	

Table 12.2   (continued)

HRM issues	Cultural determinants
Performance appraisal	
• To what extent is individual versus team effort evaluated?	Individual versus collective Hierarchy
• To what extent is goal-setting ("management by objectives") useful?	Being versus doing Time monochronic versus
• To what extent do people expect feedback? And from whom?	polycronic High versus low context
• To what extent will criticism be accepted?	
Compensation and rewards	
• Who gets what?	Equity versus equality
• To what extent should pay be linked to performance?	Doing versus being Hierarchy
What degree of pay differential is acceptable?	Control over nature Individual versus collective
• To what extent are bonuses effective?	Uncertainty avoidance
• To what extent should team versus individuals be rewarded?	Masculinity versus femininity
• How much of salary should be fixed versus variable?	
• To what extent are financial versus non-financial rewards preferred?	
Career development	
• Who gets promoted?	Being versus doing
• What determines career success?	Individual versus collective
• What types of career paths are desirable?	Task versus relationship
Internal versus external hiring?	Uncertainty avoidance
Within functions/across functions?	
Within company/industry?	
Across companies/industries?	
Between government and business?	
• To what extent are people mobile? Willing to move?	
• At what stage are "high potentials" identified? At entry?	
After 5 years?	

Source: Schneider & Barsoux (2003), pp. 152–3.

to scientific, technological, and managerial know-how across nations and cultures, divergence exists? Divergence is found in the IHRM practices of large multinational and global companies such as Phillips, Inc. of the Netherlands, Apple, Inc. of the US, and Unilever of the UK. Brewster, Mayrhofer, & Morley (2008) observe that the process of diffusion and adoption of HRM frameworks in different national, cultural, and regional contexts is not well understood and more effective theoretical frameworks need to be developed in the near future.

IMPLICATIONS FOR THE GLOBAL ORGANIZATION

Despite some difficulties in explaining the existence of divergence in HRM practices in the comparative perspective, a body of applicable knowledge and HRM methods and instruments exist. They are useful for enhancing the superiority of IHRM practices of the global organization in the worldwide context. As argued earlier, the theoretical debate about convergence and divergence of HRM practices across nations and cultures will continue to exist, and, in our opinion, is a healthy development. Human beings are products of their cultural heritages and explanations and when it comes to developing HRM systems, "when in Rome, do as the Romans" does not seem to be useful.

As more detailed case-based investigations of success and failure of various HRM practices begin to be recorded by IHRM departments of both medium- and large-scale multinationals and global organizations, we will develop better insights into the intricacies of the role of cultural variations in these practices. With the rise of global companies from BRIC and other emerging economies, we are going to encounter more bilateral and multinational flows of human resources. These human resources are likely to be from different organizational levels, and international assignments from globalized and emergent economies are going to make various IHRM practices more synergistic. In light of brain-drain from the emergent economies and former Soviet bloc countries, there is going to be a greater emphasis on circulation of talented human resources in the globalized world. This development signals two outcomes: growth of a global workforce and a reduced demand for home country nationals for international assignments.

Globalization will continue to expand, and the need to find the right person for the right expatriate assignment is going to become even more important. This is because the cost of expatriate failure can be high (Jun & Gentry, 2005). While some insights have continued to develop, not enough is known regarding why Western European and Japanese multinational and global companies report much lower rates of expatriate failure than US companies. The global orientation of Western European and Japanese companies is clearly responsible for this state of affairs (Schneider & Barsoux, 2003). The smaller size of the domestic markets in the Western European and East Asian contexts (including South Asia) makes it necessary for these companies to tailor their IHRM practices to the idiosyncratic and unique needs of the nations and cultures where they operate.

The field of international human resource management is beginning to grow, with increasing attention from leading business schools and global corporations. It is our observation that European business schools such as INSEAD, IMD, London Business School, and the University of Birmingham (UK) have been at the forefront of this movement for the past quarter-century or more. However, important developments are beginning to emerge in leading business schools such as the Wharton School, Harvard University, and the University of Michigan. It is our hope that the ideas and frameworks presented in this chapter will stimulate more research in this area, and that they will lead to enlightened methods that incorporate the important role of cultural differences in IHRM practices in multinational and global organizations.

REFERENCES

Arora, A., Jaju, A., Kelefas, A.G., & Merenich, T. (2004). An exploratory analysis of global managerial mindsets: A case of US textile and apparel industry. *Journal of International Management*, 10(3), 393–411.

Beer, M.B., Spector, P.R., Lawrence, D., Mills, Q., & Walton, R.E. (1985). *Managing human assets.* New York: Free Press.

Brewster, C., Mayrhofer, W., & Morley, M. (Eds) (2008). *Human Resource Management in Europe: Evidence of Convergence?* Oxford: Oxford University Press.

Earley, P.C. & Soon, A. (2003). *Cultural intelligence.* Palo Alto, CA: Stanford University Press.

Evans, P., Pucik, V., & Bjorkman, I. (2011). *The global challenge: International human resource management.* New York: McGraw Hill-Irwin.

Fombrun, C., Tichy, N.M., & Devanna, M.A. (1984). *Strategic human resource management.* New York: Wiley.

Jun, S. & Gentry, J. (2005). An exploratory investigation of the relative importance of cultural similarity and personal fit in the selection and performance of expatriates. *Journal of World Business*, 40(1), 1–8.

Jun, S., Gentry, J.W., & Hyun, Y.J. (2001). Cultural adaptation of business expatriates in the host marketplace. *Journal of International Business Studies*, 32(2), 369–77.

Lepak, D.P. & Snell, S.A. (1999). The human resource architecture: Toward a theory of human capital allocation and development. *Academy of Management Review*, 24(1), 31–48.

Lepak, D.P. & Snell, S.A. (2002). Examining the human resource architecture: The relationships among human capital, employment, and human resource configurations. *Journal of Management*, 28(4), 517–43.

Lepak, D.P. & Snell, S.A. (2007). Employment subsystems and the "HR architecture." In P. Boxall, J. Purcell, & P. Wright (Eds). *The Oxford handbook of human resource management*. New York: Oxford University Press.

Melian-Gonzalez, S. & Verano-Tacarante, D. (2004). A new approach to the best practices debate: Are best practices applied to all employees in the same way? *International Journal of Human Resource Management*, 15(1), 56–75.

Schneider, S. & Barsoux, J.-L. (2003). *Managing across cultures*. New York: Prentice-Hall.

Stone, D.L. & Stone-Romero, E.F. (2007). *The influence of culture on human resource management processes and practices*. New York: Psychology Press.

13. Emergent issues in managing the global organization

We live in the era of globalization. With tremendous increases of foreign direct investments in various parts of the world since the 1990s, there has been a corresponding growth of research directed at understanding and improving the functioning of multinational/global organizations. Top managers of multinational corporations are confronted with challenging issues regarding cultural differences in the way subsidiaries are designed and managed in different countries. Along with designing subsidiaries whose structures and processes are in general agreement with the broad macroeconomic environment of the host countries, it becomes crucial to develop an accurate and comprehensive body of knowledge regarding distinctive ways of motivating and leading culturally dissimilar employees. In addition, work groups of all major multinational–global corporations are being routinely composed of members belonging to different religions and cultures. To make matters even more complicated, these teams often must work longer than the typical 1950s to 1970s work teams did in most manufacturing organizations, even though the members are geographically dispersed.

Taken together, the challenges that confront multinational–global organizations are many and growing in complexity. What makes it even more difficult is the fact that, despite training in business ethics and corporate social responsibility-related topics, business leaders in many countries are engaging in corrupt and unethical practices leading to low morale in the corporations, decreased faith in the integrity of the corporation by customers, and backlashes against globalization.

In writing this book, we have attempted to address many of these issues in terms of their cultural underpinnings. We have emphasized that cultural variations are ever present in the way people organize activities and form work organizations with specialized tasks and roles to accomplish stated and derived goals. Of course, profitability is a key issue for all corporations, and it is no less important for multinational–global corporations which operate with as many as 180 subsidiaries in many countries (e.g., Philips, Inc. with a home office in the Netherlands) (Bartlett, Ghoshal, & Beamish, 2008).

WHAT ARE THE EMERGENT ISSUES?

Important challenges to multinational and global corporations can emerge from any of the facets of the global business environment. Along with relying on culture-based explanations, it is important to analyze causes and consequences of organizational phenomena, at both the macro and micro levels in terms of economic, political, and institutional factors. Undoubtedly, some of the apparent economic factors are strongly correlated with culture-specific predispositions, for example economic growth being stronger in progress-prone versus progress-resistant nations (e.g., the case of the Dominican Republic versus Haiti in the Caribbean) (Brooks, 2011). At any rate, the urge to employ culture-specific explanations for observed differences in a given organizational phenomenon across nations (e.g., differences in job satisfaction across various countries in Southeast Asia and Nordic Europe) should be coupled with a desire to look into other factors that are not embedded in the cultural context. Negandhi (1986) noted that in understanding differing patterns of management related to planning and decision-making at the upper management level in developing countries (especially in the African context), the role of political and legal contexts is paramount. It has been found that the emphasis on formal planning in organizations in Chile and Turkey was contingent on who was elected leader of the country (see Kabasakal & Bodur, 2008; Negandhi & Baliga, 1980). Along with this major consideration, other issues that have emerged and should be considered in future research on multinational–global organizations are as follows:

1. The nature of employment relationships has undergone a major transformation since the 1990s. New models of white-collar work, including telecommuting, working in virtual teams, and working from distant locations (Connley, 2009), are becoming commonplace in the developed countries and also in the global high-tech cities of the world, including places like Bangalore, India, Sao Paulo, Brazil, and Johannesburg, South Africa. During the early stages of the electronic era, social scientists were concerned with loss of personal and social identities due to extensive use of computer-mediated communication. While some of these concerns are valid, resulting in symptoms described in *Bowling Alone* (Putnam, 2000), the opportunity for networking and establishing meaningful and sometimes not-so-meaningful relationships with clients and colleagues located in distant countries have increased many-fold. These developments can influence patterns of affective and behavioral outcomes in both work and non-work. In fact, the current state of knowledge regarding

the impact of virtual relationships on individual productivity and job satisfaction-related outcomes is scant. In order for the field of cross-cultural management to provide valuable insights to top managers of multinational and global organizations (no matter where their home offices are located), it is important that more research be conducted in this area.

2. In much of the discussion in the previous chapters, the role of individualism–collectivism as the most important dimension of cultural variation has been emphasized. There is good logic behind highlighting the role of this dimension and its two important correlates of affluence and low power distance. As employees of global organizations become more affluent over time, they become more individualistic. This culture change is more pronounced at the higher echelons of management and less so at the lower levels. The role of religion and religious rituals might provide an explanation for how lower-status participants of global organizations resist possible changes in their collectivistic tendencies (Triandis, 2009). Furthermore, religious affiliation, as a dimension of cultural variation, has been identified by Georgas, van de Vijer, & Berry (2004) as part of understanding organizational behavior. In addition, one's religious affiliation tends to be independent of the cluster of attributes associated with individualism–collectivism. In a study with Catholic, Protestant, Orthodox, Jewish, and Muslim respondents, it was found that religious persons of all faiths and affiliations, in each of the 11 countries in the sample, scored high on tradition and conservative values and low on hedonism and stimulation (Hulsmans, 1994). Nations in which one religion (e.g., Islam in the Middle East and North Africa) dominates tend to have shared tendencies towards endorsing certain social behaviors (Triandis, 2009). Smith, Bond, & Kagitcibasi (2006) noted that religion as another strong source of values along with cultural and economic variations should be explored in future research. We strongly endorse this observation and urge scholars and practitioners alike to pursue this line of inquiry. This is not to say that cultural variations should be ignored. On the other hand, we believe that after decades of neglecting the role of religious differences as possible sources for imprinting people with some values that can interact with cultural variations in work contexts, the time has come to explore the importance of clashes between civilizations along the religious fault lines. Huntington's (1996) thesis on the clash of civilizations and the remaking of world order is a good example of this line of research.

3. The research literature we have reviewed in this book comes primarily from comparative analyses of work organizations across nations in

different geographical locales. During the past several years, data reported in many studies were collected by researchers employing an overarching theoretical framework—especially since the publication of Hofstede's seminal work in 1980. During the same period, anthropologically and ethnographically minded researchers emphasized the need for culture-specific, that is, emic analyses of cultures. Excellent emic studies describing specific cultural issues in Mexico (Diaz-Guerrero, 1993); the Philippines (Enriques, 1993); China (Cheung et al., 1996); the southern US (Cohen & Nisbett, 1997); Korea (Schmidt-Atzert & Park, 1999); and Japan (Benedict, 1954; Ablegen, 1958; Yamaguchi, 1994) are examples to emulate. Etic approaches also made valuable contributions, as illustrated in the works of Triandis (1972), Hofstede (1980, 1995, 2001), Inglehart & Baker (2000), and Inglehart, Basanez, & Morano (1998). Some of these have had considerable impact in generating valuable insights into the functioning of micro and macro processes in work organizations. Triandis (2000) suggested that indigenous and cross-cultural approaches should cross-validate each other.

Thus, the time has come to triangulate etic and emic approaches in order to provide a rich portrayal of the complexities of interactions between societal culture, organizational culture, and globalization. While not entirely etic in design, the Chinese Culture Connection Study (1987) is an excellent example of research giving us fundamental insights into the working of the Chinese mind and the development of capitalistic enterprises in the East. New powerful concepts may emerge from emic analyses: Confucian work dynamism is a good case in point, as was found in the Chinese Culture Connection Study. This concept has greatly aided us in understanding the rise of Chinese-style capitalism in China and has also provided insights into the workings of Chinese work organizations. A recent qualitative study (Capelli, Singh, Singh, & Useem, 2010) examined how India's top business leaders are transforming Indian global organizations. It is an example of the kind of research that can greatly advance theoretical and applied knowledge regarding the role of cultural variations and other related factors in managing multinational organizations.

4. Demographers note the growth of the elderly population in the US, Japan, China, and Western Europe. This has important implications for the economic growth of these nations along with the international competitiveness of the multinational–global corporations that are based in these countries. In our rush to focus on these issues, we forget to focus on the role of older workers and their unique concerns. A recent international comparison of retirement and late career patterns

in Western industrialized countries (Hofacker, 2010) provides valuable information into economic (i.e., retirement and medical benefit plans) and career-related (i.e., occupational obsolescence, decreasing abilities to participate in the new world of work) issues. National and cultural variations relating to the design of reward systems for these groups of workers are important for multinationals. Loyalty and organizational commitment change with age, and culture-specific variations of these phenomena are important in the management of international human resources. We believe that research involving elderly workers and working mothers, in both developing and developed countries, is very important given that their participation in the labor force is on the rise.

5. Another emergent trend that should be the focus of intensive cross-national and cross-cultural work on management is concerned with the rising tide of immigration in Western and in some non-Western economies. Since the 1960s, the liberalization of US immigration laws as well as the immigration laws of other advanced economies have created a significant growth of immigrants, both legal and undocumented. Currently in the US there are about 13 million illegal immigrants from collectivistic countries (Mexico, Honduras, Guatemala, Panama, etc.). Most are working in low-paying jobs without benefits. This group of workers has not been studied sufficiently, even though they contribute to the economies of the larger metroplexes in Western countries, such as Los Angeles, New York, Miami, London, Paris and Frankfurt. Their contributions are necessary for the effective functioning of the multinational–global organizations located in these metroplexes.

Especially important are longitudinal investigations involving the work adjustment and life-long learning processes of immigrant professionals. Immigrant professionals go through significant changes in their life experiences as they move from the cultural milieu of their home countries (typically collectivistic in orientation) to other countries. Motivation and involvement in work roles, exercising leadership, and dealing with work stress tend to be different in the case of this group of employees. Consider some facts. The latest census reports that in major US cities, about 25 percent of the population was born in a foreign country (e.g., 26 percent in Los Angeles, 25 percent in Boston, 20 percent in Chicago, and over 30 percent in Miami). Over 20 percent of the software designers and consultants in the head office of the Microsoft Corporation in Seattle, Washington are of Indian origin. While they have had significant training in Western science and technologies, they do not relate to the reward systems of Western organizations in the same way as Americans or natives of other countries.

Cultural variations in "workways" among immigrant professionals should become an important area of research given the need for integrating them into the mainstream of the work organization. Workways describe a culture's typical pattern of work-related cognitions, mental models, and practices that reflect a cultural group's ideas about what is correct, ethical, and efficient in the workplace. Sanchez-Burks & Lee (2007) provide a detailed review of the significance of this line of research pioneered by Sanchez-Burks in 2002 and 2005. The essence of workways in US subcultures is to focus on relational ideologies reflecting Puritanical protestant beliefs. *Protestant-relational ideology* (PRI) combines Lutheran teachings about the importance of work with Calvinist notions about restricting relational and social emotional concerns while working (Sanchez-Burks, 2002). Early Calvinists emphasized the need for separating emotional concerns from the work-related issues of one's colleagues and subordinates; such restrictions are often relaxed in the non-work context. Paying attention to colleagues' social emotional concerns is entirely appropriate during leisure hours and in non-work contexts (Fischer, 1989; Daniels, 1995). Thus, PRI reflects a strong emphasis favoring the relational divide between the work and non-work domains or concerns (Lenski, 1963; Bendix, 1977). Knowledge of the workways of immigrants from different cultures and how they interact with the professional relational ideologies of the West is going to be of considerable significance for multinational–global organizations. This is clearly an emergent issue and, with the exception of a few studies (Bhagat & London, 1999; Daux, 2006; Bhagat, Davis, & London, 2009; Bhagat, McDevitt, & Segovis, 2010), not much is known regarding the work adjustment and performance-related activities of immigrant professionals.

6. Cross-cultural researchers have known for a long time that nobody lives in a global culture. They live in specific cultures in the context of their nations or as immigrants in the context of their host countries. These cultures differ from each other in numerous ways and along theoretically meaningful dimensions. These dimensions have been discussed in Chapter 2. Consider the following. Plays written and produced in Germany are three times more likely to have tragic or unhappy endings as plays written and produced in the US. A large majority of people in India say that arranged marriages are highly desirable, but only 2 percent of people in Japan and the West agree. Sixty-five percent of Japanese say that they are afraid to articulate the

wrong beliefs of a co-worker or endorse a wrong practice, whereas only 25 percent of Americans are equally concerned. This is due to the tightness of norms and severity of sanctions in Japan (Triandis, 1995; Imai & Gelfand, 2009). In US elementary and middle schools, Chinese-American children perform better than other groups. During kindergarten, Chinese-American students are four months ahead of Latino children and during high school they take more demanding advanced placement classes than the average American student. They do much more homework at night, and their parents are especially driven to encourage them to excel (Brooks, 2011).

Cultural differences can produce stunning differences in the rate of growth, openness to globalization, acceptance of new ways of working, and new forms of organization. Harrison (2000) distinguishes between *progress-prone cultures* and *progress-resistant cultures* and how they shape human destiny in different geographical locales. People in progress-resistant cultures tend to depend on their native religions and rituals for making sense of their daily lives; they tend to be fatalistic. People in progress-prone cultures believe that economic growth results from collective efforts and hard work and that the gross domestic product will rise almost every year. People in progress-resistant cultures assume that economic life is a zero-sum game, and that what they were born with is what they will have all their lives. Harrison argues that people in progress-prone cultures live to work whereas people in progress-resistant cultures work to live. There is greater openness to new experiences and novel ideas in progress-prone cultures. People are more cognitively complex in these cultures; they value competition in their work roles, they tend to be optimistic, they value punctuality and place strong emphasis on educational accomplishments for themselves and their children. They do not see their families providing them with the necessary resources to live and cope with the daily challenges of life, as is the case with people in progress-resistant cultures. In progress-prone cultures people feel guilty and personally responsible when they do not complete properly an assigned task on time. They blame themselves for what happens to them and their families, unlike people in progress-resistant cultures, who externalize guilt and blame authority figures and the government for their misfortunes.

We believe that further research on Harrison's (2000) thesis is going to yield important insights into how economic globalization is received and absorbed across nations. East Asian nations like Japan, South Korea, China, Singapore, and Vietnam have achieved significant rates of growth since they learned the techniques of management, marketing, and finance from the leading countries of the West. In contrast, countries in the Middle East (e.g., Iraq, Iran, Egypt, Libya, Lebanon) have had the same opportunities to absorb Western know-how to improve the effectiveness of their organizations but have not done this as much as the cultures of East Asia. The rise of the Arab Spring (2011) has included revolutions to force political elites to abandon authoritarian and progress-resistant practices in favor of democratic and progress-prone methods.

Since the dawn of the 20th century, major conflicts have appeared in the Middle East and North Africa concerning the role of fundamentalist Islamic thought and the growth of industrialization and modernization. Allawi (2009), a renowned scholar of Islam, notes that Islam in the 1950s was more open to embracing modern ideas and practices rooted in Western physical and social sciences compared with the Islam of the 1990s. He advances the notion that the Arab–Israeli war of 1967 was perhaps the major cause of this shift in Islamic thinking regarding the role of modern Western social science and particularly the role of globalization led by the US and its Western allies. The loss of the war resulted in loss of face of the political leaders of countries such as Egypt, Syria, Lebanon, and Iraq, and precipitated the shift toward seeking refuge in the "permanent knowledge" (knowledge that comes from God) structure of Islam, as opposed to the "changeable knowledge" (knowledge that comes from science and experiment). Recent research by Ginges, Hansen, & Norenzayan (2009) reports that fundamentalist Muslims who attend a mosque regularly are more likely to approve various sanctions against women (e.g., women should not be allowed to drive cars without the presence of their husbands or other male relatives, women cannot hold the position of Imam). They are also more likely to approve of suicide attacks against Western embassies and establishments, including those objects and pleasures of modern life that do not reflect fundamentalist Islamic values. A caveat is in order—since the findings are based in laboratories, one needs to exercise caution when generalizing the findings to other groups. Islam is enormously heterogenous (Allawi, 2009; Triandis, 2009), and some Islamic countries (e.g., Turkey, Malaysia, and Indonesia) are tolerant of globalization and its accompanying values and practices while other countries are less tolerant. Therefore, it is safe to assume that it is not the existence of Islam *per se* that provides hindrance to the progress of globalization and effective functioning of global organizations. However, the themes discussed in Friedman (2002) and Triandis (2009) suggest that some sects of Islam believe so strongly in the superiority of permanent knowledge, derived from the Koran, that they include many individuals who are anxious, intolerant, and opposed to globalization, global organizations, and modern values. In Nigeria, the Boko Haram sect (which means "Western knowledge is sinful") is certainly not going to accept globalization.

For global organizations to function in those parts of the world where Islamic fundamentalism exists, it is necessary to be cautious and not assume that Western cultural patterns will be accepted. Marketing practices which reflect the equality of the sexes, or depict physical affection or love among the customers should be discouraged, if not censored. This part of the world is in a state of flux and while different types of commentaries are emerging regarding the future of the Arab Spring, we are not in a position to fully assimilate this stream of diverse information. Therefore, it is hard to predict the extent to which globalization and the functioning of global organizations are going to be accepted in these parts of the world (for details regarding this topic, see *Megatrends in World Cultures* (2006), Special Issue of the *Journal of International Management*).

A related area of research that should occupy the interest of organizational researchers is the relationship between economic globalization and culture change. Does globalization, especially increasing economic interdependence among the members of the countries of the World Trade Organization, tend to produce selective cultural changes in the lives of people who are participating actively as important players in the global economy? Multinational and global organizations are everywhere, including in the progress-resistant cultures. Therefore, it is crucial for future researchers to investigate the nature of the basic differences between progress-prone and progress-resistant cultures. Multinational corporations have a lot to gain from advanced knowledge on the workings of these cultures, in those places where they have encountered turbulent times and political uncertainties.

7. Our final suggestion concerns the use of suitable research methodologies in the collection of cross-cultural and cross-national data relevant to the management of global organizations. Much of the research reported in this book has been collected by administering research instruments to managers and blue-collar workers in work organizations in different countries. This stream of research is likely to continue, if not intensify, due to major advances in the administration of questionnaires and research instruments by computer-mediated means, which can reach a larger group of respondents in many countries. An excellent discussion of the methods and measurement-related issues in cross-cultural management is provided by Leung (2008).

The problem that has plagued cross-cultural management research stems from the fact that researchers have collected data from people as concomitant sources of cultural information on individuals and societies. This tendency leads to the ecological fallacy—use of insights from one level of analysis to draw inferences at other levels of analysis (Hofstede, 2001; Meyers, Gamst, & Gaurino, 2006; van de Vijver, van Hemert, & Poortinga 2008). For example, if a group of researchers is interested in finding the effects of collectivism as a cultural syndrome in the relationship between a formal organizational leader and his or her followers, then the "leadership style" of the manager should be assessed separately—not from the perspective of the followers. Much organizational research could provide more insightful results if creative methods for collecting culture-specific data at the level of the society, work organization, and work group were employed.

A related example is the influence of institutional corruption on honest behaviors on the part of customer service representatives of a marketing organization. The finding that institutional corruption is related or predictive of dishonest behaviors on the part of customer service personnel (i.e., taking bribes in facilitating exchange of merchandise, etc.) does not allow for predictions about individual-level variables like conscientiousness and honesty on the part of these employees or the nature of behavior involved in transacting with customers. Another example concerns a situation when a researcher is interested in knowing whether individualism or collectivism as a cultural syndrome influences the nature of interpersonal bonds that develop among fellow workers in work groups. While data on both individualism and collectivism and the nature of interpersonal bonds may be collected relatively easily from the individuals in the work organization, there is no guarantee that the psychological processes at both the individual (i.e., micro) and the collective (i.e., macro) level will be the same. In these kinds of situations, information about the size and density of various close personal relationships to which an individual belongs provides information about a different category of variables which may correlate with both the macro-level construct of cultural syndrome and the micro-level construct of closeness of interpersonal bonds.

Another phenomenon called the Simpson paradox may appear at different levels of analyses (Waldmann & Hagmayer, 1995; Fiedler, 2000). The sense of this paradox is that different patterns of relationships may appear between variables of interest at different levels of analyses involving cross-cultural data. That is, when decomposed, relationships may not be present or may be present in directions opposite to the hypothesized predictions. Sometimes, there may be negative relationships or no relationship between constructs at separate levels (Fiedler, Walther, Freytag, & Nickel, 2003). We suggest that these issues should be considered as carefully as possible before conclusions are drawn from cross-cultural research. In fact, research involving the methodology of participant observation techniques and qualitative methodologies (i.e., ethnographic techniques) should be employed in the early stages of research design. Insights from such studies can identify culture-specific (i.e., emic) constructs in interesting and often unanticipated ways. Such research is likely to yield valuable information regarding the complex interplay of cultural variations and organizational behavior. For more information on this topic, see Van de Vivjer & Fischer (2009).

There have been significant advances in cross-cultural psychology in this decade. The 2002 Special Issue of the *Psychological Bulletin, Handbook of cultural psychology* (Kitayama and Cohen, 2007), *Cambridge handbook of culture, organizations, and work* (Bhagat & Steers, 2009), and *Handbook of international management research* (Smith, Peterson, & Thomas, 2008) provide detailed discussions of important avenues for meaningful theory construction and data collection on various aspects of the functioning of global organizations. We do not lack a systematic body of knowledge in the area of cross-national and cross-cultural variations in the management of work organizations. What is needed is a strong will to engage in innovative research to go beyond what we know and make greater contributions to the effectiveness of the multinational–global organizations of tomorrow. Only then can economic globalization benefit mankind at large and also uplift poor people in developing countries.

REFERENCES

Ablegen, J.C. (1958). *The Japanese factory*. New York: Free Press.
Allawi, A.A. (2009). The crisis of Islamic civilization. New Haven, CT: Yale University Press.
Bartlett, C., Ghoshal, S., & Beamish, P. (2008). *Transitional management*. Boston, MA: McGraw-Hill Irwin.
Bendix, R. (1977). *Max Weber: An intellectual portrait*. Berkeley, CA: University of California Press.
Benedict, R. (1954). *The chrysanthemum and the sword*. New York: Routledge.
Bhagat, R.S. & London, M.L. (1999). Getting started and getting ahead: Career dynamics of immigrants. *Human Resource Management Review*, 9(3), 349–65.

Bhagat, R.S. & Steers, R.M. (2009). *Cambridge handbook of culture, organizations, and work*. Cambridge: Cambridge University Press.

Bhagat, R.S., Davis, C.A., & London, M.L. (2009). Acculturative stress in professional immigrants: Towards a cultural theory of stress. In A. Antoniou, G. Chrousos, C. Cooper, M. Eysenck, & C. Spielberger (Eds). *Handbook of managerial behavior and occupational health* (pp. 345–62). Cheltenham, UK and Northampton, MA, USA: Edward Elgar Publishing.

Bhagat, R.S., McDevitt, A.S., & Segovis, J.C. (2010). Immigration as an adaptive challenge: Implications for lifelong learning. In M.L. London (Ed.). *Handbook of lifelong learning* (pp. 402–21). New York: Oxford University Press.

Bond, M.H. (2009). *The psychology of the Chinese people*. New York: Columbia University Press.

Brooks, D. (2011). *The social animal: The hidden sources of love, character, and achievement*. New York: Random House.

Capelli, P., Singh, H., Singh, J., & Useem, M. (2010). *The India way*. Boston, MA: Harvard Business Press.

Cheung, F.M., Leung, K., Fan, R., Song, W.Z., Zhangr, J.X., & Zhang, J.P. (1996). Development of the Chinese Personality Assessment Inventory (CPAI). *Journal of Cross-Cultural Psychology*, 24, 181–99.

Chinese Culture Connection Study (1987). Chinese values and the search for culture-free dimensions of culture. *Journal of Cross-Cultural Psychology*, 18, 143–64.

Cohen, D. & Nisbett, R.E. (1997). Field experiments examining the culture of honor: The role of institutions in perpetuating norms about violence. *Personality and Social Psychology Bulletin*, 23, 1188–99.

Connley, D. (2009). *Elsewhere, USA*. New York: Pantheon Books.

Daniels, B.C. (1995). *Puritans at play*. New York: St. Martin's Press.

Daux, K. (2006). *To be an immigrant*. New York: Russell Sage Foundation.

Diaz-Guerrero, R. (1993). Mexican ethnopsychology. In U. Kim & J.W. Berry (Eds). *Indigenous psychologies: Research and experience in cultural context* (pp. 44–55). Thousand Oaks, CA: Sage.

Enriques, V. (1993). Developing a Filipino psychology. In U. Kim & J.W. Berry (Eds.). *Indigenous psychologies: Research and experience in cultural context* (pp. 152–69). Thousand Oaks, CA: Sage.

Fiedler, K. (2000). Beware of samples: A cognitive–ecological sampling approach to judgment biases. *Psychological Review*, 107(4), 659–76.

Fiedler, K., Walther, E., Freytag, P., & Nickel, S. (2003). Inductive reasoning and judgment interference: Experiments on Simpson's paradox. *Personality and Social Psychology Bulletin*, 29(1), 14–27.

Fischer, D. (1989). *Albion's seed: Four British folkways in America*. New York: Oxford University Press.

Friedman, T.L. (2002). *Latitudes and attitudes*. New York: Farrar, Straus & Giroux.

Friedman, T.L. & Mandelbaum, M. (2011). *That used to be us*. New York: Farrar, Strauss & Giroux.

Georgas, J., van de Vijer, F.J.R., & Berry, J.W. (2004). The ecocultural framework, ecosocial indices, and psychological variables in cross-cultural research. *Journal of Cross-Cultural Psychology*, 35(1), 74–96.

Ginges, J., Atran, S., Sachdeva, S., & Medin, D. (2011). Psychology out of the laboratory: The challenge of violent extremism. *American Psychologist*, 66, 507–19.

Ginges, J., Hansen, I., & Norenzayan, A. (2009). Religion and support for suicide attacks. *Psychological Science*, 20(2), 224–30.

Harrison, L.E. (2000). Promoting progressive cultural change. In L.E. Harrison & S.P. Huntington (Eds). *Culture matters: How values shape human progress* (pp. 296–307). New York: Basic Books.

Hofacker, D. (2010). Older workers in a globalizing world: An international comparison of retirement and late-career patterns in Western industrialized countries. Cheltenham, UK and Northampton, MA, USA: Edward Elgar.

Hofstede, G. (1980). *Culture's consequences: International differences in work-related values.* Beverly Hills, CA: Sage.

Hofstede, G. (1995). Multilevel research of human systems: Flowers, bouquets, and gardens. *Human Systems Management*, 14, 207–17.

Hofstede, G. (2001). *Culture's consequences.* Thousand Oaks, CA: Sage.

Hulsmans, S. (1994). The impact of differences in religion on the relation between religiosity and values. In A.M. Bouovy, E. van de Vinver, P. Boski, & P. Schmitz (Eds). *Journeys into cross-cultural psychology* (pp. 255–67). Lisse, NL: Swets & Zeitlinger.

Huntington, S. (1996). *The clash of civilizations and the remaking of world order.* New York: Simon & Schuster.

Imai, L. & Gelfand, M. (2009). Interdisciplinary perspectives on culture, conflict, and negotiation. In Rabi S. Bhagat & Richard M. Steers (Eds). *Cambridge handbook of cultures, organizations, and work* (pp. 334–72). Cambridge: Cambridge University Press.

Inglehart, R. & Baker, W.E. (2000). Modernization, cultural change and the persistence of traditional values. *American Sociological Review*, 65, 19–51.

Inglehart, R., Basanez, M., & Morano, A. (1998). *Human values and beliefs: Political, religious, sexual and economic norms in 43 nations: Findings from the 1999–2002 World Values Survey.* Ann Arbor: MI: University of Michigan Press.

Kabasakal, H. & Bodur, M. (2008). Leadership and culture in Turkey: A multifaceted phenomenon. In J.S. Chhokar, F.C. Brodbeck, & R.J. House (Eds). *Culture and leadership across the world: The GLOBE book of in-depth studies of 25 societies* (pp. 835–74). New York: Psychology Press.

Kim, U. & Hwang, K.-K. (2006). *Indigenous cultural psychology: Understanding people in context.* New York: Springer.

Kitayama, S. & Cohen, D. (2007). *Handbook of cultural psychology.* New York: The Guilford Press.

Lenski, G. (1963). *The religious factor.* New York: Anchor Press.

Leung, K. (2008). Methods and measurements in cross-cultural management. In P.B. Smith, M.F. Peterson, & D.C. Thomas (Eds). *The handbook of cross-cultural management research* (pp. 59–73). Los Angeles, CA: Sage.

Meade, M. (1928). *Coming of age in Samoa.* New York: Morrow.

Meyers, L.S., Gamst, G., & Gaurino, A.J. (2006). *Applied multivariate research.* Thousand Oaks, CA: Sage.

Negandhi, A. (1986). Role and structure of German multinationals: A comparative profile. In K. Macharzina & K. Stehle (Eds). *European approach to international management* (pp. 51–66). New York: Walter de Gruyter.

Negandhi, A.R. & Baliga, B.R. (1980). Multinationals in industrially developed countries: A comparative study of American, German and Japanese multinationals. In A.R. Negandhi (Ed.). *Functioning of the 51 multinational corporations: A global comparative study* (pp. 152–7). New York: Pergamon Press.

Nisbett, R. (2003). *The geography of thought: How Asians and Westerners think differently and why.* New York: Free Press.

Putnam, R.D. (2000). *Bowling alone: The collapse and revival of the American community.* New York: Simon & Schuster.

Sanchez-Burks, J. (2002). Protestant relational ideology and (in)attention to relational cues in work settings. *Journal of Personality and Social Psychology,* 83(4), 919–29.

Sanchez-Burks, J. (2005). Protestant relational ideology: The cognitive underpinnings and organizational implications of an American anomaly. *Research in Organizational Behavior,* 26, 265–305.

Sanchez-Burks, J. & Lee, F. (2007). Cultural psychology of workways. In Shinobu Kitayama & Dov Cohen (Eds). *Handbook of cultural psychology* (pp. 346–69). New York: The Guilford Press.

Schmidt-Atzert, L. & Park, H.S. (1999). The Korean concepts dapdaphada and uulhada: A cross-cultural study of the meaning of emotions. *Journal of Cross-Cultural Psychology,* 30, 646–54.

Smith, P.B. (2006). When elephants fight the grass gets trampled: The Hofstede and GLOBE projects. *Journal of International Business Management Studies,* 37, 915–21.

Smith, P.B., Bond, M.H., & Kagitcibasi, C. (2006). *Understanding social psychology across cultures.* London: Sage.

Smith, P.B., Peterson, M.F., & Thomas, D.C. (2008). *Handbook of international management research.* Los Angeles, CA: Sage.

Triandis, H.C. (1972). *The analysis of subjective culture.* New York: Wiley.

Triandis, H.C. (1994). Cross-cultural industrial and organizational psychology. In Harry C. Triandis, Marvin D. Dunnette, & Leatta M. Hough (Eds). *Handbook of industrial and organizational psychology* (pp. 103–72). Palo Alto, CA: Consulting Psychologists Press, Inc.

Triandis, H.C. (1995). *Individualism and collectivism.* Boulder, CO: Westview Press.

Triandis, H.C. (2000). Dialectics between cultural and cross-cultural psychology. *Asian Journal of Social Psychology,* 3, 185–95.

Triandis, H.C. (2002). Generic individualism and collectivism. In M.J. Gannon & R.L. Newman (Eds). *The Blackwell handbook of cross-cultural management* (pp. 16–45). Oxford: Blackwell Publishers.

Triandis, H.C. (2009). *Fooling ourselves.* Westport, CT: Praeger.

Van de Vivjer, F.J.R. & Fischer, R. (2009). Improving methodological robustness in cross-cultural organizational research. In Rabi S. Bhagat & Richard M. Steers (Eds). *Cambridge handbook of cultures, organizations, and work* (pp. 491–517). Cambridge: Cambridge University Press.

Van de Vivjer, F.J.R. & Leung, K. (1997). Methods and data analysis of comparative research. In J.W. Berry, Y. Poortinga, & J. Pandey (Eds). *Handbook of cross-cultural psychology* (p. 7). Needham Heights, MA: Allyn & Bacon.

Van de Vijver, F.J.R., van Hemert, D.A., & Poortinga, Y.H. (2008). *Multilevel analysis of individuals and cultures.* New York: Springer.

Waldmann, M.R. & Hagmayer, Y. (1995). Causal paradox: When a cause simultaneously produces and prevents an effect. In J.D. Moore & J.F. Lehman (Eds).

Proceedings of the Seventeenth Annual Conference of the Cognitive Science Society (pp. 425–30). Mahwah, NJ: Erlbaum.

Yamaguchi, S. (1994). Collectivism among the Japanese: A perspective from the self. In U. Kim, H.C. Triandis, C. Kagitcibasi, S.-C. Choi, & G. Yoon (Eds). *Individualism and collectivism: Theory, method and applications* (pp. 175–8). Thousand Oaks, CA: Sage.

14. Managing the global organization in a cross-cultural perspective: the future

Developments in the world economic scene make it necessary for scholars to appreciate the role of globalization and its interplay with cultural variations. Inquiries into the nature of functioning of multinational and global organizations across cultures can come from a variety of disciplinary perspectives. For example, organizational psychologists are interested in the role of cultural shocks on adjustments of expatriates and their families in dissimilar countries; whereas those working within the sociological tradition are likely to be more interested in the convergence and divergence of organizational practices including such phenomena as the diffusion of innovation. Organizational scholars with a practical bent of mind are interested in enhancing skills like cultural sensitivity, cultural intelligence, and understanding the global mindset. Awareness of cultural differences is where it all starts. The recognition that (1) one carries a particular mental software because of the way one was brought up (i.e., socialized), and (2) that this particular mental software differs from others who grew up in different ecological and social environments is important. Such awareness is essential for the relatively trouble-free operations of multinational and global organizations across national borders and cultures. In writing this book, we have attempted to address the important issues that concern and should continue to concern the managers of multinational and global organizations. These concerns should stem not only from considerations of maximizing profits by recognizing and responding correctly to national differences in scale and scope economics, and other contributing factors (Bartlett, Ghoshal, & Beamish, 2008, pp. 87–100), but also from a genuine recognition that it is only by doing good to the communities involved that a global organization can maintain its long-term effectiveness and reputation. Making globalization work and work to meet both objectives has been a challenge that economists like Stiglitz (2006) have tried to address in a comprehensive fashion. While there are significant benefits that result from various activities inherent in the process of economic globalization, the fact is that there are good reasons for discontents as well (Sassen, 1998; Stiglitz, 2003). The discontents derive from:

- The rules of the game devised by the Davos World Economic Forum, World Trade Organization, International Monetary Fund, and other transnational organizations make globalization sometimes unfair—specifically designed to benefit the interests of the multinational and global organizations of rich developed countries and their citizens. In fact, as Stiglitz (2006) currently observes, some recent changes have been so unfair that they have indeed made some of the poor countries worse off than before they embarked on the path of economic globalization.
- The fact that globalization clearly advances "materialistic values" over other values such as concern for the environment or for life itself. Global warming, largely created by the US, Europe, and some emergent economies like China, India, and Brazil, has serious consequences for the planet and for the survival of the human race.
- The fact that globalization may have the unintended consequences of robbing the sovereignty of developing countries and their ability to make culture-specific decisions in key areas that affect their citizens' well-being. While some proponents of globalization claim that engaging Communist and authoritarian regimes in international trade and business is the best way to induce democratic values, the evidence is often contrary. Particularly in the continents of sub-Saharan Africa and Latin America, globalization has begun to erode the lifestyles of the indigenous populations and their cultural heritages.
- The fact that, while advocates of globalization claim that almost everyone is likely to benefit economically, there is plenty of evidence from both the developed countries and the developing countries that globalization widens the gap between the rich and the poor. In fact, the recent demonstrations in various cities of the US, and in particular on Wall Street in New York City, attest to the despair of Americans who feel that their economic future has been compromised by the investment bankers of Wall Street and other multinational–global companies with their ruthless practices of moving manufacturing and service jobs to lower-wage sites. Consider the distribution of income in the US. In the period 1979–2007, 1 percent of Americans received 36 percent of all income. During just the 2001–06 period the top 1 percent received 53 percent of all national income. Hedge fund managers make between $600 million and 1.2 billion *per year*. In 2006, 300,000 people had the same total

income as the bottom 180 million Americans. During 1975–2006 the improvement in the income of the poorest 1/5th of Americans was 11 percent. The next 1/5th of the distribution improved by 18 percent. The middle of the distribution, or the next 1/5th, improved by 32 percent. The top 1/5th improved by 55 percent, but the income of the top 1 percent increased by 254 percent! The net worth of the top 1 percent was $15 million; the net worth of the bottom 80 percent was $8200, and in many cases it was negative because of credit card debts (Haker & Pierson, 2010).

Other indices being equal, the countries that have more equality, such as the Scandinavian countries, have higher levels of subjective well-being than the countries that have high inequality. Both gender equality and economic equality (small ratios of the income of the top and bottom 20 percent of the population) are relevant (Veenhoven, 2008, p. 55). The evidence is very strong that within a country social pathology is strongly related to inequality (Wilkinson, 1996). One can also see the effects of inequality when a crisis occurs, as for example when hurricane Katrina hit New Orleans in August 2005. Looting and killing of innocents took place. That is an index of social pathology. Inequality results in low societal cohesion, which in turn reduces the life expectancy of some of the members of a society. In the United States there is a link between low socioeconomic status and poor physical and mental health (e.g., Schneiderman, 2000; Brim, Ryff, & Kessler, 2004). It is due to lack of affordable medical care, unhealthy behaviors, greater stress, lack of personal control, and greater hostility and depression, as well as to physical conditions such as pollution, toxins, crowding, and violence. Inequality is also seen in the discrepancies within the educational system. Private schools provide a superb education, but public schools are no longer the best in the industrialized world, as they were in the 1940s. In fact, the American test scores, compared with the scores of other industrialized countries, now show very poor performance in the sciences and mathematics. Similarly, in the US the medical care provided to the affluent is the best in the world, but the poor get care that is below the standards of Canada, Britain, or France. As a result the US has higher rates of diabetes, heart attack, cancer and so on than do those countries.

The observation that is perhaps the most important for the theses we have been advancing in this book is that globalization has forced a kind of cultural transformation of the developing countries in ways that are clearly inappropriate and often counterproductive. Globalization should not mean either complete Westernization or Americanization of economic policies, government initiatives, or organizational practices in developing countries. As long as globalization continues to have destabilizing effects on the fundamental values of the culture of developing countries, it will be resented.

The affluent part of the modern world, which includes Western Europe, North America (minus Mexico), Australia, and New Zealand, tends to be individualist and loose. Japan and segments of the population in cities around the world in developing countries also have modern perspectives, though the original cultures of Japan and most developing countries were collectivist and traces of that pattern can still be found in many perspectives and behavior patterns in these countries. Globalization makes some parts of some countries affluent, individualist, and loose. But, as Newton argued, every force produces a counter-force. Similarly, individualism produces tendencies toward collectivism, looseness tendencies toward tightness, and tightness tendencies toward looseness. Thus, in all societies there are counter-forces generated by modernity, which increase cognitive simplicity, religiosity, fundamentalism (e.g., I have the truth and will go to paradise, you are going to hell), and tightness.

The essence of modernity is openness to new experiences and to the future, non-traditional thinking (less religiosity), and the structuring of life around the clock. Cultures differ in the way they deal with time. People in modern cultures pay a great deal of attention to time (Doob, 1971; Inkeles & Smith, 1974). They also tend to use time monochronically, that is, dealing with one topic or person at one time rather than dealing with many topics and different people at the same time. Modern cultures compared with traditional cultures tend to make more of a distinction between work time and social time, and tend to use clock time rather than event time (e.g., a meeting stops when the clock reaches a certain point rather than when the event is completed).

In their extensive empirical study of modernity, Inkeles and Smith (1974) identified several elements that constitute modernity. Four of these elements are contrary to a large portion of today's Islam, though they were compatible with the Islam of the 7th to the 13th century.

First, modernity includes openness to new experiences. The Arab world during the 7th to the 13th centuries was open to new experiences, which leads to cognitive complexity, and absorbed much classical scholarship, algebra, and technology from other cultures. But now a large portion of the Arab world is relatively closed to new experiences. One clue is the number of translations into Arabic. In the past 1000 years there have been as many translations into Arabic as translations into Spanish in *one* year (*The Economist*, 2003). The accumulated total of translated books since the beginning of Islam is about 100,000, and that is about the number of books that are translated into Spanish in one year (Lewis, 2003). The Arab world currently translates no more than 330 books annually, one-fifth of the number that Greece (a country of 11 million) translates (Lewis, 2003). In short, these data suggest that there is a closed mind and cognitive simplicity in today's Arab world, in contrast to the Arab world of the 12th century.

Second, in modernity there is a readiness to adopt new behavior patterns and accept social change. Most, but not all, of Islam, on the contrary, tends to seek the older behavior patterns. Mohammed is the "model" human and most people should behave the way he did. In fundamentalist Islam the ideal is to copy the lifestyle of the Prophet, even sleep on the same side of the body as he did! It is true that other ultra-orthodox doctrines have similar rules of behavior, for example, for Jews that one should first put on the left and then the right shoe (Triandis, 2009). However, while there are no relevant data, it seems that today very few Jews follow such rules, while a good many Muslims aspire to live like the Prophet.

Third, in modernity there is an orientation toward the present and future, not the past. Fundamentalist Islam looks at the past, especially the period when the Prophet was alive and the centuries that followed, when Islam conquered North Africa, Southern Spain, and the Balkans, as the golden period. Modern people look at the 21st century (say 2050) as the important focus of their concerns. Thus, modern people are concerned with the overpopulation of the earth and the effect of global warming in 2050, but most Moslems seem to ignore such issues.

Fourth, in modernity there is trust in people one does not know. Most Arab cultures are collectivist (see Chapter 2) and collectivism is associated with distrust toward those individuals who are not members of the in-group. The in-group is usually the tribe, and in Islam the in-group usually is "other Muslims of my sect" and secondarily other Muslims. Non-Muslims are usually categorized as out-group. Only the more Western of Muslims are willing to be friends with non-Muslims. The fundamentalists do not even want to shake hands with an "infidel," let alone a non-believer.

The above observations should make management researchers and practitioners pause for a while and examine the causes and consequences of various practices that are imported from the West and implemented in the work contexts of developing countries. In addition, there is a need to be concerned with the well-being of the citizens from the globalizing countries themselves. Many citizens in rich countries such as the US, Canada, UK, France, and Australia are not sufficiently skilled to undertake the challenges of new types of work and work arrangements that inevitably come with globalization (see Chapter 2). This concern on the part of multinational and global corporations goes beyond the corporate social responsibility on an international scale. It has to do with encouraging a gradual and effective process of social and organizational change that employees, as well as the stakeholders of the corporation, can begin to appreciate. Abrupt and discontinuous changes, including rapid introduction of innovations, can cause intensive anxiety, occupational obsolescence, and stress at the individual level and conflict and stress at the work group and organizational levels. Globalization is also causing an increased overlap of the work and non-work lives of employees at all levels of the organization, and recent findings indicate that this phenomenon is taking place worldwide (Lazarova & Lowe, 2008).

The specific areas that have emerged and deserve scholarly attention are as follows:

- Culture is a complex phenomenon that influences organizational processes in all societies. Every aspect of human psychology is influenced by culture (Markus and Kitayama, 1991) and human behavior changes cultures, so that culture and psychology "make each other up" (Shweder, 1990, p. 24). The interaction between the initiatives of multinational global corporations and the cultural contexts of the societies in which they operate is an important issue confronting both advanced industrialized countries and developing ones. Research findings concerning the functioning of global organizations across dissimilar nations and cultures have and will continue to have significant theoretical and applied implications. In a related vein, while we endorse the conduct of scientific investigations of multinational and global organizations and of people working within them, we must note that for the findings to be truly helpful, they should benefit not only the corporation but should also enhance both organizational effectiveness and the well-being of employees and clients of the organization (Diener & Suh, 2000).
- The culture of nations has both enduring and changing properties. Cultures do not change much in the absence of economic development and economic globalization. As a nation becomes more affluent, or switches from one type of economy to another, it undergoes definite cultural changes. Triandis (1989) noted that as countries become prosperous, nuclear families become the dominant pattern, and people become more individualistic. During the past four decades, East and South Asian and some oil-rich Middle Eastern countries have caught up economically with Western Europe and the US. Many of the organizational practices are tending to

converge toward the Western pattern, such as selection of individuals based on merit and past performance as opposed to based on nepotism. However, many countries in Latin America and Africa have retained their management practices despite their proven ineffectiveness in the current era of globalization (Kiggundu, Jorgensen, & Hafsi, 1983). China and Japan are the second and third largest economies in the world (see Chapter 1) and many regions in these two countries are more affluent than Western countries, including the US. However, their cultural norms and organizational practices are particularistic and collectivistic in orientation: the universalism which is a major hallmark of Western cultures is shunned. Given the diversity of cultures in the world, it should not be a surprise that both convergence and divergence in organizational practices and societal norms exist.

- There is no doubt that the rapid economic growth that can accompany globalization can precipitate cultural changes: as societies become more affluent, citizens become more indulgent, open to diverse and conflicting ideologies, and political systems become more democratic.

- A country's culture (like personality traits) is harder to manage than its economy and political system. Cultural values cannot be transformed by government degree or by military intervention. A closer look at the cultural transformation of the Soviet Union shows that, despite massive propaganda, school sermons, and numerous history textbooks emphasizing the virtues of Communism, the culture did not become what Lenin, Stalin, and others hoped. The Soviet system collapsed in 1991 due to the inner contradictions of the various cultural patterns within the Soviet Union. Similarly, the cultures of multinational and global organizations (especially those which have existed for a long time such as IBM of the US, Mercedes Benz of Germany, Toyota of Japan, and Tata, Inc. of India) were not transformed overnight. Professionals working for these global companies also have their unique patterns of behavior. For example, people who grow up in a collectivist culture are likely to become allocentric, while people who grow up in an individualist culture are likely to become idiocentric. Research has shown that the fit between culture and personality is crucial for effective operation. Allocentrics do well in a collectivist culture and idiocentrics do well in an individualist culture. But allocentrics do poorly in an individualist culture (e.g., research found that allocentrics from East Germany did poorly when they moved to West Germany; Triandis, 2009), and idiocentrics do poorly in a collectivist culture, but do well in an individualist culture (e.g., East German idiocentrics did well in West Germany). In order to get an enriched picture of how global organizations evolve their value systems and practices in different nations (i.e., in various subsidiaries and networks), it is essential that we look at the complex three-way interaction among societal culture, organizational culture, and individual professional culture. Research reflecting this paradigm is rare, but a good example may be found in the work of Martin (1993).

- The role of religion in influencing the values of a nation should be understood in a much more comprehensive fashion than is now the case. Religious beliefs and practices are most resistant to change—including changes induced by economic and cultural globalization. Despite the growing importance of clashes between religions and civilizations in shaping the future of the world, not much attention has been paid by social scientists and in particular by management researchers to this topic. Large-scale surveys of religiosity and its roles in shaping the face of globalization are important and should be conducted. Such information will prepare managers of multi-national and global corporations to be more effective in managing across dissimilar cultures·

- Last but not least, cross-cultural psychologists have repeatedly noted that there is no such thing as a superior or inferior culture in a broader sense. Triandis (1994), Hofstede (1980, 2001), and other cross-cultural researchers have noted that we are all ethnocentric—it is a good idea for all of us to be acutely sensitive of our ethno-centric biases and predispositions. Learning to differentiate what is caused by a person in the work context from the general norm in a society is crucial to developing robust theories and insightful practical applications.

All in all, this book has been written to broaden our perspective concerning the role of cultural differences in managing the global organization. We have covered as many topics as we consider both relevant and important in this endeavor. It is hoped that the insights that this book provides will encourage you to begin a journey of a thousand miles with a confident first step.

REFERENCES

Bartlett, C., Ghoshal, S., & Beamish, P. (2008). *Transnational management.* Boston, MA: McGraw-Hill Irwin.

Brim, O.G., Ryff, C.D., & Kessler, W. (Eds) (2004). *How healthy are we? A national study of well-being at midlife.* Chicago, IL: University of Chicago Press.

Diener, E. & Suh, E.M. (Eds) (2000). *Culture and subjective well-being.* Cambridge, MA: MIT Press.

Doob, L.W. (1971). *Patterning of time.* New Haven, CT: Yale University Press.

Haker, J.S. & Pierson, P. (2010). *Winner-take all politics.* New York: Simon and Schuster.

Hofstede, G. (1980). *Culture's consequences: International differences in work.* Thousand Oaks, CA: Sage.

Hofstede, G. (2001). *Culture's consequences.* Thousand Oaks, CA: Sage.

Inkeles, A. & Smith, D.H. (1974). *Becoming modern.* Cambridge, MA: Harvard University Press.

Kiggundu, M.N., Jorgensen, J.J., & Hafsi, T. (1983). Administrative theory and practice in developing countries: A synthesis. *Administrative Science Quarterly,* 28, 66–84.

Lazarova, M. & Lowe, M. (2008). *Work and family: Research in cross national and international contexts.* In P.B. Smith, M.F. Peterson, & D.C. Thomas (Eds). *Handbook of cross-cultural management research* (pp. 185–200). Thousand Oaks, CA: Sage Publications.

Lewis, B. (2003). *The crisis of Islam: Holy war and unholy terror.* New York: The Modern Library.

Markus, H. & Kitayama, S. (1991). Culture and self: Implications for cognition, emotion, and motivation. *Psychological Review,* 98, 225–53.

Martin, J. (1993). *Organizational culture.* New York: Oxford University Press.

Minkov, M. (2011). *Cultural differences in a globalized world.* London: Emerald Group Publishing.

Sassen, S. (1998). *Globalization and its discontents: Essays on the new mobility of people and money.* New York: The New Press.

Schneiderman, N. (2000). Coronary artery disease. In A.E. Kazdin (Ed.). *Encyclopedia of psychology* (p. 306). New York: Oxford University Press.

Shweder, R.A. (1990). Cultural psychology: What is it? In J.W. Stigler, R.A. Shweder, & G. Herder (Eds). *Cultural psychology: Essays on comparative human development.* Cambridge: Cambridge University Press.

Stiglitz, J.E. (2003). *Globalization and its discontents.* New York: W.W. Norton.

Stiglitz, J.E. (2006). *Making globalization work.* New York: W.W. Norton.

The Economist (2003), 13–19 September, p. 6.

Triandis, H.C. (1989). The self and social behavior in differing social contexts. *Psychological Review,* 96, 506–20.

Triandis, H.C. (1994). Cross-cultural industrial and organizational psychology. In H.C. Triandis, M.D. Dunnette, & L.M. Hough (Eds). *Handbook of industrial and organizational psychology* (pp. 103–72). Palo Alto, CA: Consulting Psychologists Press.

Triandis, H.C. (2009). *Fooling ourselves.* New York: Praeger.

Veenhoven, R. (2008). Sociological theories of subjective well-being. In M. Eid & R.J. Larsen (Eds). *The science of subjective well-being* (pp. 17–43). New York: Guilford Press.

Wilkinson, R. (1996). *Unhealthy societies: The affliction of inequality.* London: Routledge.

Author index

Subject index